Innovations in Sustainability

To what extent can competition between companies encourage innovations in sustainability that have the potential to solve some of the world's major challenges? Using a series of case studies, this book pits closely related competitors against each other to examine the progress in and obstacles to the evolution of sustainable innovations in energy efficiency, solar power, electric vehicles and hybrids, wind energy, healthy eating, and agricultural productivity. It delves into the efforts of Tesla Motors to bring about a revolution in personal transportation, and the challenges Toyota and General Motors (GM) confront in commercializing hybrids. It explores the movement to healthy food by cereal companies General Mills and Kellogg's, and depicts the battles between Whole Foods and Walmart for the world's palate. By examining the experiences that particular businesses have had with sustainable innovation, this insightful book reflects upon lessons learned and encourages readers to think carefully about the challenges that lie ahead.

ALFRED A. MARCUS is the Edson Spencer Endowed Chair in Strategy and Technological Leadership at the Carlson School of Management and at the Technological Leadership Institute (TLI) College of Science and Engineering, University of Minnesota. He has published in numerous academic journals and he is the author or editor of 15 books on strategic management, business ethics, and green business. His current research focuses on sustainable innovation and cleantech venture capital.

Organizations and the Natural Environment

Series editors

Jorge Rivera, *George Washington University*
J. Alberto Aragon-Correa, *University of Surrey*

Editorial board

Nicole Darnall, *Arizona State University*
Magali Delmas, *University of California, Los Angeles*
Ans Kolk, *University of Amsterdam*
Thomas P. Lyon, *University of Michigan*
Alfred Marcus, *University of Minnesota*
Michael Toffel, *Harvard Business School*
Christopher Weible, *University of Colorado*

The increasing attention given to environmental protection issues has resulted in a growing demand for high-quality, actionable research on sustainability and business environmental management. This new series, published in conjunction with the Group for Research on Organizations and the Natural Environment (GRONEN), presents students, academics, managers, and policy-makers with the latest thinking on key topics influencing business practice today.

Published titles

Bowen, *After Greenwashing*

Forthcoming titles

Gouldson and Sullivan, *Governance and the Changing Climate for Business*
Sharma and Sharma, *Patient Capital*

Innovations in Sustainability

Fuel and Food

ALFRED A. MARCUS
University of Minnesota

CAMBRIDGE
UNIVERSITY PRESS

Shaftesbury Road, Cambridge CB2 8EA, United Kingdom

One Liberty Plaza, 20th Floor, New York, NY 10006, USA

477 Williamstown Road, Port Melbourne, VIC 3207, Australia

314–321, 3rd Floor, Plot 3, Splendor Forum, Jasola District Centre, New Delhi – 110025, India

103 Penang Road, #05–06/07, Visioncrest Commercial, Singapore 238467

Cambridge University Press is part of Cambridge University Press & Assessment, a department of the University of Cambridge.

We share the University's mission to contribute to society through the pursuit of education, learning and research at the highest international levels of excellence.

www.cambridge.org
Information on this title: www.cambridge.org/9781107072794

© Alfred A. Marcus 2015

First published 2015

A catalogue record for this publication is available from the British Library

ISBN   978-1-107-07279-4   Hardback
ISBN   978-1-107-42111-0   Paperback

For Judy,
ahavat Lebi and ezer cenegdi

Contents

List of figure and tables   *page* ix

Foreword   xii

Acknowledgments   xv

Introduction: the path to sustainability   1

Part I   Funding sustainable startups

1   Leaders of the pack: Khosla Ventures and KPCB   13

2   Scaling up: Intel Capital and Google Ventures   50

Part II   Business models

3   Follow the sun: First Solar and Suntech   87

4   Making a revolution: Tesla and Better Place   110

Part III   The macroenvironment and industry context

5   Ticket to ride: Toyota and General Motors   147

6   Blowing in the wind: Vestas and General Electric   171

Part IV   Finding customers

7   Carrying that weight: General Mills and Kellogg's   203

8   Bridge over troubled waters: Pepsi and Coca-Cola   226

Part V   Competition between mission and non-mission based businesses

9   Consensus capitalism: Whole Foods and Walmart   259

10   Sustainability's next frontier: DuPont and Monsanto   296

Concluding observations: the journey continues   332

Index   348

Figure and tables

Figure

1.1 Clean energy venture deals and US $s invested, 1995 to
2012 (United States)   *page* 17

Tables

0.1 Sustainable innovation: evolutionary stages   6
1.1 Returns to clean energy and other VC investment
categories, 2002 to 2006   18
1.2 Khosla Ventures and KPCB participation in clean energy
deals, 2004 to 2013   24
1.3 Wind startups in need of funding   45
1.4 Status of Khosla Ventures' and KPCB's clean energy
deals, 2013   48
2.1 Intel Capital's and Google Ventures' clean energy deals
by category, 2014   55
2.2 Status of Intel Capital's and Google Ventures' clean
energy deals, 2014   56
2.3 Bankrupt or acquired thin film CIS/CIGS solar cell
manufacturers   74
3.1 The decline in Chinese solar shipments to the United
States, 2011 to 2013   88
3.2 A comparison of First Solar and Suntech's financials,
second quarter 2014   94
4.1 Can Tesla achieve a break-even point with its proposed
Model E?   111
4.2 United States' luxury car sales, 2013   122
4.3 Tesla's financials compared to those of other major
automakers, July 2014   123
5.1 Largest oil reserves and producers in 2014   151

5.2 Market share of US-sold hybrid electric vehicles, 1999 to
      2013, by manufacturer   159
5.3 Sales of US hybrid electric vehicles by manufacturer,
      1999 to 2013   160
5.4 The efficiency of hybrid electric vehicles: US
      Environmental Protection Agency 2014 ratings   161
5.5 Plug-in hybrid electric vehicles: sales, efficiency, and
      battery range by manufacturer, 2014   165
6.1 Wind power revenue global change, 2002 to 2014   172
6.2 Wind power company global market share, 2010 to 2013   173
6.3 Vestas' and GE's financials compared, July 2014   174
6.4 Levelized energy costs for electric power production
      alternatives, 2012   176
6.5 Megawatts of installed wind production capacity in 20
      countries, 2003 to 2013   180
6.6 Percentage megawatt growth in wind capacity in four
      continents, 1999 to 2013   182
6.7 Global market share of top five Asian wind power firms,
      2010 to 2012   183
6.8 Global wind power firm attrition   184
6.9 Location of Chinese wind power generating capacity,
      2012   185
6.10 Wind power jobs   190
7.1 Hunger and overnutrition: the twin problems in 2010   204
7.2 The financials of General Mills, Kellogg's, and Nestlé,
      August 2014   206
7.3 Revenue changes in the ready-to-eat cereal industry, 2000
      to 2013   207
7.4 Environmental, social, and governance scores for US food
      companies   208
7.5 Healthiest and unhealthiest breakfast cereals   217
8.1 Beverage category growth in value and volume
      consumed, 2008 to 2013   229
8.2 Major world tea markets, 2008 and 2013   230
8.3 Company market share in tea in Asia, 2008 and 2013   231
8.4 Major sports and energy drink markets in the world,
      2008 and 2013   232
8.5 Bottled water consumption in developing countries, 2008
      and 2013   233

8.6 United States' bottled water revenue growth, 2000 to 2013   233

8.7 Major world juice markets and market share, 2008 and 2013   235

8.8 Coca-Cola and Pepsi global market share in carbonated soft drinks, 2008 and 2013   236

8.9 Global market share in snack foods, 2008 and 2013   237

8.10 Global and US snack food sales, 2008 to 2013   238

8.11 Soda drink market share in India, 2008 and 2013   244

8.12 Soda drink market share in Mexico, 2008 and 2013   245

8.13 Change in soda drink consumption in select Muslim countries, 2008 to 2013   247

8.14 Soda drink market share in select Muslim countries, 2008 and 2013   248

8.15 Beverage company financials compared, July 2014   254

9.1 Quarterly revenue growth and other financial indicators of major food retailers, August 2014   261

9.2 Sustainability scores of major food retailers, August 2014   264

9.3 Revenue growth in the retail food industry, 2000 to 2013   271

9.4 Comparative prices of organic food sold at Walmart and at other supermarkets   274

10.1 Benefits and controversies about genetically modified products   306

10.2 Major divisions of Monsanto, Syngenta, and DuPont, 2006   317

10.3 Agriculture chemical company financials compared, August 2014   322

10.4 Sustainability scores of major chemical companies, September 2014   322

10.5 DuPont's segments, products, markets, and sales, 2013   324

Foreword

The relationship between business and the environment has become extremely popular. Amazon lists 22,500 books under the heading "sustainable management" and 80,000 titles under "environmental management." There are of course many reasons why so many books on these topics are being published. One is that many firms are finding themselves under substantial pressures from government, consumers, employees, and the general public to improve their environmental performance. They want and need guidance as to how to accomplish this – information that such books provide.

A second reason is that a growing number of executives and investors have become persuaded that there are substantial business opportunities associated with becoming more sustainable. The very term "sustainable management" represents an effort to link improved environmental performance with long-term growth and profitability. Thus a "sustainable company" is one that has successfully managed its long-term ecological impact in a way that also assures its future financial viability, with the two goals reinforcing one another.

The claim that becoming "greener" can make a firm more profitable dominates writing on sustainable management. What makes this claim credible is that many firms have financially benefited by becoming more sustainable. As this book demonstrates, venture capital firms have prospered by investing in clean energy, investments in solar and wind power have proven profitable, there is a market for more fuel-efficient vehicles and other environmentally friendly consumer products, and many consumers want to purchase healthier food.

The stories of such business successes are certainly inspiring. But what is less clear is what lessons they have to teach. For by only highlighting "win–win" stories, the literature on sustainable management often winds up making it look too easy – just because some firms have made profitable green innovations does not mean that other firms can successfully do so. Equally important, focusing on green business successes overlooks the equally valuable business lessons from firms whose green innovations have proven disappointing.

What makes *Innovations in Sustainability* a truly innovative book is Alfred Marcus's ability to integrate his extensive knowledge of sustainable management with a sophisticated understanding of corporate strategy. As he notes in his introduction, green innovations are most usefully understood as a strategic choice. Like any corporate strategy, they involve uncertainty, or predictions about the future that may or may not prove valid. This is especially true to the extent that their successful achievement often depends on favorable public policies.

The case studies in this book are not only exhaustively researched, but they place each of the firms whose experiences they describe in a broader context. Marcus' detailed case studies enable us to clearly understand the several choices each of these firms made over time, how they affected one another, and what they have and have not accomplished – both financially and environmentally. They clearly demonstrate why the path to sustainability is so challenging and complex – in essence no different than any other corporate strategy.

By ending each chapter with a series of questions that highlight the strategic choices that now confront each firm, Marcus reminds us that sustainable business objectives are never achieved. Rather they represent an ongoing challenge; the path to profitable sustainability is an endless one. Just because a firm has succeeded in financially benefitting from green innovations in sustainability in the past or present does not mean that it will also be able to do so in the future.

Another feature that distinguishes this book from other studies of "green" business is its sophisticated recognition of the importance of the competitive context. By organizing its chapters in a way that pairs each company with a similar or comparable one, Marcus reminds us that green business strategies do not occur in a vacuum. A sustainable company must not only succeed on its own terms: its success often requires it to be *better* than its competitors. Students of business strategy understand this, but too many of those who write about successful green business strategies do not.

Innovations in Sustainability covers an enormous amount of ground; while it is organized around individual firms, few dimensions of current environmental concerns fall outside its scope. It makes fascinating reading and represents an original and much needed contribution to our understanding of the challenges facing sustainable innovations.

David Vogel
University of California, Berkeley, CA

Acknowledgments

I thank J. Alberto Aragon-Correa and Jorge Rivera, editors of this series, who urged me to write this book and Cambridge University Press' anonymous reviewers for their input. In studying sustainability and sustainable innovation my primary inspiration comes from the co-authors of the academic papers with whom I have been recently working: Ari Ginsberg of NYU, Adam Fremeth from the Ivey School, Mazhar Islam at Drexel, Joel Malen at Hitotsubashi University Institute of Innovation Research, Sue Cohen at the University of Pittsburgh Katz School, and Shmuel Ellis and Israel Drori at the Tel Aviv University Business School.

James Balch, a Carlson School MBA student, provided me with ongoing information about clean energy topics. His passion for the topic was immense. He is an indefatigable helper whose enthusiasm for the topic was infectious. I obtained much of the data that I use in the first two chapters in the book from the Cleantech Group, a market intelligence, events, and advisory services organization in San Francisco. Throughout the book I relied heavily on Greentech Media, an Internet-based information center. Euromonitor was the source of some of my information, especially about the beverage industry. CSRHub was a good source of information on corporate social responsibility.

I owe a large debt to the Carlson School where I have taught for over 30 years. All the Department of Strategic Management and Entrepreneurship members deserve mention but I will refer to just a few department members because of their outstanding contributions to matters related to the topic of this book: Andy Van de Ven for his work on innovation, and Shakher Zahra and Harry Sapienza for their work on venture capital (VC).

David Vogel, editor of the *California Management Review* and faculty member at the Haas School of Business at Berkeley, has shown that he understands well my purpose in writing this book. Other colleagues in organizations and the natural environment with whom I am close and whose work I appreciate a great deal are Sanjay Sharma, Dean of a very innovative MBA program at the University of Vermont, Magali Delmas of UCLA, Rebecca Henderson and Michael Toffel at the Harvard Business School, Mark Starik at San Francisco State, Michael Russo at the Lundquist College at Oregon, Tim Hargrave who now teaches at Simon Fraser, Frances Bowen at Queen Mary University of London, Volker Hoffman at ETH Zurich, Stefano Pogutz at Boconi, Paul Shrivastava at Concordia University Montreal, Dror Etzion at McGill, Jonthan Pinkse at Grenoble, and Rolf Wustenhagen and Jorg Grimm at St. Gallen.

As a past chairperson of the Organizations and Natural Environment Division of the Academy of Management, I owe the division a great deal. I also have been a regular attender of the Group for Organizations and the Natural Environment meetings. I believe that it was at a session in the South of France that the prospect that I might write this book first gained traction. The organizations and natural environment community has expanded greatly over the years and if I have forgotten to mention anyone please forgive me.

The *California Management Review* and the journal *Organizations and the Natural Environment* are where some of the ideas found in chapters of this book first appeared. I wrote earlier cases on Pepsi, Coca-Cola, Monsanto, DuPont, and Walmart that appeared in *Winning Moves*, a book published by Marsh Press. Libby Rubinstein, a long time editor at McGraw-Hill, who ran Marsh Press, deserves some of the credit for my understanding of these companies.

Paula Parish has been a great editor at Cambridge University Press. I also appreciate the work that Claire Wood did on the book.

The real start for the writing of this book took place while I was teaching in the MBA program at the Technion. As I teach at Carlson, the University of Minnesota's Technological Leadership Institute, and at the Technion, I owe a great deal to the many different students for the fresh insights they have provided in the classroom. The University of Minnesota Management of Technology students have been especially perceptive in what they have taught me about innovation.

Massoud Amin, long time director of the Technological Leadership Institute, is an energy expert and guru par excellence whose work on the electric power grid has been critical to making it more reliable and efficient. My conversations and other interactions with Massoud always have been enlightening.

Without a doubt, my family has been a great source of pride and support as I wrote this book. My wife Judy, a social worker by profession, is my life partner of over 40 years. I am grateful for her love, support, and especially for her patience, as the writing of this book took on great importance and often was my first priority. My sons have reached the age where I consider them intellectual peers who regularly share their wisdom with me. The older son, David, recently was appointed co-editor of *Dissent Magazine*. He also is finishing a PhD in American intellectual history at Columbia. My younger son, Ariel, works as an analyst at Spotify. He formerly worked at the *NY Times* and Linked-in. His knowledge of the Internet is unparalleled. My family is made up of humanitarians who regularly do good works. I hope they appreciate the challenges to humanity I address in this book.

Introduction: the path to sustainability

The path to sustainability has not necessarily been paved with gold, though many hoped it would be.[1] They discussed the wins available for society and wins available for businesses. The wins would be new ways of eliminating waste and introducing novel products with unique features customers would value. They viewed sustainable innovation as a sound business proposition and challenged businesses to take this road not only because it was in the vital interests of society but because it was a sound business proposition. If businesses were going to fulfill their moral obligation to society and simultaneously pursue their obligations to their financial backers and other constituencies, then they had to engage in sustainable innovation. Since the articulation of this idea more than 20 years ago, many businesses have taken up this call in whole or in part. Very few have entirely resisted it. Whether their efforts were completely sincere was the topic of Frances Bowen's book *After Greenwashing*.[2]

The aim of this book is to examine the experiences particular businesses have had with sustainable innovation during this period in order to assess and learn from these experiences and more importantly to consider the challenges that lie ahead. One element appears not to have been taken sufficiently seriously by the many previous champions of sustainable innovation. That element was risk and the importance of strategic choice in an environment of uncertainty. Like innovation of any kind, sustainable innovation has been a bet on the future. With respect to the future, humans – no matter how keen or shrewd – have limited forecasting capabilities. Their decision making is guided by passion and gut instinct as much as it is by rational calculations, and they make mistakes no matter how well intentioned they may be.

The readers of this book will become acquainted with many bold efforts by heroic and pioneering individuals to change the world for the better, but also will witness the results of many errors in the pursuit of sustainable innovation from which they can learn. After more than

20 years of attempts to achieve sustainable innovation in various organizations, it is now apparent that plans go awry, results often are more
unintended than intended, unexpected contingencies arise, and that the
individuals involved must re-examine the paths they have taken and
try to reset them to better accommodate new realities. Even the most
sophisticated technologies, the best business models, and the leadership of powerful, inspiring, energetic, and frequently highly capable
individuals do not always lead to what bestselling authors Esty and
Winston have referred to as "green gold."[3]

In the language of David Vogel, the "market for virtue," while not
non-existent, in many cases is narrow and limited.[4] To hit that bull's
eye, where sustainable innovation is possible on a wide-scale basis
and is not just a tiny niche, is a formidable task. A brutal sorting out
process of what works and what does not work has taken place. Government policies, because of the uncertainties inherent in them and
the inadvertent side effects they trigger, as Vogel points out and this
book shows, have played a substantial role in both nudging the process forward and blocking progress.[5] Neither markets by themselves
nor markets assisted by governments, as a consequence, have been
entirely up to the task of securing a future in which the planet, people,
and profits flourish and in which the environment is protected, equity
and social justice are secured, and economic growth and development
maintained.

This book consists of 20 open-ended, inter-related cases that deal
with the ongoing challenge of achieving sustainable innovation in some
of the world's largest and most prominent organizations. The cases in
this book are open-ended because the issues they raise about the sustainable journeys of these business organizations are not over, not by
a long shot. These organizations are in the midst of deciding what to
do next. The reader of this book is invited to take part in this process. What are the ensuing journeys these organizations should take
to achieve their sustainable goals and the sustainable goals of society?
The cases deal with two of sustainability's main concerns – fueling
and feeding a hungry planet – and are meant for discussion and debate
by managers, would-be managers, researchers, consultants, activists,
government officials, public policy analysts, and students about the
routes these organizations should take next. Based on their past actions
and achievements, how should these organizations adjust their goals
and take the concrete managerial steps that will better enable them

to fulfill their obligations to their stakeholders and their financial backers?

The following are among the questions that these organizations face and with which this book should help its readers grapple:

- Which sustainable options are the most promising for investors, and at which stage – early or late – should investors back them?
- Which business models should organizations use to move innovations toward broad commercialization?
- Which factors in the macroenvironment and the industry context facilitate or impede their forward momentum?
- Where will they find large enough markets for broad adoption?
- How will competitive battles among different types of organizations – mission and non-mission based – influence the results?

The investment question is covered by an in-depth analysis of the choices of the two largest private equity venture capital (VC) backers of clean energy, Khosla Ventures and KPCB, and by an in-depth analysis of the investment choices of the two largest corporate VC backers of this type of innovation, Intel Capital and Google Ventures. The business model question is covered by an analysis of the contrasting business models of two of the largest solar power startups, First Solar and Suntech, and by analysis of the contrasting business models of the two most significant electric vehicle startups, Tesla and Better Place. The macroenvironment and industry context question is raised for innovators in hybrid car technologies, Toyota and GM, and innovators in wind power generation, Vestas and General Electric.

At this point the book turns from fuel to food. The question of finding markets large enough for the adoption of sustainable products focuses on the experiences of the ready-to-eat cereal companies General Mills and Kellogg's and on the experiences of the beverage and snack companies Pepsi and Coca-Cola. The question of competition between mission and non-mission based companies has as its focus Whole Foods and Walmart, and DuPont and Monsanto.

Each question is covered by two cases and each case features two organizations dealing with a similar issue. The case studies in the book are inter-related in that together they tell a single story based on extended examples of organizations trying to cope with dual challenges of fuel and food. They are on the path to sustainability but the market for virtue is an imperfect guide.

The reader should be aware of the global dimensions of the strategic business choices organizations trying to make sustainable innovations confront, and pay special attention to the interplay of public policies in different countries, how they affect business competition, and how they influence outcomes. From reading this book, the reader should gain a sense of what might come next on the road to sustainable change. In 30 years' time, the world may be in serious trouble or it may have adequately transformed itself to deal reasonably well with the ongoing conundrums that fuel and food pose to people and the planet.

An evolutionary journey

An evolutionary model of the innovation journey informs the selection of the cases in this book.[6] The journey described is evolutionary in the sense that there are a wide variety of firms in competition with each other as well as in competition with incumbents. The lock-in of incumbents' business models and technologies provides barriers to innovative shifts in direction. Among new entrants, there is a high degree of churning. Many disappear quickly. To challenge incumbents' power, new entrants need protected spaces. If they survive, their growth often exceeds that of incumbents. The innovation journey can end in incremental adjustment with incumbents surviving as well as discontinuities that destroy incumbents' distinctive competencies.

The evolutionary perspective holds that a fitness "landscape" chooses the survivors.[7] It functions as a sorting mechanism that tests what works and what does not. Only some organizations have business designs that will become dominant. For a new design to become dominant a series of bottlenecks have to be overcome. Whether they can be surmounted is subject to substantial uncertainty. Even if in the end, particular business models and technological paradigms dominate over others, early stages are characterized by many entrants and relatively low dominance levels.

In an initial exploratory or embryonic stage, variation takes place. Uncertainty is high, many firms enter. Experimentation is rife. Competition is intense. Startups compete with mature firms. Selection is subject to shifting conditions. Business models have to adjust and change as they confront new challenges. Mature firms are at risk but so are the startups. Many startups do not survive. Retention may take a long time before a stable sorting of the winners and losers takes place and there is greater stability.

The evolutionary perspective relies on the concepts of variation, selection, and retention. Variation, selection, and retention act like a funnel. Ultimately, stabilization may happen, with convergence around particular models and technological paradigms, with some business models surviving and others being discarded, but this moment is far from inevitable.

Relying on an evolutionary approach, I divide the cases in this book into these stages (see Table 0.1): (1) variation, (2) selection's onset, (3) selection, (4) retention's onset, and (5) retention. Each stage is covered with two paired cases. The main activities in stages 1 and 2 are funding and business model testing. In stages 3 and 4 they are coping with shifts in external conditions and finding new customers. In stage 5 they are moving sustainable innovations to the mainstream.

Stage 1 involves numerous startups experimenting with concepts. Stage 2 comprises startups trying to refine their business models and establish them on a firmer footing. The next stages involve mature and early-stage companies confronting novel challenges and seeking new customers. In the final stage, mission-based firms face off against non-mission based firms for dominance. As sustainable innovation moves to the mainstream, few firms survive the first stage. Some firms succeed beyond expectation in the next stage, but in the following stages they confront new problems and challenges. For incumbents, the question is whether to exploit what they have been doing best, or explore for new sustainable options. At later stages they have to assess whether sustainable innovation has become the norm. If so, to what extent must they conform to it?

The economic exploitation and introduction of innovations into widespread use varies. Some innovations take a very long time to diffuse. Others never diffuse. Because winners and losers in the competition are determined by ex-post selection, the journey to sustainable innovation is not subject to rational planning.

The current understanding of the evolution of innovation is skeptical of the inevitability of optimal outcomes.[8] In the end, the fitness landscape determines which organizations succeed and which organizations fail, but the fitness landscape is far from perfect. The spread of inferior business models and technologies can take place because selection is not just a result of intrinsic goodness. Chance and timing

Table 0.1 *Sustainable innovation: evolutionary stages*

Stage	Main activity	Players and goals	Principal outcomes	Chapters	Case comparisons	Case comparisons
1. Variation	Funding	Numerous startups experimenting with many concepts	Very few firms survive, many fail completely	1–2	Clean energy private equity venture capital: Khosla Ventures and KPCB	Clean energy corporate venture capital: Intel Capital and Google Ventures
2. Selection's onset	Business model testing	Early-stage companies trying to build their businesses	Firms struggle, some continue on, some succeed beyond expectation, and some fail	3–4	Publicly traded US and Chinese solar startups: First Solar and Suntech	Publicly traded US and heavily funded Israeli electric car startups: Tesla and Better Place
3. Selection	Coping with macroenvironment and industry shifts	Mature and early-stage companies competing in established markets	Firms discover new obstacles to their initial successes	5–6	Hybrid vehicles and low gas prices: Toyota and GM	Unfavorable wind energy markets and weak government support: Vestas and GE

4. Retention's onset	Finding new customers	Mature companies trying to renew themselves	7–8	Firms choose between declining products and sustainable options	Advertising in sustainability: General Mills and Kellogg's	Sustainable product mix: Pepsi and Coca-Cola
5. Retention	Moving sustainable innovation to the mainstream	Non-mission based generalists facing off against mission-based specialists	9–10	Firms decide between more or less convergence	Alternatives to biotech: Monsanto and DuPont	Corporate social responsibility and sustainability: Whole Foods and Walmart

influence the outcomes, as do political and institutional biases. Innovations gain significant footholds even when they are not as efficient as the alternatives.

Embodying persistent feedback and learning, the evolutionary journey is not linear. Rather it is best understood as an emergent process that unfolds as a series of trials and errors. The prior knowledge that is needed to guarantee optimal outcomes simply does not exist. Knowledge expands from experience during the journey and affects organizational survival.

Upon reflecting on the chapters that follow, readers should judge for themselves. To what extent has the path to sustainable innovation been affected by mistake-ridden learning?[9] To what extent has it been subject to imperfect selection?

Notes

1 M. Porter and C. van der Linde, "Toward a new conception of the environment–competitiveness relationship," *Journal of Economic Perspectives* (1995): 97–118; M. Porter and C. van der Linde, "Green and competitive,"*Harvard Business Review* (1995): 120–34; S. Hart, "A natural resource based view of the firm," *Academy of Management Review* (1995): 986–1014; P. Shrivastava, "The role of corporations in achieving ecological sustainability," *Academy of Management Review* (1995): 936–60; K. Sexton, A. Marcus, K. Easter, and T. Burkhardt, *Better Environmental Decisions* (Washington, DC: Island Press, 1999); F. Reinhardt, *Down to Earth* (Boston, MA: Harvard Business School Press. 2000); S. Sharma and M. Starik, *Research in Corporate Sustainability* (Northampton, MA: Edward Elgar, 2002); W. Stead, J. Stead, and M. Starik, *Sustainable Strategic Management* (Armonk, NY: M. E. Sharpe, 2003); S. Sharma and J. A. Aragón-Correa, *Corporate Environmental Strategy and Competitive Advantage* (Northampton, MA: Edgar Elgar, 2005); D. Esty and A. Winston, *Green to Gold: How Smart Companies Use Environmental Strategy to Innovate, Create Value, and Build Competitive Advantage* (New Haven, CT: Yale University Press, 2006); P. Senge, B. Smith, N. Kruschwitz, J. Laur, and S. Schley, *The Necessary Revolution: How Individuals and Organizations are Working Together to Create a Sustainable World* (New York: Random House, 2008); P. Hawken, A. Lovins, and L. H. Lovins, *Natural Capitalism: Creating the Next Industrial Revolution* (New York: Little, Brown, and Company,2008); S. Sharma, M. Starik, and B. Husted, *Organizations and the Sustainability Mosaic* (Northampton, MA: Edgar Elgar, 2008);

A. Werbach, *Strategy for Sustainability* (Boston, MA: Harvard Business School Press, 2009); R. Orsato, *Sustainable Strategies: When Does it Pay to be Green* (New York: Palgrave Macmillan, 2009); S. Hart, *Capitalism at the Crossroads: Next Generation Business Strategies for a Post-crisis World* (Upper Saddle River, NJ: Pearson-Prentice Hall, 2010); M. Russo, *Companies on a Mission* (Palo Alto, CA: Stanford University Press, 2011); C. Laszlo and N. Zhexembayeva, *Embedded Sustainability: the Next Big Competitive Advantage* (Palo Alto, CA: Stanford Business Books, 2011); M. Blowfield, *Business and Sustainability* (Oxford, UK: Oxford University Press, 2013).

2 F. Bowen, *After Greenwashing* (Cambridge, UK: Cambridge University Press, 2014).

3 Esty and Winston, *Green to Gold*.

4 D. Vogel, *The Market for Virtue* (Washington, DC: Brookings Institution Press, 2006).

5 *Ibid.*

6 H. Aldrich, *Organizations Evolving* (Thousand Oaks, CA: Sage, 1999).

7 G. Dosi and R. Nelson, "Technical change and industrial dynamics as evolutionary processes," in B. H. Hall and N. Rosenberg (ed.) *Handbook of the Economics of Innovation, Vol. 2* (North-Holland, 2010), pp. 51–127.

8 *Ibid.*

9 *Ibid.*

PART I

Funding sustainable startups

1 | Leaders of the pack: Khosla Ventures and KPCB

Khosla Ventures and Kleiner Perkins Caufield & Byers (KPCB) were the leading venture capital (VC) investors in clean energy. They had to assess what they would do next. To what extent did the clean energy sector continue to be attractive? To what extent should they continue to invest in it? If they continued to invest, which categories should they emphasize? At what stage in the maturation of a startup should they concentrate their investments?

Clean energy consisted of energy efficiency, solar, alternative modes of transportation and energy storage, biofuels, and wind and agricultural technologies that had the potential to reduce reliance on fossil fuels such as coal and oil. These sustainable technologies had the potential to reduce noxious emissions, lower the chances of climate change, and decrease dependence on a commodity imported from unstable regions of the globe. They also might be able to build new industries and create jobs. The US Department of Energy (DOE) projected that the US and world economies would continue to be largely dependent on fossil fuels into the foreseeable future.[1] Clean energy's use expanded under the DOE's business-as-usual scenario, but its impact was not transformative. This forecast, however, could change, if clean energy made a series, or even single, major leap forward. Venture capitalists (VCs) might partially or fully fund a disruptive movement in the way energy was produced and consumed that was similar in impacts to the revolution that took place when the Internet took off. Since startups with game-changing technologies rarely had the money they needed to finance their growth and development, they often depended on VC funding.

Venture capitalists were general partners in the investment funds they created. As of May 2014, Khosla Ventures had created five investment funds and had raised $2.3 billion since its inception in 2004, while KPCB, had created twenty-nine investment funds and raised $7.4 billion since its inception in 1972. Venture capitalists like Khosla

Ventures and KPCB raised money for their investment funds from such groups as pension funds, university endowments, insurance companies, private companies, and individuals that became partners in the funds. Among the largest and best known investors in Khosla Ventures were the pension funds the California Public Employees Retirement System and the Tennessee Consolidated Retirement System.

Venture capital funds generally had a ten-year lifespan between raising money and exiting from investments they had made. The VCs' role was to find promising startups, nurture their development, and look for potential exit opportunities either through initial public offerings (IPOs) that took place on one of the world's stock exchanges or acquisitions of the firms the VCs funded by another company. For the services that the VCs rendered they typically were entitled to 20 percent of the profits if the firms they funded achieved successful exits. In the meantime, they earned management fees of two to three percent.

Examples of Khosla Venture's funds were Khosla Ventures IV and Khosla Ventures Seed B for which Khosla Ventures raised more than a billion dollars in 2010 and 2011. Examples of KPCB funds were KPCB XIV and KPCB XV for which it raised similar amounts in the same years. The focus of KPCB's latter fund was on early-stage investments, with approximately half of the money being reserved for information technology (IT). The rest was to be split between clean energy and the life sciences.

The entrepreneurs that VCs funded typically relied on basic and applied research, which might come from universities, governments, or corporate labs.[2] Their need for funding was to develop commercially viable businesses. They generally sought funding from VCs such as Khosla Ventures and KPCB after starting their businesses, the initial resources for startup mainly being dervied from their own assets as well as family, friends, or angel investors. These groups provided startups with money at very early stages to help them get started. At the next stage, the startups faced what was called the valley of death, the gap between their beginnings and the widespread deployment of the products and services they created. What VCs such as Khosla Ventures and KPCB gave them was the funding they needed to test their ideas' commercial viability in this next stage.

In taking on this task, VCs such as Khosla Ventures and KPCB put themselves at great risk, because the entrepreneurs they backed frequently failed. The complete write-off of the investments VCs made was common. Even if not completely written-off, the investments might earn little for investors. VCs such as Khosla Ventures and KPCB searched for startups that would earn extraordinary amounts of money. They looked for exceptions to this rule. Finding the exceptions was critically important to the standing of Khosla Ventures and KPCB among VC firms and to their ability to raise additional capital. Returns to VC in the first decade of the twenty-first century had fallen from the prior decade. The pension funds, university endowments, insurance companies, private companies, and individuals that backed VCs demanded accountability. Returns could fall only so much before they lost confidence.

The VCs had options other than clean energy. Their past successes were in areas such as IT, software, the Internet, medical technology, and social media. It might be prudent for them to stick to these areas as opposed to investing in clean energy. Though there was the possibility of a revolution in clean energy similar in magnitude to the one that took place in other high-tech areas in which the VCs had invested, clean energy was a risky sector in which to be involved. Yet, the nature of VC was to take risks – the bigger the risk, the greater the likelihood of return – or was this reckoning that the VCs used to justify their decisions fallacious?

A clean energy revolution

The spectacular success of VCs such as KPCB in the late 1990s contributed to the high-tech boom that so dramatically transformed the global economy. KPCB helped to fund such companies as Amazon, Intuit, Netscape, Compaq, Symantec, Electronic Arts, Juniper Networks, Cypress Semiconductors, and Citrix Systems. Thomas Perkins founded the firm in 1972. An MIT-educated engineer and Harvard MBA, he had been the head of Hewlett Packard's computer division. Disillusioned with a slow-moving corporate decision style he looked to start his own VC firm. In the process he met Eugene Kleiner, a founder of Fairfield Semiconductor Company, who became his first partner. Together they raised $8 million and over a ten-year period earned an average annual rate of return of 41.5 percent for their investors. For example, KPCB invested $1.6 million in Tandem Technologies in 1975, a company that provided ATM systems to banks, and by 1982 this company was worth $203.4 million.

The founder of Khosla Ventures was Vinod Kholsa. A graduate of the India Institute of Technology, upon graduation he tried to start a soy milk company to assist the poor in India but failed. Obtaining a master's degree in chemical engineering from Carnegie Mellon University and an MBA from Stanford, he was a co-founder of Sun Microsystems with his Stanford classmates Scott McNealy and Andy Bechtolsheim and University of California at Berkeley computer science graduate student Bill Joy. Khosla served as Sun Microsystems' chairman and first CEO from 1982 to 1984. In 1987, he joined KPCB as a general partner, only to leave KPCB in 2004 to start his own VC firm. His aim was to take advantage of innovative, outside-the-box methods to solve problems involving energy, poverty, and disease that previously had seemed intractable. The potential that VCs such as Khosla Ventures and KPCB brought to clean energy was that they could have a similarly transformative impact in this sector as they had in computer and information technology in the 1990s.

Khosla Ventures and KPCB were not the first VCs to invest in clean energy. Specialist firms that focused on the area included Nth Power, EnerTech Captial, SJF Ventures, Rockport Capital Partners, and NGEN Partners. The non-specialist firm Draper Fisher Jurvetson had also been involved. From 1995 to 1999, firms such as these had invested $100 million to $200 million in about 30 to 50 clean energy deals annually. Nonetheless, clean energy was a small part of the overall VC industry. From 1995 to 1999 the industry as a whole grew from about $7 billion invested per year to more than $50 billion. At the peak of the Internet bubble, the year 2000, an all-time record of about $100 billion was invested, mostly in Internet, Internet-related, and computer companies.When the high-tech bubble burst and the 2001 meltdown of the tech economy took place, this played havoc with the VCs' business models. The financial disturbances following 9/11 meant that the stock market was weak and very few IPOs were executed. As a consequence, VCs started to look for new investment opportunities. Clean energy was a natural candidate, one driver of its potential being climate change, which Al Gore had publicized in his movie *An Inconvenient Truth*. Gore later was to become a partner at KPCB.

The overall trend was unmistakable. Clean energy took off as a category of VC investment in the first decade of the twenty-first century (see Figure 1.1).

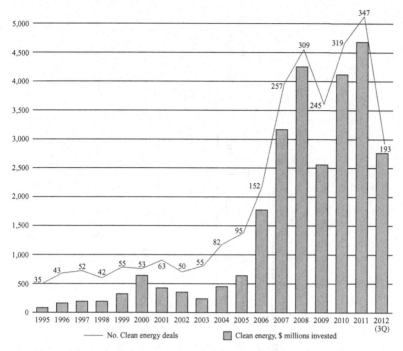

Figure 1.1 Clean energy venture deals and US $s invested, 1995 to 2012 (United States)
Source: Thomson ONE Banker: http://banker.thomsonone.com

Other than getting on a bandwagon and seeking out a fashionable category, what led VCs to choose clean energy over better established categories with longer track records, such as software, biotechnology, semiconductors, electronics, telecommunications technology, and medical devices? One reason was that returns to clean energy investments in 2002 to 2003 were very good (see Table 1.1). Three solar companies – Q-Cells, SunPower, and Suntech (see Chapter 3) – had gone public in 2004, each at a valuation of about $1 billion. Eighteen of the largest US pension funds indicated that they wanted to see more clean energy investment.[3] The California Public Employees' Retirement System dedicated $200 million to clean energy in 2004, and its sister fund the California State Teachers' Retirement System dedicated $250 million to it in 2005. The pension funds' interest was not just financial. Some of them perceived clean energy mainly in economic terms, but others touted the environmental benefits. Still others envisioned wins for both society and their bottom lines.

Table 1.1 *Returns to clean energy and other VC investment categories, 2002 to 2006*

	2002 Percentage annual return	2003 Percentage annual return	2004 Percentage annual return	2005 Percentage annual return	2006 Percentage annual return
Clean energy	26	47	13	9	7
Information technology	9	17	20	31	21
All VC categories	10	12	14	15	9

Compiled from data on the National Venture Capital Association website, December 2011

After 2003, when the returns to clean energy began to slip, encouraging signs did not completely disappear. In response to high gasoline prices, George W. Bush backed renewable-energy policies and Obama's election suggested that the issue resonated well with the public. As part of the effort to recover from the financial crisis, Congress included clean energy in the stimulus package. The Obama administration declared it a priority, setting aside more than $90 billion for this purpose. Other governments throughout the world committed close to $190 billion to clean energy and it was estimated that China would spend two to four times this amount in the coming decade.

Venture capitalists that invested in clean energy hoped that they could achieve high returns. They wished to discover and cultivate companies of comparable quality as those that they discovered and cultivated in the 1990s. Their involvement might help to usher in a global revolution in energy production and consumption similar to the revolution that took place in high tech, IT, and computers. However, obstacles to realizing this vision existed that were not present in these other industries. The energy infrastructure in place had long replacement lead times – anywhere from 15 years for motor vehicles to 50 years for power plants to 100 years and more for manufacturing facilities and buildings. Unlike the costs of scaling up the production, distribution, and installation of IT, the costs of scaling up the production, distribution, and installation of clean energy were very high.[4]

Moreover, the favorable conditions that had spurred clean energy started to wear thin. Congress' attempt to pass cap-and-trade legislation to control greenhouse emissions failed. Because of the financial crisis, many solar and wind projects were canceled. At the start of the second decade of the twenty-first century, fracking offered the potential for abundant cheap natural gas and it was widely expected to be able to produce US energy independence, a long sought-after US goal. Many renewable energy projects were abandoned. With Chinese solar power firms receiving cheap loans from their government and flooding the US market with inexpensive solar cells (see Chapter 3), US solar startups had trouble scaling up their operations and competing. The bankruptcy of solar-panel maker Solyndra, the recipient of more than half a billion dollars of federal aid, unleashed a barrage of criticism that questioned the feasibility of a vibrant clean energy sector. Though progress had been made, especially with energy efficiency, solar energy, and wind, which were starting to compete with other forms of electrical generation on a dollar-for-dollar basis, without advances in storage technologies the advances in solar and wind had limited potential. Abundant natural gas, unlike solar and wind, was not an intermittent source of power.

In general, VCs took on excessively high risks in the hope they would realize outsized gains. Though in the past their investments in the leading industries of the future had paid off handsomely – and their contribution to the creation of jobs, economic growth, and market value had been undeniable – the returns from all investments they made in the first decade of the twenty-first century were anything but impressive. According to the Kauffman Foundation, these returns that they delivered in the first part of twenty-first century were not significantly better than public markets.[5] Cambridge Associates' 2013 scorecard of VC returns showed a decade of decline.[6] During a time when the Dow Jones US Small Cap Index achieved average annual returns of more than ten percent, the VCs' average annual returns were under nine percent.

However, according to Cambridge Associates, there were differences in the performance of the investments made in the various clean energy categories.[7] Renewable power development projects performed the best, with average annual returns above eleven percent (see Chapter 2). Energy optimization – an amalgam of efficiency, lighting, transportation, smart grid, and storage – came in second, with average annual returns above five percent. Solutions involving water, waste, materials, controls, and agriculture were next with average annual returns of about three percent. The poorest performers were in a category within which the VCs had concentrated most of their investments. They had concentrated most of their investments in solar, wind, and biofuels, whose average annual returns were under one percent.

Khosla Ventures and KPCB therefore felt increasing pressure to defend the investments they had made in clean energy. In an interview in the *Harvard Business Review*, Khosla commented that the rise of clean energy technologies should not be viewed using a short-term lens.[8] In the end, trends with regard to energy prices, geopolitics, global poverty, and climate change were favorable, though many obstacles still had to be overcome. Khosla Ventures' founder maintained that within 25 years, the world would replace most fossil fuels with non-food biomass and waste or with solar, geothermal, and wind energy.

In an article in *Forbes* the firm's founder made many of the same points.[9] Acknowledging that clean energy no longer was in vogue, he blamed the media for highlighting celebrated failures such as Solyndra. He admitted that his VC firm had made mistakes, such as investing heavily in corn-based ethanol, yet he was certain that such failures were only par for the course. For VC investors these failures should not be unexpected. Those outside the VC world had to understand that VCs commonly had many failures and that a few spectacular successes justified the many investments they made that went sour.

Khosla reaffirmed that his firm would not back down. Relying on its diverse portfolio of investments, it would demonstrate that clean energy could compete with other fuels on a totally unsubsidized basis. The short-term trends VCs were experiencing, according to Khosla, were not meaningful.

The 60 Minutes' bombshell

A January 5, 2014 CBS News' *60 Minutes* segment featuring Khosla called "the cleantech crash" charged that the investments Khosla and other VCs had made in clean energy were nothing more than billion dollar tax-funded flops that created few new jobs or economic development. Khosla and other VCs, according to CBS, had overpromised and underdelivered. Worse yet, supported by tax payers' dollars, the failed startups in which they invested had been snapped up at low cost by the Chinese rivals of US companies. The United States had lost valuable intellectual property to Chinese firms, for which it paid dearly.

Khosla made a vigorous rebuttal, maintaining that the federal government had spent billions of dollars trying to find a cure for cancer and it had not succeeded, but no one maintained it should stop funding cancer research.[10] To innovate, VCs had to tolerate failure, but that should not deter them from taking risks. Glitches that some clean energy startups had encountered were temporary and could be overcome.

Khosla went on to criticize CBS for gross misrepresentation. He contradicted the assertion that he personally had invested billions of dollars of his own money into clean energy firms that were on life support to keep these companies afloat. In addition, he maintained in comparison to the half trillion dollars the federal government provided to fossil fuels, the subsidies it gave to clean energy were totally trivial. Most of the ventures DOE backed, Khosla maintained, had not been failures. Indeed, he asserted that these clean energy companies were creating new jobs and paying back the loans the government had given them. He held that the TV network just did not understand how the VC process works. His firm's overall investments in clean energy would be profitable. Though it had invested in companies with high failure probabilities, the wins were far outweighing the losses. Khosla expected 50 percent of the investments his company made to ultimately make money.

Next to Khosla Ventures, KPCB was the second largest US VC investor in clean energy. It was considered by many to be the most prestigious Silicon Valley VC. It too was subject to criticism for the investments it made in clean energy. A Reuters' article made disparaging remarks about John Doerr, KPCB's senior partner, who had helped move the firm in this direction.[11] An electrical engineer with a master's degree from Rice University and an MBA from Harvard, Doerr had joined KPCB in 1980 after a six-year stint at Intel. In a 2007 TED Talk, he affirmed that the reason for investing in clean energy was the debt his generation owed the next. However, he also proposed that the category was likely to be highly profitable. He proclaimed, that clean energy would be bigger than the Internet. In no way was it a philanthropic endeavor, but he considered it to be the biggest economic opportunity of the twenty-first century.

Despite Doerr's protests, he could not refute Reuters' contention that KPCB's clean energy losses were mounting rapidly. KPCB had not converted a high percentage of its clean energy investments into successful exits. Therefore Reuters suggested that KPCB no longer should be considered among the best US venture capital firms and the best startup firms should look elsewhere for their funding. Google, which went public in 2004, was KPCB's last major success.

KPCB set aside $100 million in a 2006 fund for green investing. The next year it doubled this amount, and the following year it created a special half billion dollar fund exclusively for this purpose. Yet KPCB's clean energy investments suffered many disappointments. The electric auto maker Fisker and the solar firm Amonix failed. Spring Networks, a smart-grid company, and Mascoma, a producer of biofuels, delayed their plans to go public. Meanwhile other VCs that concentrated on social media gained ground. Accel Partners was the main backer of

Facebook, and Charles River Ventures and Spark Capital were the main financers of Twitter. KPCB joined these deals very late and barely profited from them.

Doerr responded to the attacks against him by reaffirming his belief in the promise and the profits of clean energy.[12] In a *Forbes* article he maintained that KPCB investing was broader than well-known clean energy firms. Its investing included the backing it had given to such companies as Nest, which made a smart thermostat that ex-iPod chief Tony Fadell had designed. Its funding included as well a plant protein company called, appropriately enough, Beyond Meat. Doerr, nonetheless, admitted that he had encouraged KPCB to do too much too fast. Characterizing his style of investment as enthusiastic, he said he was proud of the companies in which KPCB invested but hated to have lost so much money. KPCB's prime objective was not to save the planet. Its prime objective was to make money for its investors. The goal was not to take advantages of clean energy opportunities but to take advantage of whatever opportunities existed that could bring profit to KPCB's backers.

Soon after this statement, KPCB was buoyed by Google's purchase of Nest for $3.2 billion. KPCB had been the architect of Nest's Series A ($15 million), Series B ($37.5 million), and Growth Equity ($80 million) funding, with Google Ventures joining in the latter stages. However, Nest soon ran into trouble. First, there was a lawsuit from disgruntled customers that claimed that Nest thermostats failed to correctly measure temperature and save consumers money. Then, Google suspended sales of Nest smoke alarms after finding that a feature that allowed a user to turn the device off with a hand gesture could be accidently activated. Another KPCB investment, Opower, an energy software company, though, went public in 2014, and it soared in value, gaining more than 21 percent on its first day of trading, giving some credence to Doerr's conviction that clean energy still had the potential to yield profits for investors as well as benefits to society.

Assessing Khosla Ventures' and KPCB's clean energy investments

Khosla Ventures and KPCB had to assess their experience investing in clean energy and what that experience would mean for their future decisions. KPCB was larger than Khosla Ventures and older. It had

Table 1.2 *Khosla Ventures and KPCB participation in clean energy deals,*
2004 to 2013

	Khosla		KPCB	
	Early stage	Late stage	Early stage	Late stage
Efficiency[a]				
Number of deals	15	13	19	39
Average amount ($m)	17.13	30.42	13.63	36.77
Solar				
Number of deals	11	6	9	12
Average amount ($m)	19.79	48.52	34.75	38.90
Transportation & storage				
Number of deals	9	8	9	31
Average amount ($m)	8.05	20.86	19.24	68.62
Biofuels				
Number of deals	33	12	13	5
Average amount ($m)	22.94	48.37	28.16	43.42
Wind & agriculture				
Number of deals	9	1	6	3
Average amount ($m)	11.88	50.00	19.50	28.33
Total				
Number of deals	80	55	56	90
Average amount ($m)	18.85	39.22	21.55	45.70

Compiled from data on Clean Tech Group Website, November 2013
[a] Includes fuel cells, smart grid, and geothermal.

a more diversified portfolio. Just eight percent of KPCB's investments
were in clean energy, while more than a third of Khosla Ventures' were
in this sector. Khosla Ventures' clean energy investments were more
focused on biofuels than KPCB's, while KPCB had participated more
in efficiency and in transportation and storage deals (see Table 1.2).
Khosla defended the priority that his VC firm gave to biofuels in the
Harvard Business Review interview by claiming that because biofuels
required less change in driving, transportation, and heating patterns,
they had fewer financial and adoption barriers.[13]

Going forward, the two firms had to decide if they were going to
continue to invest in clean energy how would they divide their bets
among the different paths that clean energy could take. They also
had to decide at what stage should they invest. Early-stage companies

had a concept under development that was not fully operational. The products or services were in testing or pilot production and in some instances might be commercially available and generating revenues. Late-stage companies had placed their products or services into production and made them commercially available. These companies were likely to be showing revenue growth, but still might not be making a profit.

Late-stage investments were more certain but less profitable than early-stage investments. For scale-up, maturity, and making their products and services commercially viable, the years clean energy firms received funding often stretched out beyond the five- to ten-year exit periods that VCs favored. A longer investment horizon was needed in comparison to the software, Internet, and computer firms that VCs previously had funded. Growth equity investments typically went to companies that needed additional time and money to mature. From 2002 to 2012, Cambridge Associates estimated that average annual returns to this category were considerably higher than the average annual return to earlier stage VC investments.[14] By getting in early, a VC stood to gain greater profits, but they also faced greater risks. From 2004 to 2013, Khosla Ventures had been involved in 80 early-stage and 55 late-stage clean energy deals, while KPCB had been involved in 56 early-stage and 90 late-stage clean energy deals.[15] To determine what they should do next, the two VC firms had to examine their past investments by category and stage, and decide how to approach the decision of which clean energy categories at which stages they should back in the future.[16]

Energy efficiency

There were many energy-efficiency options in which Khosla Ventures and KPCB could invest.[17] Khosla Venture's main early-stage investment was with Soraa, a developer of galium nitride-based semiconductors for LEDs (light emitting diodes). LEDs originally had been used as indicator lamps for electronic devices. Their potential was in the energy saving they offered if they could be used as replacements for electric lighting. They lasted 50 times longer than the typical incandescent bulb. They had low carbon emissions and slow failure rates but high initial price.

One of Khosla Ventures' main energy efficiency investments was with a company called View. Its dynamic glass product could reduce energy consumption by 20 percent by blocking solar radiation during peak summer cooling demand periods and adding insulation during peak winter warming demand seasons. These gains were significant because windows accounted for as much as 40 percent of a building's energy consumption. View took standard glass and applied a coating on the surface to build an efficient light absorbing insulating unit that was able to automatically transition to different tints and provide unobstructed views without extra glare or heat. The units adapted to external conditions automatically or could be controlled by users. The product changed from clear to tinted glass as needed, which produced costs savings and environmental benefits. As well as different coating, air space, tinting, lamination, thickness, and strength options, a range of control options were available. With these windows in place, building designs could provide for healthier indoor spaces that had the potential to improve both the occupants' spirits and their productivity. Besides Khosla Ventures, GE Ventures and Corning had invested significant amounts of money in View.

Another one of KPCB's main investments in energy efficiency was with Nest, the design-focused energy management company whose flagship product was a networked learning thermostat for home use. As indicated, Google acquired Nest for $3.2 billion in 2014. Nest began to sell its thermostats in 2011. The thermostat's operating system interacted with the user by means of the user spinning and clicking a control wheel, which unveiled menus for heating, cooling, setup, energy history, and scheduling. Nest had the capability to install software updates and added features. Google did not just buy the company because of the potential energy savings but for the platform to enter the connected home. Based on sophisticated algorithms, the smart thermostat could track the behavior and anticipate the needs of inhabitants. It was able to learn about them over time and adjust building temperatures accordingly. Opponents held that the gadgets had the potential to invade people's privacy. Google could extend the capacity to other Internet gadgets, use the data to market products of many kinds, and influence a person's behavior.

Khosla Ventures and KPCB emphasized building energy efficiency. This emphasis made sense since buildings consumed 39 percent of total US energy: 71 percent of the electricity, and 54 percent of the natural gas.[18] They were responsible for 40 percent of carbon emissions. Yet building energy efficiency consisted of a host of numerous small

fixes. These fixes had to be designed and introduced into new buildings or retrofitted into old ones. The turnover in buildings was slow.
The incentives for introduction of energy efficiency fixes had to be just
right for the owners to install the many changes that were necessary,
which included new seals, sensors, building controls, lighting fixtures
and sources, windows, insulation, appliances, and water heating and
cooling systems. Utilities played an important role. By altering their
pricing structures, increasing demand monitoring, and restructuring
billing, they could foster these changes. Some energy-efficiency technology was simple and involved nothing more than painting roofs and
asphalts white. Other energy-efficiency technology was sophisticated
and complicated, for example software that could be put in place for
monitoring and controlling buildings' energy use.

A major problem was that a good business model was needed to
entice building owners, operators, and dwellers to incorporate energy
efficiency. The new technologies had to be cost and time effective. The
payoffs, even when relatively certain, often required long lead times.
Getting renters to make changes was particularly challenging. Who was
responsible for making the changes – the owner or the tenant? The person bearing the risk was not necessarily the same as the person enjoying
the reward. Documenting the actual savings was equally complicated.
Even after an owner paid for a new system, the maintenance might be
spotty and as a consequence the anticipated gains would not be realized. When there were maintenance gaps and building systems did not
function as expected, the investments that were made did not pay off.

Only in some jurisdictions were codes in place to encourage the
changes that were needed. Even rarer were rigorous inspections to
assure compliance. Also, only some jurisdictions provided assistance
via low interest and/or subsidized loans. Government agencies such as
the US Environmental Protection Agency (EPA) had developed programs like Energy Star for testing the energy efficiency of products,
but participation in the EPA programs was voluntary. Consumers
reasons for not choosing the most energy-efficient product included
price, convenience, and the features of a product. Independent and
private sector certifying agencies such as the US Green Energy Business
Council's LEED (Leadership in Energy & Environmental Design) program played a role in promoting green buildings, but these certification
programs tended to be costly and the number of building owners that
took advantage of them, although growing, was still small.

KPBC made a number of late-stage investments in building efficiency. An example was the previously mentioned company Opower.[19] The tool that Opower used to reduce energy consumption was a social comparison report it sent to electricity users. This report showed the occupant of a building how it was doing in comparison to its neighbors. If the building occupant was doing as well as its most efficient neighbors it had a double smiley face printed in the report, if it was not doing as well as its most efficient neighbors, but better than the average, it had a single smiley face, and if it was doing worse than its neighbors, it got a frowning face. These reports, based on the research of psychologist Robert Cialdini – author of the best-selling *Influence: The Psychology of Persuasion* – had the potential to reduce energy usage by 2.5 percent, a reduction that translated into a .5 percent saving in greenhouse gas emissions. For Opower's more than 90 utility customers in 35 states and eight countries the company combined a behavioral science approach based on Cialdini's research with computer and data science capabilities to process energy-use data and derive insights about ways that individuals, homeowners, and utilities could reduce energy consumption. The reports that Opower generated not only graded customers' usage, but also motivated them to improve by giving them advice about how to save money.

Opower maintained Internet sites for customers where it offered the energy-saving tips and recommendations. It communicated directly with customers via email, text, and other formats. Its energy reports reached 32 million homes annually. The company had the capacity to analyze the data from more than 100 billion electric meters reports a year. Based on the power of its technology and the many utility customers with whom Opower was in contact, the company went public in 2014. Like other clean energy startups that went public its price immediately peaked; however, it then skidded badly.

Another late-stage investment of KPCB's in building-energy efficiency was Silver Spring Networks. It too sold thermostats, home displays, and electric vehicle chargers. Its first major customer had been Florida Power & Light in 2007. Pacific Gas and Electric Company formed a partnership with the company and became its largest customer in 2008. Spring Networks provided smart-grid software and other products to utilities and customers that enabled the utilities to manage data from customers' meters. The data showed how much money customers spent on electricity and how much money they could save if improvements were made. Silver Spring Networks went public in 2013.

Echelon Corporation, which changed its name to Elon, had gone public around the same time. Echelon, as well, had received late-stage KPCB backing. It too had a multi-application energy control networking platform for smart-grid that was designed to help customers save energy. Its network platform also could reduce outage duration and prevent outages from occurring. Neither Silver Spring Networks' nor Echelon's plans for breaking even, however, were going as expected. To gain revenue, they did not fully price their services. Silver Spring Networks' total revenue was $327 million in 2014 in comparison to Echelon's $86 million. Silver Spring Networks had 602 employees and Echelon had 192 employees; Silver Spring Networks' net losses were $171.8 million in comparison to Echelon's net losses of $17.6 million. The stock prices of both companies were unstable after they went public.

Another late-stage investment of KPCB was with OSoft. This company had facility energy-management systems that combined energy and enterprise-management systems to integrate energy use and business decisions. Its software offered distributed energy and demand-response services that enabled facilities to make rapid adjustments and better connect buildings to energy markets and the grid. The company provided a visible platform with data to analyze past decisions and collaborative tools for users to act promptly. However, competition in the building and facility energy-management market was stiff. Competitors included established companies such as Johnson Controls, Honeywell, Siemens, and ABB. To make a go of it, OSoft needed a strategic partnership with Schneider. Nonetheless, the market for the services that companies like OSoft provided, about $16 billion in 2012, was supposed to grow to $23 billion by 2017.

Another KPCB late-stage investment was Bloom Energy. This company was able to stack small solid oxide fuel cells using natural gas and oxygen close together to generate electricity. The stacked cells achieved energy-conversion efficiencies of 50 percent, very close to the 60 percent efficiencies of combined-cycle natural gas, but transmission and distribution losses were lower because the power was produced closer to a facility. The stacked units were able to yield about 100 kW of power, enough to provide for the basic needs of about 100 average-size homes. However, the cost of the units, each of which had to be custom built, was high. In 2014, they were priced in the $700,000 to $800,000 range. Without subsidies, their lifetime would have to exceed 15 to 20 years for them to be cost effective.

Nonetheless, Bloom Energy had many customers including large companies such as Google, Coca-Cola, eBay, Bank of America, Walmart, AT&T, FedEx, and Kellogg's. It employed over 1,000 people in a facility in California and made the stacked cells at a new manufacturing site in Delaware. It had a leasing program with Bank of America and Merrill Lynch to finance sales in which it installed and owned the units and provided maintenance to customers who bought electricity from Bloom for a ten-year period. The company had plans for smaller units for homes and commercial buildings that it aimed to price at under $3,000. The market for this technology was expected to grow rapidly, perhaps reaching levels of $40 billion by 2022, from the $.14 billion in revenues it had in 2013, but these were only a projection.

Another late-stage KPCB investment in energy efficiency was Transphorm. This company had a semiconductor platform for making power converters that changed AC to DC and DC to AC relying on gallium nitride (GaN), the same material used in white-light LEDs. Converters that were currently used were made of silicon and they operated at efficiencies of about 90 percent. Power losses were in the form of waste heat. Transphorm promised to reduce these losses by five percent or more.

Converters were essential parts of nearly every electrical system from simple electric motors to telecommunications equipment and personal computers. The company's first product was aimed at the data server market, which had been heavily criticized for its high electricity consumption (see Chapter 2). Transphorm's backers included Google and the billionaire financier Georoge Soros. The DOE's Advanced Research Projects Agency awarded the company a $2.95 million grant to launch a first product. Its goal to displace silicon converters, however, was not likely to be accomplished easily. Other companies that had previously attempted to do this included IBM and Intel and none succeeded. Reliability was a major issue. Servers could not fail. The ability to manufacture at high volumes and low prices was another issue. Gallium nitride was not an easy material with which to work. Transphorm's plan was to build its own factory and not depend on third-party manufacturers. It had a prototype facility in Santa Barbara, California, but this factory would have to expand if it were to meet possible demand. Khosla Ventures and KPCB also partnered in the late-stage funding of eASIC. eASIC had a gate-array design for manufacturing application-specific integrated circuits for transistors and other devices. This design reduced development costs, turn-around times, power consumption, and unit costs. It relied on a concept that brought together configurable cells customized with a single interconnect by means of a lithographic approach that permitted many patterns to be easily printed directly on a wafer.

Solar power

Khosla Ventures and KPCB invested in both solar thermal (ST) and photovoltaics (PVs). The former involved a collector amassing heat by directly absorbing sunlight for the purposes of electrical power or direct heating. It was first used for power generation in the 1980s. The largest installation in the world was in the Mojave Desert in California. Under ideal conditions when cloud cover did not obscure the sun the Mojave Desert installation's capacity to produce electricity was 354 megawatts (MW), but the sun did not always shine during the day and at night it did not shine at all, while coal- or nuclear-powered plants had the potential to produce three times or more the amount electricity any time of day or season of the year. Different ST systems existed to capture the sunlight. The most common had a parabolic collector, but there were alternatives – power towers, dishes, and Fresnel designs. Tracking systems to follow the motion of the sun increased the cost and complexity of these systems. Khosla Ventures and KPCB partnered in making early-stage investments in Areva. Areva had worked with Sandia National Laboratories to integrate thermal-energy storage into a design that used modular flat reflectors to focus the sun's heat onto elevated receivers, which allowed for a longer solar power generation cycle, one that would continue after the sun went down.

Unlike ST, PVs directly converted sunshine into electricity. When the sunlight stuck the surface of a semiconductor material from which the cell was made, it energized electrons to break loose. The freed electrons were channeled through a grid on the cell's surface to junctions where they combined to form an electric current. Semiconductor material sandwiched between printed circuit boards of glass or plastic separated the light into charges, with the negative charge captured by an inverter as usable direct currency electricity, which could be transferred to the grid. The highest level of efficiency ever obtained was about 45 percent, but the actual efficiency of PC cells in use was less than half that amount. Typically the cells were sold as panels consisting of multiple cells in a group that were oriented in the same direction.

The most common cells found in solar panels were thick-film crystalline silicon (c-Si) cells. They could achieve efficiencies in converting sunlight to useful energy of about 13 to 19 percent in use, but were subject to silicon price volatility and were heavy and hard to transport. Thin-film cells were lighter in weight than c-Si cells and were easier to mount on rooftops. However, they required more panels, sunlight, and space to generate the same amount of electricity as cells made of c-Si. Produced by depositing a very thin film of material on a suitable base, thin cells were less efficient than thick-film cells. Made of cadmium telluride (CdTe) they were 6 to 13 percent efficient in converting sunlight to useful energy. Other thin-film cells might be made of amorphous silicon, copper indium selenide (CIS), or copper indium gallium selenide (CIGS).

Failed solar manufacturer Solyndra, heavily backed by VC money as well as the federal government, had placed its bets on CIGS. With a capacity of 40 MW, the Walkdpolenz Solar Park near Leipzig, Germany, had been an early adopter of thin-film PV electrical power. High-cost silicon had been a main reason for using thin-film cells. As long as the prices of silicon were elevated, thin-film cells had the potential to be made at a lower cost, but silicon costs dropped.

KPCB made early-stage investments in Amonix, a company that employed refractive Fresnel lenses to focus sunlight onto multijunction thin-film cells. Multijunction cells stacked together more than a single cell. The system worked by layering together semiconductor materials. The sunlight entered the layer with the largest gap, while photons continued to penetrate the cells until they reached the layer with the smallest gap. Because less energy was lost in these cells, they were more efficient than single-layered ones. The Fresnel lenses had dual-axis mounting structures that tracked the sun throughout the day. Used in conjunction with concentrator optics like the Fresnel lenses, these cells had set world records. It was believed that they might be able to convert sunlight into electricity at levels approaching fifty percent efficiency. Efficiency decreased, however, as the temperature increased so the system needed cooling mechanisms and Amonix ultimately went bankrupt.

Khosla Ventures invested late-stage growth equity money in Stion, a company that manufactured high-efficiency, thin-film solar panels with technology similar to Amonix. As indicated, most solar panels only absorbed a small part of the visible light spectrum, but the Stion modules by layering two solar circuits to different parts of the spectrum, were able to absorb more of the sun's energy. Constructed with a piece of glass and thin layers of materials to form the semiconductor, one layer could absorb light and convert it into electricity and another layer could protect against rain, dirt, and snow. The multistage cells yielded better patterning and better sunlight absorption. The proprietary transparent conductor that Stion led to better electrical generation.

The company's modules, however, did not exceed 13.4 percent efficiency. Its R&D was carried out in California where it had a pilot manufacturing line. It had been aggressively recruited by the Mississippi Development Authority, so it opened a full-scale production fab in Hattiesburg in 2011. The company had a grant from the Department of Energy to scale up its production and had received backing from Taiwanese semiconductor giant TSMC, which had plans to license its technology and take part in the company's commercialization efforts. Khosla Ventures took a controlling interest in the company in 2013, but it was not commercially successful.

Low-cost silicon cells from China trumped these potentially superior Amonix and Stion designs. The Chinese government provided tax forgiveness, free land, fast-track permitting, R&D, and export financing to solar manufacturing (see Chapter 3). Wages already were low, a typical Chinese engineer earning just $7,000 per year.

Chinese solar panels originally were meant for the domestic market but the Chinese companies sold them globally in response to growing global demand. Chinese manufacturers boosted their global market share from 10 percent in 2005 to over 50 percent in 2010. In 2012, the Chinese solar manufacturer Suntech had $2.7 billion in revenue, Yingli had $1.9 billion in revenue, and Trina had $1.9 billion in revenue. These Chinese manufacturers and others were making solar-power panels for the heavily subsidized European market. European governments had far-reaching renewable energy goals. Germany's goal was to be 27 percent renewable by 2020. In 2006, it instituted a 57 to 72 cent per megawatt subsidy for renewables that would decline by 5 to 10 percent per year. Spain had similar goals and they were eliminated when the country reached its production goal. France's aim was to be 20 percent renewable by 2020. Its subsidy started at 42 cents per megawatt. Italy's goal was three gigawatts of renewables by 2016 and it had a 59 cents per megawatt subsidy that would drop 2 percent per year over 20 years. More than half of the US states had renewable energy goals, but they were not as far-reaching as the European goals and the subsidies they offered were not as generous. In the United States a key question was whether the solar panels would be mainly deployed by utilities or by private building owners. To what degree would the utilities assist in private placement, when it would mean transfer of rights to non-utility owners and loss of control?

Two of KPCB's main late-stage solar investments were in MiaSolé and Soluxe. MiaSolé was a maker of thin-film copper indium gallium selenide (CIGS) PV modules. It had notable customers such as Chevron and General Motors, and partners such as Intel. Its founders had experience in the hard disk and semiconductor industries and the process they used deposited CIGS on a flexible stainless steel substrate through a continuous sputtering process. Sputtering originated in the disk drive and architectural glass industries and it was used to deposit the thin-film material onto substrate in a vacuum. By re-engineering the manufacturing process to improve efficiency, the company exceeded early commercial production cost forecasts. By 2008, it had two 20 megawatt production lines that achieved efficiencies of 10.2 percent. Though it achieved a maximum efficiency of 20.3 percent in the laboratory, MiaSolé had problems in manufacturing cells in volume. It was hoping to surpass the efficiency of the largest US thin-film producer First Solar (see Chapter 3), but it did not accomplish this goal. It aimed for commercial scale production in 2007, but failed because of technical issues. The Chinese renewable energy developer Hanergy saved MiaSolé from bankruptcy by purchasing it in 2012. Hanergy repaid the $30 million MiaSolé owed to its creditors and acquired the company for $90 million.

Another late-stage KPCB investment was with Solexel. Led by former hard-disk drive executive Michael Wingert, its aim was to produce 20-percent efficient thick-film silicon cells at a cost that was cheaper than US thin-film leader First Solar, whose average conversion

efficiency was 12.4 percent in 2014. Other crystalline silicon manufacturers such as Yingli were in the 15 to 16 percent efficiency range. First
Solar and Yingli had high-volume production lines and were known
for the proven reliability of their cells. Solexel had yet to make this
transition to high-volume production. It planned to do its manufacturing in Malaysia and replace expensive silver in the production process
with aluminum and use about ten times less silicon than in conventional crystalline silicon cells. The cells it made were flexible and they
did not have to be supported by a frame, did not require the support of
glass, and might be offered in a format supported by an aesthetically
pleasing flexible resin and fiber carrier with a black profile that might
appeal to residential customers as they could be sold for mounting
on commercial rooftops or on the ground for electricity generation
by utilities. The company had received $17 million in DOE and NSF
grants. It had eight global developers and distributors and maintained
that its production volume was fully subscribed, but whether it would
be able to fully deliver on its goals was still to be seen.

Transportation and energy storage

Khosla Ventures and KPCB had investment opportunities in transportation and energy storage that included making improvements in
internal combustion engines (ICEs) and introducing battery-based and
fuel cell-based vehicles (see Chapters 4 and 5). The options were pure
electric or pure fuel-cell vehicles or they could be combined with ICEs
into hybrids, plug-in hybrids, or fuel-cell hybrids. Super-light materials
on the horizon would improve any of these possibilities.

Analysts rated battery electric vehicles the highest in terms of better
energy use relative to current ICEs. An MIT study claimed they could
achieve an 80 percent reduction in gasoline consumption by 2035, in
comparison to fuel cell-based vehicles whose reduction potential was
75 percent.[20] The reduction potential of plug-in hybrids was 75 percent, that of ordinary hybrids was 65 percent reduction, that of diesel
powered ICEs was 50 percent, and that of gasoline powered ICEs was
40 percent. Though battery-powered vehicles had the potential for the
highest reduction, they faced many challenges to achieving this goal:
costs, fuel storage issues, limited range, questions of reliability and
durability, lack of refueling infrastructure, and difficulties in breaking
into established markets. Unless major improvements took place, pure

battery vehicles would not be the lowest cost alternative. Popular in the early 1900s, they fell into disuse with the elimination of the crank that was needed to start conventional engines (see Chapter 5). Mass production techniques then lowered conventional ICE vehicles' costs. These advances drove battery-powered vehicles out of all but a few niche markets such as golf carts. California's 1990 zero-emission air pollution goal did not create a mass market for these vehicles despite advantages such as cleaner air, better acceleration, less maintenance, and less noise pollution.

Khosla Ventures' only transportation investment was in EcoMotors, a company that tried to commercialize an opposed-piston opposed-cylinder (OPOC) ICE. The cylinders in this engine had pistons at both ends but no cylinder heads. These engines could be arranged in modules of two or more that were connected with an electric clutch between them that engaged an additional engine when more power was needed. This company collapsed.

KPCB had a history of transportation investing. It gave early-stage backing to Next Autoworks, a startup that also offered a different take on the conventional ICE, which was liquidated in 2011. The V-Vehicle that Next Autoworks had been developing also had Google Ventures' and T. Boone Pickens' backing. Shrouded in secrecy, the aim had been to develop a high-quality, environmentally friendly and fuel-efficient car at a very competitive price largely by making innovations in design and manufacturing. The company was founded by a former Oracle executive and had as members of its top management team former high-level Mazda and Ford employees. It was going to build a state-of-the-art auto assembly plant in Louisiana's Ouachita Parish that would employ 1,400 workers relying on $67 million in grants from Louisiana's mega-fund for economic development. Once Louisiana agreed to the funding it hoped to secure additional money from the DOE's advanced transportation loan program, but Louisiana opted out when it faced budgetary difficulties and Next Autoworks had nowhere to turn.

Fisker, a luxury plug-in that KPCB funded at early and late stages met a similar fate. The founder of the firm, Henrik Fisker had designed premium cars for Aston Martin and BMW. The Karma, which he unveiled at the 2008 US Auto Show, came with a pledge that Fisker would build many of these high-volume, low-priced, plug-in hybrids. Tesla, another premium electric car company (see Chapter 4), filed suit against the company, claiming that it stole Tesla's technology. Fisker obtained a $528.7 million loan from the DOE's Advanced Technologies Vehicle Manufacturing Loan Program in 2009, after it promised to annually produce about 100,000 vehicles, create up to 2,000 factory jobs, support thousands more vendor and supplier jobs, and become a major exporter. In that year Fisker took over a previously owned General Motors assembly plant in Wilmington, Delaware, and the state of Delaware gave it $21 million more in funding

However, after using up about $200 million of the funding it obtained, the US federal government concluded that Fisker was not meeting its loan's agreed-upon milestones. The government halted Fisker's credit line in 2011. Critics maintained that it planned to create a luxury car that was out of reach of most people and was not needed. General Motors' former director of the Chevrolet Volt replaced Henrik Fisker as CEO, and the company's founder became its executive chairman. At the start of 2012, Fisker obtained additional funding, but by July of that year it no longer could continue production. The bankruptcy of its battery maker A123 Systems and the costs involved in a recall brought on the crisis. In addition, during Hurricane Sandy it lost an entire shipment of cars meant to be sent to Europe. Ultimately the Chinese parts supplier Wanxiang Group bailed Fisker out for $24.75 million after it also acquired A123 Systems with the intention to restart production of the Karma. Wanxiang Group proclaimed that its aim was to adhere to Fisker's green roots and reintroduce fun into driving.

While KPCB's investments in Next Autoworks and Fisker fell apart, its early investments in Proterra were bearing some fruit. The goal of this Greenville, South Carolina company, which started operations in 2004, was to manufacture advanced electric buses and charging stations suitable for these vehicles. By 2014, it had 130 employees and was shipping its product to communities throughout the United States including South Carolina (14 buses), Massachusetts (three buses and two charging stations), Florida (five buses and a charging station), California (14 buses and a charging station), and elsewhere.

For driving ranges to go up, batteries had to be lighter and store more energy for a given weight or volume. Many technologies were commercially available, in development, or being researched. In transportation, the promise they held was to power vehicles that could displace those that burned gasoline and diesel, while in electric power, the promise they held was to provide backup to intermittent solar and wind power. Because multiple potential pathways to improvements existed and because the pathways cut across many disciplines, investing in these technologies was challenging.

For electric power grid applications, the main batteries of interest were lead-acid, high temperature sodium-beta, and liquid electrolyte flow batteries. In grid applications, lead-acid batteries found in conventional vehicles could serve as uninterruptible power supplies in substations. They had been manufactured on a mass scale for more than a century. Outside of lead-acid, the main battery types of interest for automobiles were lithium-ion and nickel-based aqueous ones. Because of their durability, high specific energy, light weight, and relatively fast charge and discharge times, lithium-ion batteries had been commonly used in consumer electronics. A number of manufacturers including SAFT, LG Chem, SK Energy, Hitachi, AESC, A123, Enerdel, and Panasonic created high-power lithium-ion batteries.

A main investment of Khosla Ventures in batteries was with Sakti3, a developer of solid-state rechargeable lithium-ion batteries. This company formed a development partnership with Argonne National Laboratory in 2014 and received funding from General Motors Ventures. Its mission was to extend the range of electric vehicles. While the focus was on transportation applications, there also might be grid applications for this type of battery. Advances still were needed.

The main nickel-based aqueous alternatives to the lithium-ion battery were nickel-cadmium and nickel-metal hydride. Nickel-cadmium batteries were limited by cost and cadmium's toxicity. The European Union banned them. They were not a good candidate for large-scale deployment in vehicles. Nickel-metal hydride batteries, on the other hand, had found a home in hybrid electric vehicles, such as the Ford Escape and Chevrolet Malibu. However, because of low energy density compared to lithium-ion batteries, they were not likely to be widely deployed in pure electric autos.

For utility deployment, sodium-beta and liquid electrolyte flow batteries were the main alternatives to the lead-acid battery. Sodium-beta batteries included sodium-sulfur units first developed in the 1960s and commercially available in Japan. A main KPCB battery investment was in Aquion Energy, a company committed to sodium-ion technology. Another investment was with Primus Power, a company committed to a zinc-chloride flow technology. Both of these companies had received substantial support from the federal government. Bill Gates had invested in Aquion. Aquion had teamed with Siemens to test its batteries with Siemens' inverters. Primus had developed a containerized energy-storage product for utilities it called an EnergyPod. The product was scalable and transportable and could be installed in modular units. With its patented flow cell-stack system and electrode assembly it had reduced costs. Primus claimed a 20-year lifespan for the units.

Sodium-nickel-chloride batteries were in the early stages of development. In flow batteries, a liquid electrolyte drifted through a chemical cell to produce electricity. They were in the early stages of development. The R&D in these technologies had a long way to go. Sodium-beta battery R&D was trying to move in the direction of a stacked planar cell design that could cut cell costs in half. This departure from prior designs had the ability to increase both specific energy and power. The lack of specific energy and power had been a limiting factor in the use of these batteries in many applications. Research was working on packing efficiency, greater modularity, and corrosion problems. However, the designs had sealing and material selection issues. Flow R&D efforts were focused on improving the performance of commercially available products and developing new chemistries. Before there could be large-scale deployment, battery reliability and longevity had to be improved but achieving better reliability and longevity was hard to do because of toxic and corrosive electrolytes, which posed material challenges.

Neither KPCB nor Khosla Ventures had invested in potentially game-changing battery companies like Graphene Energy, which was involved in next-generation nano-tech based ultra-capacitors for energy storage. Ultra-capacitors could store and deliver energy in a very short time, making them very suitable for high power-density applications. Graphene's technology relied on a material structure of bonded carbon atoms that were densely packed in a honeycomb crystal lattice. When of high quality, this material weighed little, was strong, light, and almost transparent as well as being an excellent heat and electricity conductor. It was extremely flexible and thus had high potential for being a cost-effective, high-powered, and high-capacity energy storage solution. It could be applied in regenerative braking systems in electric and hybrid vehicles, balancing of the energy power grid, and solar and wind storage.

Neither KPCB nor Khosla Ventures had been involved in deals backing startups like PowerThru that had made their mark in older storage technologies such as pumped storage. Apparently, Power Thru's flywheel energy-storage technology was the most advanced in the world. In 2010, this firm was purchased by another startup, Pentadyne Power. Planar Energy claimed that its new generation inorganic, solid-state electrolyte and electrode-based batteries were more efficient and longer lasting than any of the other battery alternatives. Planar Energy devices also had not received funding from any VC though it was the recipient of a more than $4 million grant from the DOE in 2010. The VCs' lack of interest in these advanced energy storage technologies was surprising.

Biofuels

First-generation biofuels that used corn, sugar cane, and soy to make ethanol and biodiesel had fallen out of favor because of controversy about food versus fuel and the question of whether biofuels provided net environmental improvement. If the entire US corn crop were converted to energy production, it was estimated that it could provide just 12 percent of the gasoline the United States needed. There was not enough good arable land for this purpose.

Khosla Ventures had taken part in many biofuel investments but none matched its involvement in the second-generation company, Kior.[21] Second-generation biofuels consisted of prairie and switch grass, wood, and animal waste. This material had to be dried and fermented. More than 70 percent of the material in these substances was lignum. It had to be removed and a starch and simple sugar extracted from it. The material used for making fuel often had to be transported long distances. Over a long life cycle second-generation biofuels reduced climate change gases, but in the short term it was unclear whether their use had these advantages. Because biofuels for making the fuel were so dispersed, economies of scale in production could not be guaranteed.

Khosla Ventures investments in Kior topped $340 million as of April 2014. Kior used wood chips, which it took in on dump trucks, in order to make fuel. The wood chips were conditioned and prepared for a conversion process, fed into a device where they interacted with a proprietary catalyst system, similar to the fluid catalytic cracking used in petroleum refining. The byproducts of the process were oil, light water, gases, and coke, which were sent to a separator that removed the catalyst and recycled it. Kior touted the process as mimicking the natural cycle to make petroleum that took millions of years. The oil that was made, however, had to be upgraded and refined before it could be fed into trucks and delivered. Essentially, it was an additive to conventional gasoline made via a complex and expensive process that was as yet unable to consistently compete with the price of conventional petroleum.

The price of conventional petroleum was unstable. In the period between 2007 and 2012, prices of gasoline fluctuated from $1.61 a gallon to $4.62 a gallon. Only at the higher gasoline price ranges was Kior competitive. Early estimates of production costs varied from $0.80 to $1.90 per gallon and of the feedstock costs from $0.30 to $0.50 a gallon or higher depending on location and availability. Regulatory costs and delays had to be added. The early cost estimates were not achieved. Kior's stock price plummeted as a consequence. Other biofuel investments Khosla Ventures made also declined. Range Fuels in which Khosla Ventures participated in investments involving $161.3 million in 2006 and 2008 to produce cellulosic ethanol mandated by DOE failed to meet its target product. The company moved to a non-renewable methanol-based fuel and eventually folded.

Many of the investments Khosla Ventures and KPCB made in biofuels did not work out. For example, AltraBiofuels, a producer of starch-based ethanol from corn feedstock, in which Khosla and KPCB both made early-stage investments, was bankrupt. Both Khosla Ventures and KPCB also had been involved in early-stage investments with Amyris in 2007 and 2008. Amyris created and used synthetic biological processes to design microbes, mainly yeast, to convert plant-sourced sugars into renewable hydrocarbons. The hydrocarbons had many uses from cosmetics and personal care products to additives, lubricants, flavors and fragrances, specialty chemicals, jet fuels, diesel, and other transportation fuels. Amyris went public in January 2011. The stock peaked at about $35 a share and by January 2012 it had plunged to under $5 a share, in which range it continued to trade.

Coskata, an early-stage investment in which Khosla Ventures took part in 2006 and 2008, canceled its plan to go public in 2013 due to unfavorable market conditions. The company made cellulosic ethanol from agricultural and municipal wastes in a Pennsylvania plant using proprietary microorganisms in a licensed fermentation process that it made available for sale to other biofuel producers. Kept afloat by backing from highly competitive DOE advanced-energy projects, ARPA-E awards, and undisclosed investors, Coskata claimed that it still was on target to achieve the lowest cost per gallon of ethanol production.

Other biofuel firms highly supported by Khosla in late stages were Cilion, ETH Bioenergy, and Gevo. In 2010, Aemetis entered into an agreement with Cilion to upgrade, restart, and operate Cilion's 55 million gallon per year ethanol production plant in Keyes, California. Aemetis then acquired Cilion in 2012. Aemetis also built and operated a 50 million gallon per year plant of this type on the east coast of India. The Cilion acquisition fit into its plans to make advanced biofuels and renewable chemicals as well as ethanol and animal feed. In 2011, Aemetis acquired a biotechnology company with a patented novel aerobic marine bacterium that degrades a variety of feedstocks. They also acquired a company with a patented technology that relied on consolidated bioprocessing to convert feedstocks into chemicals and fuels. The process simplified enzyme pretreatment and yeast fermentation in a way that eliminated up-front cooking and reduced water usage. In 2008, Aemetis built a commercial demonstration facility in Butte, Montana to evaluate feedstocks subject to this process and in 2011 obtained a California Energy Commission grant to help it commercialize the technology.

ETH Bioenergy became part of Odebrecht Agroindustrial in 2012. This Brazilian conglomerate had businesses in engineering, construction, chemicals and petrochemicals and was active throughout the world. It controlled Braskem, Latin America's leading petrochemical company. A leader in the use of sugar for fuel and electricity, cultivating sugar, producing ethanol, and selling and delivering, it was able to integrate the entire ethanol value chain in one company. The company's production centers were located in a number of Brazilian states. In 2013, it had nine production units that produced 3 billion liters of ethanol and 2,700 GWh of electricity via cogeneration. In that year Odebrecht entered into a joint venture with Amyris. The joint venture provided Amryis with access to up to two million tons of sugar-cane crush capacity. Amyris then had marketing rights for the hydrocarbon molecule made at the facility. This molecule could be used in many products from specialty chemicals to cosmetics, detergents, lubricants, and diesel and jet fuel.

Gevo was another late-stage KPCB investment. This company went public in 2011 after acquiring a 22 million gallon per year ethanol production facility in Luverne, Minnesota that had been using dry-milled corn as feedstock. Gevo intended to retrofit this facility to produce isobutanol, a chemical with broad applications as a replacement for petroleum-based raw materials. Isobutanol could be integrated and added to existing refining processes without modification. Gevo cleared isobutanol with the US EPA for use as a fuel additive in gasoline. Nonetheless, like Amyris, with which Gevo may be compared, Gevo's stock quickly plunged after the company went public. Within two years, the stock price had declined about 70 percent. In April 2014, Gevo revealed that its working capital was not adequate to meet its cash requirements. The company temporarily had halted production in Luverne in 2012 after contamination issues. It only resumed output on a small scale. Gevo also had to battle with Butamax, whose parent companies were DuPont and BP, on patent infringement allegations. Even with these troubles Gevo had a number of significant accomplishments. It had channel partnerships with Land O'Lake, listed Coca-Cola and the US Air Force as customers, and had received grants from the Department of Agriculture. In 2013, the army flew a Black Hawk helicopter with a 50:50 blend of its jet fuel, and in 2014, with the backing it obtained from Total, Lufthansa agreed to do a trial test of this jet fuel.

In addition, both Khosla Ventures and KPCB were backers of Mascoma. Mascoma's consolidated bioprocessing technology made ethanol out of hardwood pulp with proprietary yeasts that did away with the need for expensive enzymes. Hardwood pulp had the major advantage of being cheap and abundant. Mascoma demonstrated its conversion process at a facility in Rome, New York where it was able to achieve a yield of 67 gallons of ethanol per short ton of pulp. However, Mascoma's plan to expand production to 20 million gallon per year in Michigan was put on hold when the major financial backer and the facility's main owner Valero Corporation refused to provide its part of the $232 million needed funding. The rest of the needed money was to have come from DOE and the State of Michigan. Mascoma was looking to achieve yields of 83 gallons per hardwood short ton at this facility. These yields translated into production at an unsubsidized cost of about $1.77 per gallon. Mascoma maintained that it could bring that number below $1 per gallon within a few years through manufacturing refinements and scale economies when the plant was expanded to 40 million gallon per year, and better use of the microorganism upon which it relied to break down the wood pulp. However, citing unfavorable market conditions, Mascoma withdrew its attempt to go public in 2013.

The fate of other biofuel startups that needed VC funding hung in the balance. After the uneven tale of progress, who was willing to back them? Who would take the next step and make investments in third-generation biofuel companies such as SBAE Industries or Algaecake Technologies, which relied on an advanced processes for making petroleum from algae?

Wind and agriculture

Both Khosla Ventures and KPCB had wind and agriculture investments. Khosla Ventures had been involved in late-stage wind investment with Nordic Windpower. This Kansas City, Missouri company developed and manufactured two-bladed, rather than the typical three-bladed, turbines. These smaller units could be used in community wind-generating sites. The company's origins were in an R&D program the Swedish government started in 1975. Prototypes had been built in various sites in Sweden. The advantages of the two-bladed systems were that they were light and affordable. They were more easily assembled and erected than three-blade systems and suffered from less fatigue. Therefore they did not require as much maintenance. In addition, they were less obtrusive and quieter than conventional three-bladed turbines and they could be located closer to population centers. Even with these advantages, in the 1990s Nordic Power had sold only five units in Europe. After selling an additional seven turbines in the United States and obtaining a $16 million DOE loan guarantee Nordic Windpower moved to Berkeley, California. Later it moved to Kansas City where it was given a $5.6 million conditional incentive package to relocate at the airport where it occupied a large former American Airlines maintenance facility. After Nordic Windpower ran out of cash in 2012 it filed for bankruptcy.

KPCB had been involved in early-stage investment in the wind company, FloDesign Wind Turbine. Now known as Ogin, the premise of this firm's business model was that while conventional wind turbines had greatly increased in size and height in recent years, their design had

Table 1.3 *Wind startups in need of funding*

Name	Description
Magenn Power	Turbine that generates energy from high-altitude sources
WindAid	Low-cost wind due to reduced mechanical belts, gears, and lubrication
Coriolis Wind	Scalable small turbines for low-wind speed environments

Compiled from data on Clean Tech Group Website, July 2010

not changed much. Standard turbines were based on the physical principles of eighteenth century windmills, which left the turbines open to the elements, while the Ogin design had a covering that enabled the turbines to take advantage of aerospace industry innovations in engine design and alter the airflow patterns through and around the turbine. The Ogin design increased energy output by as much as 50 percent while delivering useable energy in a much quieter fashion. Ogin also had been innovating in the processes of manufacturing, transporting turbines, and on-site assembly. Its modular design made possible automated parts' mass manufacture, delivered over ordinary roads in regular trucks, subassembled at sites so that project development and construction time lines were shorter and costs lower.

Other innovative wind companies, however, received no backing from either KPCB or Khosla Venture. Firms such as Magenn Power, WindAid, and Coriolis Wind (see Table 1.3) did not have any VC funding. Venture capital firms had not put much emphasis on wind.

Both Khosla Ventures and KPCB tackled major agriculture and food-related issues. Since 2010, Khosla Ventures increasingly shifted its focus to agriculture. Its 2011 investment in the Climate Corporation had a quick turnaround as Monsanto purchased the company for about $1 billion in 2014 (see Chapter 10). Both Intel Capital and Google Ventures also invested in the Climate Corporation. The Climate Corporation provided up-to-date weather, soil, and crop data at the field level to farmers on an app they could download from the Apple store or Google play. The app helped the farmers make better production decisions. If farmers upgraded to another app called Climate Pro, they could plan with greater confidence, anticipate problems, and optimize responses. An even more elaborate app called Precision Care, offered real-time actionable insights for each acre that a farmer planted. Finally, as an authorized provider of the US Federal Crop

Insurance program, the Climate Corporation was able to monetize the relationship it formed with farmers by selling them crop insurance based on variables such as the farmers' financial goals, yield variances across fields, weather perils, commodity price changes, and other risks. At the time of its sale to Monsanto, the Climate Corporation, which was founded in 2006 by ex-Google employee David Friedberg, had 100 employees.

Khosla Ventures also became part of deals that invested in Hampton Creek Foods, a developer of a bio-based egg-replacement food product. Hampton Creek Foods was dedicated to less costly and more convenient healthy food. The business model of its founder Josh Tetrick, a former college football player and Fulbright Scholar who had spent seven years working in Sub-Saharan Africa, was based on the premise that unhealthy food was cheap and healthy food was expensive and inconvenient. The purpose of his company was to provide inexpensive healthy food to people who otherwise could not afford it. Hampton Creek Foods had partnership agreements with large food manufacturers and retailers and its Just Mayo product was available in Whole Foods (see Chapter 9).

KPCB's largest participations in early-stage agricultural investment had a Chinese focus. The two largest of these investments were in Jiangxi Tianren Ecological Industrial, developer of non-petrochemicals-based natural and organic fungicides and insecticides, and Tony's Farm, a certified organic enterprise in Shanghai that has brought together growing, production, processing, sales, and after-sales services. Jiangxi Tianren Ecological Industrial had been around since 2002, and Tony's Farm since 2004, and their products were widely available commercially. These companies were meeting the need that Chinese consumers had for reliable, safe, healthy, and non-toxic foods. Chinese consumers were concerned because of so many safety scares including the industrial chemical melamine in milk powder consumed by children, illegal toxins in produce in leading supermarket chains, a highly toxic pesticide in meat dumplings exported to Japan, and tainted herbal medicines. The Chinese government admitted that as many as 100,000 people a year might be poisoned by petrochemical-based pesticides. Famers complained that pesticides often did not produce the sought-after crop yield increases. They added expense without delivering benefits. The ecofood market in Chinese cities, which could earn a very high premium, had been growing rapidly in specialty retailers and major retailers. The country had over 34 million hectares of land devoted to so-called ecofoods, either ones that had organic certification or China's own green and hazard-free labels. China had phased out many highly toxic pesticides, which created many opportunities for the firms in which KPCB had invested.

KPCB also was involved in late-stage investment in agriculture with Kaiima. Kaiima's proprietary methods of doubling the chromosomes in plants could result in high-yielding seeds that had less need for land, water, fertilizer, and pesticides for growing food and fuel crops. The processes upon which Kaiima relied took place naturally, but Kaiima made them happen more readily yielding greater cell activity, more photosynthesis, and better plant adaptations. Prior attempts to accomplish what Kaaima accomplished had produced DNA damage, which Kaiima avoided by means of its complex protocols. Its currently available products were seeds that it had created for castor oil plants. The castor oil could be used as a food additive and preservative, in medicines, in bio-based chemicals, and in biodiesel fuels. Kaiima also was testing wheat and corn seeds. In the biofuel area, it had business partnerships in Kazakhstan, China, Brazil, and Mexico.

Next steps for Khosla Ventures and KPCB

Khosla Ventures and KPCB had to evaluate what they had accomplished. After nearly ten years of clean energy investment, Khosla Ventures had focused more on biofuel investments, while KPCB had focused more on energy efficiency and transportation and storage investments. Khosla Ventures had focused more on early-stage investments, while KPCB had focused more on late-stage investments. Both companies had notable failures and they continued to have stakes in companies with some promise. What should their future priorities be?

The decisions that Khosla Ventures and KPCB would make about their future investment in clean energy depended on how well their past investments had performed. Since its inception, Khosla had a much smaller percentage of its investments result in IPOs and acquisitions (29 percent) than KPCB (54 percent), an outcome that came about mainly because KPCB was considerably older than Khosla Ventures and shared in the great success that VCs achieved in the 1990s. From 2004 to 2013, when both Khosla Ventures and KPCB were active in clean energy investing, more of Khosla Ventures' clean energy

Table 1.4 *Status of Khosla Ventures' and KPCB's clean energy deals, 2013*

Status	Kholsa Ventures, percent	KPCB, percent
Public	11	7.1
Acquired	6.9	7.1
Bankrupt	2.9	2
Out of business	4.6	5.1

Compiled from data on the Clean Tech Group website, November 2013

investments had gone public than KPCB's (see Table 1.4). Whether the higher number of IPOs meant that Khosla Ventures' investments performed better financially was uncertain because even after firms in which they invested went public, many of these firms' stock prices fell.

Going forward, Khosla Ventures and KPCB had to reconsider what was the best path to take. Should they accelerate their investment in clean energy or slow it down? Were there particular companies with whom they should become more or less involved? Were there particular aspects of clean energy investing they should emphasize and particular aspects they should avoid?

Notes

1 US Department of Energy, *Annual Energy Outlook 2011 with Projections to 2035* (Washington, DC: US Energy Information Administration, 2010).

2 A. Marcus, J. Malen, and S. Ellis, "The promise and pitfalls of venture capitalism as an asset class for clean energy investment: research questions for organization and natural environment scholars," *Organization & Environment* (2013): 31–60.

3 A. O'Rourke, *The Emergence of Cleantech* (New Haven, CT: Yale University PhD dissertation, 2009).

4 M. Kenney, "Venture capital investment in greentech industries: a provocative essay," in R. Wustenhagen and R. Wuebker (ed.) *Handbook of Research on Energy Entrepreneurship* (Cheltenham, England: Edward Elgar, 2011), pp. 214–28.

5 Kauffman Foundation, *We Have Met the Enemy . . . And He Is Us*, (Kansas City, MO: Ewing Marion Kauffman Foundation, 2012).

6 Cambridge Associates LLC, *US Venture Capital Index and Selected Benchmark Statistics: Private Investments* (Cambridge, MA: Cambridge Associates, 2012).

7 Cambridge Associates LLC, *Clean Tech Company Performance Statistics* (Cambridge, MA: Cambridge Associates, 2013).

8 D. Champion and N. Carr, "Starting up in high gear: an interview with venture capitalist Vinod Khosla," *Harvard Business Review* (2000): 93–100.

9 V. Khosla, "The big green opportunity: transforming clean tech into main tech," *Forbes* (2012): www.forbes.com/sites/toddwoody/2012/11/27/the-big-green-opportunity-transforming-clean-tech-into-main-tech

10 Khosla Ventures, "Open letter to 60 Minutes and CBS," Khosla Ventures website (2014): www.khoslaventures.com/open-letter-to-60-minutes-and-cbs

11 S. McBride and N. Groom, "Insight: how Cleantech tarnished Kleiner and VC star John Doerr," (2013): www.reuters.com/article/2013/01/16/us-kleiner-doerr-venture-idUSBRE90F0AD20130116

12 C. Gugliema and T. Geron, "John Doerr's plan to reclaim the venture capital throne," *Forbes* (2013): www.forbes.com/sites/connieguglielmo/2013/05/07/john-doerrs-plan-to-reclaim-the-venture-capital-throne

13 Champion and Carr, "Starting up in high gear."

14 Cambridge Associates LLC, *Growth Equity is All Grown Up* (Cambridge, MA: Cambridge Associates, 2013).

15 See Clean Tech Group data: https://i3connect.com/investor

16 For coverage of the status of clean energy companies, the best source is Greentech Media, see www.greentechmedia.com. Much of the discussion of specific clean energy companies is derived from stories that Greentech Media has featured.

17 A. Lovins, *Reinventing Fire* (White River Junction, VT: Chelsea Green Publishing, 2011).

18 *Ibid.*

19 A. Cuddy, K. Doherty, and M. Bos, *Opower: Increasing Energy Efficiency through Normative Influence* (Boston, MA: Harvard Business School Case, 2011).

20 MIT Laboratory for Energy and the Environment, *On the Road in 2035* (Cambridge, MA: MIT, 2008).

21 R. Nana and T. Stuart, *Kior: Catalyzing Clean Energy* (Boston, MA: Harvard Business School Case, 2009).

2 | Scaling up: Intel Capital and Google Ventures

By 2012, two trends dominated the funding of clean energy entrepreneurial firms. On the one hand, early-stage investing was declining – there was less experimentation – and on the other hand corporate investing in late-stage companies was growing. More than 50 percent of the $2.6 billion in Californian clean energy investments in 2012 came from corporations whose main focus was late-stage companies.[1] Previous involvement by corporate VCs had been lower, in 2005, just 19 percent of the $520 million invested; in 2008, 29 percent of the $3.47 billion invested; and in 2010, 40 percent of the $3.2 billion invested. Increasingly, the aim was to scale up, commercialize, and implement technologies that showed promise. Late-stage project deployment was overtaking early-stage research and testing.

Corporate investors such as Intel Capital and Google Ventures responded favorably to laws in California relating to climate change that mandated a goal of 33 percent renewable energy, which drove demand. Overall clean energy funding in California, however, had declined by close to 20 percent between 2010 and 2012.[2] Clean energy was not the only category in which Intel Capital or Google Ventures made deals. Intel Capital, for example, backed a broad range of startups in areas such as semiconductors, the Internet, and hardware, software, and services as well as clean energy. Google Ventures too had a diversified portfolio of entrepreneurial ventures in areas such as consumer, mobile, commerce, enterprise, and data and life sciences, and it was not exclusively focused on clean energy. The degree to which Intel Capital and Google Ventures should remain committed to clean energy was a question both firms had to ponder.

The parent company of Intel Capital rarely acquired a company that Intel Capital funded. Intel Capital did not have a mandate of feeding the parent company. Rather, its aim was to find the highest bidder for the companies it funded and to provide Intel with the most lucrative exit opportunities. For the third year in a row Intel Capital, in

2013 based on the number of exits it had, was the most successful US VC firm.[3] The ranking did not measure how much money Intel Capital investors earned with each exit, yet with 22 exits in 2013, Intel Capital did better than KPCB, which ranked 11th, and Khosla Ventures, which ranked 15th. The only other corporate VC firm among the top 15 was Google Ventures. With seven exits in 2013, it was tied with Khosla for the 15th spot.

Started in 2007, Google Ventures was much younger than Intel Capital, which had been making investments since 1992. As of April 2004, Google Ventures had invested in 165 companies, while Intel Capital had invested in more than 1100.[4] Google's VC arm, unlike Intel's, was a feeder to the parent company. Google purchased the startup firms that Google Ventures had funded. The best example was Google's acquisition of Nest, which Google Ventures along with KPCB backed (Chapter 1). During the negotiations for the acquisition of Nest, the involved individuals at Google Ventures had to excuse themselves to avoid conflicts of interest. As an investor Google Ventures wanted to maximize the price of the sale, but as a buyer the parent company wanted to minimize the price of the sale. Most corporate VC firms did not sell companies in which they invested to their parent companies. The average rate of acquisitions by parents of companies they funded was just three percent.[5] In its history Intel Capital's rate of buying companies it funded was just 2.7 percent. Intel Capital sold as many of the startups it supported to Cisco and almost as many to Microsoft as it did to Intel.

In light of their different investing aims and investment histories, Intel Capital and Google Ventures had to make choices about their continuing support for clean energy. Which companies should they fund and at what stages should they fund these companies? The corporate venture capital units of these companies had to reassess what was the best fit with their aspirations and expertise.

Corporate venture capital and clean energy

Corporate venture capital (CVC) could be critical in the funding of clean energy companies because of the long time it took between research, testing, and the ultimate commercialization of clean energy technologies. Unlike software and other IT startups, investors had to be patient in helping clean energy companies bridge the so-called valley of death between having a good idea and seeing it broadly adopted. This patience might be a better fit for CVCs than for private venture capitalists like Khosla Ventures and KPCB, which were under great pressure to show returns to their investors within a short time period. Corporate venture capital also might have more resources to bring to bear than private VCs. From 2010 to 2013, the median holding period for a company that received funding from a CVC was more than six years, whereas that number for a company that did not receive this type of funding was less than five years.[6] More time and resources translated into larger exits, with the median exit return for companies receiving CVC funding being greater than $70 million, compared to companies that did not receive CVC funding being around $55 million.

Corporate venture capital companies tended to make their initial investments at later stages or at the brink of startups' exits. Private VCs like Khosla Ventures and KPCB frequently brought the promising startups to the CVCs' attention and they jointly funded startups in late stages. KPCB and Google Ventures, for example, had participated in a number of close-to-exit deals together. They both had been involved in the funding of Next Autoworks and Nest (see Chapter 1). Khosla Ventures and Google Ventures had jointly funded the Climate Corporation (see Chapter 1 and Chapter 10).

Corporate venture capital companies were considered to be slower moving than private VCs because of the intense scrutiny to which they subjected startups. They had their own in-house experts in their parent companies whom they often consulted. Google Ventures had access to the world's largest datasets and cloud computer infrastructure. It relied heavily on data it collected, collated, and analyzed from the academic literature, and the past experience of startups, which it used to generate algorithms to make decisions about whether to fund companies. It tried to be logical and analytically rigorous and avoid making investments driven by emotion and intuition. Funds like KPCB started to place more emphasis on data-driven decisions but for them it might mean following how many times a startup was mentioned on Twitter or where it ranked in an app store. They were not as rigorous as Google Ventures. Some VCs were skeptical of the highly analytical approach Google Ventures used, alleging that Google Ventures did not benefit from the kind of rich experience decision makers in their firms had. The art of the deal, they maintained, was more important than the science.

Google Ventures did not dismiss these factors. It sometimes allowed intuition to override science but by and large its decision making was more analytical and rationally driven and less based on hunches than the decision making of other VCs.

In general, the due diligence that CVCs applied to the deals they made was greater than the due diligence of private VCs. Because the CVCs subjected startups to greater scrutiny, their funding of them was considered to involve a higher level endorsement than private VC funding. Utilities, which had to make commitments to provide reliable power over the long term, tended to trust startups that CVCs funded more than they trusted startups that private VCs funded. Corporate venture capital companies' backing had additional advantages. It opened up the doors of its customers to startups and provided startups with valuable relationships. Corporate venture capital backing also often opened access to the expertise within a parent company. Employees within the parent might be interested in the startup's technologies and might be searching for synergies.

Firms typically justified their CVCs as being an instrument for carrying out their innovation strategies. Corporate venture capital investments allowed them to gain access to technologies that filled gaps in existing innovation portfolios. With this access, they could better leverage existing knowledge and enter new markets. In this respect, CVCs were like R&D alliances, joint ventures, and licensing agreements. Through involvement in CVC, parent companies made staged investments, which enabled them to gradually gather information, monitor progress, and maintain flexibility until a technology's value and the size of its market were better understood. However, assimilating external knowledge generated through CVC investments was challenging because the existence of this knowledge might be perceived by in-house employees as a critique of their own efforts. For the knowledge to be used, it had to overcome the not-invented-here syndrome.

The benefits of this knowledge for the parent firm were long term. They were not easy to estimate. Many firms therefore had decided to cut back or eliminate their CVC initiatives. Corporate venture capitals' rise started in the 1990s in the midst of the high-tech boom, when many companies jumped in spurred by the prospect of quick profits. After multiple meltdowns, many companies realized that VC investing was more difficult than they had anticipated. They were reconsidering whether they should have CVCs at all. Unlike private VC, the CVC of public traded companies had to reveal the results of their investments in quarterly accounting statements. When not successful, these investments dragged down profits.

Evaluating the performance of a CVC's investment portfolio was anything but straightforward because of the complex goals that parent companies brought to the activity. Intel's goals, for instance, were not simply return on investment, but ecosystem and market development, finding new business opportunities, and identifying gap-filling technologies. By means of Intel's CVC investments the company attempted to support complementary technologies sold alongside its existing products. It invested in numerous companies whose products drove demand for its microprocessors, for example. These companies opened up new market channels that put Intel's products in a more advantageous position. More demand for these products resulted in more business for Intel. Intel also made CVC investments because it did not want to be blind-sided by new technologies that had the potential to disrupt its business.

Because of the complicated reasons for CVC investing, it was difficult to assess what CVCs like Intel Capital and Google Ventures should do next. Google Ventures and Intel Capital had many motivations for CVC investments. Nonetheless, the trend for most corporations was to start to cut back on their CVC investments. Intel retreated after the 2008 financial meltdown.[7] The peak Intel Capital deal-making years in dollar terms were 2000 and 2008. After 2008 both the number of its deals and dollar amount invested went down. In contrast, Google Ventures increased the number of deals it did in this period.

Assessing Intel Capital's and Google Ventures' investment choices

Intel Capital and Google Ventures had to make choices about their future clean energy CVC investing. In an era when most firms were reconsidering their commitments to CVC, what should they do?

Since their inception, Internet specific and software had dominated the investments both Intel Capital and Google Ventures had made. Among VC investors, software investment led the way in the first quarter of 2012.[8] Software funding grew by 39 percent and IT

Table 2.1 *Intel Capital's and Google Ventures' clean energy deals by category, 2014*

Clean energy investments	Intel Capital percent	Google Ventures percent
Advanced materials	22.8	0
Agriculture	0	7.1
Biofuels	0	9.5
Energy efficiency	39.2	21.4
Energy storage	10.5	10.1
Geothermal & fuel cells	6.3	4.7
Smart grid	13.9	7.1
Solar	6.3	26.2
Transportation	0	11.9
Wind	0	7.1

Compiled from data on the Clean Tech Group website, April 2014

services' funding grew by 33 percent, while investments in other sectors declined. The amount of funding Intel Capital and Google Ventures reserved for seed and early-stage financing also was down, while the amount of funding they reserved for expansion and later stage deals was up. In the past, Intel Capital had been more active in energy efficiency, advanced materials, and the grid, while Google Ventures had been more active in solar, energy efficiency, and transportation (see Table 2.1). Did these priorities still make sense?

If their ongoing involvement in clean energy continued to make sense, Intel Capital and Google Ventures had to decide which categories of clean energy to fund. In making decisions about which clean energy sectors to fund, Intel Capital and Google Ventures had to consider their past performance. Overall, Intel Capital's and Google Ventures had met with different levels of success (see Table 2.2). One difference between them was that Intel Capital had a greater percentage of acquisitions, while Google Ventures had a greater percentage of IPOs. About the same percentage of Google Ventures' investments were bankrupt and out of business as Intel Capital's.

Outside of clean energy, Intel Capital, an older CVC that participated in the dot.com boom of the 1990s had a stronger record of performance. More than 58 percent of its investments since inception

Table 2.2 *Status of Intel Capital's and Google Ventures' clean energy deals, 2014*

Status	Intel Capital percent	Google Ventures percent
Public	6.3	9.6
Acquired	14.6	9.6
Bankrupt	4.1	0
Out of business	2.2	6.5

Compiled from data on the Clean Tech Group website, April 2014

had resulted in acquisitions or IPOs, while only 10 percent of Google Ventures' investments had this outcome.[9]

A 2014 article by *Forbes* columnist Michael Lynch heavily criticized companies like Google Ventures for investing in clean energy.[10] He held it was the height of folly for an Internet company to assume that its innovative culture could be transferred to clean energy. In such areas as solar, wind, or electric vehicles, high-tech CVCs did not have the expertise to identify breakthroughs that corporations with far more energy experience could identify. After years of research, clean energy, without government subsidies, was not competitive.

What led Google Ventures and the CVCs of other high-tech companies to believe they could change this state of affairs? According to Lynch, Google Ventures and the CVCs of other high-tech companies should not be investing in sectors exposed to the risk of government withdrawal. The only returns that these companies' shareholders could expect from such investments were tax breaks. Once given, these tax breaks could be easily removed. The shareholders of these companies purchased stock in high-tech firms, not clean energy companies. They would be better off if Intel and Google returned the excess cash and allowed shareholders to decide if they wanted to risk their money in clean energy investing.

Business issues

What rationale did Intel Capital and Google Ventures have for investing in clean energy? Intel's businesses had been stagnant in recent years.

This stagnancy had to be contrasted with its earlier dynamism when it rose to the top of the microprocessor industry and established a near monopoly position in the lucrative PC and server markets. In 1985, Intel decided to abandon dynamic random access memory (DRAM) production. To that point, DRAM had been its main source of profits and revenues, but Japanese manufacturers had captured 80 percent of the world market, and firms from Korea were not far behind. Intel's executives reasoned that US companies could not compete with large, vertically integrated Japanese and Korean firms that were the beneficiaries of substantial government assistance.

Intel's founders were Robert Noyce, who was the co-inventor of the integrated circuit, Gordon Moore, who first coined the concept "Moore's law," and Andy Grove. Four years after the firm was founded in 1968, Noyce co-invented the integrated circuit. Moore then made his very famous prediction of an indefinite continuation of exponential growth in the number of transistors per integrated circuit and a doubling in microprocessor speed every 18 months. After exiting the DRAM business, Intel helped to make this prediction come true. In 1981, IBM selected Intel's microprocessor for its personal computer. Together Intel's microprocessor and Microsoft's operating system became the backbone of the PC. They were the well-known "Wintel" combination, which spawned the PC revolution. Up until the start of the second decade of the twenty-first century, Intel extracted more than 80 percent of its revenue and close to all of its profits from microprocessors.[11] When Intel had branched out into other areas, these other areas either resulted in losses or they made modest contributions to the bottom line. Craig Barrett, appointed CEO in 1997, had been chief operating officer (COO) under Grove. An ex-professor of engineering at Stanford, he was credited with Intel's excellence in manufacturing. He was largely responsible for Intel's ultra-efficient fabrication plants (fabs). In 1997, when Barrett became Intel's new chief executive, he launched a strategy that aimed to move Intel beyond PCs and servers and into such markets as communications, information appliances, and Internet services. By 2001, however, after about 40 percent of Intel's more than $10 billion in new investments yielded nothing, Intel had to cut back. Not only were these investments not paying off, but Intel was alienating some of its most important customers, whose turf it was invading by making these investments including major communications companies at the time, such as Ericsson, Lucent, Motorola, and Nokia. Intel made the fateful choice not to move into the cellular phone business.

Soon after Paul Otellini took over as Intel's CEO in 2005, he announced that he too wanted to branch out from its over-reliance on microprocessors. Otellini planned to have the company play a key role in a half-dozen fields. He wanted specialized chips and software for many different purposes that included integration into living-room to emergency-room platforms. Ottelini's initiatives, however, also fizzled.

At the end of the twenty-first century's first decade Intel's challenge was to find its place in mobile computing markets. The share of time people spent per day with media such as television was declining, while the use of mobile devices was rising. Portable computing devices including tablets, smartphones, and notebooks were taking over from desktop PCs. The major sellers of PCs, Intel's principal customers – Dell, HP, Acer, and others – were seeing a drop-off in PC and laptop sales. Tablets and smartphones started to outsell desktops and laptops – and Intel microprocessors were in neither.

Apple was the principal company to anticipate this development and was a central player in making it happen. Apple reinvented itself as a mobile company. The iPhone and iPad drove it to the top among global companies. Intel missed out when it had the chance but decided not to make a low-power processor for Apple's mobile devices. The margins on these low-power processors were low in comparison to the margins Intel earned for desk top and server sales. Other companies such as ARM designed most of the iPhone and iPad microprocessors. Samsung manufactured them, which meant Apple bought most of its processors from its chief global rival. Instead of pursuing this opportunity, Intel engaged in a rear-guard action of continuing to develop processors for the desk top and server markets.

For Intel, this failure to move into mobile markets was painful. In 2013, it suffered substantial operating losses trying to enter mobile markets. When the PC revolution was at its height and seemed to have no limits it made sense for Intel to throw spaghetti against the wall to see what stuck, but that period had passed. Intel no longer could take a relaxed attitude to its future. During the heyday of its dominance of the growing PC and server microprocessor market, it had the slack resources to move into diverse areas without being overly concerned about the consequences, but it no longer had this luxury. Its freedom of action had diminished.

Was there any justification for Intel's making clean energy a priority if its battle to re-emerge as an important force in the computing industry came down to whether it could compete in mobile, a struggle that some analysts saw Intel already as having lost?

Questions also existed about Google's recent business performance. Because its operating expenses were rising, its first quarter 2014 margins were down two percent from the previous year. Google had increased spending to expand the services it offered and the spending it authorized outweighed sales. Research and development expenses in the first quarter of 2014 were 14 percent of revenues. This was up from the 12 percent of revenues R&D expenses were the previous year.

Google continued to spend money on a variety of innovative programs including Google Glass, driverless cars, high-speed internet, and solar-powered drones. It also was striving to capitalize on the increase in mobile and smartphone use. Its main revenue source was advertisements and customers were not willing to pay as much per ad as they previously had paid. The small screens of mobile devices restricted the number of ads that could be displayed at a time. Even if mobile devices could track the location and other details of people using them and therefore be a platform for focused advertising campaigns, no frictionless payment system existed for customers to respond with on-the-spot purchases. Most companies that advertised on mobile did not have direct sales websites. Google also had to divest losing companies, such as Motorola, the smartphone unit that it bought and then sold to Lenovo. The sale of Motorola yielded a $198 million loss.

Both Intel and Google had to examine the value of the investments their CVCs made in clean energy, given these business challenges. Could the environmental commitments of the two companies justify the investments they made in clean energy?

Intel's environmental commitments

Though Intel had lost business ground to Apple, Samsung, and other players in the computer industry, it never gave up on its commitment to the environment. An early example of this commitment was the corporate policy to use design for the environment to improve the environmental performance of each generation of its production technologies and to ensure that all its new facilities limited their emissions. Thus in 1998, when Intel built a new manufacturing facility for advanced Pentium microprocessors in Chandler, Arizona, a suburb of Phoenix, beset by smog problems and a limited water supply, the new plant was designed to be a minor air pollution source that would emit 40 percent less volatile organic compounds (VOCs) than had been emitted by the previous generation of plants.[12] The company also agreed to limit emissions of each hazardous air pollutant the facility produced so as to provide benefits to its workers as well as the community. Intel in addition was committed to funding a reverse-osmosis water-treatment plant on site. The plant would treat more than half of the process water, meet advanced drinking-water standards, and return water to local aquifers or use it for irrigation. This $25 million plant would be almost entirely funded by the company.

Intel donated to the city the land upon which the plant was to be built and paid almost all the operating costs. The company also agreed to conserve water use on site in other ways, and to go beyond compliance with storm water regulations by pumping storm water into a retention basin, thereby decreasing the impact on groundwater. Additional environmental commitments by Intel were: to increase over time the recycling of solid waste by 60 percent and chemical waste by 70 percent; to make integrated reports of the site's environmental performance more easily available to the public; and to promote and encourage carpooling among workers. The company promised that all buildings on the campus would be set back at least 1,000 feet from the nearest residences.

These initiatives were typical of the care Intel took in minimizing its environmental impacts. Indeed, in 2009, the year Intel Capital made other CVC cutbacks, it reaffirmed its commitment to clean technology. It announced five investments in the area including a first-time investment in CPower, a company that was involved in demand response and energy efficiency. It publicized as well follow-on investments in Convey Computer, a company that was involved in energy-efficient high-performance computing, Grid Net, a company that was involved in smart meter infrastructure, Icontrol, a company that was involved in home automation and monitoring, and Powervation, a firm involved in digital power control. Intel continued to recognize the need for accelerated innovation in the domains of alternative energy production and advanced energy-management solutions because investments related to smart grid and energy efficiency had synergies with Intel's mainstream businesses. They complemented Intel's strategic objectives as well as providing benefits to utilities and consumers.

Intel also created many clean energy products. They were found in wind turbines, micro-grids, data centers, building energy controls, and home energy-management systems. In 2012, the company started tests of whole-home smart power sensors that it had developed. They would be plugged into building power sockets for the purpose of analyzing the building's power use. Intel showcased this technology in a smart-grid demonstration in Austin, Texas. Two wireless sensors plugged into regular power sockets read subtle changes in circuit voltage in appliances such as lights and air conditioning, figuring out when the electricity was used and comparing the data with overall power usage. The data were aggregated and used by utilities and consumers to improve home and building energy efficiency. The French IT consulting company Capgemini considered offering customers a tablet based on this technology that would provide cybersecurity and privacy protection as well as energy-management capabilities. Startups such as PowerMap and Navetas and the established consumer electronics company Belkin had similar devices. The Department of Energy sponsored demonstrations that would extend these systems to plug-in cars' smart-charging apps, solar panels, and energy storage. Many companies participated in these projects including Sony, Whirlpool, Best Buy, and General Motors.

In 2013, the EPA, for the third straight year, named Intel the largest consumer of green energy in the United States. The company obtained 100 percent of its power from renewable sources such as biogas, biomass, small hydro, solar and wind, producing the power on site as well as purchasing it from third parties.

Google's environmental commitments

Google was in sixth place on the EPA list, with about a third of its electricity coming from renewable sources. When Google went public in 2004, its founders Larry Page and Sergei Brin declared that their aim was to make the world a better place. Almost immediately, Google set up a separate business division called DotOrg, the purpose of which was not simply to make a profit and contribute to Google's bottom line.[13] Google placed its tax-exempt, non-profit foundation that made grants and contributions to worthy causes within DotOrg. To start the foundation's activities it gave DotOrg $90 million in Google stock. Though the foundation was in DotOrg, DotOrg's accounts were combined with the rest of the company. DotOrg therefore like the other parts of the company reported directly to shareholders. That meant it had business objectives. To achieve these objectives, it could invest in other companies or work with Google employees. In 2007, its highest priorities were making renewable energy cheaper than coal and accelerating the adoption of plug-in electric vehicles. Google also gave DotOrg one percent of Google's total equity, one percent of its total annual profits, and an initial three-year budget of $175 million.

DotOrg's campaign to make renewable energy cheaper than coal focused on solar-thermal, advanced wind, and engineered geo-thermal. Its aim was to develop enough renewable energy capacity to power a city as large as San Francisco. Unlike Google's foundation, which did not have the right to engage in politics, DotOrg did have this right and it lobbied for climate change legislation as well as acquiring a plug-in electric car fleet for employee use.

Google had employee-initiated projects organized under the title of a corporate-wide campaign that it initiated and called Google Green.[14] These projects encompassed commuting (high-tech, low-impact employee shuttles, electric corporate car sharing, and bicycles), eating (sourcing food locally, supporting sustainable seafood, and reducing waste), and buildings (eliminating toxic materials, smart design, and performance measurement including LEED [Leadership in Energy & Environmental Design] certifying its buildings). Google measured the amount of its energy that came from renewable sources. It bought carbon offsets and had a 1.6 MW PV solar array at the Mountain View campus in California that produced 3 million kWh of energy annually. It aimed to achieve a 35 percent reduction in greenhouse gases by 2012 and eventually to become carbon neutral.

Nonetheless, environmental groups such as Greenpeace criticized Google for the large amounts of electricity it consumed. They claimed that Google kept the details of its energy consumption and greenhouse gas emissions a secret. Google's response was that the information was proprietary because it could be used by competitors and it should not be forced to release the information. In 2009, *Harper's Magazine* ran an article that asserted that the real reason for the secrecy was the extent of Google's emissions, as each search on its engine released seven grams of carbon dioxide.[15] Google's retort was that it was not responsible for all of these releases; the computer user had to share in the responsibility. Google also maintained the amount of carbon dioxide released per search was two grams not seven grams as the article claimed.

With the growth in use of its data centers, the company could not stem the tide of criticism. It could not refute the assertion that its emissions were as large as the country of Laos, for example. Though each search engine's emissions were low, Gmail and YouTube use were increasing and their impacts had to be considered.

Google continued to try to defend itself by arguing that compared to other sectors in the economy, such as the petrochemical industry, it was a minor emitter. It claimed that its servers were among the most efficient in the world. They used half the energy of a typical server used by another company. Google decided to make public how much electricity it consumed. Partnering with organizations such as the Climate Savers Foundation and the Green Grid, it aimed to establish a set of best practices and make improvements in its data centers by such means as controlling airflow, adjusting thermostats, and relying on free cooling such as that the Columbia River in Oregon provided. For its efforts Google received praise from environmentalists, including Greenpeace, which urged others to follow Google's lead. Meanwhile, Google's foundation provided more than $100 million to non-profits and companies doing breakthrough utility-scale solar and wind-power projects.

In the midst of the controversy Google hired a green energy czar, Bill Weihl, a co-founder of the Climate Savers Computing Initiative, who had been involved in efforts to make computing more energy efficient. His mandate at Google was to achieve the goal of making renewable energy cheaper than coal. In the first year of his appointment he was cited as one of *Time Magazine*'s 2009 "heroes of the environment" and was interviewed by the *New York Times*.[16] In response to the question of why an Internet company was involved in alternative energy his answer was that it was because Google consumed so much energy. This consumption made Google interested in both lowering its electricity costs and increasing the reliability of the power's generation. Google too was concerned about its environmental impacts. If the costs of alternative energy were not brought down to the point where they were competitive with coal, coal's dominance would grow. Coal was responsible for 82 percent of the electricity sector's greenhouse gas emissions. For these reasons, Google was investing in renewable energy projects. It wanted to make as much money as possible while at the same time making a positive contribution to the world.

According to Weihl, Google brought to alternative energy a culture of innovation and an ability to think holistically and outside the box. It had a willingness to take risks when other companies did not. Though some people might not see the connection between Google and alternative energy, in the future they would understand that Google's participation in this sector was beneficial. Like any investor, Weihl asserted that Google was looking to back promising technologies that had the possibility of being commercialized. It asked if the technology made sense. It should not be just a science experiment. It should not violate the laws of physics. Though Google provided patient capital, its time line was not indefinite. The breakthroughs society needed to deal with climate change and make renewable energy cheaper than coal had to occur in years, not decades. Weihl maintained that Google's goal was to invest internally and externally in a diverse set of technologies that would bear fruit in a three- to seven-year time frame.

An example of Google's early investments in renewable energy was its 2006 backing of the wind power company Makani Power. This company was trying to develop a system for generating electricity from wind at high altitudes using an airborne platform. Makani was interested in employing a kite or a wing under autonomous control. The wind would pull the kite and change the angle so the energy would be obtained at less cost. Google saw promise in high-altitude wind, or even jet-stream wind, which was stronger and steadier than winds at lower altitudes. It also was examining the possibility of taking traditional wind turbines and placing them on taller towers, 200 meters as opposed to the typical 80 meters, to get stronger and steadier winds. The taller tower might be built at very little extra cost and yet might be able to reduce the cost of wind by 20 or 30 percent, which would make wind substantially less costly than coal.

In 2011, Weihl was hired away from Google by Facebook where he assumed a similar positon in that company. After Weihl's tenure, Google abandoned the goal of making renewable energy cheaper than coal, but it continued to invest in clean energy. In addition to CVC investments it made investments in the relatively profitable category of clean energy production. As a voracious consumer of electricity, with hundreds of thousands of servers, Google continued to try to find ways to reduce its environmental footprint.

The more large-scale data centers Google designed and constructed the more it invested in clean energy production. In 2014, it made its seventh and largest investment in renewable energy generation with the purchase of 407 MW of clean energy credits from MidAmerican Energy.[17] With this investment Google had increased the amount of renewable energy it financed by more than 60 percent. It owned over one billion dollars in renewable projects. Google signed the renewable energy contract with Warren Buffett-backed MidAmerican Energy, a wind generator, in Des Moines, Iowa for Google's data center located in Council Bluffs. This amount of electricity could power more than 100,000 US homes. The MidAmerican agreement also included renewable energy permits from other wind projects as well as direct purchases from MidAmerican's wind farms. Altogether, it was stated to be able to generate over 1,000 MW of power by the end of 2015.

Google started to invest in clean energy production in 2006 when it partnered with EI Solutions (later purchased by Suntech) to build a 1.6 MW solar-power system on its Mountain View campus. Most of its early investments in power generation were in renewable energy credits (RECs), which environmentalists called greenwashing because they did not directly bring new renewable generation online. Google therefore decided to increase its direct project financing efforts. In 2010, it received approval from the Federal Energy Regulatory Commission to have the right to sell and buy electricity like a utility. This move gave it flexibility in managing its onsite generation, structuring power purchase agreements, and controlling the electricity of its data centers. Among the alternative power generation deals Google made in 2010 many stand out including: a 37.5 percent early equity stake in the Atlantic Wind Connection; a transmission system to deliver 7,000 MW of offshore wind-generated electricity on the East Coast; $157 million in 270 MW of wind power constructed in Southern California's Tehachapi Mountains; $100 million in the biggest land wind farm in the world, the 845 MW Shepherd's Flat project in Oregon; $38.8 million in two North Dakota wind farms that had total capacity of 169.5 MW; and $5 million in a 49 percent stake in an 18.65 MW PV solar installation in Brandenburg, Germany.

In 2013, Google agreed to purchase all the electricity produced by the 240 MW Happy Hereford wind farm near Amarillo, Texas for one of its data centers in Oklahoma. Subsequently, it expanded its holdings in Texas Panhandle wind with a $75 million investment in Pattern Energy's 182 MW wind farm. Google also invested $168 million in the world's largest solar thermal (ST) project in Ivanpah, near the California–Nevada border.[18] This project used 347,000 sun-facing mirrors to produce 392 MW of electricity, enough power for over 140,000 Californian homes.

By 2014, Google had invested more than a billion dollars in 15 projects that had the capacity to produce two gigawatts of power. Nonetheless, unlike Intel that obtained 100 percent of its electricity from renewable sources only about a third of Google's operations were powered in this manner. Greenpeace wanted a commitment from Google to obtain 100 percent of its electricity from renewable energy.

Intel Capital's early-stage investments in clean energy

These business issues and environmental challenges provide the background for Intel Capital's and Google Ventures' investments in clean energy.[19] Intel Capital's most highly supported early-stage investments in clean energy were with the solar company SpectraWatt and the energy efficiency company Nexant. While Nexant proved to be a viable company, SpectraWatt was a failure. The immediate cause of SpectraWatt's collapse was the flooding of the solar market in 2011 by Chinese manufacturers. With their outsize capacity, the price of panels declined by more than 50 percent and the Chinese captured more than 50 percent of the California market, the fastest growing one in the United States. Many solar companies that had bet on their ability to bring down the price of solar panels, not just SpectraWatt, declared bankruptcy, closed, or were acquired at very low cost. Among more than 200 solar companies that Greentech Media identified in 2006, more than half had met this fate by 2013.

SpectraWatt's case had some unusual features. It was an internal spin off of Intel's New Business Intiatives Group and an example of technology that sprang from entrepreneurial efforts inside Intel. Though details of SpectraWatt technology never were revealed they were thought to be based on Intel's experience in processing wafers. SpectraWatt was supposed to benefit from sharing semiconductor technology and knowledge with Intel. The CEO of the company, Andrew Wilson, was a 12-year Intel veteran who had worked on photovoltaic projects within the company prior to becoming SpectraWatt's founder. He claimed that a solar cell was vastly simpler than a microprocessor. The solar industry, like microelectronics in the late 1970s, had few standards and no scale manufacturing. Therefore with Intel's global manufacturing competence and material science expertise, SpectraWatt could make breakthroughs. Its research team was made up of some of the brightest industry minds who had spent time at major research universities honing their skills. They should be able to significantly lower solar energy costs.

SpectraWatt's core business was to manufacture crystalline silicon-based solar cells not thin-film CIS/CIGS cells. The company expected to begin shipping products by mid-2009. At the time it was thought that other companies, like IBM and HP, as well as Intel were well-positioned to cut solar costs because of their high-tech manufacturing experience, large R&D budgets, and global presence. SpectraWatt did not have novel technology. It relied on silicon wafer cells, which at the time were considered more efficient. IBM and HP relied on thin-film cells. IBM's plans were to make solar panels covered with a thin film of chemical compounds on surfaces such as glass or brick by partnering with Tokyo Ohka Kogyo Co. – a manufacturer of computer chips and LCD televisions. HP, on the other hand, licensed its technology to Xtreme Energetics to help that startup company deliver rooftop thin-film solar-energy systems by baking zinc tin oxide semiconductor into glass or plastic.

SpectraWatt initially wanted to locate in Oregon and planned to ship silicon solar cells to panel makers in mid-2009, but it decided to move to New York in 2009 because of an incentive package from that state. It made the move in spring 2010 and set up manufacturing at a former chip factory. Wilson declared that the company was in great shape, its solar cells were all sold, it had no inventory, and it would hire more people in 2011 – two months before the company fell into bankruptcy and laid off more than 100 employees. When it shut down the company decided to quickly auction off its solar-manufacturing equipment because the market was flooded with so many other failed solar companies trying to sell off their used equipment. In 2013, Canadian Solar completed its purchase of what was left of SpectraWatt for about $4.95 million.

Nexant was more successful than SpectraWatt. In 2013, the Cleantech Group, a global research and advisory firm, selected Nexant as a top clean-tech company for its pioneering work on energy efficiency for the third straight year. Nexant's goal was to provide innovative renewable energy and energy efficiency solutions to help organizations improve operational and financial efficiency and reduce risk. It provided demand-side management planning, forecasting, customer billing, electronic messaging, and other services. Its customers included utilities, power producers, grid operators, and petrochemical firms. Its experts worked with local and regional partners and agencies in different parts of the world and it had a broad group of clients that included banks and government agencies as well as oil and chemical companies. In 2014, Nexant acquired the San Francisco energy consultancy Freeman, Sullivan & Company (FSC) for its capabilities in integrating demand response into utility smart-grid initiatives that complemented Nexant's software solutions. FSC had expertise in the design and evaluation of behavioral interventions in demand-response programs. It also had expertise in delivering strategic planning services and big-data solutions to utilities and regulators.

Nexant's selection as a top Cleantech company reflected a significant change among the top firms. More than one-quarter of the companies on Cleantech's 2013 list were energy-efficiency firms, an increase of seven companies over the previous year. This change represented a movement toward energy efficiency and away from solar power. It was illustrative of a shift from capital-intensive activities toward software and computer-based firms. In 2009, 20 solar companies were on Cleantech's list. In 2013, there were but six. Not every energy-efficiency company, however, was into software and data analysis. Some were LED manufacturers or were in building materials or waste-heat recovery, but unlike solar companies these capital-light firms did not require vast sums of money to build infrastructure.

Google Venture's early-stage investments in clean energy

Google Venture's most highly supported early-stage companies were solar company eSolar, and geothermal firm AltaRock Energy. As a solar-thermal (ST) company, eSolar faced serious challenges from plummeting PV prices. Photovoltaics were a less expensive method of power production and they were expected to increase their lead over ST in the coming years. Advocates maintained that large-scale ST plants (>500 MW) could rival natural gas in cost per kilowatt-hour, but the 2008 financial crisis led to a decline in funding. Environmentalists made it hard to obtain needed land permits. These developments led the utility NRG Energy to switch from ST to PV at two projects in California and New Mexico.

If PVs continued to be cheaper than ST, utilities were likely to choose the lower price alternative. Arguments for ST would depend on utilities' willingness to pay a premium. They might do so because while cloud cover tended to instantaneously drop PV plant output, ST plants produced power in a more consistent way as the turbines to which they were attached had inertia. Even more important was that ST plants could be augmented with storage systems, which might produce power at night. These systems, moreover, did not have to be battery based as eSolar with partner Babcock & Wilcox had been working on the design of a modular molten salt-based storage system with DOE support since 2010. The eSolar design used mounted mirrors called hexagonal heliostats that were programmed to move with the movement of the sun to concentrate the sunlight on salt in the tube of a thermal receiver, which was on top of a tower. The tower, about the height of a utility pole, was at the heliostats' center. With many heliostats working together, the receivers could heat salt to a very high temperature and then move it to centrally located storage (see Chapter 1). Though storage time was not indefinite, the stored energy could be used to generate electricity when needed. If successful, the molten salt-based storage system might reduce the costs of ST power and make it more competitive with PV-generated power. eSolar expected that initial commercial deployment would be in 2014 to 2015.

However, other disadvantages still hindered ST power. The US Southwest and other parts of the world offered good candidates for its deployment, but in many parts of the world it was simply not practical. eSolar therefore called for other applications. ST could be used with natural gas in hybrid systems. The company partnered with GE to bring this idea to fruition. Solar-thermal could be used in desalination systems to provide power to convert salt water to fresh water. The product was not electricity but hot steam. Hot steam could be used directly to extract petroleum or it could be used in other industrial processes.

eSolar was founded by IdeaLab's Bill Gross. IdeaLab had created and operated more than 125 companies with 40 IPOs and acquisitions since its inception in 1996. To survive eSolar crafted out additional niches in the ST business. It designed mass produced pre-fabricated heliostats at its factories. Heliostats were the basic building block of the system. They had three main components: the drive that enabled the heliostat to move in order to track the sun, the reflector module that consisted of mirrored glass, and a rigid structure to anchor them to the ground. Thousands of heliostats were found at any ST facility. eSolar had a second-generation design for heliostats with slightly larger mirrors and smaller and more easily implanted bases. The company also had streamlined the power electronics, cabling installation, and robotic cleaning to lower costs and reduce water consumption. Another eSolar advance was automated heliostat control software that was used to calibrate heliostats so they would work together. eSolar's patented system was based on a very complex algorithm based on the exact position of the sun, the heliostats, and the central collection tower. Years of research, experimentation, and testing had gone into the system.

AltaRock Energy was another major early Google Ventures' clean energy investment. This company had capabilities in enhanced geothermal systems (EGS). These systems were based on the idea that nearly anywhere on Earth, if the drilling was deep enough, it was hot and if there were the right kinds of rock, water could be injected and cycled through the system to produce steam energy. An advantage of EGS over solar and wind was that it was not intermittent and could be used to produce base-load power. The water for the injection might be the only limitation. Conventional geothermal power production depended upon high-temperature, permeable rock that had naturally occurring water circulating deep under the surface, but not many of these sites existed and drilling exploratory geothermal wells to find them was costly with the chances of discovery low. Though most land in the western United States had high-temperature rock near the surface, the rock was not permeable and there was no naturally circulating water.

AltaRock's technology was meant to overcome these problems by creating artificial geothermal systems. To create these artificial reservoirs, hydraulic pressure had to be applied to make a network of small, interconnected fractures in the rock. Water then was circulated through the network to capture heat. The process formed very small cracks in the rock with the goal of creating thousands of cracks efficient at transferring heat into circulating water. AltaRock technology was meant to create multizone stacks of such reservoirs. To stimulate a zone's development, the prior zone had to be sealed before another was stimulated. AltaRock had developed an advanced, biodegradable material made from thermally sensitive polymers to seal successive zones. Effectively blocking the zones also helped to prevent the drilling equipment from getting stuck in the wellbores.

In 2009, AltaRock suffered an embarrassment when it had to shut down a geothermal project in California because of the risk of earthquake. By its nature, the type of drilling it did created small earthquakes. The project's shutdown came after Swiss government officials permanently closed a project in Basel because it produced damaging earthquakes. AltaRock's California project's safety was then questioned because the company had not been sufficiently candid about the threat. The Basel problem, however, was unique because the digging was near a fault line. In general, earthquake risk was serious only if developers did projects near fault lines. This issue meant that great care had to be taken in many parts of California and the rest of the western United States, which were close to fault lines. These sites posed danger but they also had very good potential for geothermal development. By planting seismometers around the rock to be fractured, developers could watch if the cracks spread. Water pumps could be used to control the cracking and slipping, and if the cracks posed a danger the developers could turn off the water. The AltaRock concept allowed developers to move beyond the dry hole risks associated with conventional geothermal, where it was necessary to find existing fractures that contained economically viable flows of naturally occurring hot water. It made wide-scale geothermal development more possible, but not without new risks.

Intel Capital's late-stage investments in clean energy

Intel Capital's most highly supported late-stage investments were the solar company Solecture and the energy efficiency company Icontrol Networks. While SpectraWatt was Intel Capital's bet on thick-film crystalline silicon (c-Si) cells, Solecture (originally named Sulfurcell) was Google Ventures' bet on thin-film copper indium gallium and copper indium gallium selenide (CIS/CIGS) cells. By 2011, thin-film solar panels remained a small part of the market, accounting only for 11 percent of all solar panel sales, but production capacity was expected to grow at a rapid rate and the US DOE estimated that thin-film panels might capture as much as 38 percent of the worldwide market by 2020. This expectation led to substantial VC investment in thin film by many different firms. The three main technologies in which they invested were in cadmium telluride (CdTe), copper indium gallium selenide (CIS/CIGS), and amorphous silicon (a-Si).

Sulfurcell was a German company founded and led by physicist Nikolaus Meyer in 2001 that operated in the CIS/CIGS space. CIS/CIGS cells had some benefits that made them more appealing than CdTe or a-Si cells. Within research labs and solar modules both CIS/CIGS and CdTe cells had achieved greater efficiencies than a-Si cells, a mature technology mainly found in small devices such as calculators. A major player in the a-Si space was Sharp. The best efficiency a-Si achieved in a research lab was about 13 percent, while the best efficiency a-Si achieved in a solar module was about 8 percent. CIS/CIGS and CdTe cells had achieved efficiencies of about 20 percent in the lab and as high as 14 percent in solar modules. CIS/CIGS cells slightly outperformed CdTe cells in both settings. However, neither of these thin-cell technologies could reach the efficiencies of thick-film c-Si solar cells. Not surprisingly therefore the majority of PV modules sold in the world were c-Si. Though thin-film cells were lighter than silicon cells, they required more space to produce the same amount of energy. Typically, the installation costs also were higher and they degraded more rapidly than thick-film cells. Silicon costs, moreover, had gone down, which made silicon-based solar panels more affordable.

By 2011, the Chinese manufacturers, whom their government heavily subsidized, were using silicon-based cells to capture about a quarter of the world's PV market share (see Chapter 1). They had super-efficient factories and low labor costs. In 2011, the Chinese firm Yingli had about 6.5 percent of the global market, Trina had about 6 percent, and Sungen had more than 5 percent. The only US firm with a strong presence in the market was First Solar which used thin CdTe cells and had about 8 percent of the global market (see Chapter 3). Backed by the Walton family, First Solar had been a world-record holder for CdTe thin-film module and cell efficiency. A publicly traded company, it had power plant contracts with major utilities. Its main competitors, Abound Solar and General Electric's PrimeStar had declared bankruptcy or were failing.

Both types of thin film cells, CIS/CIGS and CdTe, had some advantages over silicon-based thick-film cells. Their temperature resistance was significantly higher than these cells and they also functioned somewhat better in the shade. CdTe-based solar panels were less costly than c-Si in some locations, mainly multi-kilowatt systems in high-temperature climates such as the US Southeast, where First Solar was headquartered.

Thin-film CIS/CIGS cells had some advantages over thin-film CdTe cells. They were slightly more efficient in converting sunlight into usable energy, but this difference was not that significant. More importantly, these cells required less use of cadmium, a heavy metal and potential carcinogen that accumulated in plant and animal tissues. However, this threat could be contained when the compound was within the confines of a solar panel, and its existence had not stopped First Solar from selling many panel cells of this kind. Nonetheless, the disposal and recycling costs of the cadmium could be dangerous and costly.

Of even greater importance was that while CdTe cells had to be placed on rigid glass substrates, this restriction did not apply CIS/CIGS cells that could be also placed on flexible substrates. In 2013, scientists at Empa, the Swiss Federal Laboratories for Materials Science and Technology, were able to place CIGS cells on flexible polymer foils and achieve an efficiency record in their laboratory of 20.4 percent. The ability to place these cells on flexible substrates was very important because it opened up many markets other than ground or rooftop collection. For example, CIS/CIGS panels could be integrated into the curved surfaces of buildings, while CdTe panels could not. An entire building, then, and not just the rooftop could be covered with solar panels. So-called building integrated photovoltaic (BIPV) technologies of this kind had much future promise.

The main disadvantage of CIS/CIGS cells in comparison to CdTe cells was that they were very hard to manufacture. Because they were hard to manufacture their costs were higher than CdTe cells. The CIS/CIGS cells therefore had the smallest market share of the thin-film technologies. Estimates in 2011 were that CdTe had a share of about

Table 2.3 *Bankrupt or acquired thin-film CIS/CIGS solar cell manufacturers*

2011
Bankrupt, closed
   Solyndra (CIGS) bankrupt
Acquisition, sale
   Ascent Solar (CIGS) acquired by TFG Radiant
   HelioVolt (CIGS) acquired by Korea's SK Innovation

2012
Bankrupt, closed
   AQT (CIGS) closed
   Odersun (CIGS) bankrupt
   Soltecture (CIGS BIPV) bankrupt
   Solibro (CIGS) Q-Cells unit acquired by China's Hanergy
   Scheuten Solar (BIPV) bankrupt, then acquired by Aikosolar

2013
Bankrupt, closed
   Avancis (CIGS) discontinuing production
   Nanosolar (CIGS) closed
   Solarion (CIGS) went bankrupt but restructured
Acquisition, sale
   Global Solar Energy (CIGS) acquired by China's Hanergy
   MiaSolé (CIGS) acquired by China's Hanergy
   NuvoSun (CIGS) acquired by Dow
   Wuerth Solar (CIGS line) taken over by Manz

Compiled from data on the Greentech Media website, April 2014

43 percent, the older technology, a-Si, a share of about 32 percent, while CIS/CIGS cells had a share of about 25 percent.

With lower silicon prices and high and uncertain manufacturing costs, CIS/CIGS fell behind other technologies. At one time there had been as many 35 different companies with CIS/CIGS plans. After Solyndra's plans to develop CIS/CIGS fell apart in 2011, many companies that either produced or intended to produce PV cells using this technology, including Soltecture, also failed (see Table 2.3). Hanergy, a Chinese company, was able to gain a strong position in the thin-film solar market by inexpensively purchasing the assets of scientific know-how of some of the most promising of these failed companies including MiaSolé and Solibro (see Chapter 1).

CIS/CIGS manufacturing problems were a result of too many options. Many processing techniques could be used – sputtering, evaporation, electrochemical deposition, nanoparticle printing, and ion-beam deposition. The processes could be broken down into additional options. Sputtering could be a two-step process (sputter first, react with selenium later), or a single-step reactive sputtering process. Evaporation could be a single-stage, two-stage, or three-stage evaporation process. The variations did not stop here. The CIS/CIGS material could be deposited on different substrates: glass, plastic, stainless steel, and aluminum. The versatility of many pathways made it difficult to find an optimal solution. In striving for differentiation, each company tried something different. They explored many pathways and experienced many dead ends. This selection process made it clearer in 2014 that the three-stage process of co-evaporation with monolithic integration on glass might prove to be superior.

Solecture, or as it was formerly known Sulfurcell, had been slow in making progress toward a solution to the challenges of higher efficiency and less expensively manufactured cells. In 2011, it produced its first panels with an efficiency of 13.4 percent. The company regarded this achievement accomplished with CIS technology a first-generation product. It was moving toward CIGS cells that would be its second-generation product. However, the company continued to devote most of its capacity to the lower efficiency first-generation product. When it finally started to ship second-generation CIGS cells to the European market, it did not disclose the cost at which these modules had been manufactured. The firm admitted that it still could not mass produce the higher efficiency cells.

Instead Soltecture tried to differentiate itself from the competition by developing comprehensive BIPV solutions for the solar construction and commercial rooftop markets. It made this choice because Germany's feed-in tariff rewarded these deployments more handsomely than ground-mounted installations. The company also designed its own racks, while it outsourced the inverters and the other pieces of equipment. It touted a growing catalog of aesthetically agreeable products that could be integrated on the sides of a building as well as ones that could be installed on building roofs. It had office and commercial building facades that it made with standardized side-dish PV cladding. It provided entire systems with racks, mounts, wiring, and power electronics – either using its own designs or configuring its components with partners. If it could not optimize on panel costs, it could optimize on overall system performance for the needs of large, flat industrial and commercial roofs. Its systems were lighter than systems consisting of silicon-based products and they were perfect for the roofs that could not bear the weight.

The surplus of silicon cells on the market led to a dramatic drop in solar module prices, which Soltecture could not overcome. To succeed the company would have required the assistance of an industrial partner who was seeking to be a major PV manufacturer. To lower costs, it needed a very high-volume standard fab design it could set up in many countries where demand made it worthwhile. Intel did not buy into this vision. It would have to invest even more into Soltecture than it already had invested and it did not reckon that this type of investment would pay off. Soltecture was part of the shakeout among CIS/CIGS cells producers. In 2012, it went bankrupt.

A second important late-stage Intel Capital investment was in Icontrol. KPCB as well made late-stage investments in this company. Icontrol software platforms were behind smart home offerings of cable companies like Comcast, XFINITY Home, Time Warner, and others. These systems allowed users to create personalized digital home systems for energy management, security, and healthcare. They integrated the functions in a tool accessible via the Internet. The meter and thermostat were easy to use. Customers had a way to monitor, control, and automate energy usage. Utilities had a means to control peak demand. The security service provided video alerts. Icontrol claimed that an average energy bill could be reduced by 10 to 20 percent. The health care service could be set up to monitor the wellbeing of the elderly. It could tell if they were awake and moving, had taken their medications, or left the premises. The system provided 24-hour connectivity to those who required extra care and was inexpensive in comparison to the alternatives.

The issue was that there were many competitors, such as General Electric and Tendril, that offered similar services. It was unclear if sufficient customers were willing to pay for it. Home energy management was a challenging market. Homes did consume a high percentage of all of the energy in the United States and much of it was wasted because people left on their lights, computers, and appliances and warmed their houses at unnecessarily high temperatures when no one was at home. Home energy-management systems, however, might cost as much as

$300 to install and they could save no more than $60 a year, therefore requiring at least five years before paying for themselves. As appliance efficiency improved, the need for these systems went down. With programmable thermostats from Nest, behavioral adjustment from OPower, and LED bulbs, the savings Icontrol's services could achieve were lower. Depending of what other functions Google might add, the $250 investment homeowners made in a Nest thermostat meant they were not likely to purchase Icontrol's services. Cable providers like Comcast, Time Warner, and Rogers sold Icontrol's systems as an additional offering to their customers relying on their well-established sales channels because it added revenue. The ultimate customer for Icontrol's products and services might be utilities who could benefit from the ability of the company's services to help the utilities manage peak-load demand, or the distinctive feature of Icontrol might be health monitoring. Its most distinctive application had yet to be determined.

Google Ventures' late-stage investments in clean energy

Three highly supported Google Ventures' late-stage investments were the solar companies Recurrent Energy and Solar Reserve and the transportation company Uber. Google Ventures' solar investments were a move in the direction of project financing. The backing that Google gave to Recurrent Energy and Solar Reserve suggested a shift in strategy to support renewable-energy project developments rather than R&D. Its investment in Uber, its biggest ever venture capital investment, suggested a major commitment to a new type of transportation system.

Recurrent Energy started by installing solar arrays on commercial roofs, but not all roofs could take the weight and property owners balked at renting their space to solar developers. Also, it was difficult to tie the arrays into the grid. The company therefore found empty lots such as old manufacturing sites or abandoned farmland for projects. It did not consider large desert fields practical because of permitting problems and distance from the grid, which overrode the inexpensive land prices. It had a portfolio of utility-scale solar power projects, most of them for utilities in markets with strong renewable portfolio goals. The company had medium-scale solar PV projects ranging in size from 20 MW to 50 MW and central scale solar PV projects ranging in size from 50 MW to several hundred. The company sold its projects based on the proposition that solar PV generated power during peak load periods, thereby providing cleaner alternatives to old fossil-fuel peaking plants. Solar PV generating costs were predictable compared to natural gas costs, which oscillated with fluctuations in natural gas prices. Even with lower priced gas being available, gas contracts of more than three years were at prices at which solar was very competitive.

KKR was Google Ventures' partner in many of Recurrent Energy's projects that Google Ventures helped to fund. Founded in 1976 and led by Henry Kravis and George Roberts, KKR was a leading publicly traded investment firm with nearly $100 billion in assets under management in 2013. Together Google and KKR invested in ten facilities in California and Arizona that Recurrent Energy had developed and managed. These facilities provided power to local utilities and municipalities under long-term power purchase agreements (PPAs). Recurrent Energy also had backing from insurance company Metropolitan Life to finance projects in Ontario, Canada. It had the right to sell the PV-generated electricity to Ontario Power Authority under a 20-year agreement it secured from the province.

In 2010, the Japanese firm Sharp purchased Recurrent Energy for $305 million. Sharp had been a leading solar-cell producer prior to the Chinese domination of the market. Since the 2011 earthquake and tsunami, which took Japan's nuclear industry offline, Japan's installation of PV panels had picked up. In 2013, the country accounted for 17 percent of the world's solar market. This development suggested to Sharp that it could revitalize its solar business. Its global market share in solar manufacturing in 2014 was fourth in the world, but Chinese solar panel maker Yingli was first with nearly ten percent of all global shipments.

Sharp's acquisition of Recurrent Energy was part of a trend in which upstream solar manufacturers such as Sharp moved downstream in an attempt to capture value from the installation of solar panels and project development. Competitors First Solar, SunPower, and Hanwha all had made downstream acquisitions. Like these acquisitions, Sharp's buying of Recurrent Energy brought together a solar module maker with a solar power project developer. Sharp could bid on projects with Recurrent Energy, and build them with its modules. Because Sharp had a longer history and was better established than Recurrent Energy, it could access capital at lower rates than Recurrent Energy.

However, as an independent subsidiary of Sharp, Recurrent Energy did not have to incorporate Sharp's panels into its projects. It could purchase the best value (price plus quality) panels from any vendor. Mostly it bought from Suntech and Yingli and not Sharp. Sharp therefore turned around in 2012 and tried to sell the company. Recurrent Energy's operating profits were not that strong and Sharp was in the midst of restructuring after losses in its flat-panel TV and TV screen business. Sharp had shifted focus to supplying high-margin smartphone maker Apple, a very demanding customer. Its 2014 forecast for LCD panels was low and it was eager to sell Recurrent Energy because the experiment had not produced the results it wanted.

Google Ventures also invested in solar company SolarReserve. It helped to provide the equity to a consortium that was involved in building a PV plant in South Africa. South African renewable capacity had grown faster than any country in the world in 2012. The cost of solar installations in that country was near grid parity. The South African project that Google Ventures helped fund was one of the country's largest. The South African Department of Energy's Renewable Energy Independent Power Producer Procurement Program had given the project a 20-year power purchase agreement. The country's target was that 38 percent of all new generation should be renewable by 2030. Its existing systems were largely coal based, they had regular blackouts, and serious updating was needed. With the price of Chinese modules low, South Africa jumped on the chance to become involved in solar power.

SolarReserve came into existence in 2008 as a partnership between US Renewables Group and United Technologies Corporation (UTC). Storage was an issue to which UTC had devoted considerable attention. In the 1990s, the US DOE had contracted with UTC's Rocketdyne division to leverage Rocketdyne's rocket-propulsion engineering capabilities in concentrating large amounts of power in small spaces. United Technologies Corporation developed a design for solar-thermal (ST) tower technology that relied on thousands of heliostats to track the sun and reflect its energy onto a receiver mounted atop a 600-feet (183-meter) tall tower. It stored some of the energy as heat using liquefied molten salt (see Chapter 10). It circulated the molten salt in a receiver where the energy heated to around 1,000°F (537°C). It then moved the energy to a large insulated tank. Because the energy could be stored as molten salt for days with little heat loss, it was available at night and on cloudy days. Rocketdyne granted an exclusive license for the molten-salt power tower concept and mirrors to SolarReserve. Thus Solar Reserve, like eSolar another firm Google Ventures had backed, had experience with this type of storage.

Another important late-stage clean energy investment Google Ventures made was in transportation. It invested growth equity money in Uber – the company that made mobile application software that connected passengers with ridesharing services and drivers of vehicles for hire. Uber's system allowed passengers to find, book, and pay for these on-demand services. Its pricing was similar to cabs, though Uber handled the hiring of the drivers and the payment, and the driver played no direct role in the transaction. If the car traveled further than a particular distance, the price was calculated on a distance basis. Otherwise it was calculated on a time basis. At the end of a ride, Uber billed the fare to the customer's credit card and told customers that no tip was needed. No option to tip existed unless the passenger personally offered it in cash.

Uber's services were available in an expanding number of cities in the United States and abroad. There were other on-demand car services, however. Lyft had raised substantial amounts of money from Andreessen Horowitz and Hallo had raised substantial amounts of money from Richard Branson. The ascent of these services took place in parallel with an interest in a so-called sharing economy, a concept that signified using technology to connect consumers to goods and services that otherwise were idle. A prominent example was Airbnb. Initially, Uber offered luxury vehicles such as Lincoln Town Cars, Cadillac Escalades, BMW 7 Series, and Mercedes-Benz S550, but after 2012 it added a selection of cars with broader appeal. Uber indicated it might expand to ridesharing and delivery.

Google's interest in Uber was related to the ongoing attention it paid to driverless vehicles and autonomous cars. Google could apply Uber's software to coordinate these vehicles. Even if the goal of a completely driverless system was unrealistic, the software and algorithms Uber created could transform transportation. They could optimize vehicle use so that fewer cars would be operating at less than full potential. The match between car availability and passenger needs could be strengthened. If a person wanted to drive alone they could obtain a comfortable seat in a small car. A group of people could obtain access to a multi-passenger van. The vehicle Uber offered for large-haul shopping trips would differ from the one it offered for a night on the town. Each vehicle would fit the traveler's requirements at the moment. The range of vehicles Uber could deliver would suit trip length and purpose. They could be put into place to remove an impediment to the use of electric vehicles – the range problem (see Chapter 4). Electric vehicles were perfect for short-distance city driving. If a traveler needed a vehicle for long-distance driving, it could be given a hybrid or gasoline-powered vehicle.

A transportation system coordinated in this way would better meet passengers' needs, consume less energy, and lead to fewer greenhouse gases than the current system. Traffic would be lighter. Fewer parking spaces would be required and there would be fewer gasoline stations. Because cities would be freer of noise and pollution, people could live in more compact and dense urban areas without sacrificing quality of life. Eliminating transportation system waste and optimizing the service travelers wanted would be a major step forward in creating a more sustainable society. Of course, this vision was a long way off. Much had to be done in the meantime to make it possible. In the short term, many cities' taxi drivers launched vigorous protests against Uber. Using their hackers' licenses, the drivers tried to prevent or limit Uber's operations. Local governments had to forge compromises that would allow both cabbies and ride sharing to coexist. For a broader transformation of the entire society and the way people lived, there would have to be much greater government involvement.

What next for Intel Capital and Google Ventures?

An important question that both Intel Capital and Google Ventures faced was the role their backing of clean energy startups would play in their futures. In comparison to other VCs were they in a better position to nurture startups and make them successful? Both Intel Capital and Google Ventures had accumulated considerable experience in the clean energy sector. They had to absorb and process what they had learned. To what extent should they continue to fund clean energy firms, what types of clean energy firms should they fund, and at what stage should they become involved in their funding?

The evidence so far with respect to the involvement of CVCs in clean-tech financing did not support the view that corporate involvement always led to good financial returns for the parent companies. In 2013, a Cleantech Group report analyzed 86 deals with this type of involvement and found that distressed exits were more common than successful ones.[20] Commercializing new technologies that originated in startups was difficult for corporations that otherwise confronted tough business challenges. These difficulties did not mean that corporations should not become involved in clean energy startups, but it did mean that they should be very clear about the role they intended to play.

Notes

1 Next 10, *Cleantech Investment: A Decade of California's Evolving Port-folio* (San Francisco: www.next10.org, 2013).
2 *Ibid.*
3 See PrivCo: www.privco.com for this rating.
4 See Thomson Reuters VentureXpert, the venture capital database that Thomson-Reuters owns and maintains http://thomsonreuters.com/financial/venture-capital-and-private-equity.
5 See Intel Capital website: www.intelcapital.com and D. Yoffie, *Intel Capital, 2005 (A)*, (Boston, MA: Harvard Business School, 2007).
6 Thomson Reuters VentureXpert: http://thomsonreuters.com/financial/venture-capital-and-private-equity
7 *Ibid.*
8 *Ibid.*
9 *Ibid.*
10 M. Lynch, "Is cleantech the smart investment for Google?" *Forbes* (2014): www.forbes.com/sites/michaellynch/2014/02/14/is-cleantech-an-appropriate-investment-for-google
11 A. Marcus, *Winning Moves* (Lombard, IL: Marsh Publications, 2009): pp. 1–19.
12 A. Marcus, D. Geffen, and K. Sexton, *Reinventing Environmental Reg-ulation* (Washington, DC: Resources for the Future, 2002), pp. 111–20.
13 M. Belinksy, *Google.org: For-Profit Philanthropy* (Cambridge, MA: Harvard Kennedy School, 2012).
14 A. Marcus and A. Van de Ven, "Managing shifting goal consensus and task ambiguity in making the transition to sustainability," in R. Henderson and M. Tushman (ed.) *Leading Sustainable Change* (New York: Oxford University Press, 2014): 298–322.

15 B. Bunker, J. Foster, J. Levine, R. Sanchez, G. Sethi, and G. Tan, *Google's Shift into Renewables* (Ann Arbor, MI: Erb Institute University of Michigan, 2012).

16 J. Marlow, "Q&A: Google's green energy czar," (2010): http://green.blogs.nytimes.com/2010/01/07/qa-googles-green-energy-czar/?_php=true&_type=blogs&_r=0.

17 See www.google.com/green/energy/investments

18 *Ibid.*

19 The discussion that follows is derived from data found on the Cleantech Group website: www.cleantech.com; stories featured in Greentech Media: www.greentechmedia.com; company analyses by contributors to the Seeking Alpha website http://seekingalpha.com; and company websites.

20 See the Cleantech Group website www.cleantech.com

PART II

Business models

3 | Follow the sun: First Solar and Suntech

Global demand for power was nearly insatiable. In the United States demand for electricity was supposed to increase by 15 to 20 percent by 2025.[1] To meet this demand, utilities needed predictable power sources. In 2014, solar represented just one percent of US electric generation.[2] With fracking and vast supplies of natural gas suddenly available, natural gas and not solar appeared to be the first choice to meet US demand. However, solar costs had come down dramatically and global investments in renewables had been growing.

To seriously contend with natural gas, the costs of solar had to come down further. Solar and wind power required storage, and government subsidies that supported renewables had to become more stable. Hit by one financial crisis after another, European countries had cut back on their generous subsidies. Germany, whose subsidies, after it chose to mothball its nuclear power plants, were the most generous, was less committed. Whenever federal government subsidies to solar or wind energy expired in the United States, Congress was indecisive about whether to continue them, especially after the debacle of Solyndra – a solar-panel producer that borrowed more than $500 million from the US government and filed for Chapter 11 protection in 2011. After the Fukushima disaster, Japan might be a promising market for solar and wind products. Its government approved a feed-in tariff in 2012 of about €0.41 per kWh.[3] Depending of how public policies in various countries evolved, they would have major impacts on solar power's future.

The latest twist in this saga was trade wars.[4] In 2011, SolarWorld, a German company that manufactures solar panels in Oregon and a company to whom Shell divested its solar business, along with seven other firms, unnamed because of fear of Chinese reprisal, targeted China for anti-competitive subsidies and the dumping of solar panels in the United States. The highest penalty the US government levied was against Chinese solar-panel manufacturer, Suntech.

Table 3.1 *The decline in Chinese solar shipments to the United States, 2011 to 2013*

	2011	2012	2013
Units	93.47 million	47.03 million	32.94 million
Value ($)	3.12 billion	2.08 billion	1.49 billion

Compiled from US Census Bureau Data

In 2011, Suntech had the world's largest market share in the production of photovoltaic (PV) modules. Together with eight other Chinese manufacturers it commanded 30 percent of the market. Second in global market share was the US firm First Solar. First Solar's largest investors were the Walton family, heirs of the huge Walmart fortune. In the late 1990s, True North venture capital, funded by John Walton, one of Sam Walton's sons, became interested in the company. Suntech, on the other hand, started in 2001 when the city of Wuxi, about 100 miles (161 km) west of Shanghai, gave Zhengrong Shi, a University of New South Wales PhD and holder of 15 solar patents, $6 million to found the company.

The countervailing trade duties the US government imposed had their intended effect. They drastically decreased the value and the volume of Chinese PV module imports to the United States (see Table 3.1). They raised average US solar module prices by 25 to 30 percent, which eased the burden on US manufacturers, such as First Solar. However, they also suppressed demand for US rooftop residential and commercial solar installations and yielded job losses in solar sales, marketing, design, installation, maintenance, and finance.

The European Union (EU) initiated action similar to that of the US government. Chinese manufacturers had to set minimum prices for their products in Europe and limit their European shipments. The Chinese government then tried to even the score. It imposed duties on the key PV cell component, poly-silicon, which often was imported into China from abroad.

SolarWorld and its co-petitioners alleged that Chinese manufacturers evaded the US tariffs by shipping their finished products through Taiwan. The latest to join the fray was India, which also attacked importers of solar cells into its country. It charged that foreign manufacturers from China, Taiwan, the United States and Malaysia had dumped products in India. First Solar, which manufactured modules in Malaysia as well as the United States, confronted limits on the business it could do in India, a country it considered essential for its global expansion.

As a result of these actions, the global market shares of Suntech and First Solar slipped. Suntech's global market share fell to 4.7 percent and First Solar's to 5.3 percent in 2012.[5] By 2013, Suntech was bankrupt, not just because of the trade wars, but as a result of a financial scandal that took place when it tried to self-finance projects in Europe.[6] With the reduction of European subsidies, the company considered self-financing the only alternative it had to expanding in Europe. Since Suntech employed more than 10,000 people in Wuxi, the Chinese city where it did its manufacturing, the government felt obliged to bail it out. Though smaller and no longer led by its founder Zhengrong Shi, the firm continued to operate.

Trade wars posed serious challenges for First Solar and Suntech. What impact would these trade wars have on their business models? How would they have to adjust them?

Differences in financing, growth, development, and technologies

Though they competed in similar markets for the same residential, commercial, and utility customers, First Solar and Suntech had very different business models. The main differences were in their financing, growth and development, and in the technologies they employed. Their strategies would have to take these factors into account.

Financing First Solar

The way First Solar had been financed was very different to the way Suntech had been financed.[7] First Solar's main shareholder was the Walton family, which owned more than four times as much of its stock than the second-largest shareholder, Los Angeles-based, Capital World Investors. The family's support during periods when the company had been engaged in money-losing R&D had been critical. Its willingness to invest for the long term had contributed to First Solar's ability to move from a venture capital (VC) backed startup to a company with $2.1 billion in revenues and profits exceeding $640 million in 2009.

Sam Walton's son John, a Vietnam Special Forces veteran, became a committed environmentalist. As the main investor in the VC firm True North, he encouraged it to buy a controlling stake in the company that became First Solar for $176 million in 1999.[8] John Walton died in a tragic airplane accident in 2005, the year before First Solar's IPO. After he died, the family continued to support the company. Its 25 percent stake in First Solar was estimated to be worth nearly $1.5 billion in 2014.[9] Though small in comparison to the family's more than $25 billion estimated stake in Walmart, it still was considerable. True North gave First Solar its first CEO, Mike Ahearn, and the company grew by selling panels in the heavily subsidized European market.

The European market was critical to the growth of solar. In the 1980s, Japan, which had few domestic energy sources, had been the first country to focus on solar energy. The government established performance standards and provided low-interest loans with the aim of increasing the efficiency of solar power cells to more than 30 percent. Sharp (see Chapter 2) and Kyocera had been innovators in amorphous silicon applications that were used in calculators and other low-power consumer devices. It was expected that they could move into larger scale electrical production. However, in a wave of austerity Japan abandoned all subsidies to solar in 2005. It no longer was a major world player in this market.

First Solar's growth and development

Mainly the result of the opening of European markets, solar achieved strong growth in the first decade of the twenty-first century (see Chapters 1 and 2). To achieve its goal of being 20 percent renewable by 2020, Germany established a feed-in tariff of €0.42 per kWh that declined gradually by 8 percent per year. To achieve its goals of being 30 percent renewable by 2010, Spain established a feed-in tariff of €0.44 per kWh. Italy, France, and Greece followed with their own renewable energy goals and subsidies. Ground-mounted utility systems dominated the market in Europe. European utilities were attracted by peak-load reductions during hot summer afternoons as well as low transmission and distribution losses when solar was placed near its point of use.

Starting in 2003, the world's solar markets grew at a pace of 43 per cent per year, the fastest among all energy sources, and this growth was anticipated to continue at an average rate of 27 percent annually through 2012.[10] However, with the financial crisis of 2008, Spain capped its solar programs and it lowered its feed-in tariff, ultimately eliminating it entirely in 2012. Spain's move alone reduced global sales by 40 percent.[11] With other European subsidies set to be reduced, First Solar started to shift its focus to California, where demand did not depend as much on subsidies, and to utility-scale projects it financed with other investors and sold to independent power producers (IPPs). The US market lacked federal incentives, but California had a goal of being 33 percent renewable based on incentives it provided and there were similar programs in many other states, the most notable being New Jersey, Colorado, Nevada, and Hawaii.[12] Not all US states had renewable goals, but collectively the US state standards amounted to a national goal of about 20 percent renewable energy by 2020. The federal government's role was in providing investment tax credits of 30 percent for systems installed before 2016. If a company did not have sufficient profits the tax credits had no value, so in 2010 Congress extended them to unprofitable companies that could take advantage of the credits. Companies such as First Solar that installed and built solar power facilities worked with independent power producers (IPPs) that had power purchase agreements (PPAs) to sell electricity at contracted prices because they were less of a risk.

First Solar moved aggressively into the US market, in 2007 acquiring US systems integrator Turner, and in 2009 buying the developer OptiSolar, another downstream integrator with a rich pipeline of projects. These types of large-scale utility installations became 70 percent of First Solar's revenues. The rest came from selling panels for placement on residential and commercial rooftops. As California and other US states began to meet their goals for renewable production, First Solar faced new challenges. Its profits shrank from $664 million in 2010 to a $40 million loss in 2011.[13] The Walton family sold shares before the collapse but did not abandon the company completely. It sold stock worth $2.2 billion, but held onto shares worth about $1.5 billion.[14] Based on its original investment $176 million it exited at the right time.

With turmoil in the industry there was substantial turnover in First Solar's executive suite. In 2012, the board hired ex-Enron executive and Texas lawyer James Hughes to lead the company. Hughes brought other ex-Enron executives into the company. He continued to close

European facilities and focused on obtaining more large-scale construction projects such as the Topaz Solar Farm in San Luis Obispo County, California and the Desert Sunlight Solar Farm near Blythe, California. Built under California's mandate to increase the percentage of power it obtained from renewable sources, these projects were eligible for federal tax credits. There was no certainty these programs could continue to sustain the momentum of First Solar's growth. United States' utility-scale solar installations expanded by almost 58 percent in 2013 and made up nearly 60 percent of solar installations, but this activity was declining, especially for large and lucrative projects.[15] Identifying suitable land with solar resources and proximity to transmission lines was a problem. It took up to three to five years to identify a good site and gain the required approvals to build. The goal of First Solar was to reduce solar's price so that it was subsidy free but that goal could not be counted on as a short-term strategy.

First Solar realized that to continue to grow it increasingly would have to tap into international markets, particularly in India and Latin America. Because the Indian market was so important, the Indian ruling on dumping was troubling. India already trailed other countries in its solar installations, in 2013, for example, installing just 950 MW of solar power in comparison to China which installed 12 GW.[16] The imposition of duties would further slow the pace of the Indian installations, a situation that India with its rapidly growing population, demand for electricity, and environmental problems, could ill afford. On the other hand, First Solar might benefit from the Indian duties, as the tariffs imposed on First Solar were significantly lower than those India proposed to place on Chinese companies, a 20 percent tariff on First Solar as opposed to an 80 percent average tariff on the Chinese manufacturers.

In 2014, First Solar announced that it had made progress in gaining business in Latin America.[17] It obtained approval from the Overseas Private Investment Corporation (OPIC), the US Government's development finance institution, and had the financing to support construction of the 141 MW Luz del Norte solar power plant in Chile's Atacama Desert. The loans would clear the way for First Solar to proceed with planning near the city of Copiapo. The Atacama Desert obtained some of the world's best concentrations of direct sunlight, presenting ideal conditions for solar-power generation.

Other than global projects of this nature, First Solar's main alternative was to expand in the domestic rooftop market, whose growth pace in the United States was outpacing that of large-scale solar installations. According to a Goldman Sachs' projection, the US rooftop solar market would expand at a rate of about 45 percent from 2013 to 2016, while utility-scale installations would grow at just 8 percent.[18] The problem with the rooftop solar market was that the light film technology that First Solar had pioneered was not well suited to this market. It required more space to produce the same amount of electricity. First Solar, a thin-film cell producer, relied on cells made of cadmium telluride (CdTe). Around 80 percent of the market in 2014 was for crystalline silicon (c-Si) based cells. Almost all Chinese producers relied mainly on c-Si, and they were a better fit for the rooftop market.

To become competitive in this market, First Solar bought a silicon-based US producer, TetraSun. This acquisition provided it with an inroad into the thick-film market. It also invested in residential distributor and installer Solar City, which had been started by Tesla's founder Elon Musk (see Chapter 4). Diversification into silicon via TetraSun positioned the company better to compete in markets such as Japan, where these panels were preferred.

First Solar also established a new panel-efficiency roadmap for CdTe cells, which aimed to increase module efficiency to around 19.5 percent by 2017 rather than the previous targeted 17.2 percent, which would mean that the efficiency of First Solar modules would equal those of silicon. First Solar's panels also might have a competitive edge in markets such as the Middle East and India, because Cd-Te panels outperformed silicon-based panels if temperatures were very hot.

Another move that First Solar made was to offer services. It could help monitor the thousands of solar power plants installed. To bolster capabilities in this domain, First Solar in 2014 acquired the German firm, Skytron Energy, the fourth-largest solar PV monitoring firm in the world. This acquisition gave First Solar the proprietary equipment and software to monitor solar power plant performance. In 2012, it opened an operations center in Arizona for data collection for large utility-scale power plants. The global monitoring market was strong, with estimates showing 90 percent market growth after 2012. In the future most of this work would be centered in Asia. Another initiative First

Table 3.2 *A comparison of First Solar and Suntech's financials,*
second quarter 2014

	First Solar	Suntech
Market cap ($)	6.96 billion	65.17 million
Profit margin (percentage)	11.58	−44.18
Operating margin (percentage)	15.16	−9.69
Return on assets (percentage)	5.24	−3.29
Return on equity (percentage)	9.77	−86.50
Revenue ($)	3.50 billion	2.68 billion
Quarterly revenue growth (percentage):	25.80%	−53.30%
Gross profit ($)	862.75 million	386.60 million
Total cash ($)	1.38 billion	473.70 million
Total debt ($)	200.94 million	2.26 billion

Compiled from publicly available quarterly report data

Solar took was to get beyond large-scale solar projects and more into small-scale commercial and industrial projects. Skytron's capabilities matched this need.

So far, a business model that relied on conservative financing had paid off for First Solar. Because it had the support of the Walton family, it had avoided using leverage to grow. Without leverage it could provide low-cost financing to projects it supported, but increasingly this business model did not make sense as the availability of funds for project financing was drying up. The availability of funds for project financing had become the major constraint on solar energy's growth.

Even with these many issues, First Solar was the most formidable player in the US solar power industry. It stood out because it had a strong financial foundation. Among US solar companies it was the only significant net-cash-positive solar-panel company.

Financing Suntech

Suntech, in contrast, was in very poor financial straits and was fighting an uphill battle for survival (see Table 3.2). According to every financial indicator, with the possible exception of revenue, where Suntech did not lag First Solar by a significant amount, Suntech was far behind First Solar. Most telling was its high level of debt and the meager amount of cash it had to support that debt. Its second-quarter revenue growth in 2014 was strongly negative. From their 2010 peak neither Suntech nor First Solar had done particularly well for investors, but since 2012, Suntech had fallen further behind, while First Solar had something of a rebound. Suntech's stock performance did not come close to the Nasdaq average, while First Solar beat that average by a substanital amount.

Zhengrong Shi, Suntech's founder, when enticed by the city of Wuxi to start his company, had been R&D director of an Australian company that was commercializing thin-film solar cells. The city government of Wuxi held a quarter of the company's equity and Shi and his backers the other 75 percent, which Suntech bought back from the city government before Suntech's 2005 IPO. Suntech's revenue grew from $85 million in 2004 to almost $2 billion in 2008.[19] Most of it (95 percent) came from the sale of solar modules, but solar cells (another four percent), and system integration (one percent) also contributed to the company's growth. About half of Suntech's modules were sold in the EU and about 15 percent in China.

This early success brought Shi great riches. With his holdings in Suntech as the foundation, he made the *Forbes* list of billionaires with net worth of more than $2 billion in 2006. A 2007 *Wall Street Journal* estimate put his net worth at over $4 billion.

Suntech's growth and development

Shi's business model was based on the belief that scale and technology were the keys to competitive advantage in the solar industry. He was very determined to reach grid parity by no later than 2012. To achieve this goal, he acknowledged, required huge capital expenditures. Most of the 2004 to 2008 growth in solar demand, from which Suntech benefited, originated in Europe. This growth in demand stimulated competition. Not only were there North American companies such as First Solar, SunPower, and CanadianSolar with which to contend, but also a host of Chinese firms – Yingli, Trina, Tianwei, LDK, Hareon, JA, and Jinko. The solar power industry's fragmentation made it hard for Shi to obtain the huge investments he needed to achieve the grid parity he was seeking. By 2008, industry capacity exceeded demand.

To control silicon prices, which rapidly increased from 2004 to 2008, a number of Suntech's Chinese rivals vertically integrated and invested in China's silicon ingot and wafer producers. Suntech made the same type of investments, but was late in taking action and therefore was hurt more than its rivals by a huge silicon glut that came into existence after the 2008 financial crisis and the temporary decline in the solar industry. In 2009, Suntech saw a 25 percent drop in revenue. Its gross margins went from 30 to 18 percent and its net margins from 23 to 4.6 percent. It had excessive debt because its investments in upstream suppliers had flopped when the price of silicon fell. Suntech's upstream investments had not held their value with the sudden glut of silicon on the market.

The upshot of this glut was that the most important input into solar cell production was 75 percent cheaper. Prices fell as a consequence. Solar panel costs declined by 50 percent, which made them very attractive to buyers, but with the banking system's weakness financing to support solar projects was scarce. Bank loans for solar projects dried up at the same time that prices fell. To deal with this problem, Suntech's competitors, including First Solar, changed their business models. They moved downstream in the value chain, endeavoring on their own and with partners to finance solar projects in North America and Europe.

Like First Solar, Suntech took advantage of renewable mandates and subsidies in US states, concentrating first on states with high electricity rates, such as California where solar was closer to grid parity. Though solar was closer to parity, it was not yet on a par with other forms of electricity production. Total non-subsidy parity did not exist in any market. First Solar made inroads in California and Suntech gained traction in New Jersey, which became a leader among US states in solar production. New Jersey was second in the nation behind California in the number of homes and businesses with installed panels.

By market share, Suntech in 2012 was the US leader in supplying modules to the non-residential PV market. It was the third-ranked supplier to the residential market. Suntech aimed to extend its reach in both domains. Like Solar First, it bid for large utility-based solar projects, and like First Solar, it also changed its business model. It started to invest in distributors and system integrators to hold onto and increase volume and margins. To participate in these deals, Suntech relied on $500 million in convertible bonds it had obtained in 2007 and 2008 for acquisitions and plant expansion. Among the acquisitions it made with these loans were solar power integrator, installer, and financing firms such as PowerLight, EI Solutions, and MMA

Renewable Ventures. Suntech created a unit called Energy Solutions that developed, financed, owned, and operated large-scale plants. It also formed Gemini Solar, a joint venture with a Spanish company for project development and investment.

In an ill-fated move, however, Suntech set up a European Global Solar Fund (GSF) to provide financing for developers.[20] With other sources of financing not available after the 2008 credit crunch, GSF asked the China Development Bank (CDB), a state-run institution, to give it a loan. To obtain the loan, CDB asked the GSF for a guarantor. Suntech agreed in 2010 to put down €554 million for this purpose but as a protection asked the GSF to post collateral for the funds, which the GSF in the form of €560 million worth of German bonds maintained it did. Suntech, struggling under a large debt burden, with large payments coming due, wanted to cash out of the GSF investment to pay down the debt. To its surprise it learned that the German bonds did not exist. Suntech's stock immediately dropped to less than $1 a share. Its market cap once above $14 billion declined to $188 million, and founder Shi's personal fortune shrunk to under $4 million. Humiliated, he was ousted from his position as Suntech's CEO.

Suntech's failure, then, was not just a consequence of falling solar prices. All Chinese producers had to face this issue. What brought Suntech down was a business model that led to a series of bad financial decisions in which Suntech was trying to self-finance solar development. These decisions resulted in the company having very high leverage.

Suntech's immoderate approach to financing was the very opposite of First Solar's caution. Believing that only by means of sufficient capacity could it achieve grid parity, Suntech borrowed very heavily to continue to grow after financial markets collapsed in 2008. Its loose financing came close to fraudulent behavior. The GSF's deception was combined with Shi starting a silicon producer. This silicon producer was called Asia Silicon. Shi gave it startup financing and purchase contracts worth more than $1 billion without revealing what he did to shareholders. Suntech's failure to disclose these dealings became the subject of a debilitating class-action shareholder lawsuit. Thus Suntech's downfall was a result of industry overcapacity, declining prices, poorly executed attempts at value-chain integration (financing projects and supporting a raw material supplier), and duplicity in the company's shareholder relations.

After the bailout that the city of Wuxi provided, Suntech's organization was very lean. The company had very few management positions; the number went from 300 to less than 100. Suntech also had to sell off holdings. Nonetheless, it was trying to adjust its business model so that it could re-gain a leadership position within the industry. The company referred to itself not just as a producer of solar panels. Like Solar First, it aspired to be an integrated provider of clean energy services. It promoted capabilities it had in solar design, engineering, manufacturing, construction, finance, insurance, operations, and maintenance. Suntech bought an inverter company. It invested in a battery storage developer. It continued to focus on downstream development projects, in line with what it had previously started and with what almost all the other major solar manufacturers were doing.

As far as global markets went, Suntech reasoned that China would be its main focus. The US and European markets had become tapped out and they were increasingly unattractive. With exports to the EU and to North America substantially reduced, the Asian market was almost all that was left and it was growing. In 2014, China became the world's largest solar market, having surpassed Germany in 2013. The attention of the global solar industry shifted away from the United States and Europe to Asia. Suntech adjusted its business model accordingly.

With its 1.3 billion plus population, China had immense potential. Turning to China instead of focusing on the more difficult global market was an obvious choice for Suntech, but there were significant barriers in the policy realm. The hurdles to be overcome were that public policies needed for expansion still were not fully in place in China. They included policies that would allow for connecting generated solar power to the national grid, adequate subsidies for this purpose, sufficient government supervision of the process, additional government-sponsored R&D to improve cell efficiency, and the need for preferential loan guarantees to customers. Though the Chinese government wanted to boost domestic demand to offset declines in Europe and the United States it had yet to adopt the kinds of comprehensive policies that would support the needed expansion. Suntech had no choice but to rely on less dependable local governments and private investors in China, who did not show signs of sufficient enthusiasm for the types of commitments that Suntech needed in order to grow.

Because of these Chinese weaknesses, its PV manufacturers had diversified their export to other destinations within Asia. Post-Fukushima Japan became the biggest export market for China's solar companies. India also had promise and so did Australia. Suntech decided to use Australia as a base for increasing its presence in the Pacific islands such as French Polynesia. If the move to these markets did not work, then the Chinese manufacturers would have to turn to South America and South Africa. Suntech had not entirely given up on the United States – it was still promising, but Europe seemed to be in permanent decline.

Suntech was planning for the cost of solar PV to rapidly catch up with the cost of coal-fired generation in China. It projected that the cost of building large-scale solar PV plants would match the cost of coal-fired generation in China by 2016, a development that would transform China's energy market. In the meantime, during the transition, how could the company manage?

The risks were high. Grid parity was a moving target. Prior forecasts of when grid parity would be reached in China had not come to fruition. Unanticipated events again could intervene. Natural gas prices in China still were five times greater than they were in the United States, but what if fracking became common in China? While solar was near to being cost competitive without subsidies in China, it still might not get there.

It would be a serious setback for Suntech if China were to develop its vast natural gas fracking potential, which was second only to the United States. The geology was more difficult to work with than in United States and water posed an even bigger obstacle, but these issues might be surmountable if the Chinese government decided that this direction was the one it wanted to take.

Technology differences

Technology differences affected First Solar's and Suntech's ability to adjust their business models. First Solar, a thin-film cell producer, relied on cells made of cadmium telluride (CdTe). The firm's founder was glass entrepreneur Harold McMaster, who in the 1980s started to work on this technology. His belief was that because of simpler processing and lower material costs, CdTe had the potential to dramatically lower solar energy costs. Making solar cells this way took years of tinkering to improve and the methods still had not been entirely perfected. Venture capital-funded companies such as Nanosolar, Mia-Solé, and Solyndra failed before they were able to drive thin-film costs down.

The advantages of thin-film CdTe solar panels were relative ease of manufacturing, absorbing sunlight at close to its ideal wavelength, and cadmium's abundance, which under most circumstances was likely to make it less expensive than silicon. However, CdTe also had many drawbacks. The most important was its efficiency. The average efficiency of CdTe solar panels in transforming the sunlight into electrical energy in 2014 was just 10.6 percent, which was significantly lower than silicon solar cells. First Solar's 2010 average efficiency of 11.1 percent allowed it to achieve the lowest cost per watt average among thin-film producers that year. The best efficiency it achieved in optimal conditions in the laboratory for CdTe that year was 16.5 percent.

Because of their lower efficiencies thin-film solar panels took up more space than thick-film panels and therefore they were less suitable for rooftop applications. The advantage of CdTe was that producing these cells was relatively simple and therefore the costs of capital for production were relatively low. Alternatives such as copper indium gallium selenide (CIGS) cells were by comparison complicated to make (see Chapter 2). Each of the many layers had to undergo careful quality inspection and control.

Yet CdTe also had drawbacks. Made of cadmium, which was highly toxic, it was combined with telluride that was less toxic than the cadmium by itself. The disposal and long-term safety of cadmium telluride was a well-known issue for which recycling at the end of useful life appeared to be a solution, though this approach was not fully accepted in the EU and China where cadmium compounds continued to be considered questionable. In China they only were allowed for export.

Cadmium was relatively plentiful, but tellurium was not. Tellurium is an extremely rare element in the Earth's crust. Most of it is a byproduct of copper production, with smaller amounts byproducts from lead and gold. Prices were volatile as producers were careful not to bring to market more than the market could bear. Researchers had found undersea ridges that were rich in tellurium but it was not known whether this undersea supply actually was recoverable.

Ongoing research focused mainly on boosting CdTe efficiencies. First Solar had been the first CdTe manufacturer to produce cells for less than $1.00 per watt. Some experts believed it might be possible to lower costs to about $0.5 per watt. With very low margins and reduced balance of system costs, an installed price might be achieved that with sufficient levels of sunlight would produce electricity at less cost than fossil-fuel electricity in many locations.

Around 80 percent of the market in 2014, however, was not for CdTe cells, but for silicon-based cells. Unlike First Solar, almost all the Chinese producers mainly relied on crystalline silicon (c-Si). Suntech had been the world's largest manufacturer of c-Si panels. These cells were expected to continue to dominate in the residential and commercial rooftop markets due to higher efficiency and lower silicon prices.

Thick film c-Si solar cells were an offshoot of the semiconductor industry and the fortunes of the cells' manufacture were intimately tied to this industry. Makers of these cells competed with semiconductor manufacturers for silicon ingots and wafers. The construction of the cells began with the purchase of the silicon, whose prices varied. Depending on prices, silicon might make up as little as 10 or as much as 40 percent of a panel's cost.

First Solar avoided this problem because it relied on CdTe cells, which helped it in the marketplace in the 2004 to 2008 period when silicon prices escalated. However, since the middle of 2009 silicon prices had fallen by 40 percent because the supply situation had improved.

After procuring the silicon, it had to be converted to cells, where penetration of the sun's rays could break free electrons, moving them through a border to a positive charge and creating electricity. Homogeneous groups of cells under a protective material such as glass had to be joined together in a frame. Balance of system expenses involved inverters, wiring and circuitry plus engineering, construction, and permitting. Balance of system costs could make up as much as 50 percent or more of a completed project's costs. Because these costs were high, it made sense for manufacturers such as First Solar and Suntech to migrate to this part of the value chain.

During periods of peak demand, as on hot summer days, silicon-based rooftop solar power operated at grid parity or better in most places in the world. The cost to generate power on rooftops was the same or lower than the cost of buying power a utility produced by other means. The solar industry's move from monocrystalline to polycrystalline silicon cells, reduced costs even more. Polycrystalline silicon was less expensive than monocrystalline because of the way it was made. The molten silicon was poured into a cast instead of being made as a single crystal. The most efficient monocrystalline solar panels available in 2014 were 22.5 percent efficient. Most silicon-based solar cell manufacturers including Suntech were moving from monocrystalline to polycrystalline cells. Further advances were expected in the next ten years.

To lower costs even more, researchers were looking at alternatives to CdTe. Silicon-based panels were more efficient than CdTe panels because they required less space to generate the same amount of power. Land costs ultimately limited CdTe for application in large utility-scale projects, but other types of thin-film cells (see Chapter 2) had potential. Unlike silicon-based cells and CdTe, they were flexible and they could be used as building materials in integrated design solutions.

Gallium arsenide (GaAs) had higher capture capabilities for equivalent wavelength than CdTe or silicon. It had the theoretical efficiency record experimentally verified under conditions of normal sunlight. GaAs cells combined lightness and high efficiency and they could be applied to building surfaces. Galium and arsenic were less rare than tellurium. There was no supply issue since the amount of material required for these cells was small. Less material reduced recycling problems. However, these cells were not yet commercially available. They were under development.

Another possibility was compound cells that had two or more kinds of materials that generated energy at different wavelength ranges (see Chapters 1 and 2). Efficiencies greater than 40 percent had been demonstrated. The higher efficiencies were obtainable through the cascading of cells. Cascading meant arranging the cells in layers. The incoming light had to traverse through each layer. Light that did not interact with cells in one layer interacted with them in subsequent layers. Because more power was made in the same amount of space, the efficiency of these stacked cells was higher than the efficiency of singly stacked cells. Many research projects were underway, but it was unclear if breakthroughs were possible because manufacturing was proving to be a sticking point.

First Solar and Suntech had to ponder these possibilities and how they might disrupt their business models. How should they hedge their bets? How should they prepare for these contingencies?

Trades wars

Another significant issue that confronted First Solar and Suntech was trade wars. Their background was China's rapid rise as a producer of components for the solar industry. Both the United States and China were committed to reducing the cost of solar-generated electricity to the level of fossil-fuel energy. How they went about it was very different. Motivated by high levels of pollution and national security concerns, the Chinese government tried to determine in the early 2000s how much it would cost to make solar power cheaper than coal. Its answer was grounded in a calculation that every doubling of PV capacity resulted in a 20 percent decline in unit cost. As this calculation had worked elsewhere, the Chinese government stepped up its efforts in solar power. With the aid and assistance of the Chinese government wind energy more than doubled its cumulative installed capacity in China from 2006 to 2009 and lowered costs (see Chapter 6). The Chinese government adopted similarly aggressive policies to nurture its solar industry.

The government's goal was to meet 20 percent of its energy needs from renewable energy sources by 2020 and it set aside over $743 billion for ten years to support the growth of domestic companies' ability to sell in global markets.[21] The Chinese Ministry of Finance set up a fund to help renewable energy companies manufacture, expand production, increase research, and export products globally. By 2008 China had become the world's largest solar-cell production country and by 2010 it controlled almost half of the global market, up from just 15 percent in 2006. These results demonstrated that the Chinese way of heavily subsidizing a massive increase in production capacity of an emerging sector had been effective.

United States' policies were quite different. For instance, in 2011, the Department of Energy (DOE) launched a SunShot initiative.[22] The stated goal was that the cost of solar power should be fully competitive with conventional energy sources by the end of the decade, but the program was far less aggressive and generous than the Chinese program. Like the energy efficiency and renewable energy programs launched in 2009 as part of the Financial Recovery Act, US-funded grants, incentives, and competitions were meant to encourage private-sector actors to commercialize technologies still in the early stages of development.

Command economies like China did not produce much innovation but when it came to marshalling of resources to expand capacity, they were relentless. But was the Chinese government engaged in unfair competition? Since clean energy was an emerging technology sector, policy assistance was required to help the new sector hold its own against existing alternatives, and the question of whether the Chinese government engaged in unfair competition therefore was complicated. To the extent that the United States and other countries also offered encouragement to solar energy, it was hard to say that the subsidies offered by the Chinese government were unfair. Were the low interest-rate loans the China Development Bank provided in violation of international trade agreements? Chinese companies maintained that they paid market interest rates for these loans, though critics argued that local governments reimbursed Chinese companies for their payments. Critics also held that Chinese companies received heavily subsidized land grants from local governments.

World Trade Organization (WTO) policies on unfair competition were not entirely clear.[23] This organization prohibited many types of incentives, but then made exceptions. It prohibited direct transfers of funds or loan guarantees, government revenue that was foregone or not collected such as tax credits, provision of goods or services other than infrastructure, income or price support, and other ways of subsidizing products and services intended for export. However, only if the subsidies created a *significant* bias for one country's goods and services over another were they viewed as having adverse effects, and only under these circumstances did they give rise to actionable claims. Actionable claims, moreover, were not the only route that a party could take. The WTO rules allowed for consultations and alternative dispute settlement procedures short of more formal charges.

The US Department of Commerce (DOC) could open an investigation and impose a countervailing duty if it found that a subsidy was received and resulted in material harm. It made preliminary determination that the foreign government had granted subsidies. Its final determination was of material harm that merited the imposition of countervailing duties. It defined dumping as selling goods in other countries at less than home market price or less than home production costs.

In 2011, on behalf of seven US solar companies, SolarWorld, a German firm that operated in the United States, complained that the Chinese government unfairly subsidized its solar manufacturers by providing them with land, electricity, material inputs, and financing them at below market rates. SolarWorld also charged that the Chinese government provided the manufacturers with direct financial support and other preferential policies. It asked for tariffs of up to 250 percent on Chinese-manufactured products. The DOC found that Chinese producers and exporters had sold cells in the United States at dumping margins ranging from 18.32 to 249.96 percent and these firms had obtained subsidies of between 14.78 to 15.97 percent. On this basis, it established countervailing tariffs and anti-dumping measures against the Chinese manufacturers of 25 to 30 percent. Estimates were that these measures would decrease overall domestic demand for solar products by 10 percent, that they would create new jobs in solar manufacturing, but result in the loss of about 10,000 jobs in solar sales, installation, and other parts of the solar business because of higher PV prices.[24] The best estimates were that the gain in manufacturing jobs probably would not be enough to offset the decline in jobs in other parts of the value chain.

The Chinese solar manufacturers initiated a similar trade action against US companies that supplied inputs to the Chinese markets. These trade wars were hurting the move toward the adoption and diffusion of clean energy. They had a negative effect on efforts to curb climate change, a cause to which both the US and Chinese governments alleged that they were committed. The United States and China were the largest greenhouse gas contributors in the world, together accounting for over 40 percent of these emissions. Chinese per capita emissions were growing at a rate of four to six times faster than per capita emissions in the United States because of growth in the Chinese economy. Trade wars were slowing introduction of technologies that might improve the situation.

With the United States and China already engaged in trade wars, other countries became involved.[25] In 2013, the European Union (EU) moved ahead with tariffs on imported Chinese solar panels in an effort to protect its own module makers. The European Commission trade head Karel De Gucht recommended that the EU impose anti-dumping charges similar to those of the United States. The European Commission's findings against Chinese solar companies were that the price of Chinese panels imported into the EU fell nearly 75 percent between 2009 and 2013. As a consequence, the number of Europeans employed in solar manufacturing, which had been rising, started to fall. The Chinese companies, the EU concluded, held almost no global market share in PVs in 2004 but controlled 80 percent of the global market by 2011.

Like the United States, EU penalties varied by the extent of the manufacturer's dumping and the extent of its cooperation with the

EU's investigation. Suntech was hit particularly hard. The 48.6 percent tariff against Suntech, one of the highest that the EU ever imposed, was a contributing factor in driving the company into bankruptcy protection after it defaulted on its $541 million bond repayment. China's PV exports to Europe went down by 18 percent in 2013.

The Taiwanese loophole

From 2008 to 2010, with Suntech leading the way, Chinese crystalline solar cell and panel imports to the United States had grown by more than 300 percent. However, after the trade sanctions the US government imposed in 2011 imports fell. Imports from Taiwan at the same time rose from a small base to more than 40 percent. In another complaint SolarWorld therefore charged that Chinese module manufacturers, to evade the tariff, had used the loophole of continuing to import to the United States through Taiwan. Taiwan, which the US government considers a market economy, was subject to less severe trade restrictions than China, which was classified as a command economy.

The DOC's 2014 finding in the case that SolarWorld and it co-petitioners brought imposed higher duties on Suntech – 35.21 percent on Suntech as opposed to 18.56 percent on Trina and an average duty of 26.89 percent on other Chinese manufacturers. Suntech protested that it had not received subsidies from the Chinese Government and that the low-price PV products the company made were the result of scale economies and good supply-chain management.

Two US trade associations claiming to represent the solar industry were in a pitched battle about this decision. Led by SolarWorld, the Coalition for American Solar Manufacturing (CASM) asserted that DOC's ruling was in response to illegal, unacceptable, systematic, unjust, improper, massive, and ever-escalating anti-competitive forms of trade and subsidies.[26] The CASM charged the Chinese government with deploying an arsenal of land grants, contract awards, trade barriers, financing breaks, and supply-chain subsidies, while impeding imports and sidestepping labor and environmental standards. The CASM argued that China had no real cost advantage. Labor was but a modest share of the costs of solar production and Chinese labor was no more productive than US labor. Massive state subsidies and sponsorship enabled Chinese manufacturers to dump modules at low cost in the United States. The trade association charged the Chinese with engaging in a systematic campaign to dismantle the US solar industry. It maintained that the Chinese government's actions had yielded thousands of lost jobs in the states of Arizona, California, Maryland, Massachusetts, New York, and Pennsylvania.

To counter these charges, a different set of US solar businesses launched the Coalition for Affordable Solar Energy (CASE).[27] This trade association was the one to which the US division of Suntech belonged. It included leading Chinese manufacturers as well as Canadian and US firms concerned that the trade wars were raising solar panel prices. The CASE declared that it was deeply disappointed with the DOC's decision. It called it a major setback for the US solar industry because it would increase prices and cut jobs in a rapidly growing sector. The negative impact of the restrictions mainly would be felt in residential and commercial markets, where low-price Chinese panels supplied more than 70 percent of the market. The CASE pointed out that the vast majority of the 150,000 US jobs in the solar industry were not in manufacturing. Most were in solar sales, marketing, design, installation, maintenance, and finance. The DOC's decision would break the momentum of job creation in this sector as the sector was on track to employ more than 350,000 Americans by 2016 and more than one million by 2020.

This split in the ranks of the US solar industry compelled the Solar Energy Industries Association (SEIA), the oldest and most prestigious solar trade association, to stake out a third position that called for a negotiated settlement between the US and Chinese governments for which the SEIA was willing to act as a broker. The SEIA agreed with the CASE that if imposed the tariffs would result in a sharp increase in the cost of solar energy in the US, slow adoption rates, and derail industry growth. The SEIA wanted the US government to revoke the tariffs for at least five years, while making Chinese manufacturers pay into a fund that would support the growth of US solar manufacturing.

The SEIA's argument did not have much sway with the Obama administration. The president affirmed that the Chinese indeed were engaged in questionable competitive practices and that his administration had to be significantly more aggressive than previous administrations in enforcing US trade laws. Members of Congress from states including Arizona, California, Maryland, Massachusetts, New York, and Pennsylvania supported the president.

Next choices

First Solar and Suntech faced many risks, For example, would First Solar reliance on CdTe technology prove to be a long-term liability? Would there be a shakeout among Chinese producers and consolidation with only some surviving? Would the Chinese market and other global markets really open up, providing new opportunities to all, or would trade wars beat down all players and create a war of all against all in a shrinking market? What should the leaders of First Solar and Suntech do? How should they adjust their business models to the circumstances that they confronted?

Notes

1 See US Energy Information Administration: www.eia.gov/electricity
2 *Ibid.*
3 See Japanese Ministry of Economy, Trade, and Industry: www.meti.go. jp/english/policy/energy_environment/renewable
4 X. Zhou, "Solar trade war II: with another wave of trade rows approaching, what's the way out for Chinese solar makers?" *Beijing Review* (Jun 19, 2014).
5 REN21, *Renewables 2012 Global Status Report*(Paris: REN21 Secretariat, 2012).
6 W. Ma and E. Glazer, "Suntech is pushed into Chinese bankruptcy court," *Wall Street Journal* (2013): http://online.wsj.com/news/articles/ SB10001424127887324557804578372082733827860
7 A. Lashinky, "First Solar rises again," *Fortune* (2014): http://fortune. com/2014/01/16/first-solar-rises-again
8 *Ibid.*
9 *Ibid.*
10 See Solar Energy Industries Association: www.seia.org/research-resources/solar-industry-data
11 See Institute for Energy Research, "Europe slashing renewable subsidies," (2014): http://instituteforenergyresearch.org/analysis/europe-slashing-renewable-subsidies-2
12 See Database of State Incentives for Renewables & Efficiency. www. dsireusa.org
13 First Solar, Inc., *Form 10-K* (Tempe, AZ: First Solar, 2010).
14 A. Lashinky, "First solar rises again."
15 See Solar Energy Industries Association: www.seia.org/research-resources/major-solar-projects-list

16 See Power Base, "List of Solar Projects in India," http://powerbase.in/project-index/solar-power-projects-index

17 See First Solar Website: www.firstsolar.com/en/About-Us/Projects

18 StreetInsider.com, "Rooftop solar volume will grow at 40% CAGR through 2016, says Goldman Sachs," (2014): www.streetinsider.com/Analyst+Comments/Rooftop+Solar+Volume+Will+Grow+at+40%25+CAGR+Through+2016,+Says+Goldman+Sachs+(SCTY)+(SPWR)+(SUNE)+(FSLR)/9589728.html

19 R. Vietor, *Suntech Power* (Boston, MA: Harvard Business School, 2012).

20 W. Ma and E. Glazer, "Suntech is pushed into Chinese bankruptcy court."

21 National Renewable Energy Laboratory, "Renewable Energy in China," www.nrel.gov/docs/fy04osti/35786.pdf

22 See US Department of Energy Office of Energy Efficiency & Renewable Energy, "Sunshot Initiative:" http://energy.gov/eere/sunshot/sunshot-initiative

23 J. Hauser, "From sleeping giant to friendly giant: rethinking the United States' solar energy trade war with China," *North Carolina Journal of International Law and Commercial Regulation* (2012–2013): 1063–1089.

24 *Ibid.*

25 *Ibid.*

26 See Coalition for American Solar Manufacturing website: www.americansolarmanufacturing.org/about

27 See Coalition for Affordable Solar Energy website: www.affordablesolarusa.org

4 | *Making a revolution: Tesla and Better Place*

Shai Agassi, Better Place's charismatic founder, was trying to make a revolution. At a 2009 TED Conference, he declared that converting to electric cars was the moral equivalent of abolishing slavery. He maintained that, like going to the moon, anything short of fully achieving this objective was a failure. Moving to electric would start a new industrial revolution.

The same revolutionary fervor, perhaps expressed with less hyperbole, came from Tesla's equally if not more charismatic founder, Elon Musk. His celebrated 2006 blog "The secret Tesla Motors master plan (just between you and me)" said that Tesla's "overarching purpose" was to "expedite the move" from a "mine-and-burn hydrocarbon economy" toward the main sustainable solution, a solar electric economy.[1] To accomplish this goal, Tesla's business model was to enter the high end of the automotive market, where customers were prepared to pay a premium, and to move down the market as fast as possible to higher unit volume and lower prices with each successive model.

Tesla's business model was to:

1. Build a sports car.
2. Use that money to build an affordable car.
3. Use *that* money to build an even more affordable car.

It cost Tesla an estimated $60,000 to build the second-generation Model S. Its aim was that its third-generation Model E, due sometime in 2017, would have a base price of $35,000 excluding any tax credit. It would have a 200-mile (322-km) battery range and it would generate an average gross margin of 15 percent.

The question was how Tesla could reduce the cost of producing the Model E to under $30,000. The Model S battery reputedly cost $15,000. A smaller battery manufactured at scale in Tesla's proposed large-scale battery factory could be priced no lower than $10,000

Table 4.1 *Can Tesla achieve a break-even point with its proposed*
Model E?

Estimated cost of building the basic Model S Tesla	$60,000
Estimated reduction incost of the battery due to smaller battery manufactured in Tesla's proposal battery giga-factory	−$5,000
Estimated lower material costs (less aluminum, plastics, and vinyl)	−$3000
Estimated lower tooling costs due to shared production with Model S	−$3000
Estimated lower component parts from ordering in larger quantities	−$4000
Estimated cost of building the basic Model E Tesla	$45,000
Proposed retail price of Model E Tesla	$35,000
Expected loss per car of sale *with* battery and without rebate and accessories	$10,000
Expected loss per car of sale *without* battery and without rebate and accessories	about $0

Author's calculations

(see Table 4.1). Less material costs might eliminate another $3,000 from the cost of the Model E. Shared tooling with the Model S could lump off another $3,000. Ordering parts in greater quantity could yield $4,000 in savings. The total savings, amounting to about $15,000 would make the cost of building the Model E $45,000 too high to sell it at $35,000 and make a profit.

The numbers did not add up, unless, of course, Tesla had a different business model in mind. For example, like Better Place, it could separate the sale of the car from the battery and make money leasing the battery and selling owners the electricity needed to drive the Model E. The car owner would have an outstanding vehicle for $35,000 or less, where fuel, maintenance, and insurance costs would be lower than with a conventional gasoline-propelled car. Anything Tesla lost on a car's sale it would more than make it up by leasing the battery and selling the owner the electricity.

Better Place, with its business model of separating car ownership from the vehicle's detachable battery, filed for a 2013 bankruptcy. At that point it had sold about 1400 Renault-built electric mid-sized sedans but had not come close to its long-term goal of bringing millions of electric vehicles to market. As Better Place ran out of cash, the nearly one billion investors' dollars poured into the company disappeared, but some of its ideas survived in the business model Tesla was adopting. For example, like the Renault-built vehicles that Better Place sold, Tesla's Model S luxury cars came with removable batteries. Like Better Place, Tesla also had swapping stations where the batteries could be replaced in a few short minutes, thereby extending the car's range and making it suitable for long trips. Tesla also had installed more than 100 Supercharger Stations, where drivers could recharge their batteries in about 20 minutes for 150 miles of additional driving. In 2014, these stations covered 80 percent of the US population. Conveniently placed on highways, near diners, cafes, and shopping centers in the United States, Tesla had started to build a similar network in Europe and Asia. Most impressively, the range of Tesla's electric vehicles was up to 265 miles (426 km), while the Renault-built vehicles that Better Place had a range of about 100 miles (161 km).

For Tesla to deliver on its business plan, it needed an affordable mid-priced car it could sell. How was it going to get there? What strategies should it pursue? What lessons, if any, should it learn from Better Place? Were there specific dos and don'ts that it should draw from Better Place's experience? How should Tesla further modify its business model to meet this goal?

Background on electric vehicles

Pre-twentieth century electrical vehicles (EVs) traveled at speeds under 20 miles (32 km) per hour and went less than 50 miles (80 km) before having to be recharged.[2] Women tended to favor them, but male drivers tended to prefer the gasoline-fueled autos powered by an internal combustion engine (ICE). The men liked speed and range.

Ironically, it was the 1910 introduction of an electric charger that eliminated the need to crank-start ICEs that led to their dominance over EVs. With mass assembly, ICEs also had a distinct cost advantage over EVs. Henry Ford made ICEs mass-assembly style in his factories and offered them for sale for $850. By 1915 more than a million ICE vehicles were on US roads and their number was rapidly rising. By 1935, virtually no EVs were produced in the United States.

Zero emissions

However, EVs made a short comeback in the late 1990s. General Motors introduced zero-emission lead-acid and nickel metal hydride (NiMH) battery cars to meet California's strict anti-pollution laws. Besides less pollution these cars had a number of advantages over ICEs. They had small motors and large battery packs, while ICEs had large engines and powertrains and a small battery. Electric vehicles' motors were nearly twice as efficient as ICE engines. The waste heat loss was less than 60 percent, compared to nearly 80 percent in ICE cars.[3] Electric vehicles also were very quiet. Unlike the complex ICE, whose powertrain had many moving parts they required little maintenance. Though some cooling might be necessary to keep the battery pack at acceptable temperature ranges, EVs' electric motors did not have to be cooled and they did not have transmissions. There was some risk of fire, but the cost of insuring an EV was lower than the cost of insuring an ICE vehicle. Electric vehicles weighed more and hence were safer. A disadvantage was the need for separate heating and air condition systems because these systems could not be hooked up to the electric motor as they connected to the powertrain in a conventional ICE.

The EVs that GM built in the late 1990s also had distinct drawbacks. Their range was no more than 140 miles (225 km). The car was not designed for optimal placement of the batteries under the vehicle's floors. The cars were small, two-seat compacts. The batteries took up lots of room and the passenger space was limited. Another issue was lack of infrastructure for charging the batteries. Public charging spots were not available and charging was very slow; on a nightly basis, it could take eight hours to recharge an EV using a special device that GM installed in a driver's home. To fully recharge the batteries using a 120-volt household outlet took 15 hours. Ultimately GM introduced 220-volt MagneChargers that could do the job in under four hours and it installed about 1,000 of these chargers in private homes and public locations such as malls.

The EV that GM built cost $35,000 and the market was confined to well-educated environmentally conscious individuals with high incomes. Less than a quarter of the public indicated that they would consider buying or leasing such a vehicle. General Motors claimed that the market was not sufficiently large for the company to make much money and it planned to sell just 300 cars per year. Perhaps, as critics maintained, it did not try to vigorously promote the product. Under pressure from the automobile companies, California weakened its anti-pollution laws and by the end of the 1990s GM recalled all the 1,138 EVs it sold and destroyed them. If the $350 million it had spent in development costs had any use, the investment GM made was considered a gateway to a non-EV alternative.[4]

Climate change and international security after 9/11

Instability in oil-producing countries and petroleum prices following the 9/11 attack revived interest in EVs. The advantages of EVs were that they not only combated pollution and reduced climate change, but they helped create independence from imported oil. Almost 96 percent of US citizens held that dependence on foreign oil was a serious problem.[5] The nearly three quarter billion gasoline-driven vehicles on the world's roads, about 80 percent of them passenger cars, were the source of a quarter of total global greenhouse gas emissions. ICEs were responsible for urban smog and pollution that resulted in asthma, heart and respiratory-related diseases. ICEs also made countries heavily dependent on oil imports from despotic governments in the world's most unstable regions.

Almost every major government therefore had created some type of incentive package for the purpose of promoting alternative forms of transportation. The US government, as part of the stimulus package, set aside $2.4 billion for electric car and hybrid technology projects. Germany planned to spend more than a half billion dollars so that a million electric cars would be on the road by 2020. The UK gave $7,500 in incentives for consumers to buy electric cars, and the Chinese government provided incentives of up to $8,800 per vehicle for taxi fleets and encouraged local governments to buy hybrids and all-electric vehicles and to invest in electric-car charging stations.

Tesla's birth and early development

Along with VC firm Compass Technology Partners, which backed Pay-Pal, Elon Musk was an early investor in Tesla, a company that had been named for the electric AC induction motor's inventor Nikola Tesla. Musk, in a 2013 Ted Talk, said that the motivation to build an all-electric car and take on the auto industry came from the recognition that the most important problem affecting the world's future was sustainable transport. The world was rapidly running out of fossil fuels and something had to be done about it. Martin Eberhard, leader of the team that started Tesla in 2003, also had concerns about US dependence on Middle Eastern oil. Musk and Compass Technology Partners provided most of Tesla's $20.5 million series A and B financing in 2004 and 2005. The company obtained $85 million more in funding in 2006 and 2007 from a consortium that included Draper Fisher Jurvetson (DFJ), JP Morgan Partners, and Vantage-Point Capital Partners, a company that also ended up backing Better Place.

Musk was a South African who had learned to program computers as a child.[6] He sold his first video game at age 12. Immigrating to Canada in 1988 he attended Queen's University and then transferred to the University of Pennsylvania where he received degrees in physics and economics. To form city guide software company Zip2, Musk dropped out of the physics PhD program at Stanford University. Compaq acquired Zip2 in 1999 for $307 million. Musk then helped to start financial services and email payment company X.com, which merged with the firm that became PayPal. eBay bought PayPal in 2002 for $1.5 billion. The money from this deal enabled Musk to help found SpaceX, a company that reflected his concerns about the fate of the planet and the potential for space travel.

Musk only became CEO of Tesla in 2008 after it failed to meet its deadlines for the Roadster sports car, which was supposed to have been its first product. At that time, the company had limited operating history, a long history of losses, and dwindling capital.[7] It had reduced its headcount and it confronted a host of patent infringement suits. When Musk took over, he invested another $40 million of his own money in the company. Building an all-electric car was not proving to be an easy task. Tesla was competing against the world's largest automakers. The US market was saturated – there were 1.17 vehicles for each licensed driver. Two of the United States' three largest auto firms were about to go bankrupt in 2009. The cars that auto companies built were complex and expensive to design, manufacture, and sell. The design of a new car might cost a billion dollars, excluding retooling and factory modifications. This process typically took four to five years. Huge assembly plants had to be built to operate at a maximum efficient scale of 100,000 to 250,000 cars per year. These plants typically were greater than 50 football fields in length and cost more than one billion dollars to build.

To sell the vehicles made in these plants, they had to be very heavily advertised in mainstream media, another large expense. Sold through dealers that had mutually exclusive relations with manufacturers and select territories, the automakers shared the profits with the dealers. They lost income because the dealers controlled service and financing, which were among the most lucrative elements in the value chain. Without ancillary offerings of this kind, the automotive business had razor-thin margins. These factors alone should have deterred a newcomer like Tesla from entering the industry. The battery technology that it needed to make EVs, moreover, was extremely expensive and consumer demand for EVs, as GM discovered in the 1990s, was uncertain.

A long-range battery

By end of the first decade of the twenty-first century, EV companies had started to settle on lithium-ion as the battery of choice. The same battery as in laptop computers, its capacity per weight was relatively high in contrast to GM's vehicle that had run on lead-acid and nickel metal hydride batteries. Hybrid electric vehicles continued to rely on nickel metal hydride and lithium-ion (see Chapter 5). The speed at which battery performance improved after the move to lithium-ion was a catalyst for Tesla's launch. The lithium-ion battery was an improvement over batteries previously used in electric cars, but it was not perfect. For use in autos, many lithium-ion modules had to be combined in a pack. Depending on how many batteries were combined in the pack, they could cost anywhere from $7,500 to $18,000. The experience curve suggested that these costs would decline at a pace of about ten percent per year, but that result was far from certain. The battery pack continued to be bulky and heavy and its placement remained a design challenge.

Tesla was as much a battery innovation company as a car company. Its designers found room for the battery pack in its cars. Some space became open because the electric motor was simpler and took up less room than in an ICE powertrain. The issue was that not only were lithium-ion batteries evolving but that other alternatives such as zinc–air and potassium-ion batteries also were progressing. There were concerns that the proven lithium reserves in the world were limited. Picking the right battery technology and supplier therefore was critical. Several suppliers had products that might be used in an EV including A123, LG Chem, AESC, Bosch–Samsung, Hitachi, NEC, Johnson Controls, and Saft. Tesla chose Panasonic, which had been GM's supplier when it introduced its EV, as its supplier.

Tesla's first car, the high-end Roadster sports car, sold for $109,000, accelerated at a rate of 0 to 60 miles (97 km) per hour in less than four seconds, and was faster than some Ferraris. It had a range of 245 miles (394 km). In comparison, the Leaf, the mid-size all-electric vehicle that Nissan made, had a range of about 100 miles (161 km). The difference mainly was due to the large battery packs the Roadster had, the 7,100 cells in the Roadster as opposed to 192 cells in the Leaf. The Chevrolet Volt plug-in hybrid (see Chapter 5) had 288 cells. While companies such as Nissan and GM used large-format prismatic cells in their batteries, Tesla, along with Panasonic, designed a battery pack around small-format cylindrical cells found in laptops. The small-format cylindrical lithium-ion battery packs that Panasonic sold Tesla yielded high energy density and supplied good storage for the batteries' weight. The drawback of the design was the thousands of weld points necessary to keep the battery pack together and the all-embracing thermal sensors and wiring needed to keep it cool.

Originally the battery packs were made in Thailand, but Tesla urged Panasonic to move production to California, near to where Tesla did final assembly. Designing the car to fit the battery was critically important. Tesla's founders were not just Silicon Valley veterans like its chief technology officer, J. B. Straubel; the design team included car specialists. The Roadster sports car was designed from the ground up by teams composed of both groups. The battery pack was placed on the floor in the passenger cabin, not in the front of the car where the engine and power train in an ICE vehicle were, in the way GM designed its EV in the 1990s. The design for car that Renault made for Better Place was similar. This placement was a more efficient use of the auto's space, and had the added benefit of providing a lower center of gravity, which meant better handling. The Tesla drive was palpably different from the drive of an ICE vehicle. It felt good, which was an important selling point.

The battery pack in a Tesla provided more than twice the range than had been available in prior EVs but it still could not compare with an ICE. If the ICE had a gasoline tank with volume enough for 16 gallons (60.6 L) and averaged 20 miles (32 km) per gallon, it could travel 320 miles (515 km) before refueling. The comparable 100 mile (161 km) or so range deficit in the Tesla car might deter some customers. The lack of charging stations and the long time it might take to re-charge the Tesla's batteries – at a regular outlet it could take 5 to 10 hours to recharge the battery pack – continued to be a problem. Tesla therefore gave customers the option of using higher-amp outlets that would double or triple the charging time. Later, it installed more than 100 supercharger stations, placed swapable batteries in the Model S, and set up a series of swapping sites to alleviate the issue.

Selling the Roadster

To sell the Roadster, Tesla did not buy advertising from the mainstream media. Instead it relied on the extensive coverage that the press devoted to the company and word of mouth. It also did product placements and purchased pay-per-click ads on websites its most likely demographic frequented. The company tried to control the information going to the public. The focus was not on the car's environmental benefits, rather its speed, styling, comfort, and handling.

A unique feature of Tesla's business model was that it completely bypassed the dealers. It relied on direct phone and Internet sales and eventually set up a string of storefronts to sell the vehicles with sales people who were on a salary and did not get paid commissions. With its direct-sales model, Tesla eliminated the intermediary so all the profits went to the company, which provided a profit boost of up to 10 percent. Since all the cars were built to order, there was no storage and little inventory cost. In addition to raising margins, Tesla avoided the negative feeling most people experienced when visiting a dealer. The company also guaranteed the resale value of its vehicles by promising customers they would provide them with resale prices similar to those they would get from a corresponding BMW or a Mercedes.

Tesla's auto service, which was not created to make money, was another way that Tesla differentiated itself from the business model of other auto firms. Unlike dealerships that relied heavily on service profits, Tesla maintained the vehicles at cost, giving customers the repose that there would not be any price gouging. It also provided an option customers valued, picking up their cars and providing a loaner should a car need repairs.

These arrangements were in conflict with the dealers' lobby. Some states had laws that only autos sold and serviced through independent dealers recognized by dealers associations were legal. In a number of states, the courts chose to allow Tesla to keep its existing company-owned outlets open but Tesla was not permitted to expand them further. In other states Tesla won its court skirmishes without its rights being diminished. The suits were ongoing but they had not stopped Tesla's momentum. In states where Tesla's right to directly sell its cars had been curtailed Tesla could set up a gallery where customers could view the cars and ask questions, but Tesla representatives could not discuss price, financing, or purchasing options with them. To finalize a deal, customers had to go to the Tesla website. States with less restrictive policies allowed customers to test drive the company's vehicles and discuss prices with the option of buying online or at the retail store.

Another advantage Tesla had was the subsidies governments offered its buyers. Tesla's vehicles were eligible for a full $7,500 federal tax credit. In addition, California offered another $2,500 tax credit. Other perks that might come with the purchase of a Tesla were reduced home electric bills, free parking, and the use of high-occupancy vehicle or carpool lanes. Hybrids, as only being partially electric, were not eligible for all of these subsidies. Despite the many factors that made the purchase of a Tesla attractive, the company fought an uphill battle in gaining customer acceptance. It took until 2009 until it sold more than 1,000 Roadsters. By 2020, EVs were expected to be only eight percent of total global automobile production, but Musk was confident and declared that EVs would be the *only* car sold in the United States by 2030 and the *only* car on road by mid-century.

From 2007 to 2011 the global electric vehicle market grew at a compound annual rate of 135 percent compared to an ICE growth rate of two percent in the same period.[8] It was projected to continue to grow at rate of 26 percent from 2012 to 2020, while the ICE market would grow at a three percent rate. Nissan CEO, Carlos Ghosn, predicted sales of a half million EVs by 2013, a level he claimed was needed for EVs to be profitable without subsidies. Worldwide, sales did not hit this target because in the mid-priced passenger car category, customers remained very price sensitive.

The Model S

Tesla's challenge therefore was to get beyond a sports car and move toward a more affordable vehicle. To accomplish this goal it accumulated a substantial amount of intellectual property, but it needed money to take the next steps. From its inception it had net losses of $236.4 billion on revenues of $108.2 million.[9] To obtain the money it needed, it made a 2008 agreement with Daimler to provide batteries and chargers for Daimler's EVs. Tesla also created a waiting list of customers who were eager to get in line to buy to the next model and asked them to pay $5,000 for the right to reserve a vehicle, a mechanism that helped Tesla to finance the Model S and one that remained in place for subsequent models.

This money still was not sufficient. In 2009, Daimler invested $50 million on its own and $82.5 million as part of consortium that included VantagePoint Capital Partners. Tesla then purchased the idled NUMMI (New United Motor Manufacturing Inc.) plant in Fremont California, a former GM–Toyota joint venture that had produced a half million cars a year at its height. Tesla was fortunate to be able to buy it for $42 million. The purchase of the NUMMI plant was financed through a $50 million Toyota capital injection and an agreement to share information and cooperate with the Japanese automaker. It would have taken another carmaker a billion dollars or more to create this facility de novo. Tesla's goal was to fully use the facility, to produce half a million cars a year there by 2017 or 2018. In the short term, it aimed for an output of about 21,000 cars with the potential to expand production up to 100,000 vehicles. To make the Model S, Tesla bought production equipment at a discount from struggling manufacturers and made the cars' plastic parts in house with its own injection-molding machines. The US Department of Energy (DOE) also helped, kicking in with a low-interest loan of a $500 million as part of the financial recovery package. Finally, battery-maker Panasonic made a $30 million investment in Tesla in 2010.

The Model S that Tesla made with the money it collected was a huge success. *Consumer Report* gave the Model S the highest rating it ever gave to a car and it won the magazine's 2014 Car of the Year award.[10] The magazine lauded the Model S not only for its styling, handling, and fuel efficiency but also for its safety. The car competed in the same category as the Audi A6 and the BMW 5 Series but it accelerated from

0 to 60 miles (97 km) per hour ten percent faster. Due to the precision of its electric powertrain, it had outstanding traction. The rigid flat battery pack on the bottom of the car provided superior handling and created space for an all-glass panoramic roof. With the small electric motor positioned above the rear axle, the Model S offered rear-wheel drive at no extra cost. It had no key and automatically unlocked when approached. When the driver put on the seatbelt the car started. Its sophisticated touch-pad screen could be used to adjust suspension, steering, and other aspects of the drive. When the electric charge was low the Model S warned drivers and told them where to go to recharge. The car could be bought with two alternative battery packs. The larger 85 kWh cost more than the 60 kWh ($89,900 as opposed to $69,900), but had additional range, up to 306 miles (492 km) at average speeds of 55 miles (89 km) per hour.[11]

With superchargers installed throughout the United States and increasingly in Europe and Asia drivers never were very far from a place where to replenish their batteries for 150 miles (241 km) of additional driving in about 20 minutes. Superchargers were near amenities like diners, cafes, and shopping centers so that travelers could stop for a quick rest and some food and have the vehicle re-charged by the time they were finished. The 85 kWh battery pack could be charged for free at any supercharger, unlike gasoline stations where the driver would have pay to fill up. Drivers who had the 60 kWh battery pack could buy this service for $2,000 or $2,500 depending on whether they bought the service at the time of sale or after. The Model S came with removable battery packs, and Tesla had set up swapping stations where battery packs could be replaced in a few minutes.

Reservations for the Model S grew at a 64 percent compound annual growth rate from the time the car was introduced in 2009 until 2012. The biggest success was in Norway where it was the top seller of all cars. A number of conditions in Norway were ideal for the Model S: no sales tax (i.e. VAT); toll-free travel and the right to travel in special bus and taxi lanes; priority parking; gasoline prices typically more than $10 per gallon; and cheap electricity because of Norway's hydroelectric production. In Norway electric power charges cost approximately $0.05 per kWh, compared to $0.14 per kWh in a US state such as New Jersey. In the United States used Tesla Model Ss were selling at higher prices than new ones. A used Model S cost $99734 in 2013, which was more than the base price of either the less or more expensive Model Ss.

Table 4.2 *United States' luxury car sales, 2013*

Luxury cars	2013 sales	Price range
Tesla Model S	22,477	$69,000–89,000
Mercedes S Class	13,303	$92,000–212,000
BMW 7 Series	10,932	$73,000–140,000
Lexus LS	10,727	$71,000–119,000
Audi A7	8,483	$62,000–105,000
Mercedes CLS Class	8,032	$72,000–95,000
Audi A8	6,300	$73,000–111,000
Jaguar XJ	5,434	$73,000–116,000
Porsche Panamera	5,421	$75,000–175,000
Hyundai Equus	3,578	$59,000–66,000
Cadillac ELR	6	$74,000

See: www.forbes.com/sites/markrogowsky/2013/08/24/numbers-dont-lie-tesla-is-beginning-to-put-the-hurt-on-the-competition

The reason was the car's scarcity. Very few used Model Ss were available.

Some of Tesla's most visible EV competitors such as Fisker (see Chapter 1) and Think went bankrupt or stopped production. Tesla raised its first year's sales target from 20,000 to 21,000 vehicles. In 2010, it did an initial public offering (IPO), with the stock price jumping 40 percent. Daimler was pleased as it owned about ten percent of the company. In 2013 Tesla raised an additional $1 billion in a common stock offering, which it used to pay off its below interest loan from the US DOE. The company returned the money to the government nine years before it was due.

By the spring of 2014, Tesla had sold more than 31,000 vehicles in the auto industry's highest margin luxury niche. Its prior year US sales were greater than the Mercedes S Class, the BMW 7 Series, the Lexus LS, and the Audi A7 (see Table 4.2). Largely because of the Model S's introduction, Tesla, as of July 2014, had a very successful two-year run on Wall Street. Its stock price grew at a greater than 600 percent clip. Its 25 percent gross margins surpassed all automakers except Honda. However, its operating margin remained in negative territory. It lost more than $135 million, while all the other automakers, including GM, were profitable (see Table 4.3). Its quarterly revenue was growing at an 11 percent pace, but this growth rate, while greater than that of

Table 4.3 *Tesla's financials compared to those of other major automakers, July 2014*

	TESLA	GM	FORD	TOYOTA	HONDA	NISSAN
Market cap ($)	27.14 billion	60.17 billion	67.58 billion	190.15 billion	63.06 billion	40.51 billion
Employees:	5,859	219,000	181,000	338,875	198,561	142,925
Quarterly revenue growth	0.11	0.01	0.01	0.13	0.13	0.08
Revenue ($)	2.07 billion	155.95 billion	147.14 billion	251.52 billion	115.94 billion	102.62 billion
Gross margin	0.25	0.11	0.12	0.19	0.26	0.18
Operating margin	−0.05	0.03	0.03	0.09	0.06	0.05
Net income($)	−135.06 million	3.03 billion	6.53 billion	17.85 billion	5.62 billion	3.81 billion

Compiled from publicly available quarterly report data.

other luxury brands, did not match the growth rate of Toyota and Honda motors in July 2014.

The rise and fall of Better Place

Better Place's founder Shai Agassi was born in 1968 and grew up outside Tel Aviv.[12] Before reaching adolescence he knew how to program computers. He began university studies at Israel's most prestigious engineering school, the Technion, at age 15. With his father, an Israeli army officer and later telecom executive, he started a software company that provided enterprise-level services for small businesses. A 1995 consulting assignment from Apple led him to Silicon Valley where he began TopTier, a company that created web portals for large Bay Area companies such as HP. SAP, which bought this company in 2001 for $400 million, asked Agassi to become head of global product development.

In 2005, Agassi was invited to be part of the World Economic Forum's under-40 age group. He responded to the forum's question about how to make the world a better place by investigating alternative transportation. His co-investigator was fellow Davos participant Andrey Zarur. Zarur was at the time CEO of BioProcessors – a company that made equipment for pharmaceutical research.

The vision and its funding

The white paper that Agassi and Zarur wrote "Transforming global transportation" maintained that widespread adoption of electric vehicles would mean a revolution like that of Watt's steam engine, Ford's Model T, the Apollo program, and the Internet. The white paper dismissed ethanol and fuel-cell technologies as impractical means to make the world independent from oil. Agassi and Zarur's idea was that the all-electric car, obtaining power from renewable sources, was the only solution. The challenges EVs confronted were their high costs, the long time it took to charge them, and their limited range. The solution Agassi developed was a simple one – separate the car from ownership of the battery. With this business model, the price of the vehicle became more affordable.

The company Agassi started to realize this vision was called Better Place. Its business model was to make money by providing drivers with charging services at less cost than gasoline. With an infrastructure of charging spots and battery swapping stations in place, drivers' concerns about range would be eliminated. Because the average miles a person drove was less than 50 miles (80 km) per day, the average driver would need to use the swapping stations only in exceptional cases. The model for the swapping stations was that they would be completely automated and they would not require drivers to get out of their cars. The whole process would take less than the amount of time necessary to refuel a gasoline powered car. Drivers would buy subscriptions for charging services based on their estimates of how much they drove. They would be offered different service plans – for instance, all-you-can-drive for $500 a month, a fixed monthly amount of driving for $350 a month, or pay-as-you-go, which would expose customers to the risk of fluctuating electricity prices. Without the battery, the price of an EV was as low as the price of a gasoline-driven vehicle. Better Place would own the batteries and earn its revenue by providing the electric charging services. Admittedly, much of the world's electricity was generated by burning coal, but the goal was to promote renewable energy and have customers buy only clean electricity from renewable sources.

With this business model in hand, Agassi left SAP in 2007.[13] Encouragement for his ideas came from Israel's then President Shimon Peres and Prime Minister Ehud Olmert. Olmert held out the possibility that the Israeli government would support Better Place if Agassi could secure $200 million in funding and a major auto producer's backing.

Agassi went about trying to achieve these goals. The company's first investor was Maniv Energy Capital, which had been set up in 2005 by Michael Granoff, a Northwestern trained MBA and lawyer, to explore opportunities in new energy technologies. Granoff also was a founder of Securing America's Future Energy, a Washington-based advocacy group. Later, he became part of Better Place's management team, handling investor relations and public policy. Granoff introduced Agassi to Idan Ofer, who at the time was board chair of Israel Corporation. This company had been formerly state-owned. Ofer's family gained control of it in 1999. Though Israel Corporation had interests in shipping (ZIM), oilfield services and refining (Inkia Energy), power (IC Power), chemicals and fertilizers (Israel Chemicals), and autos (Quros), the company also sought opportunities in renewable energy. Ofer had been a co-founder of the Carbon War Room, a Washington-based organization focused on using market mechanisms to create a carbon-neutral economy.

Agassi had about an hour to make his pitch to Ofer. He told him that Better Place's business model was premised on keeping the price of the car low by selling it without the battery. He compared the contracts that customers would have with Better Place to cell-phone subscription services. Instead of minutes, owners of the car would pay Better Place for miles. Ofer asked for a copy of the working paper that Agassi and Zarur wrote. Agassi believed that Ofer had not been impressed by his presentation. As he left the room, he was surprised to hear Ofer say "put me down for 100" – by which Ofer meant that Israel Corporation would invest $100 million in the company. Better Place's Series A funding came shortly thereafter from a consortium that included besides Israel Corporation, Edgar Bronfman Sr., Israel Cleantech Ventures, James Wolfensohn, Morgan Stanley, Musea Ventures, and VantagePoint Capital. Together they provided Better Place with the $200 million it needed. To the $200 million, Ofer contributed another $30 million from his personal fortune.

Partnering with an auto company and marketing the car

With the funding to get started, Better Place now had to find an auto company with which to partner. Its business model was not to make the car but to provide the electric charging infrastructure it would need. Israel's then President Peres arranged a meeting between Agassi and Carlos Ghosn, the CEO of Nissan and Renault. Ghosn at the time wanted to overtake Toyota, the leader in hybrid technology (see Chapter 5), by going fully electric. He promised Agassi that Renault would develop an electric version of the mid-sized passenger car Fluence for Better Place. The cars would cost Better Place about $25,000. The battery packs, with a range of about 100 miles (161 km) and an expected lifetime of eight to ten years, would be purchased from A123 Systems and AESC for another $7,000 to 12,000 per vehicle. Better Place agreed to acquire the rights to 100,000 of these vehicles to sell in Israel and Denmark between 2011 and 2016. In these countries, Better Place would price the cars after taxes at around $35,000. In Israel, where the tax rate on an equivalent mid-size Honda was 78 percent, the all-electric Fluence would cost about the same as the Honda. In

Denmark, where the tax rate on this type of car was 180 percent, the equivalent vehicle would cost close to $50,000. Because the Fluence was all electric, the Danish government would waive all taxes. Though the price was low in both countries, many consumers bought used cars and avoided the new car market altogether.

Better Place went back to the Israeli government and asked for a subsidy of $150 million to produce the Fluence in Israel. If Agassi had obtained the subsidy, he might have been able to lower the cost of the car and sell more of them, but the Israeli government turned down his request. Renault set up its factory in Turkey. The Israeli government provided tax breaks to EV buyers but it did not fully extend the tax breaks to fleet purchasers. For the most part, the cars Israelis drove were a perk from employers, who bought the cars in bulk for corporate fleets. The Israeli government gave the fleet managers a discount for hybrid electric vehicles but not for fully electric cars.

Better Place's early marketing efforts were directed toward the fleet managers. It tried to sell them on the environmental benefits of the cars and on cutting dependence on foreign oil, but the company quickly realized that it also had to make a case for the car based on cost. About 200,000 cars of all kinds were bought in Israel each year.[14] Consumer research suggested that 20 percent of Israel's 1.2 million car owners would consider an EV, but they preferred if they did not have to put any money down and they could buy the car with monthly payments. They also reported that they did not find the Fluence especially appealing. They wanted other options. Fleet managers' attitudes were similar. They were not satisfied with a single model. They also tended to be interested only if their companies paid for employees' fuel expenses, they had parking lots where Better Place could install chargers, and their companies had environmental agendas. From the beginning, Better Place had to acknowledge that limited car choice was a problem. The Renault auto that Ghosn promised to sell Better Place had little pizzaz and the car's lithium-ion battery packs did not provide substantially better range than those GM had used in its failed efforts to induce California drivers to buy EVs in the late 1990s. Renault promised to add more models in the future. It had plans for all-electric SUVs, mini-vans, sports cars, and compact vehicles, but Better Place did not have a written agreement that Renault would fulfill these promises.

Approaching other automakers

After making the deal with Renault, Agassi approached other major automakers, but none of them agreed to supply him with cars. He tried to entice German carmakers, Daimler and BMW, to be partners but they did not go along. Like their US counterparts, European manufacturers were subject to environmental guidelines issued by the EU to reduce pollution and control carbon emissions. The EU also had guidelines that encouraged investment in sustainable transportation. However, with their own plans for pursuing electric vehicles, the German manufacturers with whom Agassi was in touch did not consider his idea to be a good fit. Daimler-Benz had partnered with Tesla. It had committed $350 million in 1997 to a program with Canadian firm Ballard Fuels to create a hydrogen fuel-cell engine. It had its own plans for an electric vehicle. Agassi thought that the German companies tended to oppose new ideas they did not invent themselves.

The most promising lead Better Place secured was with GM. Granoff arranged for a meeting, which took place in Detroit in 2008. General Motors had a secret team investigating EVs and studying Tesla. The company's own history with an EV had ended in failure. The executives' understanding of Toyota's difficulties in building market share for the Prius made them wary. They doubted that Better Place offered customers a good value proposition. Like the German automakers, these executives had their own view of what GM should do. It should continue pursuing a partially electric car like the Chevy Volt plug-in, because with its back-up engine this car provided customers with confidence they would not run out of power (see Chapter 5). The GM executives therefore turned Agassi down. Not yet interested in going fully electric they made Agassi a counter-offer. If Better Place would redesign its charging network to be compatible with the Volt battery, they would allow Better Place to manage their charging system. For Better Place, this proposal made no sense because the Volt had a back-up gasoline engine and the need for on-the-road charging was minimal. Better Place wanted a single world charging standard interoperable with all other charging systems and not one that might end being exclusive to GM. According to Better Place, utilities, car manufacturers, and battery developers should adhere to protocols set up by the International Organization for Standardization (ISO) and open up their access to optimize adoption speed.

Better Place also faced many competitors who also were producing and selling charging systems. Coulomb Technologies, an electric-car service provider founded in 2007, was in the process of setting up charging stations in nine regions in the United States. The driver paid it a fixed amount for access and on top of that paid a sum of money to a utility for electricity. Elektromotive, a UK company that had partnerships with Renault-Nissan and Mercedes-Benz, pursued a similar strategy. These chargers were not super-fast like Better Place's or Tesla's and they took up to eight hours for a car to be fully charged.

Better Place did not reach out to the startup electric car maker, Think Global, in Norway, which was developing a sub-compact fully electric car, nor to REVA, which was developing an affordable electric car in India, nor to Fisker, at that time still struggling to get off the ground in the United States. No record exists of approaches it made to other US automakers or to Toyota and Honda, which manufactured in the United States. The company did not try to ally with Tesla nor did Tesla try to ally with Better Place, and without a US partnership of some kind, Better Place was unable to obtain funding from the US government.

Installing infrastructure in Israel and Denmark

The key task for Better Place was to demonstrate that its business model could work in Israel and Denmark. In itself this task was massive. Everything had to take place at roughly the same time – enough cars sold at the same time batteries were available and charging spots and swapping stations in place. To assure coordination, software had to be created to synchronize the system. Software also was needed to monitor and bill customers for energy use. It was also needed for the car's digital dashboard, for heating, air conditioning, audio, and GPS systems, and for alerting drivers how much electricity they had consumed and where the nearest charging and swapping systems were. Better Place had to create this software itself or buy it from vendors. It contracted out the billing system to Amdocs, an Israeli company that worked for cell phone companies and created its own navigation system called Oscar for the operating system for the car.

Better Place's business model rested on the assumption that in countries such as Israel and Denmark, where the price of gasoline was above eight dollars or more per gallon, it could price the electric service it offered at rates lower than drivers otherwise would have to pay to fill their tanks. However, this model only worked if Better Place sold enough vehicles to achieve economies of scale. Otherwise the infrastructure would not receive enough use and it would be too expensive.

Better Place sold the cars online, by word of mouth, and by relying on the positive publicity it generated. It also spent money on a visitors' center in Israel and some radio, TV, and print ads, but it could not afford the expensive mainstream media blitzes traditional automakers gave to a new vehicle. For the business model to work, Better Place would have to install thousands of charge spots in garages, retail spaces, streets, and homes. Its estimate was that it would need two charge spots for every car it sold, with each charge spot costing as much as $1,000 depending on how difficult it was to mount and connect.

Better Place also needed to set in place the switching stations. Its switching stations were a novel feature of its network of which it was very proud. They could replace a depleted battery in less than five minutes with a fully charged one. Cars moving along the conveyor belt had their batteries swapped in less time than it took to refuel at a gasoline station. Each swapping station had the capacity to change 12 batteries per hour. Better Place estimated that it would need at least 40 stations at key locations to service 100,000 cars in locations the size of Israel or Denmark. In comparison, in 2010, Israel had about 1,000 gasoline stations and Denmark had about 2,000 gas stations. By virtue of this fact, drivers' confidence in being able to fill up at a gasoline station always would be higher than their assurance they could get to a swapping station in time. The swapping stations therefore had to be very carefully located. Better Place built 30 such stations in Israel. They covered the entire country. Each cost more than a traditional gas station. For it to be run effectively, it required cost-effective stocking of expensive batteries. Despite the careful planning, busy Tel Aviv stations might be subject to congestion during periods of peak use. The difficulties in setting up the stations had not been anticipated. The original estimate for how much each station would cost ballooned from half a million dollars to two million dollars.

Better Place's business model also depended on cooperative utilities willing to work with the company. The utilities had to have excess power and want to expand their power sales. In Denmark, the Danish Oil & Natural Gas (DONG Energy) company, flush with excess wind energy that otherwise would be wasted if it was not immediately consumed, was eager to work with Better Place. The batteries in the cars Better Place sold were ideal storage devices for the excess power. Israel's national utility was not as eager to cooperate. Most of the electricity it sold came from imported coal and oil. With respect to Agassi's suggestion that it should rapidly expand solar energy production in Israel's Negev desert it was lukewarm. When Israel discovered natural gas fields near its territorial waters, this proposal was off the table. Israel was in the process of converting its electricity production from coal and oil to natural gas.

Initiatives in other countries

Clearly, the startup challenges Better Place faced in Israel and Denmark were great. Yet Better Place, buoyed by a second investment round of $350 million that included the participation of HSBC, Lazard Asset Management, Morgan Stanley, and VantagePoint Capital Partners, turned its attention to initiatives in other countries. It engaged in such discussions with more than 20 other countries. The results were specific plans to act in six places. Better Place announced plans to do business in Canberra, Australia's capital, in 2008. Canberra would be the base for its national roll-out in Australia. The company would begin constructing charging spots and swapping stations throughout Australia in 2011.

In 2008, Better Place joined together with Bay Area mayors. Based on a nine-step policy initiative, the goal was to make their region the US EV capital. Better Place would make investments in charging spots and swapping stations totaling more than one billion dollars. In the same year Better Place publicized an initiative with the governor of Hawaii to bring an electric car network to that island, promising to begin infrastructure construction within a year and to start selling EVs by 2010. The aim was to install 50,000 to 100,000 charging stations and 20 swapping stations by 2012. The final two initiatives were in Asia. In 2010, Better Place established a partnership in Japan to construct swapping stations to support electric taxis in Tokyo. It also began work on a large infrastructure project in Guangzhou, China.

Each location required a different operational blueprint. Each necessitated extensive preparations. Calculations had to be made about how many new car owners would have to choose EVs and the numbers of subscriptions that Better Place would have to sell to break even It all depended on local taxes, the price of gasoline, and the price of electricity, which varied by location – the bigger the gap between gasoline and electricity prices, the more attractive a location. Local utilities also had to be willing to cooperate. Each initiative had different laws with which to cope. Regulatory permission had to be granted. Different procedures had to be followed with respect to securing the property rights, the swapping stations, and constructing the infrastructure. Better Place's plan was to own 51 percent of the operating companies in each location and the other 49 percent would be independent. The operating companies were expected to get local funding to help them finance their initiatives.

Better Place's R&D team was in Israel, while its top management team was located in Palo Alto, California. Despite the idealistic vision, and that the employees were very well paid, they were frustrated by the company's management style and structure. Agassi hired a team of management experts, led by a former Boston Consulting Group employee, to try to turn this situation around. In the midst of the sorting out process, Agassi moved back to Israel. The company's chief financial officer and general counsel, who lived in the Bay Area, quit. For two years, Better Place operated without anyone in these positions.

Bankruptcy

At the start of 2012, Better Place was losing more than a half million dollars a day. It had orders for just 100 cars, most of them bought by its employees. Despite Better Place's raising close to a billion dollars, time was running out.[15] Sales were not picking up quickly enough. At the mid-year board meeting, Zarur, Agassi's early collaborator, asked Agassi to leave the room and suggested that the board immediately hire a CFO and operations director and confine Agassi to the role of figurehead, chair of the board. Reluctantly, the board agreed, and asked Idan Ofer, of Israel Corporation, the entity with the biggest investment in Better Place, to tell Agassi. Agassi – furious at Zarur for turning against him – managed to convince Ofer that this step was mistaken. In disgust, board member Alan Salzman of VantagePoint Capital, quit the board. Agassi asked for a bridge loan to keep the company going. For months, he reported that he had been desperately trying to raise more money. He did obtain a $56 million loan from the

European Union's investment bank, most of which had to be spent in Denmark. He also revealed that money might be available in California and in an entirely new country, the Netherlands, where Better Place had not yet held extensive discussions. Without a bridge loan, he admitted that the company would be insolvent.

Ofer apparently was sympathetic to Agassi's request, but he pointed out that Israel Corporation had been a public company since 1982 and that its books were audited. With Agassi at the helm, he could not provide Better Place with more money. Ofer again offered Agassi the position of chair but told him he no longer could be CEO. Agassi refused and Ofer removed him from this position. Ofer helped to raise another $100 million from Israel Corporation and appointed Evan Thornley, head of the company's Australian operations, as CEO. Thornley tried, but could not get out of contracts Better Place had with its suppliers. As a startup, to secure the contracts, there were cancellation penalties and Better Place owed the suppliers more than $100 million. The billing system it purchased from the software firm Amdocs alone was an $80 million liability. To break even, Better Place would have to rapidly sell 30,000 cars. Its 2012 operating loss was $386 million. When Thornley did not make sufficient progress, he was ousted.

Dan Cohen, a former Israel Corporation executive, replaced Thornley. Choosing to focus only on Israel and Denmark, one of his first decisions was to close the Australian division. Better Place picked up the pace of its fleet sales in Israel by promising to buy back cars when the leases expired. Altogether it sold more than 1,400 cars in Israel, but this improvement in sales, given its dire financial condition, was not enough. Bleeding cash, the company had no choice but to declare bankruptcy. As Better Place's largest shareholders, Israel Corporation and Ofer owned 12 percent of the company. The losses they had suffered were very great, but they also lost patience and refused to provide more support.

Upon declaring bankruptcy, Dan Cohen issued this statement:[16]

This is a very sad day for all of us. We stand by the original vision as formulated by Shai Agassi of creating a green alternative that would lessen our dependence on highly polluting transportation technologies. While he was able with partners and investors to overcome multiple challenges to demonstrate that it was possible to deliver a technological solution that would fulfill that vision, unfortunately, the path to realizing that vision was difficult, complex and littered with obstacles, not all of which we were able to overcome. The technical challenges we overcame successfully, but the other obstacles we were not able to overcome, despite the massive effort and resources that were deployed to that end. The most important thing of all was that the intention was the right one. The purpose and concept of the business was to deliver a positive change in the world in which we live. We know that there is no certainty in any venture. It requires daring, courage, determination, and resources in order to turn a venture into a sustainable business. The vision is still valid and important and we remain hopeful that eventually the vision will be realized for the benefit of a better world. However, Better Place will not be able to take part in the realization of this vision.

The attempted rescue

The drivers of Israel's Better Place cars organized a new ownership group to try to keep the company alive. Very satisfied with their driving experience, they did not want to give up their vehicles. Some of the benefits they associated with owning an EV were the relatively low leasing, purchasing, maintenance, insurance, and electricity costs, the ease of using the charging and swapping stations, though it did take planning, and the road service. A big plus was no need to go to environmentally unfriendly gasoline stations. Another plus was the significant reduction in noise pollution. The owners, though, wished that some other automobile model, rather than the Renault Fluence, was available. The Fluence was not enough to cover the entire market for EVs. There had to be other options. Another drawback was that an owner needed a permanent parking place at home. The requirement that every Better Place car owner have a dedicated parking space limited the car's market potential.

The consortium of owners of Better Place cars made a valiant effort to save the company. They reduced costs by shutting down the computer center that Better Place had built in Spain to monitor the many cars the company anticipated it would sell. The system was relocated to Israel with scarcely a glitch. The owners also achieved savings by shutting down lightly used swapping stations. An advantage of swapping was that it permitted improvements in battery technology on existing cars. If range improved, fewer trips would require a swap, and the need for swapping stations would be lower. If the Fluence battery had the range of the Tesla, the cost overruns that came about because of the need to build so many swapping stations would not have happened.

After making these savings, the consortium of Better Place drivers calculated that they still needed to sell a total of at least 7,000 cars to reach a break-even point. Two issues then arose. First, the Israeli Minister of Transportation, beholden to Israel's car import monopoly, did not give the consortium the right to import cars. About 350 sold vehicles were sitting on the docks of the Ashdod port and some still had not left the Renault factory in Turkey. During the bankruptcy period, time had elapsed and the cars no longer were current models. According to Israeli law, they no longer could be sold as new cars. The Israeli Supreme Court ordered the Transportation Ministry to issue an exemption. However, to avoid misleading consumers, the cars' year of manufacture had to be explained to potential buyers who, if deciding to buy, would have to confirm in writing that they had been told. In addition, verification was needed that the cars remained in good working order.

The Supreme Court's exemption came too late because of a second issue. Renault announced that it was changing its EV engineering focus to fixed-battery cars leaving the Fluence with its swappable battery on indefinite hold. Without an ample supply of switchable battery cars, the switching stations in Israel had little value. Renault made the decision to give up despite reports by analysts that rapid growth in swapping and charging stations would drive high adoption rates of EVs in Europe. Without a dependable supply of cars any plan the owners' consortium could devise was unworkable and they had no choice but to pull out.

Tesla's moves

While these events were taking place, Tesla was making a series of moves of its own, the end results of which were unknown. Tesla had set up and was continuing to establish a series of supercharger stations in North America, Europe, and Asia that delivered 170 miles' worth of battery capacity in under a half hour. It had the capacity to launch swapping stations, like Better Place, that removed one battery pack and replaced it with another in a few minutes; this was less time than it took the average driver to refuel at a gasoline station. Because of the superior range of Tesla's vehicles – they had almost three times the range of Better Place's cars – Tesla did not have to install as many charging and swapping stations as Better Place did to achieve the same coverage. Tesla claimed, for example, that the hundred or so superchargers it had installed in North America provided coverage for as many as 90 percent of US drivers. Better Place, in contrast, needed up to 40 swapping stations to establish similar coverage in countries the size of Israel or Denmark.

The extent to which Tesla could maintain or expand the range of its vehicles as it downsized into less luxurious niches, then, was very important. It neutralized the need to install expensive charging infrastructure. The trade-off Tesla had was that more battery capacity was costly and made a vehicle more expensive and harder for a consumer to afford, thus limiting the size of the market; yet it also reduced the need to create and manage a large and expensive infrastructure. Most drivers would prefer expanded range over having to recharge their batteries more often, making battery capacity a very important need that Tesla had to fulfill.

Selling to the global middle class

Tesla had to create batteries that had greater range for fewer dollars. Its business model now that it had the successful Roadster and Model S was to make cars for a mass market. Only a small percentage of the world's ten million top one percent earning households, who could reasonably afford a car that sold for more than $69,000 would buy the Model S. The gasoline-free mass-market car that Tesla intended to produce, renamed the Model III after a dispute with Ford over calling it the Model E, had to be priced as a family sedan in the $35,000 range. The market for this vehicle still would be restricted, mainly to households earning more than $100,000 per year. In the United States with its growing income inequality, this segment was shrinking. To achieve its goals, Tesla would have to rely on the growth of the global middle class. Customers who fit this profile, however, had other luxury and semi-luxury brands from which to choose including the Mercedes C Class line, which had a base price of $36,000. Moreover, with the countries that offered EV subsidies strained fiscally, Tesla could not count on them continuing their subsidies. If the global middle class did not grow and subsidies were reduced, Tesla's road ahead would be difficult.

In the EV market, Tesla faced a number of competitors. With an anticipated range of 200 miles, the Model III was stated to be released in 2017, but BMW already had entered this market. The all-electric BMW i3, which was on sale in the United States in 2014 was a city car with a range of 100 miles. With a $7,500 federal tax credit it retailed for under $35,000. For customers concerned about its limited range, BMW offered a $4,000 option, a small gasoline motor that functioned as a range extender. The car had a boxy style, but BMW was investing in other electric and hybrid cars and had created a state-of-the-art green factory in Leipzig to produce them.

The problem Tesla confronted was that in the non-luxury niche where it was heading it faced greater competition and lower margins, which put more pressure on the company to lower the costs of the most expensive single element in its cars, the battery. From 2009 to 2013 it grew its revenues from $413 million to over $2 billion, while at the same time it made vast improvements in its margins and lowered its operating losses.[17] As it downsized its vehicle offerings, could it stay on course? The next generations of its cars, if they were to appeal to the world's middle class, could not be priced at more than $35,000 – but if priced at this level could Tesla sell these cars profitably?

Lowering battery costs

Tesla did not sell its electric cars as two-seat boxy vehicles for environmentalists as had GM in the 1990s, but as objects of desire that far exceeded a buyer's expectations for styling, handling, speed, safety, resale value, and maintenance. Critics, however, pointed out that the need to buy expensive tire replacements did not fit with low maintenance costs. Yet the buyer experience was vastly different. Tesla sold cars in company-owned stores that had the atmosphere of Apple outlets. As the technology improved, the software and batteries could be upgraded.

Battery improvements were the key. With scale, would cost and range improvements obey an exponential-like Moore's curve? Battery costs were expected to further decrease with advancements in technology and achievement of economies of scale, which would enable Tesla to manufacture and offer cheaper models for low-cost third-generation vehicles targeted at a mass market. The company's cylindrical-form battery had an edge that other manufacturers, such as Daimler and

Toyota, could not match. Tesla was likely to benefit from increased demand for its batteries from other manufacturers.

The giga-factory Tesla planned to build was meant to achieve cost reductions in batteries and accelerate the pace of battery innovation.[18] The financing would come from a $1.6 billion convertible debt offering. Tesla was supplying $800 million of convertible senior notes that were due in 2019 and $800 million that were due in 2021. It predicted that the new factory would be able to produce batteries for 500,000 vehicles – doubling worldwide capacity by 2020, which would lower battery prices by 30 percent. The company needed 10 million square feet (929,000 m^2) of factory space and more than 6,000 workers for the factory. The potential customers were not only automakers – as the batteries could be adapted for a wide variety of uses, including buses, delivery trucks, tractors, earth moving machines, and forklifts. They also could be used in lawn mowers, tools, and as storage for solar systems like those sold by Solar City, another company that Musk had founded and continued to have major investments.

Panasonic was the most likely partner in the factory but also mentioned was Samsung. Negotiations with these partners were likely to be sticky with regard to the question of profit sharing. Components (foils, cathode materials, anode materials, separators, electrolytes, etc.) that Tesla and whoever became its partner could not provide could lead to supply-chain issues. Did suppliers have the capacity to provide these components for such a large enterprise? The availability of lithium and other minerals and their prices also could be a problem. To flawlessly coordinate all the technical competencies needed for the factory to run well could be a challenge. Another issue might be inflexibility in such a highly automated enterprise, whose main goal was to lower costs. If better methods or materials become available, the tightly synchronized system might stand in the way of change. Thus the factory could become obsolete before it was fully paid for. Other issues could arise. The giga-factory could have problems getting permitted and built on time or on budget. Texas, Arizona, New Mexico or Nevada, and California were competing for the factory by offering subsidy packages. The extent of these subsidies could have an important impact on the investment.

Other risks associated with such a large endeavor were external. For example, fuel-cell technology could surpass batteries as the technology of choice in cars. Both Toyota and GM still were pursuing this alternative actively (see Chapter 5). With new finds in conventional petroleum or advances in the production of oil from shale, gasoline prices could rapidly decline creating a high hurdle rate for electric-powered vehicles. At the same time that gasoline prices became cheaper ICE vehicles might become significantly more efficient, hence raising the bar for EVs even further. On-the-road vehicles could move to fracked natural gas, which could price electricity out of the market. Electricity prices themselves, because of climate change or air pollution issues, could rise, making EVs increasingly unattractive. Another risk was that Tesla and other EV producers would not be able to install enough charging and swapping stations to reduce range anxiety. Then demand for the batteries produced in the giga-factory would not be sufficient.

Further developing Asian and European markets

To create demand for its EVs, markets outside the United States would have to be developed. Tesla was vigorously exploring external markets. The potential market of greatest importance was China.[19] Chinese rivals that made EV vehicles, such as BYD, Chery, and BAIC, had made progress but they were hindered by a perception of low quality. One of Tesla's main liabilities was that because it did not produce its cars in China its customers were not eligible for the generous incentives that the Chinese government gave. Another issue was that a very high percentage of Chinese electricity was generated using coal, and thus Tesla could not make a strong claim that the Model S was a low-emission vehicle. One estimate was that it took more than 75 pounds (34 kg) of coal to charge the car just once. Another issue was the lack of charging and swapping stations and service. Tesla was in discussion with the China Petroleum & Chemical Corp., known as Sinopec, to overcome this obstacle by building charging facilities initially in large cities such as Beijing, Shanghai, Hangzhou, Guangzhou, Shenzhen, and Chengdu. Sinopec, a stated-owned enterprise, would be an excellent partner in helping Tesla reach the goal of a nationwide charging station network.

In China, Tesla benefited from the snob factor. Among China's newly rich, Tesla was perceived as a very prestigious brand. The company's cars had a reputation for outstanding quality and reliability.

Tesla's aim was to double the number of Model S vehicles it sold in 2014 compared to 2013. It hoped it could reach sales a figure as high as 8,000 in China. Only 11,375 EVs in total were sold in China in 2013 so for Tesla to reach this goal would be difficult. Nonetheless, it was opening a dozen sales outlets in China, including a flagship store in Beijing. Mainly because of the import taxes, the Chinese price for the models was almost 50 percent more than the price in the United States and considerably higher than domestic brands – but in line with Audi's S5 and BMW's 5 Series that also were subject to the import taxes.

Tesla's plan was to build cars in China. To achieve this goal it would have to form a joint venture with a Chinese manufacturer, which put it at risk of losing its trade secrets. Chinese companies could copy Tesla's battery innovations and sell vehicles for less than Tesla – and Tesla would have little recourse. The Chinese 2006 "Long-term program for the development of science and technology" emphasized indigenous innovation and making China a powerhouse in technologies such as EVs by 2020.

Another option would be for Tesla to hone in on Germany, the largest luxury-car market in the world, and try to take share from domestic producers. However, despite Germany's vaunted environmentalism, from 2010 to 2013 only about 10,500 EVs had been sold in that country. Tesla's goal was to build sales to about 10,000 Model S cars in Germany. As elsewhere in the world, its major competitors would be German carmakers who made the BMW 5 Series, the Mercedes-Benz E-Class and Mercedes-Benz S-Class, as well as Toyota, which made the Lexus hybrid.

In 2014, Tesla started to make cars for left-hand driving countries. The major markets that fit this category were UK, Japan, Hong Kong, Australia, India, and South Africa. In the UK the same £5,000 incentive for which the Tesla was eligible was awarded to plug-in hybrid cars. The Mitsubishi Outlander, a plug-in hybrid SUV, was a major competitor. Australia was another market where Tesla was optimistic it could do well. An issue Tesla faced in countries that drove on the left-hand-side of the road was lack of chargers, swapping stations, and service. The EV infrastructure was under-developed. Japan had its own electric car makers so penetrating this market would be difficult. Tops sellers were the Leaf and Outlander. Hybrids and plug-in hybrids were quite popular. Hong Kong, India, and other south Asian markets had long-term potential. Drivers in Gulf nations could afford expensive EVs, but they had cheap oil. As in the Gulf nations, high temperatures were an obstacle to EV penetration. Lithium batteries were not well suited for these climates. Nonetheless, Tesla estimated that the market for left-hand driving countries was about 2,500 a significant boost to its overall sales since its total 2013 sales were not quite above 23,000.

Giving patents away and what comes next

By announcing in 2014 that Tesla would *not* initiate lawsuits against anyone who in good faith wanted to use its technology, it was trying to accelerate the path to sustainable transportation.[20] Platform-shifting category creation rested on the idea of cooperative competition. When this strategy worked, massive disruption was possible. Other innovators had opened up their intellectual property in similar ways. The personal computer market was divided among numerous proprietary technologies and operating systems when IBM introduced its PC in 1981 – using technology from Intel and Microsoft anyone could access. Other companies such as Compaq, Dell, and Gateway made PCs using this platform. Google's Android mobile operating system also grew by creating a bigger total market where there would be more opportunity for everyone. It made sense for Tesla to build both the category (EV) and the company (Tesla). Once the market expanded, it could out-execute competitors and achieve a dominant position. Its aim was for the small-cell cylindrical technology it employed in its battery packs to become the standard for a thriving industry that consisted of many players. The intention was to accelerate the movement of EVs into the mainstream so that Tesla would be a dominant player in a large and growing niche – and not the dominant player in a small niche (less than one percent overall EV penetration in the auto market in 2014). This move was necessary for Tesla to have an outlet for the battery packs it planned to make in the giga-factory. The giga-factory would create supply, while Tesla's opening up its patents to competitors would create the demand needed to meet the supply.

Tesla kept adjusting and readjusting its business model. The moves it so far had made had the potential to unleash a revolution in the auto industry. However, there were obvious pitfalls, as the example of Better Place so vividly illustrated.

What could Tesla learn from Better Place's failure? How should it adjust its business model to avoid a similar fate? What steps should it take to guarantee that its vision ultimately would become a reality?

Notes

1 E. Musk, "The secret Tesla Motors master plan (just between you and me)," (2006): www.teslamotors.com/blog/secret-tesla-motors-master-plan-just-between-you-and-me

2 D. Etzion and J. Struben, *Better Place: Shifting Paradigms in the Automotive Industry* (Montreal, Canada: McGill University, 2011): www.oikos-international.org/academic/case-collection/free-cases

3 *Ibid.*

4 A. Marcus, *Strategy, Ethics, and the Global Economy* (Chicago, IL: Irwin, 1996): pp. 421–430.

5 D. Etzion and J. Struben, *Better Place: Shifting Paradigms in the Automotive Industry.*

6 T. Friend, "Plugged in: can Elon Musk lead the way to an electric-car future?" *New Yorker*, (2009): www.newyorker.com/magazine/2009/08/24/plugged-in

7 E. Van Den Steen, *Tesla Motors* (Boston, MA: Harvard Business School, 2013); J. Foroughi, A. Casscells, and M. McNichols, *Tesla Motors: Evaluating a Growth Company* (Palo Alto, CA: Stanford University, 2013).

8 See EV Obsession: http://evobsession.com/electric-car-sales-increased-228-88-2013

9 See extensive coverage given to Tesla on Seeking Alpha: http://seekingalpha.com

10 W. Oremus, "Tesla finally won the one car award that counts most," *Future Tense* (2014): www.slate.com/blogs/future_tense/2014/02/25/consumer_reports_top_overall_pick_of_2014_the_tesla_model_s_of_course.html

11 See the Tesla website: www.teslamotors.com

12 J. Boomis, A. Racek, J. Turner, and B. Van Abe, *Better Place: Charging into the Future?* (Ann Arbor, MI: Erb Institute University of Michigan, 2010); E. Ofek, *Speeding Ahead to a Better Place* (Boston, MA: Harvard Business School, 2012).

13 M. Chafkin, "A broken place: the spectacular failure of the startup that was going to change the world," *Fast Company* (2014): www.fastcompany.com/3028159/a-broken-place-better-place

14 *Ibid.*

15 *Ibid.*
16 See K. Kloosterman, "Israel's Better Place EV company dies and files for bankrutpcy," *Green Prophet* (2004): http://www.greenprophet.com/ 2013/05/israel-better-place-bankrupt; "Death of Better Place: Electric Car Co. to dissolve," *Jerusalem Post* (2013): www.jpost.com/Business/ Business-News/Death-of-Better-Place-Electric-car-co-to-dissolve- 314380; A. Rabinovitch, "UPDATE 2-Electric car venture Better Place files to wind up company," *Reuters* (2013): www.reuters.com/article/ 2013/05/26/betterplace-idUSL5N0E704E20130526
17 See the Tesla website: www.teslamotors.com
18 D. Sparks, "Why Tesla's next big thing could flip the auto industry upside down," *The Motley Fool* (2014): www.fool.com/investing/general/2014/ 10/05/why-teslas-next-big-thing-could-flip-the-auto-indu.aspx
19 E. Wesoff, "Tesla's deal architect on the giga battery factory and the EV market," (2014): www.greentechmedia.com/articles/read/Teslas- Deal-Architect-on-the-Giga-Battery-Factory-and-the-EV-Market
20 See coverage of Tesla giving away its patents on Seeking Alpha: http:// seekingalpha.com

PART III

The macroenvironment and industry context

5 | Ticket to ride: Toyota and General Motors

The challenge that Toyota and GM confronted was the extent to which they should commit to alternative vehicles in light of changes in the macroenvironment and the industry context in which they operated. They had to make their choices in light of serious global environmental, energy, and security concerns that could affect oil prices. To what extent should they forego their reliance on vehicles propelled solely or almost exclusively by gasoline? Their choices included both hybrids and fuel-cell vehicles, but they could not overlook improving conventional gasoline-powered vehicles. If they committed to alternative vehicles which types should they be? Given the global uncertainties and rapidly evolving industry context, what would best fit their future plans?

Global uncertainties

Toyota and GM faced a range of vehicle choices including hybrid electric vehicles (HEVs), plug-in hybrid electric vehicles (PHEVs), and fuel-cell vehicles (FCVs). However, they also could focus on making improvements in the autos they already sold that were propelled by the internal combustion engine (ICE). An ultra-efficient gasoline engine and/or auto body that relied on cutting-edge technologies was possible. This vehicle, though not free of emissions, might prove to be highly energy efficient. To develop an ultra-efficient conventional engine, additional advances were needed in sophisticated electronic timing and sensing devices, advanced aerodynamic engineering, regenerative braking, and other areas. Many of these features later could be incorporated into hybrids and fuel-cell vehicles should that be necessary. An advanced diesel engine also was possible. Diesels might be a viable alternative in Europe and other parts of the world where they already were in widespread use and perhaps they could gain greater acceptance in the United States. This approach also might yield lower pollution and more fuel efficiency.

What should Toyota and GM do? How serious should they take the alternatives to the ICE? Among the alternatives – which ones should they emphasize and to what degree? In making these choices, the automakers had to consider important factors such as climate change, the demand and supply for petroleum, and global security, which affected the external environment in which they operated. As these factors played out, a number of different scenarios were possible.[1] They had to make their choices in light of these different scenarios.

Climate change

Burning fossil fuels put greenhouse gases into the atmosphere that trapped heat and warmed the globe. Heat waves and other weather events, from storms and hurricanes to droughts, could be the result. Ice caps could melt and sea levels rise by as much as 20 feet (6.1 m). Most scientists accepted that the phenomenon was for real but, especially in the United States, some still contested the claim, arguing that the evidence was not strong enough to definitively conclude that the concentration of greenhouse gases in the atmosphere would lead to catastrophe. Proponents pointed to an increased incidence of extreme weather-related events. Opponents objected and maintained that the risks were exaggerated. Any attempt to limit or eliminate the fossil fuels that provided 90 percent of the world's energy was folly. It would yield economic disaster – job losses, recession, and high inflation.

Scientists had detected that by the end of World War II approximately a billion metric tons of carbon had been emitted into the atmosphere and that by 2008 this number had grown to more than 7 billion tons, but how would this increase in greenhouse gases affect the planet? This question was complicated. Impacts on agriculture might be mixed because of longer growing seasons, but also less arable land and drier soils. Low-level cloud cover shielded the sun from the Earth and cooled the planet, while high-level cloud cover trapped the heat from the sun and warmed the planet. Greenhouse gases, moreover, did not act in isolation. Complex feedback occurred between these gases and the other factors that affected global climate. Even modest warming could destabilize ocean currents such as the Gulf Stream that carried warm water from the equator to the north Atlantic and moderated the temperature of Britain and the Scandinavian countries.

All scientists agreed that a distinction must be made between natural fluctuations in the weather that regularly occurred and more fundamental alterations that took place over a longer period. How hot or cold it was on a particular day was not as important as these long-run patterns. The consensus view was that the more greenhouse gases emitted, the higher the increase in average global temperatures would be, but scientists were uncertain about how abrupt and extreme the changes would be and how prepared people would be to adjust to them. Would rich nations adjust better than poor nations? If humans were able to adjust, could plants and animals?

Climate change could force governments to make rapid cutbacks in the dependence on fossil fuels. The efforts policy-makers so far had made to prevent climate change from taking place, however, had ended in stalemate. In December 1997, representatives from 160 countries met in Kyoto, Japan to deliberate about a treaty that would limit the world's greenhouse gas emissions. Based on the 1992 Rio Treaty signed by US President Bush and ratified by Congress, they agreed that the nations of the world had common but differentiated responsibilities for the problem. This deceptively simple phrase led to continuous controversy about who was responsible for climate change and who had to bear the burden of reversing it.

For developing countries the highest priority was economic growth, not curbing global greenhouse emissions. Their view was that industrialized nations had to act first. Energy use by industrialized nations such as the United States was the main cause for the rise of greenhouse gases in the atmosphere. These nations accounted for 90 percent of the historic accumulation of greenhouse gases in the atmosphere. Yet the US Congress failed to endorse the Kyoto treaty and to pass legislation to curb greenhouse emissions on the grounds that the future of global warming would be determined by what happened in developing nations such as Brazil, India, and China, where three quarters of the world's people lived. The developing world had higher rates of population and economic growth, which meant they would lead the world in future greenhouse emissions increases. The developing world's share of the global concentration of greenhouse gases in the environment was expected to pass the industrialized nations' share before 2040 if not sooner. Given this ongoing controversy between the interests of developed and developing nations, serious global action on climate change tended to get bogged down in debate and inaction.

The demand and supply for oil

Another factor that was weighing heavily on the automakers was global demand and supply for oil. In the world as a whole, growth in energy use for transportation continued to swell. It was stimulated by rising demand for private automobiles in countries such as China. From 1978 to 2008, the number of private automobiles owned by Chinese consumers increased by more than 100 percent, from less than 500,000 in 1978 to more than 70 million in 2011.[2] Approximately half of the estimated increase in demand for energy in the world was expected to come from China. Already in 2008, it had become the world's second-largest oil consumer, after the United States, and it was fast catching up. Like China, other Asian nations such as India, Indonesia, and Malaysia understood that rising standards of living depended on increased energy use. Oil consumption in North America, Western Europe, and the developed nations in Asia that were part of the Organization for Economic Cooperation and Development (OECD) such as Japan had peaked, but no country in the world was willing to voluntarily relinquish the many benefits that the use of oil provided.

In the decades after 1980, the Organization of Petroleum Exporting Countries' (OPEC) market share in oil had eroded because of an increasingly diverse supply base. Non-OPEC nations, such as Russia and Canada, played an important role in providing the world with oil.[3] The North Sea oil discovery reduced pressure on prices. Little increments added to the global petroleum market made a big difference. However, as of 2013, plentiful North Sea oil was starting to dry up and the OPEC nations remained best endowed oil nations in the world. The world's largest oil reserves were found in Venezuela, Saudi Arabia, Canada, Iran, and Iraq (see Table 5.1), while the world's largest producers were Russia, Saudi Arabia, the United States, and China. If not for instability and terrorism, Iraq had the capability of producing more than 6 million barrels per day. Nigeria and Libya, plagued by turmoil, also could not fully tap their abundant reserves.

On the surface, OPEC's oil reserves appeared very substantial. However, since cartel production quotas were based on reported reserves, OPEC nations had incentives to exaggerate how much oil they actually

Table 5.1 *Largest oil reserves and producers in 2014*

Largest oil reserves			Largest oil producers		
Rank	Country	Reserves (millions of barrels)	Rank	Country	Output (barrels per day)
1	Venezuela[a]	297,570	1	Russia	10,730,000
2	Saudi Arabia[a]	267,910	2	Saudi Arabia[a]	9,570,000
3	Canada	175,200	3	United States	9,023,000
4	Iran[a]	157,300	4	Iran[a]	4,231,000
5	Iraq[a]	140,300	5	China	4,073,000
6	Kuwait[a]	104,000	6	Canada	3,592,000
7	United Arab Emirates[a]	97,800	7	Iraq[a]	3,400,000
8	Russia	80,000	8	United Arab Emirates[a]	3,087,000
9	Libya[a]	48,014	9	Mexico	2,934,000
10	Nigeria[a]	37,200	10	Kuwait[a]	2,682,000

[a] Organization of Petroleum Exporting Countries (OPEC) member
Compiled from US Energy Information Administration statistics

had in the ground. Transparency did not exist. The actual reserves of the OPEC states had not been fully verified by independent experts. For example, extraction costs of Persian Gulf oil were supposed to be very low. Questions, however, arose because decades' old reservoirs such as the Saudi's did not flow as easily as they did when they were young. The Ghawar field, the Saudi's largest, with greater than 50 percent of its oil, already was more than 50 percent exhausted.[4] As additional depletion took place, extraction costs were likely to grow.

Non-OPEC member Canada's potential for oil production was high but a large percentage of its reserves were in the form of non-conventional liquids such as oil sands and ultra-heavy oils, where the environmental impact was great and the costs of extraction high. OPEC member Venezuela could increase its production capacity at a fraction of the cost of non-OPEC member Canada. At odds with Western nations, non-OPEC Russia had relinquished its oil reserves to oligarchs who controlled their oil companies as nationalized or semi-nationalized subsidiaries of the post-Communist regime. Caspian output in countries to the East and South of Russia appeared to be promising but had their limits since exporting routes for this oil – whether by pipeline or by sea – were not well established. With Vladimir Putin increasingly using oil as a tool for advancing his personal political interests, there was no guarantee that Russia could be relied upon as a global energy supplier.

United States' exploration in the Gulf of Mexico suffered from adverse environmental and safety issues that the disastrous BP oil spill highlighted. The most optimistic forecasts for the Alaska National Wildlife Refuge were only about 10 billion barrels. United States' production was growing because of its reliance on enhanced extraction methods. As oil fields reached a 50 percent exhaustion level, it was necessary to move from inexpensive primary retrieval to expensive secondary and tertiary recovery. The United States had made this move and increasingly it was tapping into old fields that long since had been abandoned. Prior to World War II, oil companies only removed about ten percent of the oil in a field. With the assistance of vast infusions of water, they were able to expand this amount to 30 percent or more after the war ended. By 2014 they could extract another 30 percent or more by using gas, carbon dioxide, chemicals, and engineered microbes to remove the oil. Some fields resisted these methods. Wherever they were applied, they raised extraction costs. Yet, overall these methods had vastly increased US supplies and production; they led to the fracking revolution that resulted in temporary gluts in oil availability and stable or falling prices in the fall of 2014.

Oil companies spent huge amounts exploring for new oil, but even the improved technology for discovering this oil that they had did not prevent them from producing many dry holes. Each year as existing petroleum reserves were consumed, the world needed additional replacement oil. The controversy about so-called peak oil (greater than half the oil in the ground of a particular nation being exhausted) was an old one. Many economists held that resource limits did not exist, that it all depended on prices, and that the oil in the ground never would be exhausted because whenever prices rose the technology of extraction would get better and lower the extraction costs. Geologists and petroleum engineers disagreed and argued that after about a half of the oil in the ground was exhausted, extraction costs could not be simply or easily lowered.

In the United States peak production was once taken for granted. Peak production had been reached around the year 1970, and since then the United States had been increasingly reliant on foreign oil, but with secondary and tertiary recovery and fracking this trend was being reversed. Within a 50-year time frame, peak production in other nations, upon which the United States depended, was possible. It was uncertain if secondary and tertiary recovery and fracking could revive the reserves of other nations in the same way that they so far had revived US reserves. Even if a reversal in peak production was possible, the price of oil, historically low in the United States in December of 2014, could rise.

The US Department of Energy's (DOE's) long-term projections of oil prices assumed that Saudi Arabia could produce 18 million to 22 million barrels per day by 2020 to 2025.[5] However, it was unclear if Saudi Arabia could produce this amount of oil. The Saudis and other OPEC nations were not holding back on delivering oil in December 2014, driving down the price in a way that made alternatives such as fracking less attractive. If the DOE was not correct about the Saudi's potential reserves, then demand for oil would overtake supply earlier than assumed, perhaps as soon as 2020 rather than 2035 or so as the DOE anticipated.

War and global politics might interfere with these forecasts. The future of many of the nations upon which the world relied for petroleum was very uncertain; they had despotic regimes and their ongoing stability was far from guaranteed. In the past, there had been supply interruptions during the Yom Kippur War Arab oil embargo, Iran's fall under President Carter, Iraq's war with Iran, the Iraqi invasion of Kuwait, and the United States' attack on that country after 9/11. The Persian Gulf nations with most of the world's oil reserves could go in many different directions. They could stay much as they were or radicalize. There could be al Qaeda-like, Iran-like, or far worse revolutions in these countries driven by Islamic extremists from groups such as ISIS, or they could modernize and become more open and democratic. Whatever direction they headed, there would be impacts on oil prices.

With this many factors at play, it was hard to predict what the supply picture looked like, what prices would be, if they would rise slowly, precipitously, or not at all, and when such changes might take place. If alternative sources of fossil fuels were found and growth in the world's developed countries stalled, the price of petroleum might go down rather than up.

Three scenarios

Getting a grip on future oil prices was a key factor in any calculation automakers had to make about investing in petroleum-powered vehicles and their alternatives. At least three scenarios, if not many more, were possible.[6] A middle-of-the road scenario had OPEC producers in the Middle East still holding significant reserves though they were stretched thin and pumping near capacity. Enhanced drilling and fracking in the United States and the unconventional oil reserves in Canada would take up the slack and keep prices relatively steady. Oil prices would be high enough to stimulate renewed exploration and production activity both within OPEC and among non-OPEC producers that would bring new supplies to the market. Canadian oil sands development already was resulting in almost a million barrels per day of oil being produced with much more expected in the future.[7] Fracking in the United States also was resulting in bonanza-like conditions based on investments in unconventional US sources such as western shale. If these investments continued to pay off, it would mean increased oil supplies and automakers would be able to operate much the same as they had in the past. Any run up in prices would have a time limit and not be permanent.

A pessimistic scenario, on the other hand, was that though modern seismic techniques had made exploration efforts more reliable and efficient, no gigantic new fields would be found. Even if found, bringing new supplies to the market would be expensive and it would take much longer than expected because these promising finds were in politically unstable areas. Neither new supplies of oil nor petroleum from aging or unconventional oil fields or fracking would be able to accommodate expected increases in demand. If this pessimistic scenario were correct prices would rise over time and stay high for a long period. The question was when the tipping point would take place and when high oil prices would be permanent. If governments increased oil taxes because of climate change damage or otherwise took this threat seriously and acted to curtail oil consumption because of it, the tipping point could come sooner. If the global economy fell into a major recession because of high oil prices, the slump in demand would bring prices down again, however.

An optimistic scenario, on the other hand, suggested that with high prices, new supplies would be quickly introduced. The new supplies would not necessarily be hydrocarbons of some type that released climate-damaging gases. Rather, major technological breakthrough in alternatives to fossil fuels would take place and permanently change the entire situation. Another surprise like fracked natural gas might be on the horizon, or alternatives to oil and to natural gas such as renewables might become cost effective and plentiful and lessen oil dependence to the point where prices were seriously and permanently lower (see Chapters 1 to 3). The revolution that might take place also could be in energy efficiency. Electric power generation could be streamlined, waste eliminated, and fuel needs substantially reduced. As part of the same process, motor vehicles also might become much more efficient with EVs superseding gasoline-powered vehicles as the typical consumer's transportation mode of choice (see Chapter 4).

As different factors rose to the forefront at different points in time, all three scenarios might play a role at some point in the future. These scenarios were not mutually exclusive. There could be alternating periods of rising, falling, and stable prices. Against the backdrop of these uncertainties, Toyota and GM had to make their decisions. To what extent should they offer their customers vehicle alternatives that were less petroleum reliant? So far, the main options they had focused on were regular hybrids, plug-in hybrids, and fuel-cycle vehicles. Had they emphasized these options sufficiently? Should they raise or lower their commitment to them? Did they have other choices?

The market for hybrids

By combining battery-powered electric motors with conventional ICEs, HEVs achieved better fuel economy than conventional cars in a number of ways. When the hybrid stopped, the ICE shut down. As it slowed, the batteries captured waste energy in the form regenerative braking. At slow speeds, the gasoline engine either shut down or it powered the vehicle alongside the electric engine. At high speeds, the electric motor and the ICE shared in the vehicle's propulsion. Reducing the ICE's size and power by adding an electric motor had benefits. The increased fuel economy meant that hybrids emitted less greenhouse gases and caused less pollution than conventional vehicles. However, because of the need to add batteries and an electric propulsion system, hybrids weighed and cost more than conventional vehicles. Buyers of HEVs faced the trade-off of how many miles would they have to put on their vehicles before they would see a positive economic return. Working in their favor was that with the exception of countries with very low gasoline prices and very high electric rates, the price of the electricity was almost always lower than the equivalent price of gasoline. Under these conditions, hybrids ultimately cost less than ICEs to own and operate.

Prius' entry into the hybrid market

The Toyota Prius was the world's top selling HEV. Besides the Prius, Toyota had introduced hybrid versions of the Camry, Lexus, Avalon, and Highlander. Since hybrids first came on the market, the number of registered hybrids in the United States had surpassed two million.[8] Japan superseded the United States as the country with the most registered hybrids in the world in 2009, but the United States came in a close second. United States' drivers bought nearly a half million hybrids in 2013.

During the 1990s, the US government spent $240 million per year for six years funding a group of US car manufacturers. Called the Partnership for a New Generation of Vehicles (PNGV), the objective was to developing a new fuel-efficient vehicle.[9] Out of this effort came the GM Precept and the Ford Prodigy. General Motors showed its hybrid prototype, the Precept, at the 2000 Detroit auto show. The Precept, like Ford's prototype, the Prodigy, achieved PNGV's 80 miles per gallon (34 km/L) aim. These prototypes were "American cars" – that is they were not tiny vehicles, but big roomy mid-size sedans. The Precept prototype was designed to be extremely aerodynamic and comprised of lightweight materials such as aluminum and polymer composites. The internal pumps were very efficient and the tires were rigid to forestall frictional losses. The car was powered by two electric motors plus a diesel engine and ran two-thirds of the time using the electric motors. Of course all of this came at a cost. A commercial model was likely to be significantly more expensive than petroleum-powered vehicles. General Motors and Ford concluded that Americans appeared to like the idea of more fuel-efficient vehicles, but most were unwilling to pay the extra cost for them.

Toyota, operating with different reasoning, moved forward with its own hybrid concept. Toyota's prototype car made its first appearance at the Tokyo Motor Show in 1995. Called the Prius –

the Latin word means the ascendance of a new era – the car used high-voltage batteries in the rear as a power source and electric motors in the front as the propulsion system. Californian designers did the styling. The first commercially available Prius went on sale in 1997 in Japan. At its introduction, it won Japan's the Car of the Year. In 2000 hybrid vehicles, marketed with an emphasis on their environmental benefits, grew in popularity. Honda was the first to sell such a car in the United States, the two-seat Insight. The Insight achieved 70 miles per gallon (29.8 km/L), and was priced at around $19,000. In 2002, Honda introduced another hybrid under the Civic brand. However, Toyota's Prius, which was sized between a Corolla and a Camry and priced at about $20,000, was more popular than either of these cars. It did not hurt that hybrid owners were eligible for a $2,000 US federal tax deduction. Toyota executives reported that the company broke even financially. In 2002, Americans bought more than 36,000 of these cars. Viewed as a percentage of total US vehicle sales, however, these sales amounted to just 0.24 percent of the total 2002 US auto market.

In 2003, Toyota completely redesigned the Prius. Redistributing the mechanical and interior space, it significantly increased rear-seat room and luggage compartment space. The US National Highway Traffic Safety Administration (NHTSA) gave the car a five-star driver and four-star passenger safety rating. The US Insurance Institute for Highway Safety scored its safety as good overall even when competing with much larger vehicles. The battery pack had a 150,000 mile warranty. As for the EPA, it rated the new Prius more environmentally friendly than the previous one. For all these reasons, Toyota's second edition of the Prius was a success. Toyota could not make enough of them and consumers experienced long waits before they got their cars. The development effort led to 530 patents, some of which Toyota licensed to Nissan and Ford.

European sales started in 2000. While Japan and the United States had strong hybrid markets, Europeans preferred diesel vehicles as a way to lower their energy consumption. Companies such as Mercedes and Volkswagen developed new-generation diesels that used electronic controls and fuel-injection systems to increase fuel efficiency and reduce noise and pollution. At the time these vehicles did not comply with US pollution rules. The diesel electric hybrid that GM and Ford had pioneered therefore did not gain traction

The Prius was introduced into China in 2005 but sales were disappointing. Low sales were blamed on the high price, about the equivalent of $15,000 higher than the same car in Japan or the United States because of high import duties.

Toyota's dominance

The third-generation Prius debuted at the 2009 North American International Auto Show and sales began in Japan that year. The car again won the Japanese Car of the Year Award. Its new body design was very aerodynamic and the car received a very good safety rating. Toyota cut its price so that it could better compete with the Honda and Toyota's hybrids became the world's leaders.

The total US 1999 to 2013 market share for Toyota's HEVs was 71 percent. Honda's total US market share was 12 percent; Ford's was 10 percent, GM's 3 percent, and Hyundai's 3 percent (see Table 5.2). In 2013, Toyota's US HEV market share was 67 percent. Ford was in second place with 15 percent market share. Though Honda introduced the Insight, the first HEV into the market, in 1999, its US market share had dropped to four percent. General Motors' 2013 market share had fallen from eight percent in 2012 to five percent in 2013. Hyundai, which did not make HEVs in 2011, had a market share of seven percent in 2012 and the same market share in 2013.

Ford almost doubled the number of hybrids it sold in 2013 compared to 2012 (see Table 5.3). The number of hybrids Honda sold in the United States peaked at about 44,000 units in 2007. In 2013 Honda sold fewer than 20,000 of these vehicles. General Motors' hybrid sales peaked at about 34,000 units in 2012. In 2013, its sales fell to about 25,000 vehicles, while Hyundai advanced from selling no hybrids in 2011 to sales of almost 36,000 hybrids in 2013.

A major reason for Toyota's dominance was that its vehicles generally had the best miles per gallon in their class (see Table 5.4). At low speeds Toyota's HEVs did not require ICE use; so long as there was enough charge, they could be propelled by the electric motor alone. Honda hybrids did not work this way; at all speeds the ICE and battery shared the task of powering the vehicle. Toyota's hybrids therefore were called full hybrids, while Honda's were referred to as mild hybrids. To propel the hybrid by electricity alone, Toyota's hybrids had to have bigger battery packs than Honda's, but their gasoline engines were smaller and they relied on sophisticated software that shifted the vehicles from electric to gas in a way that minimized fuel

Table 5.2 *Market share of US-sold hybrid electric vehicles, 1999 to 2013, by manufacturer*

	Toyota Percentage	Honda Percentage	Ford Percentage	GM Percentage	Hyundai Percentage	Other Percentage
1999	–	100	–	–	–	–
2000	60	40	–	–	–	–
2001	77	23	–	–	–	–
2002	56	44	–	–	–	–
2003	52	48	–	–	–	–
2004	64	32	4	–	–	–
2005	70	21	9	–	–	–
2006	76	15	9	–	–	–
2007	79	10	10	1	–	–
2008	77	10	6	4	–	3
2009	67	12	12	6	–	3
2010	69	12	13	3	–	3
2011	67	12	10	2	–	9
2012	72	4	8	8	7	1
2013	67	4	15	5	7	2
15-year total	71	12	10	3	3	1

Compiled from US Energy Information Administration statistics

Table 5.3 *Sales of US hybrid electric vehicles by manufacturer, 1999 to 2013*

Company	Toyota	Honda	Ford	GM	Hyundai	All hybrids sold	Percentage of all vehicles sold
1999	–	17	–	–	–	17	0.000001
2000	5,562	3,788	–	–	–	9,350	0.0006
2001	15,556	4,726	–	–	–	20,282	0.0014
2002	20,119	15,916	–	–	–	36,035	0.0024
2003	24,600	23,000	–	–	–	47,600	0.0032
2004	53,991	27,215	2,993	–	–	84,199	0.0056
2005	146,560	43,356	19,795	–	–	209,711	0.014
2006	191,742	37,571	23,323	–	–	252,636	0.0177
2007	277,623	35,980	25,108	5,175	–	352,274	0.0255
2008	241,072	31,493	19,502	11,454	–	312,386	0.0237
2009	195,545	35,691	33,502	16,134	–	290,271	0.0279
2010	189,187	33,547	35,496	6,759	–	274,210	0.0237
2011	178,587	31,582	27,114	5,049	–	268,752	0.0211
2012	313,844	18,166	32,543	34,069	30,838	434,498	0.0301
2013	331,708	19,511	72,795	25,066	35,680	495,685	0.0319
Total	2,185,696	359,126	292,171	103,706	86,191	3,087,961	0.0145

Compiled from US Energy Information Administration statistics

Table 5.4 *The efficiency of hybrid electric vehicles: US Environmental Protection Agency 2014 ratings*

Manufacturer	Miles per gallon	Manufacturer	Miles per gallon
Toyota		*Honda*	
Prius	50–42	Civic & Insight	45–42
Camry	41–40	Accord & CR-Z	47–37
Lexus and Avalon	42–20	Acura	38–30
Highlander	28		
Ford		*General Motors*	
Fusion	42	Chey Malibu	29
C-Max	40	Chevy Impala	29
Lincoln	38	Buick LaCrosse	29
Escape	32	Buick Regal	29
Hyundai			
Sonata	37–38		
Kia Optima	37–38		

Compiled from US Environmental Protection Agency data

consumption. Ford licensed the technology from Toyota. With Chrysler, GM developed a full hybrid system of its own, but it had not installed it in the HEVs it sold. Ford's hybrids therefore got better gasoline mileage than GM's.

Hyundai's hybrids also were mild ones. The norm for hybrids prior to Hyundai's entering the market were nickel hydride batteries. Hyundai's HEVs were the first non-plug-ins to use lithium polymer batteries. These batteries were similar to those found in laptops and electric cars (see Chapters 1 and 4). However, the polymer used in the batteries' electrolyte allowed for thinner and lighter casings, which increased the HEV's cargo space and interior volume. These lithium polymer batteries delivered the same power with a quarter of the weight and 40 percent less volume than nickel hydride batteries. They were ten percent more efficient than nickel hydride batteries and also discharged more slowly, maintaining available power up to 1.7 times longer than the nickel hydride batteries. A question for Toyota was should it switch to lithium-ion batteries? Could it maintain its dominance in this segment without making this switch?

The Chevy Volt

For all intents and purposes GM had abandoned the HEV. It had tried to market mild versions of the technology in Tahoe, Sliverado, Yukon, Sierra, Cadillac, and Saturn models, but did not have much success. The best it did was sales of close to 5,000 Saturn Vue hybrids in 2007 (See Table 5.3). It had sales of close to 4,000 Chevy Silverado hybrids in 2008, but it never sold more than 5,000 of these cars in a single year. By 2013, GM had phased out of these models. The only hybrids it had left that were producing sales of any quantity were the Chevy Malibu and Buick hybrid assists, which together had sales of 25,000 car sales in 2013.

To compete with the popular Prius and the new Nissan Leaf, which was an all-electric vehicle (see Chapter 4), Chevrolet launched the Volt in 2010. As an extended-range vehicle the Volt ran on its battery until the charge dropped to a particular level and then the ICE kicked in to extend the vehicle's range. The Volt's regenerative braking also contributed to fuel efficiency. As rated by the US EPA, the Volt was the most fuel-efficient car that had a gasoline engine sold in the United States, quite an accomplishment for GM. With different styling the car was sold as the Vauxhall Ampera in the UK and the Opel Ampera in the rest of Europe. General Motors' vice-chair Robert Lutz had been the main developer behind the Volt. Inspired by the Tesla's Roadster (see Chapter 4) and lithium-ion battery progress, he initially proposed an all-electric vehicle, but Jon Lauckner, GM's vice-president for Global Vehicle Development, dissuaded him with the argument that the batteries would cost too much and that without enough public charging stations, buyers would be anxious about vehicle range.[10] For range extension, Lauckner suggested a smaller battery and a small ICE.

The concept

General Motors debuted a concept car at the 2007 North American International Auto Show that ultimately evolved into the Volt. It was the first time for a major automaker to showcase a plug-in hybrid. The design was vastly different from the electric car that GM had marketed in the 1990s to comply with California's pollution laws. That car had been a two-seater (see Chapter 4); it was cramped because of the need for space for its bulky lead-acid batteries. The car GM unveiled in

2007 was a family-size sedan that comfortably seated four passengers. The size of the battery pack was relatively small because of advances in lithium-ion technology. General Motors targeted 40 miles (64 km) of all-electric range, because research showed that 78 percent of daily US drivers did not travel any more than 40 miles (64 km) per day. Charging was to take place overnight at home. With a 12-gallon fuel tank, the vehicle had a potential driving range of 640 miles (1,030 km) (battery plus ICE).

General Motors planned to produce the car in the United States in a factory in Michigan. The car featured advanced plastics to reduce its weight. Being lighter meant that it was relatively fast. General Motors tried to standardize components so they could be used in future electrically propelled vehicles. General Motors found a partner for its battery in the South Korean firm LG Chemical, while Toyota relied on Panasonic for the Prius' nickel hydride battery. The US startup A123 Systems, a US battery firm that ultimately failed and was purchased by a Chinese company, had competed for the GM contract. General Motors did extensive battery testing that included 50,000 real-world miles and ten years of use under a variety of extreme weather conditions. The federal government assisted in the battery's development. General Motors obtained $106 million and LG Chemical $151.4 million in grants. The batteries were cooled and had a thermal management system to ensure even temperature distribution for maximum performance and durability. A 2009 Presidential Task Force on the future automobile in the United States, nonetheless, criticized GM for being "at least a generation behind Toyota."[11] General Motors was spending a significant amount of money to leapfrog Toyota, but it had not figured out how to reduce vehicle costs to be competitive.

The $7,500 federal government rebate, combined with GM's leasing offers, made the Volt relatively affordable, but the car still was expensive in comparison to its gasoline-powered peers. Only in comparison to other electric vehicles, such as those of Tesla and Nissan, was the Volt reasonably priced. Many buyers had to budget for an additional $2,000 as their homes needed electrical upgrades for the car to plug into 120 or 240 VAC (voltage alternating current) residential outlets. The ICE engine needed premium grade high-octane gasoline. Controversy arose about the Volt's payback period. It varied a great deal depending on the cost savings projected and different future gasoline prices. It also depended on how much a person drove.

After the Volt was introduced in 2010, it won numerous awards such as North American Car of the Year in 2011. In range-extended mode, for trips of 100 miles (161 km) and more, it had the lowest cost per mile of any car on US roads including the Prius and the Civic and Hyundai hybrids. Based on data collected through its OnStar system, General Motors reported that Volt owners drove 900 miles (1448 km) or a month and a half, between fill-ups.[12] The media, though, raised concerns about a battery pack fire following a National Highway Traffic Safety Administration (NHTSA) crash test. After investigation NHTSA concluded that no discernible defect could be found. The 2011 Volt obtained a five-star overall crash safety rating from the NHTSA and was named Top Safety Pick by the Insurance Institute for Highway Safety.

General Motors' dominance and its continued challenges

With the Chevy Volt and Cadillac ELR, which was also a plug-in hybrid electric vehicle (PHEV), GM was on the leading edge of this technology, selling more than 60,000 of these vehicles after they were first introduced (see Table 5.5). While batteries in HEVs were charged by the ICE's waste heat, PHEVs had an additional way to charge them. They could be connected to external power sources such outlets on walls or charging stations. Plug-in HEVs therefore could achieve roughly twice the energy efficiency as HEVs. General Motors was the first major auto company to offer a PHEV for sale and its PHEV technology outperformed that of Toyota, which also had a product in the PHEV market in terms of the EPA's combined miles per gallon (MPG) rating. Ford as well as Toyota had products in this market, but the GM models substantially outsold both companies' offerings.

General Motors admitted that it would lose money on the Volt, but not as much as $50,000 per vehicle as some claimed. Along with the Opel/Vauxhall Ampera models sold in Europe, GM's PHEVs had sales of about 70,000 units worldwide at of the end of 2013. Around 5,000 customers across Europe had reserved the right to buy an Amperas by the middle of 2011, with fleet or business customers representing 60 percent of these reservations. In 2011 Opel announced that the Ampera would be offered at a uniform price throughout Europe of $56,920 including the VAT (the sales tax). A total of 7,000 orders were received

Table 5.5 *Plug-in hybrid electric vehicles: sales, efficiency, and battery range by manufacturer, 2014*

Model	Launch	US sales (units)	EPA rated (miles per gallon)	Battery range (miles)
Chevrolet Volt	2010	63,167	98	35
Cadillac ELR	2013	396	82	35
General Motors, total sales		63,563		
Toyota Prius plug-in hybrid	2012	34,138	95	11
Toyota, total sales		34,138		
Ford C-Max Energi	2012	13,456	88	20
Ford Fusion Energi SEL	2013	12,324	88	20
Ford, total sales		25,780		
Honda Accord plug-in hybrid	2013	706	115	13
Porsche Panamera S e-hybrid	2013	567	50	16

Compiled from US Department of Energy and Environmental Protection Agency statistics

by the spring of the following year, with Benelux countries, Germany, and the UK being the top markets.

The Volt and Opel/Vauxhall Ampera models became the world's top-selling PHEV cars. Over half of the Volt's 2012 sales were in California, where the state government offered an additional tax rebate of $2,500 besides the one the federal government offered. On top of the economic incentives, in California the Volt was eligible for valuable high-occupancy vehicle lanes stickers. The projected resale value of a 2011 Volt was very good. It was about $17,000 after 36 months, the length of a typical lease. With the $7,500 federal tax credit, which effectively reduced the car's price to $33,500 the $17,000 resale value represented 51 percent of the Volt's original value.[13] In 2011 the Toyota Prius also had a projected resale value that was very good, 46 percent compared to its original value after 36 months

Although the Volt's 2011 to 2012 sales increase was substantial, it was less than GM executives wanted. General Motors overproduced the car in 2011 and 2012, and had to temporarily halt production in these years. The Volt was the world's best selling PHEV, but it was one of Chevy's lowest selling cars.[14] It declared that its investments in the Volt would pay off when the innovative technologies it had placed in the car were transferred to its other vehicles. General Motors also hoped the car would create a green image that could rival that of Prius. When operating in all-electric mode the Volt produced no tailpipe emissions. However, the clean air benefit was mostly local with both HEVs and PHEVs because, depending on the source of the electricity used to recharge the batteries, the air pollutant emissions shifted to the electricity generation site.

The Volt went on sale in China by late 2011 with prices starting at $78,000.[15] However, the Chinese government refused Chevrolet Volt owners access to $19,000 in government subsidies unless GM agreed to transfer intellectual property to a Chinese joint venture. The Chinese government wanted access to at least one of the car's three core technologies – the electric motor, electronic control, or power storage device. Because of high import duties and lack of subsidies, Volt sales in China were low. The projections were that alternative vehicles would constitute as much as ten percent of global sales by 2020 and China's appetite for this type of vehicle would expand, but was the effort to expand sales in China the type of initiative that GM could sustain given other challenges it confronted?

The question GM faced was how much more to invest in the PHEV given its weak financial position, safety recalls, and the liabilities resulting from these recalls. It still had to be concerned about other auto manufacturers dominating the PHEV space that it had pioneered. It did not want to let its lead slip as Honda had let its lead slip in HEVs. Yet, almost all of GM's profits came from building full body high-horsepower trucks and cars for US consumers. With a weak financial position and major recalls, to what extent did it make sense for it to invest in a technology whose main pay-off was likely to be long term? But if it did not make this investment would Toyota or some other auto manufacturer take control of the category?

A fuel-cell vehicle

The dilemmas Toyota and GM faced had to be examined in light of other options, one of which was fuel-cell vehicles (FCVs). In June of 2014, Toyota made the unexpected announcement that rather than move toward all-electric vehicles, it would rely on fuel-cell technology rather than ICEs as the power source for on-board hybrid electric motors. Fuel cells depended on oxygen from the air and hydrogen and from a vehicle's tailpipe. They emitted few pollutants other than water and heat. Producing hydrogen with methods available in 2014, however, was an energy-intensive process that involved the release of greenhouse gases from the burning of natural gas.

Ironically, in the past Toyota had not been a major supporter of FCVs. Its push into hybrids had been the major initiative it took. General Motors had been the major backer of FCVs not Toyota. In 2005, GM announced that it had invested more than a billion dollars in FCV technology and was looking forward to the launch of a fuel-cell model in 2010 called the Sequel.[16] General Motors' representatives then referred to hybrids as a poor solution to the fuel-economy problem because HEVs had the potential of reducing fuel use by just 25 percent, while FCVs were capable of 50 percent reductions.

General Motors was calling on the US government to help create a massive hydrogen filling station infrastructure. It continued testing FCV vehicles and, in 2013, it formed an alliance with Honda. Honda already sold the FCX Clarity fuel-cell sedan in limited numbers and was planning a new fuel-cell car, with a more powerful fuel cell. However, GM put off the timetable for introduction of FCVs into commercial use until 2020. Toyota was talking about a much more rapid introduction.

Embracing the fuel cell and facing objections

Toyota became a major FCV backer, while cash-strapped and recall-battered GM had less interest. Toyota, basing itself on its success with hybrids, was confident that drivers would want to embrace the hydrogen fuel-cell technology. The leader of Toyota's push into FCVs, was the same engineer, Satoshi Ogiso, who led the Prius project.[17] Ogiso was very optimistic that Toyota would succeed with this technology. He believed that Toyota was meeting the same type of skepticism that greeted its move into hybrids and would overcome this skepticism. Fuel-cell vehicles had become common in applications such as forklifts and buses. They were much greener than hybrids. It was only a matter time before they became a practical means of auto transportation.

The Toyota announcement that it was embracing fuel-cell technology was unanticipated because like other automakers it too had struggled to make fuel-cell technology affordable. Despite decades of research underwritten by industry and government the main obstacle, other than lack of fueling stations, was the vehicle's cost. Fuel-cell vehicles did enhance Toyota's green image. They would help the company meet the regulatory demands of California and other US states that were calling for zero or very low emission vehicles, but they were very expensive.

Toyota's early FCV designs shared many features with hybrids. The vehicle came equipped with nickel-metal hydride batteries along with the fuel cell. The fuel cells and the batteries powered the motor singly or in parallel. At low speeds the vehicle ran on battery power. At high speeds or accelerating from rest, the batteries and the fuel cell together supplied the power. The switching mechanism was the same technology Toyota placed in its other hybrids. With a fuel cell replacing an ICE the additional reduction of emissions could be more than 50 percent. The FCV also benefited from regenerative braking.

Nonetheless, it was a surprise that Toyota let its deal to obtain lithium-ion batteries from Tesla expire and implied that its main focus would be on FCV hybrids that used the older nickel-hydride technology. Toyota had acquired a substantial stake in Tesla. Its investment was $50 million and it was involved in a $100 million joint-development deal for a vehicle with a Tesla electric powertrain. Tesla was supposed to supply 2,500 of the powertrains to Toyota and Toyota had publicly suggested that the deal would be the start of much broader collaboration. Toyota, however, was dissatisfied with initial sales of its all-electric Rav4 sport utility vehicle. Despite a low-cost lease and loan it offered buyers, sales did not pick up. Instead, Toyota decided that it would sell a four-door FCV sedan priced at $70,000 – a car that it would introduce into Japanese and California markets in 2015, where they would face immediate competition from the Hyundai Tucson Fuel Cell SUV, the first mass-market fuel-cell vehicle.

Though Toyota's FCV would cost more than most hybrids, it would not be priced higher than most EVs. The advantage of FCVs was that, unlike EVs, they did not need a long recharge. The vehicle's power could be restored in a matter of minutes, but that depended on drivers being able to locate nearby refueling stations. To back up the sale of FCVs Toyota also would have to support a rapid build-up of refueling infrastructure. The Japanese government under Prime Minister Shinzo Abe buttressed Toyota's plan to move into FCVs as part of the government's plan for economic growth and promised to subsidize infrastructure creation and car sales.

Nonetheless, critics had many objections to FCVs. First, PHEVs' range was better than FCVs.[18] While the range of a typical FCV was about 300 miles (483 km), the 2014 Chevy Volt with a tank of gasoline and a charged battery had a much higher range. Second, because of the way the hydrogen fuel was created, almost 80 percent of the energy was lost in the conversion process. Third, while an electrical charge station might cost $15,000 to 60,000, FCV refueling stations cost more than $2 million a piece. There already were close to 1,800 public electric charging stations in California. Elsewhere in the United States there were more than 8,000. Fast chargers provided for an 80 percent re-charge in less than 25 minutes. Why should funding for EV infrastructure be in competition with funding for FCV infrastructure? What was the benefit of diverting funding to FCV refueling when hydrogen fuel costs were nearly the same as gasoline and electricity costs were half or a quarter as much of either of these options?

What next?

Given their options, what should Toyota and GM do next? With issues such as climate change, oil demand and supply, and various possibilities in front of them, how should they plan for the future? To what extent should their emphasis be on HEVs, PHEVs, FCVs, conventional ICEs, or EVs? To hedge their bets against an uncertain future, which combinations of investments in alternative vehicles should they make?

Note

1 See A. Marcus, *Strategic Foresight* (New York: Palgrave Macmillan, 2009).
2 "Number of private cars in China exceeds 70 million," *People's Daily Online* (2011): http://english.peopledaily.com.cn/90001/90776/90882/7446361.html
3 A. Marcus, *Controversial Issues in Energy Policy* (Newbury Park, CA: Sage, 1992).
4 M. Simmons, *Twilight in the Desert: the Coming Oil Shock and the World Economy* (Hoboken, NJ: Wiley, 2006).
5 See US Energy Information Administration, "Analysis and projections" www.eia.gov/analysis/projection-data.cfm

6 Marcus, *Strategic Foresight.*

7 See US Energy Information Administration, "Canada" www.eia.gov/countries/cab.cfm?fips=ca

8 See US Energy Information Administration, "How many alternative fuel and hybrid vehicles are there in the United States?" www.eia.gov/tools/faqs/faq.cfm?id=93&t=4

9 A. Marcus, *Business Strategy, Ethics, and the Global Economy* (Chicago, IL: Richard D. Irwin Publishing, 1996): pp. 421–31.

10 NBCNEWS.com "Detroit to unveil Volt electric concept car," (2007): www.nbcnews.com/id/16503845/ns/business-autos/t/gm-unveil-volt-electric-concept-car/#.VD19hvldV8E

11 J. Green and J. Hughes "BM's Volt Electric said still in plans after Obama orders cuts," *Bloomberg* (2009): www.bloomberg.com/apps/news?pid=newsarchive&sid=aCJOCuv6_jg8

12 J. Ross, "GM says Chevy Volt owners have logged over 100-million electric miles," *Autoblog* (2012): www.autoblog.com/2012/12/06/gm-says-chevy-volt-owners-have-logged-over-100-million-electric

13 C. Jensen "Toyota and Lexus are back on top in Kelley Blue Book Resale Value Survey," *The New York Times* (2011): http://wheels.blogs.nytimes.com/2011/11/16/toyota-and-lexus-are-back-on-top-in-kelley-blue-book-resale-value-survey/?ref=automobiles

14 M. Maynard, "Stunner: GM may be losing $50,000 on each Chevrolet Volt," *Forbes* (2012): www.forbes.com/sites/michelinemaynard/2012/09/10/stunner-gm-may-be-losing-50000-on-each-chevrolet-volt

15 K. Bradsher, "Hybrid in a trade squeeze," *The New York Times* (2011): www.nytimes.com/2011/09/06/business/global/gm-aims-the-volt-at-china-but-chinese-want-its-secrets.html?pagewanted=all

16 M. Hanlon, "GM builds the Sequel advanced hydrogen fuel-cell concept vehicle," *gizmag* (2006): www.gizmag.com/go/6072

17 S. Ogiso, "Toyota hybrid world tour," Toyota – USA Newsroom (2013): http://pressroom.toyota.com/releases/2013+thwt+ogiso.htm

18 "Hydrogen cars: the car of the perpetual future," *The Economist* (2008): www.economist.com/node/11999229

6 | Blowing in the wind: Vestas and General Electric

Headquartered in Aarhus, Denmark, Vestas Wind Systems began in 1945 as a steel technology company founded by Peder Hansen.[1] The company moved into household appliances, agricultural equipment, and hydraulic cranes before dedicating itself to wind turbines in 1979. Since 1989, its exclusive focus had been on wind turbines. After it merged with Danish wind turbine manufacturer, NEG Micon, in 2002 it became the world's largest manufacturer, seller, installer, and servicer of wind turbines.

The massive US conglomerate General Electric (GE) had a venerable history in electricity and electric lighting going back to Thomas Edison. Though it participated in many industries including oil, gas, nuclear power, aviation, health, transportation, and the media, under Jack Welch, CEO from 1981 to 2001, it evolved into one of the world's largest global lenders and a powerful financial services firm. Its wind power assets were acquired from Enron in 2002, during that company's bankruptcy proceedings. Without abandoning its ongoing commitments to fossil fuels, GE, under Welch's successor, Jeff Immelt, initiated a program christened "Ecoimagination" – devoted to renewable energy and other clean technologies. By 2009, GE had become the world's second largest wind-power company behind Vestas.

Was wind power, the industry in which the two companies competed, an attractive industry? How could they alter their strategies to more effectively take advantage of the opportunities it offered? In deciding what to do, they had to consider the industry's performance, substitutes to wind, their customers, new entrants to the industry, suppliers, and the competition between them and other industry players. In the short and long term what actions should they take? What strategies should they pursue?

The 2002 to 2014 growth of the global wind-power industry, though rapid, was unsteady (see Table 6.1). Revenue in 2003 expanded by 180.3 percent in comparison to 2002, but in 2003 it declined by

Table 6.1 *Wind power revenue global change, 2002 to 2014*

Year	Added revenue million $	Percentage growth
2002	905	0
2003	2,537.10	180.3
2004	1,222.90	− 51.8
2005	4,219.00	245
2006	5,336.10	26.5
2007	9,640.20	80.7
2008	14,404.00	49.4
2009	13,087.50	− 9.1
2010	7,785.60	− 40.5
2011	8,862.20	13.8
2012	15,198.30	71.5
2013	5,712.20	− 62.4
2014 (first six months)	10,231.00	79.1

Compiled from US Department of Energy statistics

51.8 percent in comparison to the previous year. In 2009 it went down by 9.1 percent, in 2010 it fell by 40.5 percent, and in 2013 it plummeted by 62.4 percent. The main reason for the 2013 plunge was that the US Congress failed to extend tax incentives. A drop of more than 90 percent in new US wind capacity installation pulled down global growth. However, in the first six months of 2014, demand for new wind-power installations rebounded and the industry was in the midst of its best year since 2008.

Vestas lost its historic lead in global wind market share to GE in 2012 (see Table 6.2), as GE took advantage of a robust US market to surpass Vestas, but with the collapse of the US market in 2013 Vestas again regained the top position and GE fell to sixth place among major wind companies. Though Vestas reacquired the lead in market share, the total 2013 market was a third less than it was in 2012. Vestas made massive changes to regain the lead. It closed 12 factories and laid off about a third of its workforce, including doing away with 3,000 jobs in Scandinavia in order to eliminate billions of dollars in debt and annual losses.

From 2008 and 2014, the stock price performance of both companies trailed the S&P 500 average by more than 50 percent. Vestas'

Table 6.2 *Wind power company global market share, 2010 to 2013*

Company	Country	2013 Market share percentage	2012 Market share percentage	2011 Market share percentage	2010 Market share percentage
Vestas	Denmark	13.20	14.00	12.70	14.80
Goldwind	China	10.30	6.00	8.70	9.50
Enercon	Germany	10.20	8.20	7.80	7.20
Siemens	Germany	8	9.50	6.30	5.90
Suzlon	India	6.30	7.40	7.60	6.90
General Electric	United States	4.90	15.50	7.70	9.60
Gamesa	Spain	4.60	6.10	8	6.00
Revenue, million $		5,712.20	15,198.30	8,862.20	7,785.60
Revenue growth, percentage		−62.40	71.50	13.80	−40.50

Compiled from US Department of Energy statistics

Table 6.3 *Vestas' and General Electric's financials compared, July 2014*

	Vestas	General Electric
Market value ($ billion)	9.27	254.9
Profit margin (percentage)	1.13	8.86
Operating margin (percentage)	5.73	11.54
Revenue ($ billion)	8.42	146.12
Quarterly revenue growth (percentage)	17.10	3.20
Net income ($ billion)	0.95	14.85
Total cash ($ billion)	1.47	10.50
Total debt ($ billion)	0.83	378.70

Compiled from publicly available quarterly report data of the two companies

stock market losses mounted from 2011 to 2013, but after that it made a come back. General Electric's margins were far better than Vestas', but Vestas' July 2014 quarterly revenue growth rate of 17.1 percent was far better than GE's 3.2 percent quarterly revenue growth rate (see Table 6.3). General Electric's large size and diversification gave it resources and options than Vestas did not have. As a conglomerate competing in many businesses, GE could leave the wind-power industry, while as a company solely devoted to wind Vestas did not have this option. These factors weighed heavily on Vestas' and GE's management as they decided what to do next.

Substitutes

Wind faced a host of substitutes. In 2014, the most formidable one was natural gas. Though the cost of wind power had declined by more than 80 percent since the 1990s it could not match the rapid drop in US natural gas prices. If wind was to compete with low-priced US natural gas, its costs had to fall even further.

The relative ranking of the costs of natural gas, wind, and other forms of power generation was hotly debated. Levelized energy cost (LEC) calculations compared the total 20- to 40-year lifetime costs of different ways of generating electricity.[2] These costs included those of the initial investment, operation and maintenance, fuel, and capital. Key assumptions had to be made about financing, deployment times, demand, and capacity. Regional differences existed that might be related to steam reservoir, hot water, dam and waterfall availability, fuel source distance, transportation costs, proximity to pipelines, wind intensity and speed, days of sunshine, and the land available for energy development. They also might have to do with people's tolerance for environmental and safety risks, the degree of public approval or disapproval for various technologies, and the ability of interest groups to mount campaigns for and against them. In each jurisdiction there were different government regulations and subsidies.

Levelized energy cost calculations were generic formulations that tried to accommodate such differences. Making many assumptions about conditions that might prevail in the future they smoothed them over, averaged them out, and combined differences. More an art than a science, they gave a rough sense of the relative costs of different forms of electricity generation at a particular point in time. As such, they were useful to decision makers. Governments and electric utilities commonly relied on them as a starting point in their assessments. Because of the uncertainties, LEC calculations might avoid a single best estimate of the costs of different ways of generating electricity, offering instead a sense for the range of possibilities with median, minimum, and maximum figures that gave decision makers the ability to evaluate a range of possibilities.

A study by the US Department of Energy (DOE) in 2012 showed that hydropower at the median was the least-cost alternative (see Table 6.4). The problem with hydropower was finding sufficient good sources for development. The next best option was combined-cycle natural gas followed by coal. The problem with the latter was the emissions, both conventional air pollutants that caused respiratory and health problems and greenhouse gas emissions that led to climate change. With several EPA regulations to go into effect in the United States, coal did not seem to be a promising alternative. The regulations included a proposed cross-state air pollution rule, a mercury and air toxics standard, the imposition of emissions costs for sulfur dioxide, nitrogen oxides, carbon dioxide, coal, and potential greenhouse gas regulation.

Next in order came onshore wind, followed by nuclear, geothermal, biomass, and integrated coal gasification. The problem with nuclear was the long lead times in permitting and construction, and public fears of the technology after the Chernobyl and Fukushima incidents.

Table 6.4 *Levelized energy costs for electric power production alternatives,*
2012

	Median ($/MWh)	Minimum ($/MWh)	Maximum ($/MWh)
Hydropower	20	20	120
Natural gas combined-cycle	50	10	70
Coal pulverized and scrubbed	50	10	120
Onshore wind	60	20	120
Nuclear	60	40	120
Geothermal	60	40	140
Biomass	70	10	170
Integrated coal gasification	80	60	180
Offshore wind	100	70	200
Solar thermal	200	60	300
Solar photovoltaic	280	150	590

Energy Information Administration, Annual Energy Outlook 2012. June 2012,
DOE/EIA-0383(2012)
MWh = megawatts per hour

The problem with geothermal was finding sufficient reservoirs that
could be practically developed (see Chapter 2). Geothermal projects
also were capital intensive and required long lead times. Investments
made in 2012 would not produce power for at least six years.

For all these reasons, onshore wind was projected to be less costly
than coal by 2020. These estimates led many decision makers to conclude that wind and combined-cycle coal were the best current alternatives. Wind facilities were relatively easy to construct and could be
flexibly added to existing generating capacity. In particular regions,
such as Texas and the eastern United States, they might be less expensive than coal or natural gas, but because the wind did not blow all
the time, back-up generation was required. If the back up was coal
or oil based, wind might yield more environmental damage than it
prevented.

Natural gas could be relied upon to take up the slack when the wind
was not blowing strongly. Natural gas and wind were good comple-
ments. Natural gas' capital and transmission costs were low and its
fuel costs were high, while winds' capital and transmission costs were
high and its fuel costs were low. But natural gas was not carbon free,

and therefore nuclear also had to be considered. Another carbon-free option was to construct a vast array of wind farms and solar generators throughout the world to assure that, so long as the wind or sun were available and transmission was in place, the need for storage would be limited. This plan to make the world's power supply more constant and dependable required the building of sufficient transmission to connect the widely dispersed sources. The building of transmission was both costly and controversial. Still another carbon-free option depended on making breakthroughs in storage technology, but such breakthroughs had been promised in the past and had not come to fruition (see Chapters 1 and 4). If different this time, then LEC estimates would have to be adjusted. The bottom line was the uncertainty that industry executives and government officials faced regarding the costs of alternative models of electrical power generation and the role that wind would play.

Subsidies

Government subsidies affected whether decision makers leaned toward or away from wind. All forms of energy were subsidized. An estimate of annual US subsidies to fossil fuel in 2014 was $37.5 billion.[3] The US federal government provided a six percent deduction from net income for businesses engaged in qualified fossil-fuel production activities. Small and independent producers had the right to resource-depletion allowances. All companies could write off drilling expenses in the year they were incurred rather than writing them off over time, and all companies involved in fossil fuels could obtain credits for the taxes they paid to foreign countries. Outside the United States, the estimated annual subsidies were $21 billion. None of the estimates took into account the military, climate, environmental, and health impacts of fossil fuel use.

Subsidies lowered producers' costs, increased profits, led to lower consumer costs, and were well entrenched. In 2014, politicians concerned about ballooning budget deficits tried cutting back on them in Malaysia, Indonesia, Egypt, and India but faced angry citizen pushback. In the United States a main controversy was the subsidies wind and other types of renewable energy obtained. The government had offered wind-power producers a tax credit of 2.2 cents per kilowatt-hour. There were calls to make wind power subsidy free.

Encouragement for wind and other renewables had a long history in the United States. Oil shocks and environmental concerns in the 1970s stirred the public's interest. Congress passed the 1978 Public Utility Regulatory Policies Act (PURPA), which mandated that utilities interconnect with renewable power facilities and buy the power at a price equivalent to the avoided costs. The 1992 Energy Policy Act provided a production tax credit (PTC) of 1.5 cents per kWh for renewable production, a credit that expired many times and was renewed for one- and two-year time periods. Drama over extension created boom-and-bust cycles in the wind-power industry, with a rush to finish projects prior to expiration and forced slowdowns thereafter. In 2003, prior to expiration, 1,687 new megawatts (MW) of wind had been installed, but in 2004 after expiration only 400 MW of wind-energy capacity was installed (see Table 6.1).[4]

The American Recovery and Reinvestment Act of 2009 (ARRA) extended the PTC at the rate of 2.2 cents per kWh for produced power and gave developers cash grants for property costs covering up to 30 percent of their capital investment. In 2012, with uncertainty raging about extension, developers added new wind-power generation capacity at a rapid rate. General Electric, whose main markets were in the United States, did particularly well. Opponents maintained that the cost of the subsidy – estimated to be $2 billion a year through 2022 – was far too high.[5] The PTC expired and was not extended in 2013, and the president of the American Energy Alliance, who represented oil, coal, and natural gas interests, called the decision a huge victory for taxpayers. Debt-ravaged Spain and the German government also reduced their subsidies to renewable energy.

Grappling with the winding down of US subsidies for wind power, Vestas warned that it would have to scale down operations and lay off more than half its 3,000 US workers. Uncertainty about the future had lowered demand for wind and substantially reduced industry revenues in 2013. However, in 2014 a loophole was found, an eligibility criteria adjustment that allowed projects that had commenced construction in 2013, and that continued construction until 2016, to remain eligible for ten years of tax credits. Unlike previous subsidies, these projects did not have to actually produce any power. They just had to be involved in the construction of wind-power capabilities. As a result in the first half of 2014 there again was growing demand for wind in the United States with anticipated revenue increases for companies such as Vestas and GE in the US market.

Customers

With these factors in the background, Vestas' and GE's executives had to decide on which parts of the global market they should concentrate (see Table 6.5). If focused on the United States, should they expect that favorable policies that had helped the industry in the past would continue to be in place? If focused on the rest of the world, which countries should they emphasize?

The United States

From 2009 to 2013, the five-year average annual growth rate for wind energy in the United States had been 19.5 percent.[6] During this period, wind provided 31 percent of all new US generation capacity. From 2011 to 2013, the states of Iowa, Minnesota, North and South Dakota made up more than 80 percent of all new US generating capacity. Wind's growth in the Pacific Northwest, Plains states, and Midwest was especially impressive, but what would happen next was uncertain because many of the best sites for wind generation in these regions had been taken. If the US economy stumbled, as it had in Europe, would wind-energy development in the US decline? Spokespersons for the industry called for steadier and more certain policies that would end industry boom-and-bust cycles and allow for more rapid resolution of transmission controversies.

Most US states had their own incentives and tax credits in place to promote wind energy. More than half of them also had renewable portfolio standards (RPS), which required utilities to produce a percentage of their electricity (depending on the state from 4 to 30 percent) from renewable sources within a particular timetable.[7] As long as utilities tried to meet these standards, the US wind industry had experienced growth, but by 2009 to 2010, most states already had commissioned enough renewable energy to meet the portfolio goals. Cutbacks in large capital investments also took place due to the lingering effects of the recession. In 2013, wind-power capacity growth in the United States came to a virtual standstill because of uncertainties related to the PTC, but the US market came back in 2014 because of the eligibility adjustment that allowed projects to qualify for tax credits. So long as the US wind market in 2014 was in recovery mode, Vestas rededicated itself to US manufacturing and hired hundreds of new workers in Colorado. To better compete with Vestas, Siemens also expanded its US workforce, but would the surge in US orders be permanent?

Table 6.5 *Megawatts of installed wind production capacity in 20 countries, 2003 to 2013*

Country	2013	2012	2011	2010	2009	2008	2007	2006	2005	2004	2003
China	91,324	75,324	62,364	41,800	25,104	12,210	5,912	2,599	1,266	764	567
US	61,108	60,007	46,919	40,200	35,159	25,170	16,819	11,603	9,149	6,725	6,370
Germany	34,660	31,308	29,060	27,190	25,777	23,903	22,247	20,621	18,428	16,629	14,609
Spain	22,959	22,796	21,673	20,623	19,149	16,740	15,145	11,630	10,028	8,263	6,202
India	20,150	18,421	15,880	13,065	10,926	9,587	7,850	6,270	4,430	3,000	2,110
UK	10,531	8,445	6,556	5,204	4,051	3,288	2,389	1,963	1,353	888	684
Italy	8,551	8,124	6,737	5,797	4,850	3,736	2,726	2,123	1,718	1,265	904
France	8,254	7,564	6,640	5,970	4,492	3,404	2,455	1,567	757	386	248
Canada	7,698	6,200	5,265	4,008	3,319	2,369	1,846	1,460	683	444	322
Denmark	4,772	4,162	3,927	3,749	3,465	3,160	3,125	3,136	3,128	3,124	3,110
Portugal	4,724	4,525	4,083	3,706	3,535	2,862	2,130	1,716	1,022	522	289
Sweden	4,470	3,745	2,798	2,163	1,560	1,067	831	571	509	452	404
Brazil	3,399	2,508	1,429	931	606	339	247	237	29	24	24
Poland	3,390	2,497	1,616	1,180	725	472	276	153	73	58	58
Australia	3,049	2,584	2,005	2,020	1,712	1,494	817	817	579	379	197
Turkey	2,959	2,312	1,799	1,329	801	333	207	65	20	21	21
Netherlands	2,693	2,391	2,328	2,269	2,229	2,225	1,747	1,559	1,224	1,078	908
Japan	2,661	2,614	2,501	2,304	2,056	1,880	1,528	1,309	1,040	896	506
Romania	2,599	1,905	826	462	14	8	8	3	1	1	1
Ireland	2,037	1,738	1,614	1,428	1,260	1,245	805	746	495	339	186
Total	320,526	284,696	239,035	196,570	159,921	123,255	95,966	76,181	61,068	49,666	41,336

Source: www.thewindpower.net/statistics.countries_en.php

It was uncertain what the main US buyers of wind-energy turbines – utility companies, independent power producers, and households – would do.[8] Independent power producers (IPPs) constituted an estimated 40 percent of the market but the line between them and utilities was blurred, because the IPPs generated energy that they typically sold to the utilities and other end users. Before starting a project they needed a guaranteed power purchase agreement (PPA) from utilities or these parties. Some companies were involved in both parts of the market. For example, NextEra Energy, the largest generator of wind power in the United States, was both an IPP and a major utility (Florida Power and Light). It was the largest US and global owner and operator of wind-project assets and the second largest US developer. Other large owners, operators, and developers of wind energy, such as Iberdrola (Spain) and MidAmerican Energy (Iowa), followed a similar model as wholesale power producers and utilities.

Among US utilities Xcel Energy, headquartered in Denver and covering territory in Colorado, Minnesota, Texas, and Wisconsin, had commissioned the most wind-power generation. MidAmerican Energy in Iowa, backed by Warren Buffet, came in second place, followed by Southern California Edison and Pacific Gas & Electric in California, and American Electric Power in Ohio. In 2013, 80 percent of US wind energy came from 12 states, with Texas being at the top of the list.[9] Among states, other big purchasers were California, Iowa, and Minnesota. Fifteen states had installed over 1,000 MW of wind capacity. Nonetheless, financing and electricity demand still were low because of the recession, which made future markets uncertain. The states confronted transmission congestion problems and the prevalence of cheap natural gas. Because of energy efficiency there was weak power demand, which resulted fewer PPAs.

Global

From 2003 through 2013, competitive pressures that existed among wind-power companies and technological advances resulted in steadily falling wind energy prices. Demand grew nearly everywhere in the world (see Table 6.6), but the direction in which the market was headed in 2014 and thereafter was unclear. Depending upon public policies and other factors in different parts of the world, different regions had different prospects. The prospects for the Chinese market seemed to be

Table 6.6 *Percentage megawatt growth in wind capacity in four continents, 1999 to 2013*

Year	North America percentage growth	South America percentage growth	Asia percentage growth	Europe percentage growth
1999	51.2	71	21.8	75.4
2000	1.6	11.8	29.4	40
2001	64.2	33.5	23.6	30.5
2002	10.6	− 1.5	16.1	34.7
2003	35.5	45.1	26.7	23.5
2004	7.4	13.9	46.4	20.9
2005	37.8	11.6	47.8	17.8
2006	33.1	227.5	51.9	18.7
2007	42.2	11.2	50.5	17.5
2008	47	33.8	54.3	15.5
2009	40	92.8	60.8	14.5
2010	15.6	41.7	49.6	13.3
2011	19	49.5	40.6	10.6
2012	27.2	64.4	19.7	13.7
2013	5.1	36.5	18.8	10.9

Compiled from data collected by the World Wind Energy Association: www.wwindea.org/home/index.php

high because of the massive pollution in that country's cities. In 2010, wind-energy industry revenue dropped in the United States, with China becoming the leader. However, by 2012, the Chinese market slumped because insufficient transmission had been built to link the power to users. The Indian market had promise, but because of contradictory policy signals it had not made much progress. Europe, on the other hand, faced retrenchment as it started to revise previously favorable renewable energy policies.

Globally, the International Energy Agency (IEA) forecast that the amount of electricity generated from wind would grow more than four-fold between 2009 and 2020, but whether this goal would be reached was uncertain.[10] New markets outside the developed nations had to be developed. In the absence of significant US and European growth, GE and Vestas looked to global markets to take up the slack. To better compete in China, for instance, GE formed a joint venture with

Table 6.7 *Global market share of top five Asian wind power firms, 2010 to 2012*

Country	Company	2012 percentage	2011 percentage	2010 percentage
India	Suzlon Group	7.4	7.6	6.9
China	Goldwind	6.0	8.7	9.5
China	Guodian United Power	4.7	7.4	4.2
China	Sinovel	3.2	9.0	11.1
China	Ming Yang	2.7	3.6	3.1
Total		24.0	36.3	34.8

Derived from data in "Renewables 2013: global status report": www.ren21.net/portals/0/documents/resources/gsr/2013/gsr2013_lowres.pdf

Chinese power-equipment company Harbin Electric Machinery. The two companies worked together to make onshore and offshore GE-designed turbines. General Electric had a minority stake in the venture, with 49 percent ownership. This partnership built on an existing GE–Harbin relationship to produce large gas turbines in China. It involved the sharing of blade, tower, and control technologies, with Harbin having a 49 percent stake in GE's Shenyang Wind factory and GE and Harbin planning to build a plant in Jiangsu for offshore turbines.

New entrants

The main new entrants to the wind-power industry were Asian firms. Five Chinese and one Indian company captured more than one third of the global market share in 2010 (see Table 6.7), but by 2012 their global market share had slipped to under a quarter. To enter the wind-power industry these Asian companies had to overcome many obstacles. They had to contend with companies such as Vestas and GE that had worldwide reputations and relationships. They needed significant capital to set up manufacturing facilities. Their entry into the market nonetheless ended up eliminating many European and North American competitors. There had been as many as 149 wind-turbine manufacturers in the world, but by 2014 just 101 remained (see Table 6.8). As the wind-power industry became a commodity business and low-cost

Table 6.8 *Global wind power firm attrition*

	Original number	No longer exists, or acquired	2014 number
Germany	30	16	14
Denmark	10	8	2
USA	16	8	8
Netherlands	10	4	6
France	9	3	6
Spain	7	3	4
Canada	3	2	1
India	16	2	14
United-Kingdom	1	1	0
Panama	1	1	0
China	18		18
South Korea	6		6
Italy	4		4
Norway	3		3
Argentina	2		2
Finland	2		2
Japan	2		2
Belgium	1		1
Brazil	1		1
Czech Republic	1		1
Egypt	1		1
Iran	1		1
New Zealand	1		1
South Africa	1		1
Switzerland	1		1
Turkey	1		1
	149	48	101

Derived from The Wind Power data: www.thewindpower.net/manuturb_manufacturers_en.php

competitors did away with the advantages European and North American companies had, consolidation took its toll. With competition for future business increasingly hinging on less than fully tapped global markets, the push to keep costs down was continuing.

Table 6.9 *Location of Chinese wind power generating capacity, 2012*

Province	Megawatts added	Cumulative megawatts
Inner Mongolia	1,647	20,270
Gansu	617	7,096
Shandong	1,290	6,981
Liaoning	640	6,758
Xinjiang	3,146	6,452
Heilongjiang	623	4,887
NingJiang	885	4,450
Shanxi	1,309	4,216
Shaanxi	583	1,293
Guizhou	683	1,190

Derived from 2012 China Wind Energy Outlook data: www.gwec.net/wp-content/uploads/2012/11/China-Outlook-2012-EN.pdf

Chinese firms benefited from their country's commitment to wind energy. The country installed more wind generating capacity than nuclear power and had ambitious plans to keep growing its wind generating capacity. The United States overtook Germany in 2008 to become the world's leader in megawatts of installed wind production capacity, but its leadership position was short lived as by 2010 China surpassed the United States. In 2013 China had installed one third more wind capacity than the United States and two thirds more capacity than Germany (see Table 6.5). Competition in the Chinese market was intense. Both Vestas and GE had to contend with domestic Chinese competitors. The Chinese firm Goldwind captured more than ten percent of the wind market globally in 2013, putting it in second place behind world market share leader Vestas (see Table 6.2).

Though the country had a large land mass and was very crowded it potentially could meet all of its electricity demand from wind by 2030. To overcome the problems of limited land and crowding, it located the bulk of its wind resources in distant provinces such as Inner Mongolia and Xinjiang (see Table 6.9). China's problem was in making this wind operational. These distant provinces were not close to population centers and China lacked sufficient transmission to move the electricity. A law passed by the National People's Congress required that Chinese utilities purchase the electricity, but China had not connected all its wind power to the grid. United States' wind farms yielded 40 percent more energy from the same capacity as China's wind farms because China's power sources were not well connected.[11] This problem led to an 18 percent drop in new wind-power construction in China in 2012.

So far neither Vestas nor GE had been very successful in cracking the Chinese market. Domestic firms, all relatively new to the market, installed about 80 percent of China's wind capacity in 2013.[12] Goldwind's market share was the largest in China. It had 23.3 percent, followed by Guodian United Power with 9.25 percent and Ming Yang with 7.9 percent. Other Chinese wind companies were Envision and XEMC with market shares of about 7 percent. Goldwind, the largest Chinese company, came into existence in 1998. It was strongly identified with Xinjiang province, an autonomous region in the country's northwest. In 2013, China's largest additions to its wind generating capacity were in this province, which was China's largest Chinese administrative division by land mass. Spanning over 1.6 million kilometers it had borders with Russia, Mongolia, Kazakhstan, Kyrgyzstan, Tajikistan, Afghanistan, Pakistan, and India. Only about five percent of the province was fit for human habitation and it was China's largest oil- and natural gas-producing region, home to diverse ethnic groups, and with a majority Muslim population.

In 2007, Guodian United Power restructured as a state-owned enterprise in Beijing. Previously it had been called Longwei Power Generation Technology Service Company. It had joint ventures with Westinghouse and Siemens. Part of one of the largest integrated power-generation corporations in China it engaged in the development, operation, and management of many generation assets other than wind. Its wind energy assets were scattered throughout the country.

The most troubled of the Chinese companies was Sinovel. Established in 2005 in Beijing, it became the largest Chinese turbine manufacturer but rapidly lost its leadership positon. In 2013 it ran afoul of a law in the United States for stealing trade secrets. Its Chairman Wang Yuan was forced to resign and the company also came under Chinese regulatory scrutiny for its accounting practices. Its profits were low and demand for its products started to decline. Sinovel moved toward specializing in offshore wind development, supplying turbines to Shanghai Donghai Bridge Wind Farm, Asia's first large offshore wind development. Unfortunately, China was having trouble meeting its offshore goals, offshore wind energy was not advancing as fast as the Chinese government hoped, and Sinovel was getting most of the blame.

Mingyang Wind Power, in contrast, was located in the southern Guangdong Province, China's most populous province, with more than 100 million people. This province had China's greatest concentration of industry. This company worked closely with German design firm Aerodyn Energiesysteme on its turbines. It had eight production facilities and service centers throughout China and sought to accelerate its business development both within China and overseas. In 2012, it formed an alliance with India's Reliance Group to co-develop clean energy projects in that country.

All of these companies were trying to improve the quality of their products so that they could compete globally not just on the basis of the price. Their weakness was that they were dependent on the growth of the Chinese market. If that market was not thriving, their future was not assured.

Suzlon, the Indian wind-power company, often outperformed Chinese companies in global competition. Suzlon's roots were in an experiment of its founder Tulsi Tantie who had owned textile properties. A factory he owned confronted rising power costs and poor power availability and in 1995 he set up a wind farm, an experience that gave his company the know-how to be involved in wind power. By 2014, his company had built nearly half of India's wind installations. Though located in the Pin Pune region of India, its reach was global. Employing over 10,000 people, it had a comprehensive product portfolio that involved manufacturing blades, generators, panels, towers, and building offshore turbines. The company had capabilities in project management, installation, operations, and maintenance services. It had R&D and technology centers in Germany, Denmark, and the Netherlands, and an international sales office in Aarhus, Denmark, where Vestas was located.

Suppliers

The supply chain for wind was complex. Needed was not only wind but land, access to transmission, skilled workers, and companies that supplied a variety of inputs and complementary services. A critical factor in the amount of energy a wind farm was able to generate was how regularly and how steadily the winds blew. Sites able to achieve

50 percent or more capacity factors due to strong and ceaseless winds were rare. More common were capacity factors of 25 to 50 percent. Weather and wind-speed models that were created prior to construction were not always correct. What was considered a productive site during the planning stages might turn out not to be one during operation – lowering an asset owner's revenue and profits.

As time passed, most of the best sites for wind in the United States and Europe had been identified. Newer sites with less strong and ceaseless wind had to be exploited. United States' average wind-power projects built in 2011 were located in areas with wind conditions 16 percent less productive than prior projects. However, more power might be generated at these sites than at older sites because of improvements in technology. The site's wind generating capacity might be lower, but the new technology better captured the wind's energy than old technology. The issue was that new technology was likely to cost more than old technology and prices had to reflect the use of this technology.

Another important factor was the site had to be close to transmission to absorb the energy. If far from transmission, a site's value was diminished. Obtaining access to productive sites close to transmission was not easy. In exchange for access, landowners might charge very high rental income. Farmers might insist on the right to grow crops and graze cattle and thereby interfere in some ways with the turbines. Developers also often encountered non-financial problems at productive sites because of citizen opposition. Citizens might not like the noise, or they claimed that their views were impaired, or birds and other animals were endangered. Developers had to overcome these protests and zoning issues.

If a generating source was close to existing transmission lines and no upgrades were needed, the costs of a project would be lower, but linking projects to the transmission lines was a challenge. Requests by wind-energy developers for permission to interconnect might be delayed or denied, which added to project costs. The US electric transmission grid was aging rapidly and the existing infrastructure suffered from congestion and overuse. A high percentage of promising wind resources were located in remote areas where new transmission investment was needed but often was not feasible. In creating new transmission, NIMBYism ("not in my backyard") posed just one of the many challenges. Another point of contention was who paid for connection costs – the wires, poles, and transformers – was it the wind energy developer or the user of the energy?

Staff and vendor inputs

After land, developers needed skilled staff (see Table 6.10). Workers in the wind-power supply chain were involved in many different trades including:

- aluminum
- circuit boards and electronic components
- engines and turbines
- iron and steel
- semiconductors
- steel framing, rolling, and drawing
- electric power transmission
- electrical equipment manufacturing

Shortages often existed for jobs that required the highest levels of experience and responsibility. In the United States, wages consisted of about 17 percent of the costs of a wind-power development.[13] They grew by about ten percent annually in the years 2009 to 2014 – largely because of shortages in high-level skills.

Because of rapid industry growth, many kinds of workers were in demand. As in the case in other sectors, Indian and Chinese firms had an advantage over US companies as the wages they paid were lower. This advantage, however, was offset by high shipping costs. Transporting large and heavy turbines with blades larger than a huge commercial jetliner's wingspan and towers as high as a football field across oceans was expensive, complicated, and rarely feasible. Thus there were good reasons to locate wind manufacturing near the locations where the turbines were installed. As the European market faded and the US market became more active, Vestas shut down factories and laid off workers in Europe and hired workers and built factories in US locations where the demand for wind energy was growing. General Electric had an advantage in the United States because most of its workers and facilities were located near sites where wind was installed. A reason for its strong grip on the US market was this proximity.

Though hard to pin down, estimates had been made that as many as 100,000 people were employed in the wind-power and associated

Table 6.10 *Wind power jobs*

Field of activity	Job
Manufacturing and assembly	Highly qualified chemical, electrical, mechanical & materials engineers dealing with R&D issues, product design, management, and quality control of production process.
	Semi-skilled and non-skilled workers for the production chains.
	Health and safety experts.
	Technical staff for the O&M and repair of the wind turbines.
	Other supporting staff (including administrative, sales managers, marketing, and accounting).
Management	Project managers (engineers, economists) to coordinate the process.
	Environmental engineers and other specialists to analyze the environmental impacts of wind farms.
	Programmers and meteorologists for wind-energy forecasts and prediction models.
	Lawyers and economists to deal with the legal and financial aspects of project development.
	Supporting staff (administrative, sales managers, marketing, and accounting).
Construction inspection, maintenance, and repair	Technical staff for operations, maintenance, and repair.
	Electrical and civil engineers for the coordination of construction works.
	Health and safety experts.
	Specialists in the transport of heavy goods.
	Electricians.
	Staff specialized in wind-turbine installation, including activities in cranes, fitters, and nacelles.
	Semi-skilled and non-skilled workers for the construction process.
	Other supporting staff (including administrative, sales managers, and accounting).

Table 6.10 (*cont.*)

Field of activity	Job
Operations and sales	Electrical, environmental, and civil engineers for the management of plants.
	Technical staff for the O&M of plants, if this task is not subcontracted.
	Health and safety experts.
	Financiers, sales, and marketing staff to deal with the sale of electricity.
	Other supporting staff (including administrative and accounting).
Other specialized activities	Programmers and meteorologists for the analysis of wind regimes and output forecasts.
	Engineers specialized in aerodynamics, computational fluid dynamics, and other R&D areas.
	Environmental engineers.
	Energy policy experts.
	Experts in social surveys, training, and communication.
	Financiers and economists.
	Lawyers specialized in energy and environmental matters.
	Marketing personnel, event organizers.

Adapted from Bureau of Labor Statistics, Measuring Green Jobs: www.bls.gov/green/home.htm

industries in the United States. When Vestas set up factories in the United States it promoted their job creation. States and localities competed for the factories because Vestas promised to hire workers who left jobs in hard-hit manufacturing industries. To better compete with GE, Vestas spent one billion dollar building six factories in Colorado. The argument for extending PTC, which Vestas made to US lawmakers, was the need to maintain and create jobs. Vestas threatened that the job losses would be substantial if the government did not extend the subsidy. In 2013, it cut 2,300 jobs globally or ten percent of its workforce, including 500 jobs in the United States. It cautioned that it would have to lay off another 1,600 workers if there was a slowdown in US orders. General Electric also issued notices of potential job losses. There were estimates that because of the 2013 slowdown in orders, manufacturers of turbines and other components would have to shed as many as 10,000 workers. General Electric noted that 35,000 US workers might lose their jobs if Congress did not extend the PTC.

About 500 US manufacturing firms spread over 40 states made the 8,000 or so components needed by the industry.[14] Of these, over 60 were dedicated suppliers. As US-based capabilities rose, the import fraction of wind power products went down from over 70 percent in 2006 to 2007 to less than 30 percent in 2012. Purchases from the supply chain represented the wind industry's largest cost.[15] Total cost of purchases increased as the price of components, especially those containing steel, rose in the 2009 to 2012 period. Previously companies such as Vestas and GE had absorbed the price increases for components such as steel in order to grow. They wanted to keep their prices down and maintain their market share. Because of uncertainty about the costs of steel, they started to use less expensive composite materials. Vestas made its wind turbine blades from high-strength lightweight carbon fiber supplied by a company called Zoltek, and GE obtained similar material from a company called TPI.

With orders down, GE had little choice but to cut back on its supply-chain commitments. It admitted that some makers of the gearboxes, towers, and blades that it used would not survive. It scored them on their efficiency, quality, price, and the strength of their balance sheets, and maintained that it would only do business with the best of them. From its remaining vendors, a core of about 200, it captured better terms because of how it had graded them.

Offshore capabilities

The growing scarcity of land with high potential for wind forced developers to take seriously more expensive offshore wind installations. The offshore movement began in Europe where the number of locations with good wind speeds and turbines close to transmission had nearly been exhausted. Throughout Europe, in countries such as France, Germany, the UK, and Denmark, where renewable energy remained a priority, targets were set to boost offshore development. Despite higher initial and operating costs, offshore wind farms might make economic sense because offshore wind tended to be stronger and steadier than it was onshore. The economic viability of offshore wind still had to be proven, however. The cost gap relative to onshore wind was substantial. If offshore wind could achieve grid parity was not certain. Because parity was far off, the US Department of Energy did not expect offshore wind to make a significant contribution to power generation in the United States until 2030.[16]

Both Vestas and GE had been slow in developing the capabilities they needed to participate in offshore development. The turbines had to be larger and stronger, and the transmission and interconnection was more complicated, and other barriers existed. Siemens in alliance with the Chinese companies Goldwind and Shanghai Electric had the lead. Sinovel also was a major player, but it had mixed success. Vestas created a joint venture for offshore wind turbines with Mitsubishi Industries, while GE was in the midst of purchasing Alstom's energy businesses, with Alstom's onshore weakness being matched by offshore strengths that GE did not possess.

Seeking the economic development and associated jobs, advocates for offshore wind fought the advocates for onshore wind to obtain benefits from governments. The US Department of Energy Advanced Technology Demonstration Project initiative recognized the need for innovative offshore technology to lower costs and gave awards to more than a half dozen projects. Out of its efforts came the first offshore wind turbine in the United States, which was deployed in 2013 by the University of Maine. Twelve other offshore projects covering all the US coasts, including the Great Lakes, were in the works. Cape Wind was the first offshore wind project in the United States to be granted the right to use federal waters. It gained that right in 2011, after nearly ten years of a highly contentious permitting process, where the Alliance to Protect Nantucket Sound vigorously fought the project.

Competitors and next steps

Competition in the industry was high as firms such as Vestas and GE competed with each other on turbine price, quality, and service. Large turbines used to power utility-scale commercial and industrial projects constituted about 70 percent of the market.[17] Mid-scale turbines and small-scale wind turbines that powered homes and small businesses were about 30 percent.

A turbine's nameplate capacity was an important part of the competition. It represented the turbine's maximum potential energy output.

If the turbine operated at or near full capacity it commanded a higher price and yielded more profit. Firms that could provide turbines that were more efficient and had longer product life usually also were able to gain competitive advantage. Project management, maintenance, and support service skills also played a role. Almost all firms in the industry, including Vestas and GE, offered services in product procurement, construction, and support. They had to help their client gain access to the best quality wind, secure good land, deal with transmission issues, control labor costs, and manage vendor relations.

Besides Vestas and GE, the two German companies Siemens and Enercom as well as the Spanish firm Gamesa were well-regarded industry players with long histories. The global market share of Siemens and Gamesa had been slipping, but that of Enercom had been growing because it won projects in Brazil and was doing increasingly well in North America. Siemens was a latecomer to US markets but it did a fair amount of business with MidAmerican Energy, the Iowa utility majority owned by Warren Buffett's Berkshire Hathaway. Technologically Siemens was advanced. It introduced a bolted-steel maintenance-free design that reduced tall tower costs. The bent-steel plate shells and other parts could be delivered to project sites by standard size trucks for onsite assembly. The broad base increased stability. Gamesa had been in the wind turbine business since 1994. It had installed turbines in more than 35 countries and in 2014 employed over 6,000 people.

The original players in the industry were from Europe and the United States but the industry now had a high level of globalization and the older players in the industry had to contend with vigorous Asian rivals. European and US markets were saturated. They could level off or decline while markets in Asia and other parts of the world might take off. No matter where they were based, all companies established facilities overseas and expected foreign-based companies to establish facilities in their home countries.

Vestas

As Vestas struggled to cope with these changes, it suffered from management shake-ups and large layoffs. It took aggressive measures to minimize costs, but was known mostly for high quality, with the best intellectual property in the industry and more patents than any other firm. Vestas' turbine designs were the industry's best. The innovations on which it worked involved greater height, more aerodynamic and bigger blades, variable pitches, gearbox improvements, and better coatings – innovations that would reduce the price per megawatt of generating electricity and increase availability and turbine-capacity factors.

The technology of wind turbines had dramatically improved. Whereas a wind turbine of the early 1990s might have had a 20 to 25 percent capacity factor, a turbine in 2014 might have a 40 percent capacity factor in reasonably good wind and up to 50 percent capacity in the best wind conditions.[18] Vestas turbines lost less than two percent of the unharvested wind passing through them. They regularly outperformed in the industry in terms of overall efficacy. There were questions whether they could do any better. The industry had become commoditized, with low-cost bids typically winning contracts. Vestas took the high-quality route and refused to participate in bidding processes if prices were too low and its operating costs were too high for it to make a profit. Its profits already had fallen because of declining demand and workforce restructuring. To obtain new business, Vestas was trying to deliver solutions for low-wind speed sites in China. Other initiatives that it was taking included its first dedicated offshore product.

While Vestas' turbine business was barely profitable – it usually posted operating losses or low operating profits – its service business was quite profitable, often achieving operating profits levels of 16 percent or more. As more wind turbines were installed, the company could evolve in this direction. In a sign that it was focusing more on service, it announced that it could render this function to non-Vestas turbines. A path it could take was to concentrate on service delivery, remove itself from the low-cost turbine business, and focus on high-cost turbines, but this strategy was not likely to support its more than 20,000 global workforce.

General Electric

A reason for GE being one of the world's most admired companies in the 1990s had been the performance of GE Capital but, in 2014, revenue growth and profits were falling in this part of its business while they were trending higher in the non-financial industrial sector. In light of the global financial collapse of 2008, GE had been trying to shift from finance and back to its core industrial businesses. In 2014, the company was in the midst of downsizing GE Capital and spinning off its credit card, lending, leasing, and real estate assets, while it acquired most of Alstom's energy assets including Alstom's TGV train offering. In that year, GE's Oil and Gas division was doing especially well. Its Power & Water division, of which GE Energy was a part, was performing adequately, but GE's wind revenues had dropped substantially, a decline that could lead GE in two directions. On the one hand, it could try to achieve innovations in wind that might alter the rules of the game and revitalize this business. On the other hand, it could de-emphasize wind in comparison to its other energy initiatives and gradually sell off or rededicate its wind assets.

In support of the first option, GE was working on a truss-structured, fabric-covered turbine blade that could be shipped in containers and assembled economically onsite even as the blades continued to get bigger. Using these blades with taller towers would enable GE to deliver more power production at a lower cost. The three-dimensional tower had struts that locked together and was able to bear heavy burdens with limited material and support. The 120-meter tower used 20 to 30 percent less steel than older 100-meter towers, because the broad base needed less support. General Electric housed advanced power electronics and battery storage inside the tower's base, which protected them from weather and vandalism. Concrete could substitute for steel if the project was near a concrete source, thus lowering costs even more. To pursue this project GE had an ARPA-E grant from the US Department of Energy.

In another initiative, GE was to get more involved in managing the variability that renewable sources introduced into electrical-power systems. Integrating renewables with gas-fired power continued to be a challenge. Vestas and Siemens as well were using sensors to obtain better automated control of a turbine's multiple computer systems. With the use of sensors, remote operators could wirelessly manage variables such as erratic wind and grid changes that automated systems were unable to entirely control. Full application might be able to cut the cost of integrating wind into the grid by as much as 30 percent, which at a 100-megawatt project translated into savings of as much as a half billion dollars per year. A key element was efforts to find ways to better assimilate and use weather data and to improve turbine performance at lower wind speeds in recognition of the fact that the sites with the best wind speeds had been taken.

Rather than upping its stakes in wind, GE could decide to exit the field. It could concentrate instead on the more profitable segments of its power business, particularly gas turbines, gas engines, and the network needed to support them. It could expand its support for the oil and gas industry, rather than become further involved in wind energy.[19] If wind was not attractive, there was less reason to stick with it. Unlike Vestas, GE had the option to leave.

Unconventional fracked gas and shale oil offered GE many opportunities, some of which it already was exploring. It could build off the base of partnerships it had formed with major industry players such as Chesapeake Energy. It also could help in opening the market for fracking and shale oil in parts of the world like China. General Electric could become more active in converting the gas feedstock into fertilizers, chemicals, plastics, and a wide range of other products. It could assist in making natural compressed natural gas (CNG) and liquefied natural gas (LNG) transportation more accessible. The purpose of these initiatives would be to establish the key linkages that would further expand and integrate a global natural-gas network.

General Electric was committed to making the gas system more intelligent by adding new digital and software technologies. It also could work on mitigating environmental concerns and meeting the many protective regulations that existed and were expected as fracking became more common. It was not just natural gas that offered GE unique business opportunities. The company might get further involved in the oil industry. It could apply its expertise to drilling rigs, pressure pumping, water sand, chemical handling and processing, and drill pipes. It could assist in making continuous improvements in these areas to lower their costs, increase their productivity, and boost sustainability. General Electric had the capabilities to operate in these areas. Unlike Vestas, it did not have to be a major player in wind.

Finally, GE could look elsewhere in the domain of alternative energy. It already had announced that it was trying to making fundamental advances in fuel cells (see Chapter 5). It could proceed further with this type of work. Fuel cells relied on chemical reactions that involved hydrogen molecules and oxygen to produce energy. The attractiveness was the abundance of these chemicals in nature. Yet commercial viability had eluded fuel-cell efforts. General Electric had made progress with the solid oxide fuel cell, increasing overall efficiency by 95 percent when it configured the system to capture the waste heat produced by the process.[20] The GE fuel cell used stainless steel rather than rare platinum metals. The fuel-cell generated electricity anywhere there was a supply of natural gas. It was an important advance upon which the company could move forward.

Rather than continue to exploit wind technology, GE could search for game changers in a wide variety of different areas. As a large diversified company, this option was open to it, but it was not an option open to Vestas.

Next steps

As the market for wind continued to evolve the two companies had to decide what they were going to do next. In what ways should they change their commitments to wind?

- How should they handle the politics of subsidies?
- Which parts of the world provided the best opportunities?
- To what extent should they consider partnerships with new entrants and old industry players?
- Should offshore be a direction in which they continued to turn?
- Where should they focus their R&D and in which parts of the industry should they be involved?
- Should it be in service of some kind rather than building and installing new turbines, but what kind of service business was the most viable?

Notes

1 See T. Steenburgh and E. Corsi, *Vestas' World of Wind* (Boston, MA: Harvard Business School, 2011).
2 See *Lazard's Levelized Cost of Energy Analysis – Version 8.0* (New York: Lazard, 2014).
3 Oil Change International, "Fossil fuel subsidies: overview," (2014): http://priceofoil.org/fossil-fuel-subsidies
4 See US Department of Energy – Energy Efficiency & Renewable Energy, *2012 Market Report on Wind Technologies in Distributed Applications* (2013): p. 62.
5 American Energy Alliance, "Thanks to big wind the hidden cost of wind energy may get even more expensive," (2013): http://american energyalliance.org

6 American Wind Energy Association "US wind energy market reports for 2013," (2013): www.awea.org/Resources/Content.aspx? ItemNumber=875&navItemNumber=621

7 See DSIRESOLAR, "Database of State Incentives for Renewables & Efficiency: Current RPS Data," (2014): www.dsireusa.org/rpsdata/index.cfm

8 See L. Isokowitz, "High winds: a strengthening US Economy and demand for electricity will benefit the industry," *IBISWorld Industry Report 22111d*, Wind Power in the US (2014).

9 See Earth Policy Institute, "Data highlights" (2013): www.earth-policy.org/data_highlights/2013/highlights37

10 International Energy Agency, *World Energy Outlook 2010* (Paris, France: International Energy Agency, 2010).

11 M. Davidson, "Transforming China's grid: integrating wind energy before it blows away," *The Energy Collective* (2013): http://theenergy collective.com/michael-davidson/259871/transforming-china-s-grid-inte grating-wind-energy-it-blows-away

12 "Goldwind dominates in China – CWEA," *Recharge* (2014): www .rechargenews.com/wind/asia_australia/article1358574.ece

13 See Isokowitz, "High winds."

14 *Ibid.*

15 *Ibid.*

16 See US Department of Energy: Energy Efficiency & Renewable Energy, *20% Wind Energy by 2030: Increasing Wind Energy's Contribution to US Electricity Supply* (Oak Ridge, TN: US Department of Energy, 2008); and Navigant, *Offshore Wind Market and Economic Analysis: Annual Market Assessment* (Burlington, MA: Navigant Consulting, 2013).

17 See Isokowitz, "High winds."

18 Z. Shahan, "Wind turbine net capacity factor: 50% the new Normal?" *Clean Technica* (2012): http://cleantechnica.com/2012/07/27/wind-turbine-net-capacity-factor-50-the-new-normal

19 P. Evans and M. Farina, *The Age of Gas and the Power of Networks* (Fairfield, CT: General Electric, 2013).

20 "The new power generation: this fuel cell startup could spark a revolution," *GE Reports* (2014): www.gereports.com/post/92454271755/the-new-power-generation-this-fuel-cell-startup-could

PART IV

Finding customers

7 | Carrying that weight: General Mills and Kellogg's

Companies such as General Mills and Kellogg's had to decide to what extent they would treat healthy foods as a threat or an opportunity. To what extent should they shift their portfolio of products in this direction? Both companies had many brands. They competed vigorously for the world's leading market share in ready-to-eat cereals. General Mills had yogurts (Yoplait), soups (Progresso), flour and cake mixes (Gold Medal and Betty Crocker), snack foods (Chex Mix, Fiber One, and Gardetto's), and vegetables (Green Giant). Kellogg's had snacks such as Pringles and Cheez-It, cookies such as Keebler, Famous Amos, Hydrox, and Mothers, and breakfast foods including Eggo Waffles and Pop-Tarts. Both companies also had nature bars. General Mills' sold them under the Nature Valley and Larabar labels, while Kellogg's sold them under Nutri-Grain and Bear Naked labels. Kellogg's had meat and egg substitutes such as MorningStar Farms, Natural Touch, Gardenburger, and Worthington.

Both companies purchased firms whose main mission was to provide healthy options. General Mills bought Cascadian Farm and Kellogg's bought Kashi. Cascadian Farm, in the mountains of the state of Washington, and Kashi, mainly located in the suburbs of San Diego, were far from the Midwest headquarters of General Mills in Minneapolis and Kellogg's in Battle Creek, Michigan. They operated separately and independently of the two food companies that had acquired them.

Consumer tastes seemed to be shifting toward foods that were promoted as healthier options. For instance, consumers increasingly wanted high-protein, low-carbohydrate "foods on the go." General Mills and Kellogg's for years had been trying to meet consumers' demand for more convenience, but had been slow to recognize the consumer preference for added protein. To what extent should General Mills and Kellogg's add to or subtract from their existing holdings, increasing or decreasing the degree to which they appealed to consumers looking for healthy alternatives?

Table 7.1 *Hunger and overnutrition: the twin problems in 2010*

Undernutrition	Overnutrition
About 104 million children in the world were underweight.	About 1.5 billion people were overweight, of whom 500 million were obese.
Undernutrition contributed to about one third of all childhood deaths.	About 43 million children under age five were overweight.
Stunting, an indicator of chronic undernutrition, thwarted the development of 171 million children.	Growing rates of maternal overweight were leading to higher risks of complications in pregnancy and obesity in children.
13 million children were born with low birth weight or prematurely due to maternal undernutrition.	At least 2.6 million people died each year from being overweight or obese.

Adapted from G. Gardner and B. Halweil, *Underfed and Overfed: The Global Epidemic of Malnutrition* (Washington, DC: Worldwatch Institute, 2000): www.worldwatch.org/nearly-two-billion-people-worldwide-now-overweight

Hunger and obesity: twin nutritional problems

In 2000, Worldwatch Institute, a Washington, DC-based think tank, announced that for the first time in human history, the number of overweight people was about equal to the number of underweight people.[1] Since 1980, the world's underfed population had declined to roughly 1.1 billion, while the number of overweight people had increased to about 1.1 billion. Both groups had high levels of sickness and disability, curtailed life expectancies, and low productivity levels. Both suffered from a lack of the essential nutrients and dietary elements a person needed for healthy living.

From 2000 to 2010 the number of overweight people had grown to 1.5 billion (see Table 7.1). Obesity's public health impact made up more than half of the world's disease burden. Overnutrition and obesity were linked to cancer, heart disease, and diabetes. These twin nutritional problems demanded attention from an already overly stretched global health care system.

As developing countries continued to struggle with malnutrition, developed nations had to cope with an obesity epidemic. In the developing world, there were more than 100 million underweight children in 2010, nearly one in three. In Africa, the number of underweight children was rising. Hunger and inadequate nutrition resulted in the early deaths for infants and their impaired physical and mental development. In the United States, on the other hand, more than half of the adults were overweight, and about a quarter of the population was obese. Among children, more than 20 percent were overweight. Because of obesity, liposuction was the most common form of cosmetic surgery among adults – with 400,000 operations per year.[2]

Excessive eating was beginning to make rapid inroads in the developing world. The population of overweight people in developing nations had expanded rapidly, more than counterbalancing declines in hunger.[3] Consider South Africa, a country where 60 percent of women and 25 percent of school children were overweight, yet 20 percent of all children suffered from malnutrition. In developing countries, overnutrition was growing rapidly in urban areas. In some countries the poor were gaining weight faster than the rich. Still battling infectious diseases, health care systems in developing nations were likely to be overwhelmed by a growth in diseases such as heart disease and diabetes. Organizations in the United States, such as the American Heart Association, spread awareness about the link between obesity and heart disease, diabetes, and cancer, but who was spreading this awareness in countries such as Guatemala, India, and South Africa?

The main opportunity for General Mills' and Kellogg's' growth might lie in the developing nations. If they chose to expand further in developing nations, how should they do so? Should they stay away from the types of foods that had been associated with obesity in developed nations? Should they try to limit their sales to options that were considered healthy? Or should they provide consumers the world over with choice, and allow consumers to pick the types of food they wanted to eat?

Economic and social performance

The economic performance of General Mills and Kellogg's was driving the push for them to expand abroad. Neither company's performance in recent years had been stellar. In US and European markets they both suffered from declining demand for most of their products. Moreover, globally they both competed with the Swiss behemoth Nestlé, a company that was much larger and had greater reach than either of them. Unable to establish a presence for its cereals by itself in overseas markets, General Mills had formed a partnership with Nestlé. Nestlé's 2010 to 2014 stock market performance slightly topped that of

Table 7.2 *The financials of General Mills, Kellogg's, and Nestlé,
August 2014*

	General Mills	Kellogg's	Nestlé
Market value ($ billion)	32.60	23.22	245.90
Employees	43,000	30,277	333,000
Quarterly revenue growth (percentage)	−0.03	−0.01	−0.05
Revenue ($ billion)	17.91	14.64	99.42
Gross margin	0.36	0.44	0.48
Operating margin	0.16	0.22	0.15
Net income ($ billion)	1.82	1.84	10.51

Compiled from publicly available quarterly report data of the companies

General Mills and these two firms performed at a level about the
same as the S&P 500 average. The stock of Kellogg's was in positive
territory, but its performance significantly lagged that of Nestlé and
General Mills.

Given that both General Mills and Kellogg's had to confront the
much larger Nestlé, were they competitive at their current sizes (see
Table 7.2)?

General Mills and Kellogg's also competed with Pepsi in cereals
(Quaker) and snack foods, and Pepsi employed more than 275,000
workers globally and 150,000 in the United States. Pepsi generated
about $65 billion in revenue in comparison to about $18 billion for
General Mills and $15 billion for Kellogg's (see Chapter 8). One advan-
tage that Kellogg's had was that it was more profitable than General
Mills (see the gross and operating margins in Table 7.2) but the stock
market had not rewarded it because the stock market was more interested in its growth than its profits. Where were the world's food giants
going to find sources of new revenue?

The ready-to-eat cereal industry in which General Mills and Kellogg's competed was mature and declining. It had experienced little
growth and had been in the process of consolidating for many years.
From 2000 to 2013, the ready-to-eat cereal business saw nine years
of industry-wide decline in revenue in comparison to only five years
of growth (see Table 7.3).[4] The industry-wide $11 billion in revenue
in 2013 was 20 percent lower than the industry-wide $13.7 billion

Table 7.3 *Revenue changes in the ready-to-eat cereal industry, 2000 to 2013*

Year	Revenue $ million	Growth percentage
2000	13,729.4	0.0
2001	13,149.3	−4.2
2002	11,486.2	−12.7
2003	13,213.7	15.0
2004	13,763.6	4.2
2005	12,035.0	−12.6
2006	10,877.9	−9.6
2007	11,080.2	1.9
2008	11,853.4	7.0
2009	12,217.9	3.1
2010	11,307.5	−7.5
2011	11,059.5	−2.2
2012	10,957.7	−0.9
2013	10,956.6	0.0

IBISWorld "Cereal Production in the US," Industry Report 31123 (2014).

in revenue in 2000. Among General Mills' many divisions, its cereal segment was its worst performing segment in 2013. This segment's revenue was off by $70 million in comparison to the previous year.

Food industry consolidation had allowed General Mills to acquire Pillsbury from Diageo in 2000 and Kellogg's to acquire Pringles from Procter and Gamble in 2012. Without Pillsbury's added revenue of about six billion dollars and Pringle's added revenue of about 1.5 billion dollars, General Mills and Kellogg's would have been much smaller companies. July 2014 quarterly results for General Mills and Kellogg's were disappointing. Falling behind consensus estimates, General Mills' revenue dropped 3 percent and its share price fell by 3.7 percent. North American sales of Kellogg's were down 3.7 percent and its share price fell by 6 percent. Neither company ranked that well on environmental, social, and governance indicators (see Table 7.4). General Mills was third among the top-seven food companies in the United States and Kellogg's was sixth. Would improvement in this area have a positive effect on the two firms' bottom lines?

Table 7.4 *Environmental, social, and governance scores for US food companies*

	Total score	Greenhouse gas emissions (million metric tons)	Energy consumption (trillion Btus)	Total water use (millions of gallons)	Total waste (1 = high intensity, 0 = low intensity)	Investments in operational sustainability
Campbell	48	769	3	24,820	0	$16 million
Con Agra	48	1924	6	49,697	1	No data
General Mills	42	1011	3	16,200	0	No data
Hershey	36	326	No data	6,473	0	No data
Smucker	26	No data	No data	No data	No data	No data
Kellogg's	26	No data	No data	No data	No data	No data
Kraft	19	No data	No data	No data	No data	No data

	Women employed percentage	Women managers percentage	Women on board percentage	Community spending	Independent directors percentage
Campbell	45	36	33	$52.6 million	93
Con Agra	40	30	18	$41.3 million	91
General Mills	No data	No data	31	$153 million	92
Hershey	No data	20	9	$9.4 million	91
Smucker	No data	No data	23	No data	62
Kellogg's	No data	No data	27	$61 million	82
Kraft	No data	No data	27	No data	82

Adapted from Bloomberg Professional Finance and ESG Platform July 2014

Industry conditions

Though the combined market share of General Mills and Kellogg's in ready-to-eat cereals held steady at more than 60 percent, there were other important players in the industry. Between them Quaker (acquired by Pepsi in 2001; see Chapter 8) and Post (a unit of Kraft) had a combined market share of close to 18 percent in 2014.[5] To capitalize on consumer shifts to natural, healthy products, Quaker and Post both had brands that contended in this niche. Quaker's brands in the niche were slimmer than Post's and included Quaker Oats, Chewy Granola Bars, and Mother's Natural Foods, while Post, whose historic brands were Grape Nuts, Raisin Bran, and Honey Bunches of Oats, acquired Attune Foods, a manufacturer of premium natural organic cereals and snacks under the labels of Uncle Sam, Erehwon, and Peace Cereal in 2012, and in 2013 added the assets of the Hearthside Food Solutions and Premier Nutrition, which sold protein shakes and nutritional supplements. After many years of declining revenue Post's US sales grew by more than six percent in 2011.

During the recession, US consumers turned to inexpensive generic cereal alternatives, such as Malt-O-Meal and Gilster-Mary Lee. MOM Brands (formerly called Malt-O-Meal) controlled about five percent of the US ready-to-eat cereal market in 2014.[6] Its knock-offs of major company brands (Crispy Rice, Honey Buzzers, Toasty O's, Tootsie Fruities, Toasted Cinnamon Twists, Honey Graham Squares, etc.), sold under its own and private store labels, did exceptionally well during the recession and immediately after it. Its success was related to the cereals' minimal packaging and a low marketing budget that allowed MOM Brands to keep its prices affordable. Another generic producer, Gilster-Mary Lee, had generics that mimicked major company brands such as Corn Flakes, Honey Frosted Flakes, Toasted Oats, Fruit Whirls, Cinnamon Oats, and Krispy Krunch. It was Walmart's store brand main supplier and it had about four percent of the US ready-to-eat cereal market.

Cereal companies not only faced high levels of competition from generics. They confronted a host of breakfast substitutes – fruit, eggs/omelets, bread, pancake/waffles/French toast, bacon, yogurt, real or veggie sausage, and bagels – that also increased in popularity after the recession. Consumers, who started to eat more in restaurants when the recession was over and their incomes rose, did not return to the

packaged cereal brands of General Mills and Kellogg's. Both companies engaged in heavy marketing to differentiate their products, but
neither staged a comeback. General Mills and Kellogg's assumed that
the only way they could counter the threats they faced was to do
more marketing, an old industry formula for combating low growth.
When these companies faced limited opportunities for growth, they
differentiated their brands more to make them stand out based on
minor innovations. The marketing budget of both General Mills and
Kellogg's picked up in the years from 2009 to 2014. It accounted for
about seven percent of their revenues in 2014.[7]

Relying on a host of marketing techniques including television and
social media ads, in-store banners and signs, and website, General
Mills and Kellogg's engaged in aggressive marketing of their products.
To attract and maintain the attention of children, they advertised pre-
sweetened cereals with colorful cartoon characters and flashy designs.
For adults, the message was somewhat different. More health related, it
tended to emphasize a cereal's nutritional qualities such as high fiber,
low fat, and reduced cholesterol. When this message did not work,
the cereal companies resorted to the same methods they used with
children.

The main customer of both firms was Walmart (see Chapter 9).
Walmart put unrelenting pressure on them to contain costs and made
it difficult for them to maintain decent margins. To pay for increased
advertising, both companies wanted to raise prices but Walmart limited how high their prices could go. General Mills sold more than 30
percent of its merchandise to Walmart and Kellogg's sold more that 20
percent of its merchandise to Walmart. The prices of key raw materials
such as flour, corn, wheat, and sugar were subject to volatility despite
supply contracts to facilitate production planning. Both companies
had serious long-term cost reduction programs. Kellogg's closed many
factories and announced lay-offs of 2,000 workers over four years to
bolster its US profits and deal with lagging demand.

To compensate for declining US sales, both companies looked to
overseas' markets. From 2012 to 2013, General Mills' global sales
expanded from $4.2 million to $5.2 million, while its domestic revenues grew hardly at all. In the same period, Kellogg's grew its overseas
business in such regions as Latin America by 5.5 percent and Asia by
3.0 percent, while its US morning foods' segment declined in revenue

by about 2 percent and its US snacks segment declined in revenue by nearly 3 percent. To grow abroad, both companies looked to acquire foreign companies. For example, one of General Mills' biggest acquisitions was a 2012 deal for Brazilian food maker Yoki Alimentos that had a strong share of that country's salty snack market. A big part of the global expansion plans of Kellogg's involved Pringles. Both companies found the snack market abroad promising and there were major opportunities in snacks in Latin America and Asia (see Chapter 8).

Emerging markets were an important opportunity for mature companies such as General Mills and Kellogg's to accelerate revenue growth that had stagnated because domestic markets were saturated. General Mills generated $6.6 billion of its sales outside the United States in 2014. Its global sales amounted to 35 percent of its total sales, with $2.2 billion of the sales in Europe, $1.2 billion in Canada, and $1 billion dollars of sales in both Latin America and Asia. The growth in its overseas business since 2009 had been a very important part of its strategy. Increasing Latin American and Asian urbanization abroad meant a higher percentage of women entering the workforce, which companies like General Mills and Kellogg's reasoned would drive up demand for convenience foods such as cereals and snacks.

Both General Mills and Kellogg's were trying to pick up the pace of their growth in Latin America and Asia. But if they were going to expand overseas how were they going to do it? To what extent should they follow, adjust, or abandon business models that had brought them success in the United States?

Sugar, salt, and fat

The past business models that General Mills and Kellogg's used to grow their US sales had led them to many controversies, but perhaps the bitterest and the longest standing of these controversies concerned the ingredients they used in foods that they sold. Ironically, the late 1800s founder of Kellogg's, the medical doctor, John Harvey Kellogg, had been a health-food fanatic. In an attempt to wean US eaters off fat-filled bacon-rich breakfasts he created the world's first ready-to-eat cereals.[8] Moving back to Battle Creek, Michigan from the east coast, where he had a medical practice, he opened a spa where guests cleansed themselves by indulging in a pure food and exercise regimen. John Harvey Kellogg looked down on sugar, considering it a major cause of health problems, abhorred salt, disliked fat, and tried to limit or prevent intake of them. His invention, Corn Flakes originally had no sugar, salt, or fat in it. His brother Will, in a contested case that went to court many times, took the Corn Flakes' recipe from John and made the original product more appealing by adding sugar.

General Mills' earliest wheat-based (Wheaties) products were different from Kellogg's corn-based ones. Post, the originator of the coffee substitute Postum, also moved into cereals with the barley-based Grape Nuts. A perennial laggard behind Kellogg's and General Mills, to catch up Post made the bold move in 1949 of introducing sugar-coated cereals such as Sugar Crisps, Crinkles, and Corn-Fetti. Not to be outdone, Kellogg's and General Mills also introduced sugar-coated brands such as Sugar Crisp, Corn Pops, Frosted Flakes, and Sugar Smacks. Immensely popular with the baby boom generation, these brands were a major reason for the cereal manufacturers' post-war success.

Before Harvard nutrition professor Jean Mayer shook up the industry in 1969, the only objection to sugar-coated brands was tooth decay. No one expected Mayer to associate cereals so directly with obesity, which he presciently called the disease of a civilization.[9] In a column running in newspapers throughout the country, he asked if the popular sugar-coated cereals General Mills, Kellogg's, and Post sold were really candy and not food. The industry's reaction was to play down the role of sugar in its advertising, but it made few changes in how it formulated its products until the beginning of the twenty-first century when the obesity epidemic reached larger proportions.

As Michael Moss related in his bestselling book, *Salt, Sugar, and Fat*, at an industry conclave of the CEOs of all the major food companies in Minneapolis in 1999, Michael Mudd, at the time a vice-president for global corporate affairs at Kraft, made a 114-slide presentation that called upon the industry to do far more to deal with obesity.[10] He warned of obesity's health effects, listing the following as consequences – diabetes, heart disease, hypertension, gall bladder disease, osteoarthritis, breast, colon, and uterus cancer. He told the assembled executives that the media blamed them for the problem. Playing a short take from the PBS *Frontline* documentary called "Fat," he showed another Harvard professor, not Mayer, condemning the industry for its excessive use of sugar, salt, and fat.

Mudd noted that the food industry had lost the support of the American Heart Association and the Cancer Society. He cautioned that the Center for Disease Control and Prevention and the Department of Agriculture also were beginning to turn against the industry. His plan of action was for the food industry to rely on the expertise of its scientists to create foods without excessive amounts of these ingredients. He proposed that the industry encourage the role of exercise and police itself lest it be over-regulated by government.

Moss's account of what occurred next was based on the recollections of three participants at the meeting.[11] No written account exists. According to these participants, Stephen Sanger, then General Mills CEO, squashed any backing Mudd might have generated for his ideas with the comment that the typical consumer did not want food that was healthy. Sanger opined that the consumer wanted food that tasted good and the industry had acted responsibly by providing a wide variety of choices. Why should it change if consumers liked its products as they were? Why should it abandon practices and business models that had taken so long to perfect? The industry had weathered storms in the past – an example Sanger gave was trans-fat – and this storm too would blow over.

In an email to Moss that Moss included his book, Sanger claimed he did not recall the meeting, but the testimony of participants was inconsistent with General Mills' and his own longstanding commitment to good nutrition. In the email he maintained that as CEO improving nutrition was a consistent high priority as shown by introduction of whole grains, fiber, and nutrients, and reduction of fat, salt, sugar, and calories, corporate nutritional objectives and metrics, reformulated light products, and advertising nutritional improvements to consumers. However, he maintained that consumers were only responsive if taste was maintained.[12]

A spokesperson for General Mills, Tom Forsythe, revealed to Moss that company efforts to make good tasting low-sugar cereals were hit and miss until a 2007 technological breakthrough that permitted a 14 percent across the board reduction in sugar.[13] Forsythe as well was convinced that it was not possible to sell healthy products that did not also taste good.

Changes at General Mills and Kellogg's

In 2007, General Mills promised that the highest amount of sugar in its products advertised to children under twelve would be 12 grams per serving or less.[14] Products with more than 12 grams of sugar such as Count Chocula, no longer would be advertised. In 2010, the company went further and promised to lower the amount of sugar in cereals for children to ten grams per serving. In 2007, Kellogg's announced that by the end of 2008 it no longer would advertise its products to children under age 12 unless the products met the company standards per serving of less than 200 calories, less than 2 grams of saturated fat, 0 grams of trans-fat, less than 230 milligrams of sodium, and less than 12 grams of sugar. Kellogg's also announced new nutrient labels that it would put on the front of its cereal boxes.[15] After these announcements, the company reformulated many of its original recipes, including those for Fruit Loops, Apples Jacks, and Corn Pops. It reduced the sugar content by one to three grams and added fiber to many cereals. General Mills under the Fiber One brand also sold fiber-added products in categories from yogurt to pancakes. Critics, however, pointed out that high fructose corn (HFC) syrup was replacing sugar and it was found in many cereals.[16] Many cereals contained HFC including Frosted Rice Krispies, Apple Cinnamon Cheerios, and others. Numerous health experts warned that HFC was as bad as sugar. It also was associated with diabetes and heart disease, and increased the body's triglyceride and cholesterol levels and blood pressure.

General Mills and Kellogg's made other plans to fight obesity. In 2009, both affirmed their commitment to help people achieve a healthy weight. They joined together with retailers, non-governmental organizations, and other food and beverage manufacturers in the Healthy Weight Commitment Foundation (HWCF).[17] The purpose of the foundation was to conduct a national, multi-year campaign to reduce obesity – especially among children. The foundation promoted healthy weight through a balance of fewer calories and increased physical activity. At a news conference to publicize its launch, the chief executive of Kellogg's, David Mackay, announced a $20 million contribution to encourage food makers to reconsider the way they sold their products.

The foundations of the two companies also were participants in anti-obesity campaign. In collaboration with the Academy of Nutrition and

Dietetics Foundation, the General Mills Foundation awarded Champions for Healthy Kids grants. Organizations such as Boys & Girls Clubs obtained grants of up to $50,000 to continue their program to improve nutrition and physical fitness among youth. The W. K. Kellogg Foundation funded researchers to study obesity and supported magazines that published the researchers' work.

Efforts such as the HWCF and these foundations, however, were criticized because their theme was personal responsibility. Critics maintained that by emphasizing personal responsibility manufacturers like General Mills and Kellogg's could avoid accountability for making junk food so appealing.[18] The food industry spent billions of dollars to develop products and packaged, advertised, and marketed them to entice people to buy. Bombarded with commercials for unhealthy foods that contained too much salt, fat, and sugar, most people relented. They did not have enough will power for personal responsibility. The critics argued that companies enticed people to buy nutritionally empty products and in exchange donated to better eating and exercise campaigns whose results were hard to measure.

Some progress

Public interest groups acknowledged that that the cereal makers had made some progress but they contested its significance. The concern of the Yale Rudd Center for Food Policy and Obesity was advertising sweet-coated cereals to impressionable young children on prime television and other media.[19] Its 2012 report argued that the cereal companies made but little progress in reformulating their products. The report analyzed 47 children's brands and found that cereals marketed to children had 85 percent more sugar, 65 percent less fiber, and 60 percent more sodium than those marketed to adults. It estimated that the average sugar content of cereals marketed to children had dropped just 2 grams, from 14 grams to 12 grams per serving, a decrease equivalent to about a half a teaspoon of sugar. The top cereal brands marketed to children still had about the same amount of sugar as in donuts. The cereal companies' main advertising target, moreover, was African-American and Latino children who had disproportionately high obesity rates.

The biggest offender, according to the Yale Center, was General Mills.[20] Six of the ten cereals with the worst combined nutrition and marketing scores were General Mills' products, while three were from Kellogg's and one was from Post. General Mills was responsible for about 60 percent of the cereal ads aimed at children, the most children-targeted advertising of any cereal company. The products it advertised most extensively to children (Cinnamon Toast Crunch, Honey Nut Cheerios, Lucky Charms, Cocoa Puffs, and Trix) were significantly less nutritious than other cereals it sold. This report also criticized General Mills for being among the most vociferous opponents of a Federal Trade Commission's voluntary proposed marketing principles.

A General Mills' spokesperson responded to the report by asserting that cereal was one of the healthiest breakfast choices a person could make.[21] Ready-to-eat cereals had fewer calories and less fat and cholesterol than most breakfast options and therefore the company was part of the solution not the problem. If the problem was obesity, then cereal should be advertised more and not less to children because frequent cereal eaters, including those who ate sweet cereals, had healthier body weights according to a US Department of Health and Human Service study that the General Mills spokesperson cited. The General Mills' spokesperson pointed out that people who ate a breakfast of any kind consumed less fat and more fiber.[22] Children who ate breakfast had better focus in school and people who consumed whole-grain cereals had healthier body weights. However, critics maintained that these people did not have to eat cereals like Lucky Charms or Chocolate Cheerios to get these results. They also maintained that the serving size on cereal labels was very misleading. For instance, Cheerios only had 100 calories per serving – but most children ate two to three cups of cereal at a sitting, which meant that their actual caloric and sugar intake was much higher than the caloric and sugar intake printed on the label.

A joint 2013 paper by employees of General Mills, Kellogg's, and the US Department of Agriculture in the academic journal *Procedia Food Science* documented progress the cereal companies allegedly had made.[23] Calculating the mean 2005 to 2011 sugar, salt, and fiber values for ready-to-eat breakfast cereals they found the sugar levels had decreased by 7.6 percent, but not the 14 percent that General Mills had maintained. Salt levels had fallen by 11.2 percent and fiber levels increased by 13.4 percent. These researchers maintained

Table 7.5 *Healthiest and unhealthiest breakfast cereals*

General Mills	Kellogg's	Post
Winners (5)	Winners (2)	Winners (2)
Cheerios	Ali-Bran	Shredded Wheat
Fiber One	GoLean Cereal (Kashi)	Grape Nuts
Wheaties	Losers (11)	Losers (4)
Total	Honey Smacks	Oreo O's
Wheat Chex	Corn Pops	Cocoa Pebbles
Losers (8)	Apple Jacks	Fruity Pebbles
Franken Bern	Eggo Cereal Maple Syrup	Waffle Crisp
Trix	Smorz	In-between (3)
Basic 4	Froot Loops	
Count Chocula	Cocoa Puffs	
Reese's Puffs	Mini-Swirlz Cinnamon Bun	
Cookie Crisp	Frosted Krispies	
Golden Grahams	Frosted Flakes	
Lucky Charms	Rice Krispies Treats Cereal	
In-between (9)	In-between (8)	

Adapted from ACalorieCounter ratings: www.acaloriecounter.com/breakfast-cereal.php

that these trends were positive and would have a significant effect on public health. Indeed, in 2014, new federal data showed a 43 percent decline in obesity rates among children age two to five over the prior decade.

The website ACalorieCounter also carried out a systematic comparison. It examined the websites of 51 breakfast cereals. Of these 51 cereals, 9 were viewed as winners – that is they had positive nutritional content – and 23 were viewed as losers – that is they had negative nutritional content (see Table 7.5).[24] The criteria applied to the winners were they contained no trans- or saturated fats, little or no sugar, and higher levels of fiber, protein, and whole grains, while the criteria applied to the losers were that they contained trans-fats and had ten or more grams of sugar not coming from fruit. Five General Mills' products were included among the winners, one product from Kellogg's, one Kashi product, and two Post products. Eight General Mills' products were included among the losers, eleven Kellogg's products, and four Post products. None of these companies were offering more healthy cereals than unhealthy ones. The choices they provided were tipped in favor of unhealthy categories.

Continued marketing controversies

General Mills and Kellogg's faced continuous controversies about marketing claims. On the one hand, the two companies stood to benefit from the health halo effect. When a label claimed that a product was low sugar, low fat, or low cholesterol, consumers felt smart when they bought the product. They thought that they had done something good for themselves. However, the foundation of the health claims on which they made their decisions often was contested. For example, consumer advocates wanted to know if General Mills could support the contention on the Cheerios box that the product was clinically proven to help reduce cholesterol.

To support this claim General Mills referred to a study on the effects of whole-grain oats on cholesterol reduction. The high concentration of fiber in whole-grain oats helped to lower cholesterol. It also had seven B vitamins, vitamin E, nine minerals, including iron and calcium, and twice the amount protein that was in wheat or corn. However, the oats in Cheerios were not whole grain. They were made of whole oat flour. It was impossible to shape whole grains into tiny cereal rings. Cheerios also were enriched with modified corn starch, sugar, salt, trisodium phosphate, calcium carbonate, monoglycerides, and wheat starch. Health specialists asked were the effects of Cheerios on a person's health the same as the effects of whole grains? Was General Mills being fully honest in its claim of health benefits?

Kellogg's

General Mills never had been sued for this claim. Kellogg's, on the other hand, had been sued often for the claims it made about its products. In 2009, it alleged that Mini-Wheats were clinically shown to improve children's attentiveness by 11 percent. When the court case was over, the company had to pay $4 million in compensation to the plaintiffs in a class-action suit.[25] In 2010, Kellogg's again was sued for unreliable representation. In this instance, it had to do with its Nutri-Grain energy bars.[26] An advertisement featured salads, water, and healthy people exercising, suggesting that a Nutri-Grain yogurt bar contributed to health, good looks, and wellness. The slogan, "eat better all day" that appeared in the commercial referred to the calcium and whole grains in the bar, but the bar also had trans-fats, which caused diabetes and heart disease. Kellogg's maintained that the suit had no merit but the US District Court of Southern California found for the plaintiffs.

Again, in 2012, Kellogg's had an issue with how it represented its products. The Advertising Standards Authority (ASA) censured it for making the website claim that sugar was not related to obesity or ill health.[27] Kellogg's tried to answer critics by publishing information on the Coco Pops' site that was meant to tell children the truth about sugar. The company stated that a panel of world health experts reviewed all the scientific evidence and concluded that high sugar intake is not related to obesity or the development of diseases such as heart disease, diabetes, high blood pressure, or cancer. Nor was high sugar content connected to behavioral problems, such as hyperactivity. The ASA accepted Kellogg's summary of the study as credible but concluded that the company overstated the certainty of the scientific conclusions and forced Kellogg's to change the website's wording.

In 2012 Kellogg's agreed to drop the terms "all natural" and "nothing artificial" from its Kashi products as part of a class-action lawsuit.[28] Philip and Gayle Tauber had founded Kashi as a breakfast food firm that produced nutritionally balanced products that relied on whole grains and seeds in 1984. The company name was a combination of kosher and Kushi. The Kushis were a Japanese couple that brought macrobiotics to America. Kellogg's purchased Kashi in 2000 and operated it independently. In April 2012, a grocer in Rhode Island discovered that Kashi used genetically engineered and non-organic ingredients. When he removed the products from the store he posted pictures on his website and sent out notifications to social networks. Kellogg's also donated $790,000 to the campaign against California's Proposition 37, which asked if voters wanted foods containing genetically modified (GM) organisms to be labeled.

Customers did not like Kashi's use of the word "natural." The Food and Drug Administration (FDA) did not regulate use of the term and had not opposed its use of the term so long as a food did not contain added color, artificial flavors, or synthetic substances. Plaintiffs that brought the suit in California in 2011 against Kashi argued that its products contained unnatural ingredients such as pyridoxine hydrochloride, calcium pantothenate, and soy oil processed using hexane, a component of gasoline. Though such ingredients did occur naturally, the food companies relied on synthetic versions. Kashi's sales, which had started to decline before the controversy, fell even more. Consumer disaffection was a result of a number of factors. They lost faith in the company because it was not being wholly transparent. They also lost faith because they believed they were buying from a small company when, in fact, Kashi was part of a large multinational enterprise. Kashi responded by trying to move in the direction of removing all GM ingredients from its products (see Chapter 9). However, with only one percent of US cropland dedicated to organic crops and 70 percent of all foods sold in the United States having some GM ingredients making such a transition would be very difficult.

General Mills

General Mills ran afoul of consumers for its formulation of Greek yogurt.[29] Traditional Greek-yogurt makers Chobani and Fage thickened the yogurt by straining it. Yoplait thickened it by adding milk protein concentrate. Consumers became aware of the difference because of a campaign by Chobani and its founder, Hamdi Ulukaya. Greek yogurt rose from 2 percent of the overall US yogurt market in 2007 to 43 percent in 2013. Chobani was the segment leader with over one billion dollars in revenue in the US yogurt market. Yoplait's market share topped out and started to slip. The overall US yogurt market was worth $6.1 billion in 2013 and Yoplait had lost its leadership position in this market to Dannon. General Mills' failure to be completely honest with consumers about how its Greek yogurt differed from traditional yogurt hurt sales. When the company reformulated its Greek yogurt its market share for both Greek and general yogurt again grew.

General Mills also tried to dispel consumer concerns about GM ingredients in its cereals.[30] In 2014, it announced it was making Cheerios free of this content. The change only affected original Cheerios. It did not affect any of the other varieties such as Honey Nut Cheerios. General Mills chose Cheerios because the main ingredient was oats, a crop not grown from GM seeds, so making the change just meant finding new sources for the cornstarch and sugar that were in Cheerios. General Mills revealed that because of the high hurdles it would be unable to make Honey Nut Cheerios and other varieties without relying on GM inputs.

In 2014, a class-action suit maintained that General Mills' fruit snacks misled consumers into believing that they were healthy and nutritious.[31] The plaintiffs attacked Fruit Roll-ups, Fruit Gushers, and Fruit by the Foot for being filled with trans-fat, sugar, and food dye. They criticized the products for not having significant amounts of real fruit. Their complaint maintained that calling the products fruit was misleading because they were not substantively different from candy. In a motion to dismiss the suit General Mills tried to counter these arguments by asserting that the labels of fruit-flavored snacks did not affirm that the products were healthful. Other than a claim about vitamin C and low levels of fat, General Mills admitted on the label that the products were not healthy.

General Mills tried to capitalize on its Green Giant brand. It already had started to create vegetable chips of various kinds for a healthy consumer's palate. Again, in conceptualizing this product, the issue that stood out for the company was taste. The advantage of a vegetable chip was the use as primary ingredients of whole-grain corn flour along with sweet potatoes or bell peppers. To achieve a decent taste in the Green Giant Chips, General Mills included six to seven grams of fat per serving along with the 140 calories. This formulation made the veggie chips just a tad healthier than typical potato chips, which had nine grams of fat and 150 calories. Most health experts agreed that excessive snacking added unnecessary calories to US and global diets and was a major cause of obesity. The entire snack category might be a dead end if the US and global obesity problem persisted and grew.

Protein-rich products

In response to customer demand, both General Mills and Kellogg's tried to provide more protein-rich products.[32] Consumers were responding to low-fat, low-sugar, and no-cholesterol messages and were looking for more protein in their foods. A product with protein in the brand name, however, did not have to contain a minimum amount of protein according to FDA regulations. Only if the label made the claim that the product was a good source of protein did the product require at least five grams of protein per serving. General Mills and Kellogg's had to be very careful about the extent to which their enriched protein products actually were protein-full.

Protein was seen as building muscle, helping people lose weight, and giving them a pick-up. These foods obtained a boost from Greek yogurt, which was rich in protein and was feeding the craze. However, the degree to which US consumers actually needed additional protein was questionable. Most ate more than enough meat giving them all the daily protein they required. Additional protein intake might contribute to weight gain, exactly what most US consumers wanted to avoid.

General Mills' Nature Valley had pioneered the granola bar. By 2014 it had become a $0.7 billion a year business. In market share, General Mills had first place in this category with Nutri-Grain; the Special K bar from Kellogg's being in second place. In 2012 General Mills successfully started to market Nature Valley Protein bars. In 2014 it introduced Fiber One Protein bars and Larabar ALT Protein bars. Kelloggs' plans were to launch Breakfast to Go drinks that had both ten grams of protein and five grams of fiber. The problem with this rush to protein-rich foods was that it might land General Mills and Kellogg's right back in the thicket of the controversy about high-fat, high-sugar, and low-fiber products. Websites warned that most protein bars were loaded with sugar and fat. Unless they had at least 20 grams of protein for less than 200 calories they should be viewed as candy and not a meal replacement.[33]

The website Everyday Health rated nine protein bars and Nature Valley's came in last place.[34] Although the Nature Valley bar had only 190 calories, it also had only 10 grams of protein plus 6 grams of sugar and 3.5 grams of saturated fat. It far underperformed the best protein bar, QuestBar, which had 160 calories, 20 grams of protein, 0.5 grams of saturated fat, and only 2 grams of sugar. In the category of sugar the Special K Protein bar did even worse. It had fewer calories than the Nature Valley bar, 180 compared to 190, and it had the same amount of protein and saturated fat, but its sugar content was 15 grams, which was far more than the Nature Valley Protein bar.

At both General Mills and Kellogg's a concern for taste was in conflict with a concern for health – even in the health conscious protein-rich category. Anxious that their protein bars might taste bad to consumers because of the added protein, the two companies deemed it necessary to load the bars full of sugar and fat.

The next set of challenges

What should their companies do next? They needed new customers and new business opportunities but where should they turn? If snacks were not the answer, what was? How were they going to deal with the issue of taste? What role should global expansion play in their future plans? How should they communicate the message that the products they sold were healthy?

Notes

1 G. Gardner and B. Halweil, *Underfed and Overfed: the Global Epidemic of Malnutrition* (Washington, DC: Worldwatch Institute, 2000): www.worldwatch.org/nearly-two-billion-people-worldwide-now-over weight

2 A. Sha, "Obesity," *Global Issues* (2010): www.globalissues.org/article/558/obesity

3 U. Friedman, "Two-thirds of obese people now live in developing countries," *The Atlantic* (2014): www.theatlantic.com/international/archive/2014/05/two-thirds-of-the-worlds-obese-people-now-live-in-developing-countries/371834

4 See B. Carter, "Whole Grains: IBISWorld Industry Report 31123, Cereal Production in the US" (2014).

5 *Ibid.*

6 *Ibid.*

7 *Ibid.*

8 M. Moss, *Salt, Sugar, Fat* (New York: Random House, 2014).

9 *Ibid.*

10 *Ibid.*

11 *Ibid.*

12 *Ibid*, p. 358.

13 *Ibid.*

14 C. Zhu, R. Huang, and M. Cohen, "Product reformulation and advertising abeyance: using voluntary marketing initiatives to reduce childhood obesity," *NYU Stern School of Business* (2012): https://editorialexpress.com/cgi-bin/conference/download.cgi?db_name=IIOC2012&paper_id=496

15 "Tracking how industry responds," *Yale University Rudd Center for Food Policy & Obesity* (2014): www.yaleruddcenter.org/what_we_do. aspx?id=103

16 See A Calorie Counter, "Breakfast cereal compared: cereals from Post, Kellogg's and General Mills" (2013): www.acaloriecounter.com/ breakfast-cereal.php

17 See the Healthy Weight Commitment Foundation (HWCF) website: www.healthyweightcommit.org

18 See D. Cohen, "A desired epidemic: obesity and the food industry," *Washington Post* (2007): www.washingtonpost.com/wp-dyn/content/ opinions/index_20070221.html

19 J. Harris, M. Schwartz, K. Brownell, V. Sarda, C. Dernbek, C. Munsell, C. Shin, A. Ustjanauskas, and M. Weinberg, "Cereal facts 2012: limited progress in the nutrition quality and marketing of children's cereals," *Yale University Rudd Center for Food Policy & Obesity* (2012): www. yaleruddcenter.org/archive/publications.aspx

20 *Ibid.*

21 See Kitchen Stewardship, "Cereal: 'One of the healthiest breakfast choices'" (2011): www.kitchenstewardship.com/2011/10/03/cereal-one-of-the-healthiest-breakfast-choices

22 *Ibid.*

23 R. Thomas, P. Pehrsson, J. Ahuja, E. Smieja, and K. Miller, "Recent trends in ready-to-eat breakfast cereals in the US," *Procedia Food Science* (2013): www.ars.usda.gov/SP2UserFiles/Place/80400525/Articles/ ProcediaFS2_20--26.pdf

24 See A Calorie Counter, "Breakfast cereal compared."

25 B. Kennedy, "Kellogg pays for iffy Mini-Wheats claims," (2013): www. msn.com/en-us/money

26 J. Byrne, "Nutri-Grain legal challenge has 'no merit,' says Kellogg," *Food Navigator-USA*. (2010): www.nutraingredients-usa.com/ Regulation/Nutri-Grain-legal-challenge-has-no-merit-says-Kellogg

27 Advertising Standards Authority, "ASA adjudication on Kellogg marketing and sales company," (2012): www.asa.org.uk/Rulings/Ad judications/2012/3/Kellogg-Marketing-and-Sales-Company-(UK)-Ltd/ SHP_ADJ_172001.aspx#.VEUqw_ldV8E

28 S. Strom, "Kellogg agrees to alter labeling on Kashi line," *The New York Times* (2014): www.nytimes.com/2014/05/09/business/kellogg-agrees-to-change-labeling-on-kashi-line.html?_r=0

29 M. Hughlett, "General Mills sued over whether Yoplait greek yogurt is yogurt," *Star Tribune* (2012): www.startribune.com/business/ 162301436.html

30 B. Horovitz, "Cheerios drops genetically modified ingredients," *USA Today* (2014): www.usatoday.com/story/money/business/2014/01/02/cheerios-gmos-cereals/4295739

31 N. Arumgam, "'We never said they're healthy': General Mills files to dismiss fruit snacks lawsuit," *Forbes* (2012): www.forbes.com/sites/nadiaarumugam/2012/03/29/we-never-said-theyre-healthy-general-mills-files-to-dismiss-fruit-snacks-lawsuit

32 S. Nassauer, "When the box says 'protein,' shoppers say 'I'll take it'," *Wall Street Journal* (2013): http://online.wsj.com/news/articles/SB10001424127887324789504578384351639102798

33 See for example, "Do you know what's in your protein bar?" *The Oz Show* (2011): www.doctoroz.com/blog/lisa-lynn/do-you-know-whats-your-protein-bar

34 W. Myers, "9 smart protein-bar picks," *Everyday Health* (2013): www.everydayhealth.com/diet-and-nutrition-pictures/smart-protein-bar-picks.aspx

8 | *Bridge over troubled waters: Pepsi and Coca-Cola*

Shareholder patience with the slow growth of Pepsi and Coca-Cola only went so far. As global trends went against them and their competition intensified, they faced the question of how to find new customers. Increasingly, they turned to sustainability to set them apart. They hedged their bets by acquiring the assets of alternatives to their carbonated soft drink (CSD) and snack products. These efforts legitimated the types of foods and beverages they sold against critics who attacked the foods and beverages for lacking nutritional value and putting an undue burden on the world's environment.

To what extent were Pepsi's and Coca-Cola's commitments to sustainability assisting them in finding new customers? Should they grow, decrease, or alter their sustainability programs' direction? How could they better align a commitment to sustainability with their obligation to shareholders to grow their businesses?

Saturated markets

The core North American and European CSD market on which the Pepsi and Coca-Cola heavily depended was saturated. Demand for sugary soft drinks was dropping. Carbonated soft drink volumes were down by an estimated three percent in 2013, the ninth straight year of their decline and more than twice their 2012 contraction, and most marketing firms forecasted a continuing decline in CSD consumption in North American and European markets.[1] With the average American consuming more than a daily 12-ounce (296 ml) portion of these drinks in 2014, and attacks on them from figures such as Michelle Obama and former New York mayor Michael Bloomberg so prevalent, there was little hope that Pepsi and Coca-Cola could significantly raise US consumption.

Thirty US states had proposed soda taxes, but because of intense industry lobbying none had been passed. The Center for Science in the

Public Interest (CSPI) released an educational video featuring Coca-Cola-liking polar bears that drank too much soda, got diabetes, and had their legs cut off.[2] Attacks on sugary soft drinks were unrelenting and consisted of charges such as the following.

- Whereas the American Heart Association recommended no more than nine teaspoons of sugar per day, the equivalent of 16 teaspoons was in a twenty-ounce (591 ml) soda serving.[3]
- Children who frequently drank sugary soft drinks suffered from dental problems, diabetes, asthma, headaches, ear infections, depression, joint and muscle problems, and developmental delays.
- Calories from sugar-sweetened beverages, because they had no protein or real nutrients, did not satisfy people's real craving for food. As soda consumption grew so did obesity.
- Obesity in the United States had gone up dramatically. More than a quarter of the US population was obese. Obesity increased the risk of diabetes, heart disease, arthritis, asthma, and certain types of cancer. Those who developed diabetes were more likely to suffer from gum infections, kidney disease, hearing impairment, blindness, amputation of toes, feet, or legs, and Alzheimer's disease.
- The medical costs for people who had diabetes were substantially higher than those for normal weight people, with more than half of those costs paid publicly through Medicare and Medicaid.
- Diabetes and obesity imposed not only a huge cost on the medical system but also a loss in productivity, disability, and premature death. The average medical expenditure for people who had diabetes was more than twice that for those without the disease.

With these attacks being so insistent, a surprise was that diet drink consumption also was falling. Diet soda sales also were in a protracted slump that was likely to continue. Diet and low-calorie soda sales fell by more six percent in 2013.[4] A debate had arisen about whether the sweeteners they included adversely affected a person's metabolism. Despite FDA testing and its assurances that artificial sweeteners were safe, growing numbers of Americans did not consider them healthy.

Hedging their bets

Pepsi and Coca-Cola hedged their bets by acquiring the assets of alternatives to soft drinks and snacks. Via joint ventures, acquisitions, and investments of various kinds, they moved outside their mainstream businesses and became involved in selling teas, juices, sports and energy drinks, bottled water, juices, and other categories of beverages. Pepsi partnered with Unilever to market Lipton Teas. It bought Tropicana, Gatorade, SoBe, Naked Juice, and Izze. It started its own line of bottled water, Dasani. It spent billions of dollars on a Los Angeles-based coconut-water company, a Russian dairy and juice maker, and a fortified water company in the UK. Coca-Cola partnered with Nestlé to market Nestea. It bought MinuteMaid. It bid for Gatorade but failed to acquire the company. Instead it started a brand of its own, Powerade. Coca-Cola also started its own line of bottled water, Aquafina. Coca-Cola bought Odwalla juices and snack bars. In 2007, Coca-Cola did a study that found that found that 20 percent of the sales and 50 percent of the growth in the beverage industry came from small, independently owned brands, a third of which were less than five years old.[5] That year, Coca-Cola launched its Venturing & Emerging Brands (VEB) division to nurture relationships with and invest in startups. Coca-Cola bought Fuze tea and fruit drinks, Glaceau vitamin water, Zico coconut water, and Innocent, a British-based juice maker. It made a 40 percent investment in Honest Tea, acquired a 10 percent stake in Green Mountain Coffee, and partnered with Core Power, the high-protein drink.

Though promising, these investments had yet to produce the kinds of results that Pepsi and Coca-Cola regularly attained from CSDs. About 60 percent of Coca-Cola's US revenues came from CSDs, compared to roughly 25 percent for Pepsi, yet the two strongest brands in Pepsi's portfolio, the ones that produced greatest percentage of its annual revenue, continued to be Pepsi and Mountain Dew, which were CSDs. Market share in the alternative beverage segments that Pepsi and Coca-Cola used to hedge their bets remained highly fragmented. The alternative beverage segments were not dominated by Coca-Cola and Pepsi in the manner that the CSD market was dominated by these companies. Two ways existed to evaluate beverage consumption trends – dollar value sold and liters consumed (see Table 8.1). In growth in the amount consumed, CSDs were in last place. The highest growth, of about 45 percent from 2008 to 2013, was tea sold in bottles and cans. Sports and energy drinks and bottled water were next. Juice was near the bottom. At the very bottom in terms of growth in volume consumed were CSDs. However, in terms of dollar value sold CSDs

Table 8.1 *Beverage category growth in value and volume consumed, 2008 to 2013*

		Dollar value		Liter volume	
Category	Growth percentages	2008$ million	2013$ million	2008 million liters	2013 million liters
Tea	47.7	31,907	47,139		
Tea	45.0			22,527	32,670
Sports and energy	42.4	32,550	46,365		
Sports and energy	32.7			12,713	16,873
Bottled water	34.0	81,484	109,226		
Bottled water	35.4			180,023	243,720
Juice	20.2	85,562	102,877		
Juice	15.4			55,687	64,249
Carbonated soft drinks	16.0	157,793	183,037		
Carbonated soft drinks	5.4			155,324	163,712

Derived from Passport Euromonitor International: http://portal.euromonitor.com/portal/magazine/homemain

Table 8.2 *Major world tea markets, 2008 and 2013*

Country	2008 Millions of liters consumed	2013 Millions of liters consumed
China	8,398.20	14,956.30
Japan	5,559.20	5,787.30
United States	2,105.50	2,739.50
Indonesia	1,006.90	1,456.30
Vietnam	184	818.2
Germany	789.6	759.5
Taiwan	660.4	718.1
Italy	461	469.6
Thailand	96	418.5
Russia	288.3	370.3
Canada	290.2	361.7
Hong Kong	250.4	313.4

remained in the lead. What should Pepsi and Coca-Cola do? What mix of drinks should they offer?

Tea

Not surprisingly the tea market was very strong in countries such as China, Japan, Indonesia, and Vietnam as well as the United States (see Table 8.2). However, in countries such as China, where tea was popular, local brands like Ting Hsin and Uni-President dominated. Only in Japan did Coca-Cola have much market share (see Table 8.3).

To respond to the challenge Coca-Cola tried to innovate with tea products that addressed the problem of obesity. It introduced a brand of tea called Enviga, which was supposed to burn 60 to 100 calories per three 12-ounce (355 ml) servings, but this claim was disputed and the introduction of the product stalled.[6] The buzz behind Enviga, developed in partnership with Nestlé, was that it might actually take off rather than put on pounds. This buzz stimulated media hype, but the scientific evidence came from a single non-peer reviewed study Coca-Cola and Nestlé sponsored that a University of Lausanne researcher carried out adjacent to Nestlé's headquarters in Switzerland. The study involved 32 healthy, normal, non-overweight 18- to 35-year-olds, whose energy expenditure was measured through the metabolic heat that came from their bodies after they drank a placebo

Table 8.3 *Company market share in tea in Asia, 2008 and 2013*

Country/brand	2008 Market share, percentage	2013 Market share, percentage
China		
Ting Hsin	25.7	23.7
Uni-President	12.2	15.4
Japan		
Ito En	21.5	28.2
Coca-Cola	23.6	21.9
Indonesia		
Sinar Sosro	74.3	63.2
Beverage Partners	12.4	14
Taiwan		
Uni-President	25.4	27.3
Vitalon Foods	12.3	12.2
Vietnam		
Tan Hiep Phat	42.5	43.5
JG Summit	26.3	25.8

Derived from Passport Euromonitor International: http://portal.euromonitor.com/portal/magazine/homemain

or Enviga. Coca-Cola warned that Enviga was not a diet pill and had to be consumed as part of a healthy diet along with regular physical exercise. Under these conditions it would give a slight boost to body metabolism. The company's claim was that Enviga was made from proprietary tea leaves from a plantation in India, which had more epigallocatechin gallate (EGCG) content (the substance that led to weight reduction) than other teas. The US FDA, however, rejected efforts to claim that Enviga or other green tea products reduced the risk of cardiovascular disease or cancer.

Sports and energy drinks

In the sports and energy category, the consumption leader was the United States (see Table 8.3). However, consumption of this beverage category, though slumping in Japan, was taking off in countries such as China, Indonesia, Thailand, and the Philippines. The world's dominant brand was a Pepsi product, Gatorade.[7] Though it had slipped

Table 8.4 *Major sports and energy drink markets in the world,*
2008 and 2013

Country	2008 Millions of liters consumed	2013 Millions of liters consumed
United States	5,417.00	6,635.40
China	857.3	1,575.90
Japan	1,745.40	1,565.80
United Kingdom	532.3	673.2
Indonesia	292.5	551.5
Thailand	363.4	531.3
Germany	280.1	380.9
Mexico	264.7	372.4
Philippines	68.5	331
Vietnam	113.7	323.5

Derived from Passport Euromonitor International: http://portal.euromonitor.com/
portal/magazine/homemain

from a market share of 36.8 percent in 2008, Pepsi continued to be
first in global market share in 2013 with 30.7 percent. In the United
States it had 54 percent of the market, down from 66.2 percent in
2008. Coca-Cola was second in global market share in this category
with 17.8 percent in 2013 and second in US market share with 20.1
percent. Its global market share was slightly down from 2008, but in
the United States Coca-Cola had made progress since 2008 when its
market share had been 16.6 percent. Red Bull, an Austrian firm, and
Monster, formerly called Hansen Natural, made significant gains both
in the United States and globally. Red Bull's global market share was
6.5 percent and its US market share was 7.4 percent, while Monster
had a US market share of 11 percent and a global market share of
5.4 percent.

Bottled water

Bottled water's health benefits were touted in developing countries
because of a lack of clean tap water. In these countries global demand
for bottled water was rising (see Table 8.5). Both Pepsi and Coca-Cola
invested heavily in their bottled water brands. In the United States,
where it was considerably more expensive than treated tap water,

Table 8.5 *Bottled water consumption in developing countries, 2008 and 2013*

Country	2008 Millions of liters consumed	2013 Millions of liters consumed
China	16,642.80	31,686.40
Nigeria	12,036.60	22,236.90
Mexico	14,863.80	19,953.00
Indonesia	11,895.50	16,638.10
India	2,734.30	8,042.70
Brazil	4,444.00	6,373.50

Derived from Passport Euromonitor International: http://portal.euromonitor.com/portal/magazine/homemain

Table 8.6 *United States' bottled water revenue growth, 2000 to 2013*

Year	Revenue $ millions	Growth Percentage
2000	5,132.00	0
2001	5,279.70	2.9
2002	5,572.40	5.5
2003	5,738.70	3
2004	5,947.40	3.6
2005	7,053.10	18.6
2006	8,489.70	20.4
2007	8,493.10	0
2008	8,586.20	1.1
2009	7,993.70	− 6.9
2010	7,785.30	− 2.6
2011	7,986.60	2.6
2012	8,301.50	3.9
2013	8,351.90	0.6

bottled water, however, showed signs of weakness. After the economic downturn, US consumers cut back their spending on bottled water and sales contracted (see Table 8.6).

Neither Pepsi nor Coca-Cola was the world's leader in this category.[8] Danone, which sold bottled water under the brand names

Evian, Aqua, Volvic, and Badoit, had this distinction with 10.3 percent of world market share in 2013. Danone owned such brands as Yili Aqua in Indonesia, Sehat in Malaysia, Brunei, and Singapore, and Robust and Bonafont in Mexico, and had majority ownership of China Wahaha water products. Coca-Cola was in second place in global market share in bottled water in 2013 with a 7.7 percent share, Nestlé was in third place with a 7.3 percent share, and Pepsi was in fourth place with a 3.6 percent share.

In the United States, Nestlé, with a market share of 22.9 percent, had the top position in bottled water.[9] The company had 75 different brands with local brands accounting for about two-thirds of its US sales. It participated in this category through such brands as Perrier, Vittel, San Pellegrino, and Poland Spring. Weakness in the US and European markets, however, had hampered its performance. Its global and US market shares fell. Coca-Cola was second in the US market in bottled water with 11.4 percent of the market in 2013, down from 14.5 percent in 2008, and Pepsi was third with 6.0 percent of the market in 2013, down from 8.8 percent in 2008. Both in the United States and abroad the bottled water market was fragmented with many small companies participating. To stand out in this market Pepsi innovated with Propel Fitness water, a product that was stocked full of vitamins and antioxidants and was sold in Walmart and other discount grocers.

Ready-to-drink juices

From 2008 to 2013 growth in the consumption of ready-to-drink juices advanced in developing countries such as China and Mexico, while it fell in the United States, Russia, and Germany (see Table 8.7). Coca-Cola, with a global market share of 12.1 percent and a domestic market share of 19.7 percent in 2013, had the lead. It gained market share in the United States in this period. Pepsi, in second place with a global market share of 6.1 percent and domestic market share of 9.7 percent, lost market share. Many companies participated in this market and it too was very fragmented.

Carbonated beverages

In contrast to other categories Coca-Cola and Pepsi dominated the CSD market. Between them the two companies controlled around

Table 8.7 *Major world juice markets and market share, 2008 and 2013*

Major juice markets		
World markets	2008 Millions of liters consumed	2008 Millions of liters consumed
China	10,033.90	15,983.10
United States	9,781.30	9,027.30
Russia	3,059.00	2,883.30
Germany	3,178.40	2,723.90
Mexico	1,930.30	2,626.40
Japan	2,373.80	2,572.50
Market share		
Companies	2008 Market share, percentage	2013 Market share, percentage
Global		
Coca-Cola	10.4	12.1
Pepsi	6.2	6.1
Ting Hsin	1.3	3
United States		
Coca-Cola	15.9	19.7
Pepsi	12.3	9.7
Deutsche SiSi-Werke	7.7	6.5

Derived from Passport Euromonitor International: http://portal.euromonitor.com/portal/magazine/homemain

70 percent of the global market and about 65 percent of the North American market in 2013 (see Table 8.8). Coca-Cola capitalized on its brand name, extracting slightly more market share in dollars than in volume consumed. Coca-Cola was ahead of Pepsi in the CSD category in every region in the world. Nowhere in this category was its market share lower than 38 percent, and nowhere did Pepsi have market share greater than 32 percent. The closest contest was in North America. Since 2008, Coca-Cola's global market share had gone up in every region in the world, while Pepsi's had declined in every region except the Middle East and Africa.

Table 8.8 *Coca-Cola and Pepsi global market share in carbonated soft drinks, 2008 and 2013*

Region	Coca-Cola's 2008 percentage dollar value	Pepsi's 2008 percentage dollar value	Coca-Cola's 2013 percentage dollar value	Pepsi's 2013 percentage dollar value
World	49.1	19.9	50.9	19.0
Asia Pacific	52.1	22.1	54.5	19.8
Eastern Europe	37.2	16.5	40.3	19.6
Latin America	55.9	13.7	59.0	13.3
Middle East and Africa	50.3	27.7	49.3	31.9
North America	39.2	29.8	37.9	26.6
Western Europe	54.0	11.6	53.5	11.8

Derived from Passport Euromonitor International: http://portal.euromonitor.com/portal/magazine/homemain

To maintain its lead, Coca-Cola pursued product innovation. Zero was the company's most successful brand launch in 20 years. Its success followed the failure of C2, a drink with about half the carbohydrates and calories of Coca-Cola Classic, which was meant for weight-conscious consumers who did not like Diet Coca-Cola. In the rollout of Zero, Coca-Cola was careful to get bottler input about customer reaction. The ads for Zero had two people seeking legal advice on how to sue Coca-Cola back to the Stone Age for taste infringement, a charge that stemmed from the alleged similarity in taste between Zero and Coca-Cola Classic.

Snacks

While Coca-Cola led the world in market share in CSDs, Pepsi had a large snack division, Frito-Lay, upon which to fall back, in which it was dominant. In snacks, Pepsi dominated globally and in North America with major brands like Lay's and Ruffles potato chips, Dorritos and Tostitos tortilla chips, Cheetos, and Fritos corn chips (see Table 8.9). General Mills and Kellogg's (see Chapter 7) were distant followers in second and third place respectively. In 2012, more than 50 percent of Pepsi's total revenue came from snacks. Carbonated soft drinks were 31 percent and other beverages 19 percent. Activist investor Nelson

Table 8.9 *Global market share in snack foods, 2008 and 2013*

Company	2008 Percentage dollar value	2013 Percentage dollar value
Global		
Pepsi	28.1	29.1
General Mills	0.7	1
Kellogg's	0.1	2.5
United States		
Pepsi	45.6	44.3
General Mills	1.8	1.9
Kellogg's	0.1	3.2

Derived from Passport Euromonitor International: http://portal. euromonitor.com/portal/magazine/homemain

Peltz pressured Pepsi to split up the snack and beverage divisions so that shareholders would benefit, but Pepsi's management resisted.[10]

Carbonated soft drinks were 70 percent of Coca-Cola's revenues in 2013 while the rest of its revenue came from beverages. Juice was ten percent of the total, bottled water nine percent, sports and energy drinks five percent, teas three percent, and all other drinks under three percent.[11]

Pepsi's dominance of the snack food category was a curse as well as a blessing. The company faced nutritional challenges in this market as well. The problem in the case of the snack foods was not so much that sugar contributed to obesity and heart disease, but that salt and fats were such important ingredients. Consumers also had become wary of the negative health effects of eating foods high in sodium and trans-fats. According to the Centers for Disease Control and Prevention, 90 percent of people in the United States ate more sodium than needed for a healthy diet, which put them at risk for high blood pressure and cardiovascular diseases.[12] The demand for snacks still was high (see Table 8.10) but it was changing. Increasingly, consumers asked for healthier snacks made with little or far less salt and no trans-fats.

Performance with a purpose

Pepsi's CEO Indra Nooyi dealt with the criticism of the CSDs and snack foods sold by her company by articulating a vision she called

Table 8.10 *Global and US snack food sales, 2008 to 2013*

Dollar value of sales (millions)	2008	2009	2010	2011	2012	2013
World	95,454	95,940	102,668	111,941	115,884	119,261
United States	28,352	29,569	29,963	31,256	32,911	34,031

Percentage growth in sales	2007–08	2008–09	2009–10	2010–11	2011–12	2012–13
World	0.5	7.0	9.0	3.5	2.9	4.7
United States	4.3	1.3	4.3	5.3	3.4	3.6

Derived from Passport Euromonitor International: http://portal.euromonitor.com/portal/magazine/homemain

performance with a purpose. Nooyi, CEO since 2006, was a vegetarian and the first woman and non-US born person to hold the job. She did not accept Pepsi's responsibility for the obesity crisis – that she blamed on sedentary life styles – but she did believe that a large and powerful corporation like Pepsi should be part of the solution.[13] The company should be part of the solution not by selling fewer products but by selling products that were both good for people and tasted great.

Steven Reinemund, CEO at Pepsi from 2000 to 2006, had tipped Nooyi as his heir.[14] Reinemund, the efficiency expert, had worked together with Nooyi for many years. Nooyi was known for vision and having good negotiating skills. She closed the 1998 deal to purchase Tropicana and played a critical role in the 2000 acquisition of Quaker, which brought Gatorade into Pepsi's fold. She was the company's corporate strategist. Her aim as CEO was to position Pepsi for the future. Nutrition would play a much more central role. Products that Pepsi referred to as good for you, those made of grains, fruit, nuts, vegetables, and dairy, would become a $30 billion part of Pepsi's portfolio, rather than the $10 billion part they were in 2010.[15] With an aging population and people focused on health, Nooyi understood nutrition to be an opportunity. Healthy food categories would continue to grow faster than less healthy categories. Via the application of science and technology, Nooyi believed that foods could be made healthier and they could taste good at the same time. She also believed that they could become more affordable.

Pepsi already sold packaged nutrition in brands such as SoBe Lifewater, and the Naked line. Products under these brands were crammed full of vitamins and antioxidants. In addition, Pepsi had enhanced Gatorade's line of sports drinks so that they met a person's specific physiological or metabolic needs before, after, and during exercise. All the foods Pepsi sold Nooyi believed might evolve into delivery vehicles for health benefits. She touted Pepsi's new Tropolis products as an example.[16] The company was putting carrots and fruits with a little oatmeal in drinkable form as snacks for children and adults in squeezable containers.

The task Nooyi set before Pepsi's scientists and technicians was to re-engineer foods so that they would have less salt, fat, and sugar.[17] Pepsi employed top-notch experts to accomplish this goal. It built world-class laboratories and expanded its R&D budget. The scientists worked on a salt crystal, the fifteen-micron crystal, that would produce the same taste but with less salt. The company tested it on its Walkers brand of chips in the UK, but was cautious about using the ingredient in other products because it was not certain that people would be satisfied with the taste. Pepsi developed new technology that reduced the amount of oil absorbed by potato chips and built a sophisticated method of taste-testing to experiment with sugar substitutes. It was hoping to create a natural, zero-calorie sweetener that tasted exactly like sugar. In fulfilling the goal of profit with a purpose Nooyi promised that Pepsi would reduce the amount of salt and sugar in its products by 25 percent by 2015.[18]

Pepsi also initiated a major advertising campaign known as Pepsi Refresh. The company donated $20 million to people with uplifting ideas about how to change the world. Winning proposals were those that received the most votes on Pepsi's website. Eighty million people made their preferences known on the website and Pepsi heavily advertised what it was doing on TV hoping that it would bring more sales to its products. The funded projects assisted many people. They helped the homeless. They built school playgrounds, established education programs for teenage mothers, and carried out many other worthy activities. No matter, Pepsi's sales did not increase. After the Refresh project started, Pepsi continued to lose market share to Coca-Cola, which advertised its products as having no other purpose than being indulgent treats. As a consequence, the financial community began to question Nooyi's judgment. Since she had become CEO, Pepsi's performance was lackluster along a number of dimensions. The company's stock price declined, while Coca-Cola's gained. Analysts asked whether she took shareholder interests sufficiently into consideration when she made her pronouncements.[19] Nooyi defended herself by claiming her job was not to pay attention to quarterly numbers but to gaze into the future and understand the challenges Pepsi inevitably would have to confront in coming decades. She asserted, "You don't dance like a dervish to the old music but think about different dances."[20] Her campaign that Pepsi perform with purpose, however, did not release the company from the sting of health-minded critics, some of whom asserted that the best way for people to consume healthier foods was for Pepsi to go out of business.

Coca-Cola's rejoinder

Recognizing consumers' rights to choose lifestyles and make dietary choices, Coca-Cola responded by providing factual, meaningful and easy-to-understand information about nutrition and engaging in initiatives to encourage people to live active, healthy lifestyles. To facilitate choice, it provided fact-based data about its products on its labels and websites that were meant to assist customers in meeting their nutritional and energy requirements. Coca-Cola's foundation sponsored education programs about the importance of a balanced diet in many countries including South Korea, Italy, and China, and it promised to apply product development expertise to the issues of malnutrition and obesity. Yet the company was emphatic that diet was not the only cause of obesity. The main culprit was a lack of physical activity. On its website, it proclaimed that a high level of fitness was the strongest predictor of cardiovascular health. Therefore it dedicated itself to improving physical activity and fitness. It celebrated the more than 280 active, healthy living programs it sponsored in over 115 countries worldwide.

Globally Coca-Cola assisted in solving the problem of malnutrition with nutrient-enhanced beverages that it introduced under the labels of Nurisha and Vitingo. Examples of these products it introduced included:

- NutriBoost Dairy and juice drink fortified with essential nutrients (Thailand and Vietnam)

- Pulpy Super Milky fortified with whey protein and fruit bits (China)
- NutriJuice fortified with four vitamins and minerals to provide children with iron (the Philippines)
- Kids+ Orange Juice with essential nutrients for children, including vitamins A, C, D, E, and calcium (the United States)
- Antiox, fortified with antioxidants from fruits (Spain).

Stinging criticisms, motivated by the belief that a company like Coca-Cola could not honestly sell healthy products, put Coca-Cola's new ventures under a veil of suspicion. The Center for Science in the Public Interest (CSPI) sued the company in 2009 on behalf of vitamin-water drinkers, charging that it deceptively marketed Glacéau drinks as healthy when they contained as much sugar as ordinary sodas.[21] Coca-Cola indicated that it might start to gradually move away from supersize drinks back to its older and smaller sizes. The proof of its commitment was an experiment with smaller package sizes. It offered five-ounce (148 ml) mini bottles and cans that had less than 100 calories and sold for around 50 cents. It renegotiated its bottler contracts, basing them on total dollar revenue and not sales volume, a move that would take away some of the incentive that the bottlers had to sell large-sized portions. Coca-Cola tried to show that it did not depend on people's gluttony to grow, but critics saw its moves as tokenism. If it did not immediately remove jumbo-sized containers from convenience and grocery stores, the critics maintained that Coca-Cola simply was not serious. However, for Coca-Cola to immediately replace the 50-ounce (1,479 ml) Double-Gulps at 7-Eleven and the 2-liter bottles, which accounted for 75 percent of its US soda sales would be difficult.

To appease the critics Coca-Cola started to test-market an all-natural stevia-based low-calorie cola called Coca-Cola Life. It made the product available in Argentina, Chile, and the UK to see how consumers would respond. Its concern was the product's taste. It did not believe that stevia taste was satisfactory in colas and was concerned that US consumers would not accept stevia-sweetened drinks. When the company tried a vitaminwater–stevia combination, Coca-Cola received irate posts on the company's Facebook page.

At the same time that the company engaged in these efforts, it recommitted to the US soft drink market with a two-year, one-billion-dollar marketing blitz designed to put the sparkle back into CSDs. Playing on people's emotions, it placed the 250 most common names of US teens on Coca-Cola bottles, hoping that this maneuver would get them to buy the drinks. The 2014 Super Bowl commercial in which children of different ethnicities sang "America the Beautiful" in their native languages increased CSD sales among young people ages 19 to 24. Pepsi also decided that it had to ramp up the advertising and marketing of its flagship cola and other soda brands. The year 2014 was considered to be a watershed for the company. Could Pepsi regain market share from Coca-Cola after losing it for so many years?

Global competition

Whereas Pepsi excelled in snacks, Coca-Cola excelled in overseas sales. The US and West European markets were mature, but other global markets still were open. The best hopes for expansion therefore might not lie in the United States; rather they might exist globally. Global markets, however, were not always easy ones to crack.[22]

India

India had been one of Pepsi's top overseas priorities, but the company became the target of repeated charges about its abuse of the country's scarce water resources. The charges were that its consumed excessive amounts of water and that its sodas contained water soaked with dangerous pesticides that poisoned people. This campaign gained momentum in 2006 just as the Indian-born Nooyi became CEO.

Water had a special meaning and place in Indian culture where bathing was a sacred act and drinking clean water was a means to improve well-being, comparable to taking health supplements in the United States. Overpumping and poor management, however, made water scarce, and poor sewage, industrial waste, and pesticide polluted it. Sunita Narain, a New Delhi activist and follower of Gandhi's nonviolent tactics championed the charges against Pepsi. The Centre for Science & Environment (CSE), which she directed, provided evidence of a toxic assault by US multinationals. The CSE studies revealed that Pepsi's soft drink brands were 30 to 36 times below EU standards for water purity. The CSE maintained that multinational Indian-produced soft drinks were unfit for human consumption and caused cancer and birth defects. It declared that samples of Pepsi and Coca-Cola drinks it tested in the United States did not have the same dangerous residues.

Indian government studies reported high pesticide levels in milk, rice, and other staples as well as soft drinks. The government therefore planned to stiffen its water standards. The CSE, however, accused Pepsi and Coca-Cola of sabotaging these efforts. These accusations helped to incite a global movement against multinationals in India in which protestors smashed both Pepsi and Coca-Cola bottles in the streets. Several Indian states banned or restricted their sales. Pepsi was especially hard hit and suffered double-digit sales declines.

Nooyi went to India and publicized the company's initiatives to improve water quality and the environment. She repeatedly asserted that Pepsi was a company with a soul and emphasized its investments in educating communities in how to farm better and collect, retrofit, and recycle water. She defended Pepsi by pointing out that it often helped villages dig new wells or harvest rainwater and it taught villagers better agricultural techniques. She noted that soft drinks and bottled water accounted for less than 0.04 percent of the industrial water usage in India.

The charges against Pepsi and Coca-Cola later proved to be baseless, because the CSE tests had been carried out on water entering the Pepsi and Coca-Cola plants and not on the companies' finished products. Nevertheless, both companies started to engage in extensive efforts to preserve and improve water quality in India and other developing countries.

In India, Coca-Cola vigorously marketed its products. Its salespeople went house to house in New Delhi, handing out free bottles of Coca-Cola and Fanta. It hosted gatherings of large numbers of retailers to show them the coolers and refrigerators the company would loan them. Pepsi and Coca-Cola fought a head-to-head battle for dominance from 2008 to 2013. Coca-Cola came out ahead, but local company Parle Bisleri continued to be strong (see Table 8.11).

Mexico

In this country Coca-Cola and Pepsi faced the rise of local brands. The upstart Kola Real, part of the Aje Group, surprised both companies.[23] Based in Peru, Kola Real had success in creating a product a lot like Coca-Cola, but cheaper. The family-run firm moved to Venezuela and Ecuador, and then targeted Mexico. In Mexico, soda consumption per capita was even greater than in the United States. Mexico represented

Table 8.11 *Soda drink market share in India, 2008 and 2013*

Company	2008 Percentage dollar value	2013 Percentage dollar value
Coca-Cola	24.1	24.7
Parle Bisleri	24.5	23.6
Pepsi	21.2	20.4
Manikchand	5.6	4.1
UB	0.6	3.2
Parle Agro	3.8	2.8

Derived from Passport Euromonitor International: http://portal. euromonitor.com/portal/magazine/homemain

more than ten percent of Coca-Cola's global sales, and Coca-Cola's control of the Mexican market had been solid prior to Kola Real's entry. The ex-Mexican president, Vicente Fox, had been a Coca-Cola executive. What made Kola Real's entry into Mexico easier was the switch to plastic bottles. The company put its Big Cola product in large plastic bottles and sold it at a steep discount in supermarkets. Supermarket chains were growing in Mexico. Because the margins in supermarket sales were low, they were not a favored Coca-Cola outlet. They were less than ten percent of soft drink sales, but their share of the market was growing. Walmart had arrived on the scene with supercenters that combined discount merchandising and groceries. It identified low-cost local alternatives to Coca-Cola. Kola Real's entry strategy was to compete on price. The same bottle of Coca-Cola that cost about $1 in the United States cost about $1.40 in Mexico. Kola Real had a similar product that it sold for 80 or 90 cents.

Within a year of opening a plant in Mexico, Kola Real built market share in the country. Its operations did not rely on frills. It did little advertising. Instead word of mouth stimulated interest. Kola Real distanced itself from Coca-Cola's distribution system and had its own way to get product to the market. Hundreds of leased trucks moved product from the two dozen distribution centers it owned and operated. Its sales staff pushed its sodas into large grocery stores and small shops in rural locations.

Coca-Cola's response was to listen more to the advice of local business partners and adapt its products and advertising more to local

Table 8.12 *Soda drink market share in Mexico, 2008 and 2013*

Company	2008 Percentage dollar value	2013 Percentage dollar value
Coca-Cola	38.6	39.1
Danone	18.5	20.8
Pepsi	18.0	16.9
Aje	3.0	2.7
Dr Pepper Snapple	2.5	1.9
Consorcio	1.8	1.7

Derived from Passport Euromonitor International: http://portal. euromonitor.com/portal/magazine/homemain

tastes. The company delegated additional product development and marketing responsibility to local managers, and developed and promoted local executives in the place of expatriates. It increased its acquisition of local brands. It aimed its marketing at trend-setting Mexican teenagers, but it faced difficulties from Mexico's Federal Competition Commission, which accused it of paying retailers to exclude competitors' products.

Other companies followed Kola Real's lead. An Ecuadorian company launched a low-price cola called El Gallito, or Little Rooster. Mexico's Guadalajara soccer club introduced a brand, which it called Chiva Cola. In Brazil, the world's third-largest soft drink market, local companies also emulated Kola Real's successes. Nonetheless, Coca-Cola held on. From 2008 to 2013, it continued to dominate the Mexican market with a market share close to 40 percent (see Table 8.12). Pepsi's market share was falling and Aje made but a small dent on Coca-Cola's overall leadership.

The Muslim world

In the Muslim world, activist groups called upon consumers to boycott US products such as Coca-Cola and to use Muslim products in their place.[24] Extremist vigilantes in Pakistan's North-West Frontier Province regularly destroyed signs advertising foreign goods. Local brands' revival came on the heels of resentment toward US cultural imperialism. The Iranian cola company, ZamZam, became an emblem of opposition to the United States.

Across Europe, Muslim alternatives to Coca-Cola also sprouted up. Tawfiq Mathlouti, a Tunisian-born French businessman, set up Mecca Cola, which sold a Coca-Cola look-alike product that relied on the slogan – don't drink stupid, drink with commitment. The company promised that 20 percent of its profits would go to charities, such as Palestinian causes and European Muslim organizations. Other Islamic alternatives on the European market were Qibla Cola and Muslim Up. Qibla, named after the direction in which Muslims pray, started in the UK and it also promised to use its profits to help Muslim charities. The company estimated it could sell one million bottles in Britain and had plans to expand to Scandinavia, Turkey, Pakistan, and Egypt. Muslim Up, started by three Frenchman of Tunisian origin, was operating in Britain, Germany, Belgium, and Italy as well as France.

Coca-Cola tried to place some distance between itself and its country of origin, repositioning itself as a supranational brand – global in nature, uniform throughout the world, and not particularly American. It maintained the stature and implied quality of a product associated with the United States, but did much else to merge with local cultures by adapting product packaging, serving sizes, and flavors. To improve its global image, it introduced new worldwide graphics to convey its core values of authenticity, energy, and refreshment for fun-seeking young people. It enhanced its local ties by doing community service projects such as giving educational grants to local charities. It donated to the Palestinian Authority and gave money to local environmental organizations.

Pepsi tried to match these activities, selling its products as US brands, but with a distinctly local orientation. It was a major sponsor of local sports teams. It garnered the support of local celebrities. It sought out prominent local business people and gave them exclusive distribution rights. It recruited senior management from local talent and initiated many community projects.

With the exception of Iran in 2012 to 2013, the consumption of soda drinks grew rapidly in predominately Muslim countries from 2008 to 2013 (see Table 8.13). Pepsi did well in Saudi Arabia, Egypt, and Pakistan; Coca-Cola dominated Iran, Morocco, and Turkey; and local firms that had the upper hand in Algeria and Morocco (see Table 8.14). In nearly every Muslim country they had a strong presence. Local

Table 8.13 *Change in soda drink consumption in select Muslim countries,*
2008 to 2013

Percentage sales growth	2008–09	2009–10	2010–11	2011–12	2012–13
Pakistan	8.9	6.2	9.3	7	7.4
Algeria	11.1	11.5	11.1	10.8	11
Egypt	11.5	9.9	1.6	1.8	0.4
Iran	5.8	6.5	8.4	6.7	–7.6
Morocco	6.7	7.5	9.2	9.1	9.2
Saudi Arabia	4.2	–8.1	8.3	7.1	6.5
Tunisia	8.4	11.3	16.4	10.8	9.6
UAE	5.2	4.6	2.5	5.7	6.7
Turkey	6.3	5.9	7.4	2.5	3.2

Derived from Passport Euromonitor International: http://portal.euromonitor.com/
portal/magazine/homemain

producers, such as those active in Muslim countries, stood in the way
of greater dominance by Coca-Cola and Pepsi. Large multinationals
such as Pepsi and Coca-Cola had to buy homegrown brands to expand.
They had to cater to local tastes and preferences and establish and
maintain strong local distribution outlets.

Environmental stewardship

Pepsi and Coca-Cola also had to compete vigorously in the realm of
environmental stewardship. The two main areas in which they tried to
stand out were in their use of water and support for greenhouse gas
emission reductions.

Water

In 2005, Coca-Cola's then CEO, E. Neville Isdell, declared that the
company had a responsibility to conserve the water it used in its
own operations and to make water more available to the communities around it. Worldwide the company was a major user of water,
devouring more than 73 billion gallons of the precious liquid annually. The main ingredient in its 500 plus beverages was water. On its
web page Coca-Cola declared that achieving water security might be

Table 8.14 *Soda drink market share in select Muslim countries, 2008 and 2013*

Country	Company	2008 Percentage dollar value	2013 Percentage dollar value
Pakistan	Nestlé	21.3	24.8
	Pepsi	23.2	24.0
	Coca-Cola	20.3	22.3
Algeria	Ibrahim & Fils Ifri	15.6	17.3
	Coca-Cola	9.7	9.1
	Hamoud Boualem	7.7	7.9
Egypt	Pepsi	29.7	30.5
	Coca-Cola	26.6	28.0
	Nestlé	8.6	9.1
Iran	Coca-Cola	17.2	21.8
	ZamZam	21.2	13.8
	Pepsi	10.6	12.8
Morocco	Coca-Cola	41.8	34.9
	Holmarcom	24.1	33.9
	Danone	5.0	6.2
Saudi Arabia	Pepsi	39.4	33.1
	Makkah Water	4.1	7.5
	Coca-Cola	11.5	6.7
Tunisia	Société Frigori- fique et Brasserie	28.6	31.6
	Cije	30.2	21.9
	Société d'exploitation des Eaux	15.5	21.6
UAE	Pepsi	17.5	19.0
	Masafi	15.9	17.5
	Al Ain Dairy	10.8	12.3
Turkey	Coca-Cola	21.3	20.6
	Danone	2.0	10.6
	Nestlé	8.3	10.0

Derived from Passport Euromonitor International: http://portal.euromonitor.com/portal/magazine/homemain

humanity's most crucial task and it called upon world governments to re-examine the use of water in agriculture, to make investments in cities where pipes leaked, and in general to optimize water's use.

The company pointed to its own water stewardship programs in treating and recycling wastewater and replenishing the water it used in its beverages. In 2006, it reported that its water usage was down by 9.4 percent worldwide since 2002, while at the same time it produced 10 percent more liquid beverages.[25] The company spent two million dollars on the Global Water Challenge, a coalition of corporations and organizations based in the United Nations Foundation. In Kenya, where rural access to clean water was restricted, it introduced water-purification systems and storage, and taught hygiene lessons in schools on using chlorine-based solutions to kill diseases. It set up similar programs in 36 other countries including India.

Partnering with the Nature Conservancy, Coca-Cola found that the largest portion of the water it used took place before manufacturing – in the cultivation of ingredients. As a result, it also started to work more closely with the farmers and processors of sugar, corn, and other ingredients. It committed not only to reducing its own water consumption but also to reducing the water consumption of those in its supply chain.

Not to be topped by these efforts, Pepsi as well augmented its activities. Like Coca-Cola, it pledged support for the United Nation's declaration of water rights and incorporated the pledge into its operations. In 2007, the company set a global goal to decrease water use by 20 percent per unit of production by 2015, which it was well on the way to achieving. Both Coca-Cola and Pepsi told the public about their efforts to consume less water through enhanced conservation and efficiency. To publicize their efforts, they worked with NGOs and other organizations, issued reports, and launched web pages. In moving in this direction firms such as Pepsi and Coca-Cola were not just acting altruistically. They were responding to investors' concerns about diminishing water resources and the potential risks to companies that were major water users such as Coca-Cola and Pepsi. Investors such as the pension fund of the Norwegian government and the California Public Employees' Retirement System wanted more disclosure about issues relating to water use. They wanted to know how water shortages might hurt the businesses of companies like Coca-Cola and Pepsi, and they wanted these companies to reveal how they were addressing the issue. When Coca-Cola and Pepsi tightened up their operations to use less water, they tended to save money. Projects of this nature generally had positive impacts on their bottom lines. Using less water typically meant using less energy and it therefore lowered costs.

Coca-Cola and Pepsi also benefited from the positive public relations. The push they made to use less water helped them do better in corporate social responsibility (CSR) rankings. The reputational as well as operational advantages provided the incentives for carrying out these activities.

The goal guiding the programs was to reduce their overall water footprint, defined as the total amount of water embedded in their finished products. To the credit of the two companies they recognized that establishing a credible accounting for this footprint was not easy. It was not easy because measurements had to be estimated at so many different production stages. In creating beverages there were many different steps. To measure only the water residing in a beverage's base was not sufficient. In addition to the water needed for producing and distributing the beverage, it was necessary to measure the water that might have been used to grow sugar, corn, other flavors, and ingredients. How far back in this process did analysis have to go? The goal of water neutrality, or net-zero water use, was probably unattainable because accurate assessment of a beverage's comprehensive footprint was not possible.

Climate change

The pressure for disclosure applied to climate change as well as water use. The US Securities and Exchange Commission (SEC) had issued guidance about climate-related risks. Coca-Cola's involvement in the climate change issue also was related to persistent water issues in India.[26] The towns of Kaladera in the water-poor Rajasthan District and Plachimada in the water-poor Kerala District blamed precipitous water-level declines in their aquifers on Coca-Cola bottling plants. Pepsi had similar charges brought against it. Coca-Cola denied responsibility shifting the blame to droughts that might have been brought on by climate change. Droughts not only threatened water supplies on which Coca-Cola depended. Along with the floods that might be unleashed by climate change they added risk to growing corn, sugar, and the other ingredients on which Coca-Cola relied. The price of these essential raw materials had the potential to rise dramatically.

The unpredictability of these prices was an alarming development as it meant that the economic impact of global warming extended backward into the supply chain. Global warming also could affect consumers' standard of living. Coca-Cola and Pepsi relied upon a growing global middle class to sell its products. If this middle class was economically vulnerable to climate-change disruption, demand for the beverage makers' products would go down. Coca-Cola, as a consequence, was keen on lobbying countries to adopt more climate-friendly policies. Along with other companies it was active in this effort. However, the determination of Coca-Cola and other companies to have such policies enacted was thwarted in most countries in the world. In the US, lawmakers were uncomfortable with these policies. Developing countries in Asia, such as India and China, which depended heavily on coal, though understanding the importance of climate change, had as their first priority the need to improve their teeming populations' standard of living. Even Western European nations reconsidered climate change policies they had established because of ongoing economic malaise and hardship.

The key focus of Pepsi's climate change agenda was energy. The company acquired its first renewable energy certificates (RECs) in 2007. This step brought it to the forefront of US green power buyers. It purchased enough renewable energy to offset electricity use at all of its US operations, thereby achieving a top position on the EPA's list of greenest energy users. Another Pepsi commitment was to green buildings. Its Gatorade facility in Virginia obtained gold level Leadership in Energy and Environmental Design (LEED) from the US Green Building Council (USGBC). Overall, the company promised to slash fuel and electricity use by 25 percent and reduce water use by 20 percent by 2015 compared to 2006 levels and, like Coca-Cola, it pledged to remove hydrofluorocarbons from vending machines.[27]

Coca-Cola was one of the earliest members of the Global Greenhouse Gas Register of the World Economic Forum – joining in 2005. Along with the World Business Council for Sustainable Development and the World Resources Institute the Forum adopted a greenhouse gas (GHG) protocol, which aimed to harmonize GHG accounting and reporting standards. In 2005 the Carbon Disclosure Project acknowledged Coca-Cola's improved response to the World Registry of Corporate GHG Emissions it distributed to institutional investors concerned about climate change. Coca-Cola's Commitment 2020 plan included goals of reducing its carbon footprint one percent from a 2007 baseline, minimizing water use, and phasing out hydrofluorocarbons, the powerful greenhouse gases used as refrigerants, by 2015.

Coca-Cola also was committed to recovering 100 percent of its packaging waste and increasing recycling. Part of the packaging initiative was to introduce sustainable bulk packaging systems such as refillable steel tanks or bags-in-boxes (BIBs) for the syrups it delivered to bottlers throughout the world. Pepsi as well was making the packaging of its products more sustainable, looking for innovations in making packaging lighter and recycling and searching for alternative materials, such as the inclusion of at least ten percent of recycled polyethylene terephthalate (PET) in the primary soft drink containers it used in the United States. Its Naked Juice products sold in the United States had a 100 percent recycled PET container and Pepsi was launching a green PET bottle in Canada.

Social and economic performance

While Coca-Cola took market share from Pepsi in many world markets, Pepsi rose higher in ratings of corporate citizenship. It did so by moving brands into various good-for-you categories, embracing broader-than-bottom-line purposes, and trying to succeed with good-cause initiatives. Though Coca-Cola was not a laggard in these areas, it was more cautious. The priorities of Muhtar Kent, who became Coca-Cola's CEO in 2008, were more business-like in nature than the priorities of Pepsi's Nooyi.[28] Coca-Cola generally stuck to business performance first and put social concerns second. The environmental, social, and governance (ESG) disclosure score published in Bloomberg's Professional database showed that Pepsi surpassed Coca-Cola. Given the direction CEO Nooyi had given the company, this achievement was not accidental.

Both Coca-Cola and Pepsi disclosed their GHG emissions and had the data verified. The data revealed that Coca-Cola's GHG intensity was about 30 percent higher than Pepsi's. They showed that its water intensity was nearly 3.5 times greater than Pepsi's. Pepsi had 31 percent representation of women on its board versus Coca-Cola's 24 percent. Pepsi also outperformed Coca-Cola with regard to board independence, but Coca-Cola slightly outspent Pepsi with regard to charitable contributions. The 2011 Dow Jones Sustainability Index saw Pepsi as the leader in the food and beverage sector, while it no longer listed

Coca-Cola, one among a number of well-known companies dropped from the list. With Nooyi's strong championing, sustainability was a major focus at Pepsi but clearly, improving the nutritional profile of Pepsi's products still was a major challenge.

Bottler acquisition and other moves

Pepsi rearranged its relationships with its bottlers and Coca-Cola soon followed. In 2009, Pepsi completed a $7.8 billion acquisition of its two largest North American bottlers. By integrating their operations into the company, Pepsi saved money and enjoyed a boost in revenue. Pepsi revenue growth was achieved by this acquisition, which masked weak performance in other areas.

Coca-Cola followed suit in 2010. Muhtar Kent himself had been a bottler and understood their needs. He had been European chief of Amatil, an Australian-based bottler that operated on the European continent. When he returned to work for Coca-Cola in 2005, his main job was collaborating with the bottlers to boost their sales. When promoted to president of international operations, he focused on establishing better relations with bottlers. Prior to his tenure as CEO, the bottlers often felt abused by Coca-Cola. Coca-Cola had squeezed so much money out of them that they were seriously in debt and no longer could invest sufficient amounts of money in market development. Coca-Cola's $13 billion purchase of the largest of its North American bottlers, active not only in the United States but also Western Europe, gave it more control over the production and distribution and allowed it to reduce expenses. Along with this acquisition came revenue and market share.

Prior to Coca-Cola's and Pepsi's acquisition of the bottlers, the two companies had engaged more in marketing and product development than manufacturing. They sold beverage concentrate and syrup to the bottlers who did the capital- and labor-intensive work of making and distributing the finished beverages. In the short term the bottler acquisition raised both firms' revenues, but this move also lowered profitability. After Coca-Cola and Pepsi acquired the bottlers, their companies were larger and more complicated to run. They were less flexible and perhaps also less capable of innovation.

Sodastream's home carbonation products reduced the utility of Pepsi's and Coca-Cola's purchase of the bottlers. SodaStream was

Table 8.15 *Beverage company financials compared, July 2014*

	Pepsi	Coca-Cola	Dr. Pepper Snapple	Monster
Market capitalization ($)	140.42 b	181.62 b	11.89 b	14.44 b
Employees	274,000	130,600	19,000	1,240
Quarterly revenue growth	0.01	−0.01	0.01	0.09
Revenue ($)	66.54 b	46.22 b	6.04 b	2.35 b
Gross margin	0.53	0.61	0.59	0.53
Operating margin	0.15	0.24	0.2	0.28
Net income ($)	6.84 b	8.37 b	728.00 m	404.55 m

Compiled from publicly available quarterly report data of the two companies
b = billions; m = millions

an alternative to traditional sodas. Its system, which allowed customers to turn their tap water into carbonated drinks, sidestepped the bottlers. By sidestepping bottlers, it provided frequent imbibers of carbonated beverages with cost savings. The idea of a self-made soda was not entirely new at Coca-Cola. In 2009, it introduced a touch-screen Freestyle soda fountain machine that offered more than 100 drink options as a standard machine at some fast-food restaurants. To deal with the SodaStream challenge, Coca-Cola planned to partner with Green Mountain, a company in which it already had invested. Under the partnership, Green Mountain would produce a Keurig Cold brew system that would allow customers to make carbonated drinks by themselves. These technologies took away the need for bottlers. The unit price of soda made from a Keurig or a Sodastream machine was lower than the unit price of store-bought bottled beverages.

Wall Street did not reward Pepsi and Coca-Cola for their purchase of the bottlers. Both companies performed below the S&P stock market average from 2009 to 2014. The big winner was upstart Monster, which returned more than three times more to investors than Coca-Cola and Pepsi during this period (see Table 8.15). Monster, previously Hansen Juices, expanded its product lines and flavors. In 2013, it launched nine new product lines. Demand for energy drinks in the United States was anticipated to grow. In 2014 Coca-Cola therefore engaged Monster in a strategic partnership, acquiring a minority interest of about 17 percent in the company.[29] Coca-Cola transferred ownership of its energy drink business, including the NOS, Full Throttle, Burn, Mother, Play and Power Play, and Relentless brands to Monster in exchange for Monster's health and wellness drinks, its Hansen's, Peace Tea, and Hubert's Lemonade brands. Coca-Cola became Monster's preferred distribution partner and Monster became Coca-Cola's exclusive energy-drink affiliate.

Next steps

If consumers remained wary of sugar and artificially sweetened drinks, where would Pepsi and Coca-Cola find new customers? Pepsi's and Coca-Cola's sustainability accomplishments deserved praise, but to what extent did these activities augment their ability to find new customers? What goals for their sustainability and market growth should these companies have? Which products should they emphasize? Where should they sell these products? How should the products be delivered to customers? How should Pepsi and Coca-Cola achieve their sustainability goals and at the same time satisfy their shareholders' need for high returns?

Notes

1 See W. McKitterick "Fizzling out: soda producers will refresh product lines to decelerate falling demand," *IBISWorld Industry Report 31211a, Soda Production in the US* (2014).
2 C. Suddath and D. Stanford, "Coke confronts its big fat problem," *Bloomberg Business Week* (2014): www.businessweek.com/articles/2014–07–31/coca-cola-sales-decline-health-concerns-spur-relaunch
3 Y. Wang, P. Coxson, Y. Shen, L. Goldman, and K. Bibbins-Domingo, "A penny-per-ounce tax on sugar-sweetened beverages would cut health and cost burdens of diabetes," *Health Affairs* (2012): http://content.healthaffairs.org/content/31/1/199.full?sid=e7cdd71b-93a1–47b3–872d-359a235498ea; American Heart Association, "Sugar 101," (2014): www.heart.org/HEARTORG/GettingHealthy/NutritionCenter/Sugars-101_UCM_306024_Article.jsp
4 McKitterick, "Fizzling out: soda producers will refresh product lines."
5 Suddath and Stanford, "Coke confronts its big fat problem."
6 B. McCay and C. Terhune, "Coke's Enviga: it may burn calories, but it isn't a cure for a bulging belly," *Wall Street Journal* (2006): http://online.wsj.com/articles/SB116070042671191408

7 See Euromonitor International, "Sports and energy drink market research," Market research for the soft drinks industry (2014): www.-euromonitor.com/sports-and-energy-drinks

8 See Euromonitor International, "Bottled water market research," Market research for the soft drink industry (2014): www.euromonitor.com/bottled-water

9 *Ibid.*

10 M. Esterl and D. Benoit, "Peltz's trian fund renews push for PepsiCo split," *Wall Street Journal* (2014): http://online.wsj.com/news/articles/SB10001424052702303636404579393481783495514

11 McKitterick, "Fizzling out: soda producers will refresh product lines"

12 Centers for Disease Control and Prevention, *Salt* (Atlanta, GA: 2014): www.cdc.gov/salt

13 J. Seabrook, "Snacks for a fat planet," *The New Yorker* (2011): www.-newyorker.com/magazine/2011/05/16/snacks-for-a-fat-planet

14 A. Marcus, *Winning Moves, Cases in Strategic Management* (Lombard, IL: Marsh Publications, 2009): pp. 119–39.

15 Seabrook, "Snacks for a fat planet."

16 *Ibid.*

17 *Ibid.*

18 *Ibid.*

19 *Ibid.*

20 *Ibid.*

21 S. Gregory, "Is vitaminwater really a healthy drink," *Time* (2010): http://content.time.com/time/business/article/0,8599,2007106,00.html

22 Marcus, *Winning Moves.*

23 *Ibid.*

24 *Ibid.*

25 See Coca-Cola Company, "Water stewardship and replenish report," (2014): www.coca-colacompany.com/water-stewardship-replenish-report

26 Marcus, *Winning Moves.*

27 See Pepsico, "GHG emissions: energy use and emissions," (2014): www.pepsico.com/Purpose/Environmental-Sustainability/GHG-Emissions

28 C. Burritt and D. Stanford, "Coca-Cola to purchase bottler in $12.3 billion deal (Update2)," *Bloomberg* (2010): www.bloomberg.com/apps/news?pid=newsarchive&sid=ayIm0dQClBNA

29 M. Esterl, "Coca-Cola buys stake in Monster beverage," *Wall Street Journal* (2014): http://online.wsj.com/articles/coke-buys-stake-in-monster-beverage-1408049780

PART V

Competition between mission and non-mission based businesses

9 | *Consensus capitalism: Whole Foods and Walmart*

John Mackey, charismatic founder and long-time CEO of Whole Foods, referred to the business model that he followed as conscious capitalism.[1] First and foremost this model meant that Whole Foods pursued a higher purpose than just maximizing the wealth of its shareholders. However, a better description of the kind of capitalism in which both Whole Foods and Walmart were engaged might be called consensus capitalism. All companies in the second decade of the twenty-first century had to profitably grow to please their shareholders and at the same time had to pursue a sustainability agenda that could convince external stakeholders of their rectitude.

The capitalism that both Whole Foods and Walmart practiced had converged, a convergence that signified that the major challenges that the two firms confronted were not entirely different. Whole Foods had to increase the size of its market while it continued to enhance its image as a company that was, to use Mackey's words, heroically trying to change the world. Walmart, as well, despite its immense size, had to meet shareholder expectations to grow and be profitable while at the same time it had to improve its reputation for corporate social responsibility, if not as heroically as Whole Foods, then by means of practical steps that had meaning for its workers, the environment, and communities.

No matter how much these companies had achieved they still had far to go on their journeys toward sustainability. They had to become more sustainable while also meeting the expectations of their shareholders. The dilemma they faced was how to deal with the challenge of achieving this broad agenda. What should their plan of action be? What should they do next?

How to stand out

Whole Foods and Walmart were finding it increasingly more difficult to stand out. While Whole Foods was best known for its gourmet natural

259

foods, Walmart was best known for its low prices. The distinctive difference between them, however, was starting to blur. The pressure on Whole Foods was to lower its prices and the pressure on Walmart was to offer the healthier eating fare for which Whole Foods was celebrated. With its partnership with Wild Oats, Walmart was moving into Whole Foods' turf and offering a line of certified organic foods at much lower prices than Whole Foods.

In addition, both companies faced major competitors that were growing faster than either of them. Whole Foods had to be especially apprehensive about copy-cat chain Sprouts Farmers Market and Walmart had to be particularly anxious about warehouse giant Costco. In August 2014, Sprouts Farmers Market was growing twice as fast as Whole Foods and Costco's growth was seven times that of Walmart (see Table 9.1). Neither Whole Foods nor Walmart were growing as fast as Kroger. Perennial Walmart rival, Target, despite its serious data breach, had two times Walmart's quarterly growth rate in August 2014.

From 2009 to 2014 neither the share prices of Whole Foods nor Walmart did better than the S&P 500. Kroger was the only grocer that did better than the S&P 500. From an investor's perspective it was the best performing company in this category. The 2014 stock market performance of Whole Foods put it at the bottom among retail grocers. It trailed Sprouts Farmers Market and Walmart, though ahead of Target, and trailed Costco.

Whole Food's margins continued to be high, but investors were concerned that such high margins could not be sustained. Falling margins were likely partly because of the competitive pressure from upstart Sprouts. As of August 2014, Sprouts had 163 stores, mostly in the southwest and western United States, and was growing 12 percent annually. Sprouts kept its prices down by eliminating frills and having simpler operations than Whole Foods. It did not engage in activities such as providing free samples or offering freshly cooked food to entice customers.

Prior to Sprouts' emergence, Whole Foods had enjoyed close to a monopoly status in the premium health-food store niche. It now faced growing competitive pressure not only from Sprouts but from grocers like Kroger that were also selling the same natural and healthy foods, as well as from Walmart, the dominant US grocer in terms of market share. These companies all had full lines of these products

Table 9.1 *Quarterly revenue growth and other financial indicators of major food retailers, August 2014*

	Whole Foods	Sprouts Farmers Market	Walmart	Costco	Kroger	Target
Quarterly revenue growth	0.10	0.20	0.01	0.07	0.10	0.02
Revenue ($)	13.91 b	2.71 b	480.48 b	109.60 b	101.34 b	73.23 b
Gross margin	0.36	0.30	0.25	0.13	0.21	0.29
Operating margin	0.07	0.07	0.06	0.03	0.03	0.05
Net income ($)	572.00 m	84.62 m	15.45 b	1.98 b	1.53 b	1.51 b
Employees	56,700	14,000	2,000,000	103,000	375,000	366,000
Market cap ($)	14.14 b	4.64 b	243.87 b	53.07 b	24.93 b	38.07 b

Compiled from publicly available quarterly report data of the companies
b = billions; m = millions

that were priced more affordably than similar items found in Whole Foods.

Walmart, the world's largest retailer, operated close to 11,000 stores in many formats in more than 25 countries and sold its products in discount stores, supercenters, Sam's Clubs, neighborhood markets, and on the Internet. It made broad assortments of merchandise available to customers – not just food – everything from pet supplies to consumer electronics – all of which it sold at everyday low prices (EDLP).

Walmart was synonymous with its big-box stores, but not all consumers had the same appreciation for the big-box retailing experience. The company therefore operated through several store formats ranging from relatively small express stores in Mexico to cash-and-carry warehouses in India. The problem with the smaller store formats was that it was hard to achieve the supply-chain efficiencies for which Walmart was so well known. Target was showing an increasing ability to catch up with these supply-chain efficiencies and to match Walmart on price. Walmart also was chasing Amazon, which had a stronger presence on the Internet.

In terms of overall resources Walmart totally dominated Whole Foods. In 2013 Whole Foods Market operated just 362 retail stores, of which 347 were located in 40 US states and the District of Columbia, eight in Canada, and seven in the UK. A premium natural and organic supermarket, Whole Foods offered 2,600 store-brand natural and organic products to customers and sold them specialty and organic coffee, tea, and drinking chocolate through a subsidiary called Allegro Coffee Company.

In the realm of social responsibility the images that Whole Foods and Walmart tried to project did not entirely match the reality. Whole Foods touted its dedication to natural foods and proudly displayed the many environmental awards it had won on its website and elsewhere, but it regularly was criticized for among other matters the hyperaggressive way that it had expanded that had leveled smaller health-food chains and cooperatives. Similarly, Walmart in its growth had upended numerous smaller and weaker competitors. However, Walmart was in the process of introducing innovative green business standards to which it expected its suppliers in the United States and overseas to conform. If these efforts would work was yet to be determined.

Despite the efforts Whole Foods and Walmart made to stand out in the domain of social responsibility, the most comprehensive and objective assessment group CSRHub rated neither company as doing that well (see Table 9.2).[2] CSRHub evaluated 12 indicators of employee, environment, community, and governance performance and aggregated and normalized this information to create a broad and consistent set of findings. The sources on which it relied included socially responsible investing firms, NGOs, government agencies, and many lists of best and worst firms. According to CSRHub, Whole Foods was tied for seventh and Walmart was ninth among the top ten major food retailers in sustainability in 2014. Both performed below food retailing's overall average, Whole Foods in every dimension except community involvement and Walmart in every dimension except the environment. Both Whole Foods and Walmart had much to prove to their shareholders and to the socially responsible investment community.

A mission-based business

As a mission-based business, Whole Foods' goal was not to just sell food but to educate its customers about a lifestyle and to encourage them to adopt a set of values. These values included community well-being and environmental awareness as well as healthy eating of high-quality natural and organic foods. Whole Foods also celebrated the win–win partnerships it maintained with its suppliers, which it claimed were opposed to Walmart whose relations with suppliers were meant to be a zero-sum game in which one party prevailed at the expense of the other.

When all the 78 ingredients that Whole Foods banned from its shelves were considered, it prohibited more than half the items that Walmart sold.[3] The decisions to ban particular ingredients derived from many factors including safety, the way the foods were manufactured, their compatibility with the company's values, and animal welfare. Whole Foods also responded to customer complaints. For example, it had not always banned HFC. It only added HFC to the list of prohibited ingredients in 2011 after customers complained. High fructose corn syrup often was singled out as a cause of high obesity rates, but biochemically it differed little from sugar, a substance that Whole Foods did not ban. Another sweetener Whole Foods prohibited,

Table 9.2 *Sustainability scores of major food retailers, August 2014*

Rank	Company	Overall	Community	Employees	Environment	Governance
1	Weis Markets	64	65	61	74	56
2	Carrefour	62	62	64	65	58
3	Winn-Dixie	62	60	53	58	75
4	Supervalu	59	55	64	59	57
5	Kroger	57	53	54	61	57
6	Safeway	56	51	58	58	57
7	Target	55	44	53	62	58
8	Whole Foods	55	56	51	58	55
9	Walmart	50	43	43	62	50
10	Costco	49	46	42	57	51
	All company average	57	54	54	61	57

CSRHub: www.csrhub.com

aspartame, had been the subject of much public debate, yet most authoritative health bodies that had examined the evidence concluded that aspartame was safe for consumption.

Simply because food items sold at Walmart contained HFC, about 14 percent of them could not be sold at Whole Foods.[4] Of the soft drinks Walmart sold, more than 95 percent contained HFC and the preservative sodium benzoate, two ingredients Whole Foods deemed unacceptable. Walmart sold Great Value 100% Whole Wheat Bread, which had seven ingredients on the Whole Foods' prohibited list. In addition to HFC, they were sodium stearoyl lactylate, ethoxylated diglycerides, datem, azodicarbonamide, ammonium chloride, and calcium propionate.

Walmart claimed it gave customers what they wanted, low prices and the freedom to decide what foods they would buy. The company had moved into groceries in the early 1990s, mainly to get customers to come into its stores more often. The average customer visited a food store about once a week, more often than they went anywhere – including church. To draw traffic, Walmart sold groceries at razor-thin margins. By 2003, this strategy had helped it become the largest grocer in the United States. Food became the most important item Walmart sold, consisting of well over 50 percent of its annual sales. With about 30 percent of the US food market, suppliers were heavily dependent on Walmart for their survival. Target, a major Walmart competitor, had to copy Walmart's strategy of combining food with other merchandise in order to maintain its rivalry with Walmart.

Though Walmart did not adhere to policies equivalent to Whole Food's about unacceptable ingredients, it did follow stricter guidelines than those mandated by the FDA and the US Department of Agriculture. Major food retailers along with Walmart had set up the Global Food Safety Initiative (GSFI) after they determined that it was necessary to strengthen and maintain consumer trust by firming up the safety of the food supply chain. Walmart voluntarily conformed to GSFI's standards.

Whole Foods' policies about unacceptable ingredients did not escape criticism. As indicated, the ingredients it banned included HFC and aspartame, but not sugar. The company took pride in its collection of specialty chocolates. It did a lively business selling sugar-filled indulgent baked goods and deserts. Its Chocolate Sandwich Cremes were knock-offs of Oreos that rivaled the Kraft product in their lack of sound nutritional value. Indeed, customers had sued the company for vastly understating the amount of sugar in its store-brand yogurt.[5] Lawyers who brought the class-action Federal Court case cited six tests by *Consumer Reports* on the supermarket chain's Whole Foods 365 Everyday Value Plain Greek Yogurt, which showed that it had 11.4 grams of sugar per 170-gram serving rather than the 2 grams that Whole Foods listed on the label. The plaintiffs sought five million dollars in damages. Forced to capitulate Whole Foods removed the yogurt from its shelves, investigated the incident and declared that its intention was to provide customers high-quality products that had accurate labeling. For those with an interest in healthier fare than its Chocolate Sandwich Cremes or its yogurt, the company gave them the choice of buying Engine 2 Plant-Strong products, a line of minimally processed snacks, breakfast items, and pantry staples.

Whole Foods' growth

Because Whole Foods had grown so rapidly by means of acquisitions, it faced criticism that it had pursued a policy of aggressive monopolization that forced many independent retailers and co-ops to cease to exist. Competitors the company swallowed included Bread & Circus, Fresh Fields, Bread of Life, Merchant of Vino, Nature's Heartland, Food for Thought, Harry's Farmers Market, and Mrs Gooch's Natural Foods Market.

Whole Foods began in 1980 when John Mackey and his then girlfriend opened Safer Way, one of a number of small health-food grocers in the Austin, Texas and merged it with Clarksville Natural Grocery. The name Safer Way was a spoof on the name of the food giant Safeway. Craig Weller and Mark Skiles, owners of Clarksville, later charged that they had been coerced to join Whole Foods by threats Mackey made that he would put them out of business.

Mackey admittedly was very competitive.[6] From an upper middle-class family he had been a basketball player in high school, and afterward a student at Trinity College in San Antonio and the University of Texas, who came close, but did not complete his degree. During his college years, he drifted in and out of various communes, worked for various health-food stores and co-ops in the Austin area, and experimented with alternative life styles. The main funding for the first Safer Way store came from a $20,000 investment from his father, the CEO of a hospital-management company, and his girlfriend, who had a $7,000 inheritance. To carry out the merger with Clarksville, Mackey obtained more funding from his father, this time for $25,000 and a matching $25,000 from a Safer Way customer. Located in a former nightclub the first Whole Foods, at 12,500 square feet and with a staff of 19, was huge in comparison to other health-food stores of its time. To fill the space, Mackey sold more than just granola and lentils. Unlike other health-foods stores, he sold liquor and meat.

In 1984, Whole Foods expanded, first into Houston and then into Dallas, where it acquired the Bluebonnet Natural Foods Grocery.[7] Then in 1988 it moved into New Orleans where it purchased another firm named The Whole Food Company. Buying Mill Valley, it set up operations in Palo Alto, California. In 1989, it bought Wellspring Grocery adjacent to the college towns of Chapel Hill and Durham North Carolina.

After Whole Foods went public in 1992 it was added to the NASDAQ-100 Index and went on a shopping spree. In the 1990s it acquired many more health-food stores and chains including:

- Bread & Circus in Massachusetts and Rhode Island
- Mrs. Gooch's Natural Foods Markets in Los Angeles
- Unicorn Village in South Florida
- Bread of Life in Northern California
- Fresh Fields Markets in the Midwest and East Coast
- Bread of Life in Florida
- Merchant of Vino in Detroit
- Nature's Heartland in Boston
- Oak Street Market in Evanston, Illinois

The key variable Whole Foods used in deciding what to acquire and where to put new stores was the number of college graduates within a 16-minute drive. In the next decade Whole Foods made many more acquisitions including Natural Abilities in Northern California, Harry's Farmers Market in Atlanta, and Fresh & Wild in the UK. The advantage of becoming bigger was the clout it gave the company with suppliers with whom it could lock up rare specialty foods and dictate terms including price. With all these acquisitions, Whole Foods became the first nationally certified organic grocer in the United States.

The owners of the health-food stores and chains that Whole Foods acquired often remained with the company. They brought expertise that Whole Foods did not have. Wellspring Grocery co-owner Lex Alexander had experience with private-labels; Bread & Circus' owner Tony Harnett had know-how in procuring seafood; and Mrs Gooch's owner Sandy Gooch had competencies in diet supplements and meat merchandising. Walter Robb, who rose to the position of CEO, had been a founder of Mill Valley.

The acquisition of Wild Oats

When Whole Foods attempted to acquire Wild Oats in 2007, Wild Oats had 109 stores in 23 US states and British Columbia. The acquisition would mean that Whole Foods would be able to gain an even tighter grip on the supply chain. Libby Cook and Mike Gilliland had started Wild Oats in 1986 by opening their first stores in Boulder, Santa Fe, and Denver – attractive markets that Whole Foods wanted to penetrate. Wild Oats had made acquisitions in other attractive markets where Whole Foods wanted to locate including Boulder where Wild Oats had purchased Alfalfa's Market; British Columbia where it bought the Three Capers Community Market; San Diego where it acquired Henry's Marketplace stores; Portland, Oregon where it purchased the Nature's Northwest chain; and San Antonio where it acquired Sun Harvest stores.

Wild Oats' image among health-food shoppers was impeccable. Perry Odak, previously of Ben & Jerry's, became CEO in 2001, but resigned in 2006 prior to the acquisition. Whole Foods was set to pay an estimated $565 million for Wild Oats and assume the company's debt of about $106 million. It would rebrand most of the stores Whole Foods Markets, convert these stores to its systems, move the employees to its payroll, and eliminate management positions. Mackey's goal was to achieve greater health-food industry consolidation. With the acquisition of Wild Oats this task would be nearly complete.

However, the Bush Administration, in an uncharacteristic moment of antitrust ardor, fought Whole Foods' purchase, contending that the merged company would unfairly dominate the market. At the same time, the Securities and Exchange Commission (SEC) began an investigation of Mackey. For eight years he had been surreptitiously logging into an Internet message board under the pseudonym, Rahodeb, which was an anagram of his wife Deborah's name. On June 21, 2006 he wrote on the message board that Wild Oats "still stinks and remains grossly overvalued based on very weak fundamentals. The stock is up now but if it doesn't get sold in the next year or so it is going to plummet back down. Wait and see."[8] While panning Wild Oats, Mackey obsessively praised his own company. By trashing his competitor he was looking for its stock price to drop at the moment Whole Foods made a bid for the company.

Until this discovery Mackey had been a media and stock-market star. Suddenly he was viewed as a shady businessman and monopolist. Alleging that the proposed acquisition by eliminating competition violated federal antitrust laws, the Federal Trade Commission (FTC) fought the transaction. It maintained that if it did not prevent the transaction Whole Foods would be able to raise prices, cut quality, and gouge customers. On his blog, Mackey explained why he thought the deal should be allowed:"If Kroger, Safeway, Super Value, or Walmart (all much, much larger companies than Whole Foods) were to acquire Wild Oats and commit their enormous capital resources to growing the company and improving its execution, then this could threaten Whole Foods' #1 leadership position."[9] A federal district court permitted the deal, but in 2008 the US Court of Appeals for the District of Columbia reversed the decision, ruling that consumers who cared about social and environmental responsibility would be adversely affected. The Court's view was that evidence indicated that Whole Foods' intention was to raise prices.

Whole Foods agreed to a settlement in 2009, selling the brand name Wild Oats, along with 32 of the company's stores and the company's intellectual property to Luberski a West Coast food distributor, otherwise known as Hidden Villa Ranch, while retaining the remainder of Wild Oats' assets. Behind Hidden Villa Ranch and Luberski was the private equity firm Yucaipa that had large interests in the grocery industry. Yucaipa, whose grocery store holdings were manifold and whose buying and selling of companies legendary, was paying increasing attention to health foods. In 1991 it acquired Alpha Beta in California, in 1994 Smitty's in Phoenix and Ralphs Grocery in California, and in 1995 Dominick's in Chicago. Dominick's then was sold to Safeway in 1996, Ralphs merged with Fred Meyer, and Fred Meyer was sold to Kroger in 1997. Yucaipa's founder and the primary agent and beneficiary of these moves was California billionaire and Democratic Party donor Ron Burkle.

After Whole Foods' acquisition of Wild Oats, the 2008 recession took hold. Whole Foods' sales and stock slid. Per capita disposable income declined and consumers pulled away from premium, organic and all-natural brands, which hurt Whole Foods' revenues. Consumers wanted bargains and turned to the less expensive private labels in grocers such as Walmart. As the recession deepened and Whole Foods' troubles worsened, the company needed new sources of capital. Leonard Green & Partners, a private-equity firm, bought 17 percent of the firm and received two seats on its board. Yucaipa purchased a seven percent stake in Whole Foods and the upshot was that Mackey had to give up the chair of the Whole Foods' board, a position he had held since the company's inception.

Prior to buying a stake in Whole Foods, Yucaipa had acquired 40 percent of the East Coast grocery chain Pathmark. Wild Oats partnered with Pathmark to bring private-label organic products to Pathmark's stores. Yucaipa also bought a stake in the Great Atlantic & Pacific Tea Company (A&P), another troubled grocery chain and rumors abounded that Yucaipa might convert old A&Ps into health-food stores that would stock Wild Oats products and undersell Whole Foods' highest margin categories.

As the recession slackened, Whole Foods, though, made a comeback. Same store revenues again grew and the company's share price advanced. From 2009 to 2014, share prices grew by a whopping 85 percent annually, but in 2014 revenues again contracted and the company's stock market value slumped by 20 percent with many analysts reasoning that the company was overpriced and due for a correction. The question for Whole Foods was how could it stop the skid. How would it react to growing competition in niches it heretofore had dominated?

Growth in the US food industry was not strong (see Table 9.3).[10] Buyers wanted ethically sourced, fresh, simple, nutritious foods, Whole Food's strength; however, they also wanted ethnic fare and new and exotic tastes and were very concerned about price. Companies such as Costco had a wide range of products at low prices. They also provided ancillary services such as gas stations, pharmacies, food courts, hearing aids, and travel. The popularity of convenience stores was growing because they were small and customers could get in and out of them quickly. Most offered some products at value prices and a few sold healthy and nutritious items. The question Whole Foods faced was why

Table 9.3 *Revenue growth in the retail food industry, 2000 to 2013*

Year	Revenue, $ million	Growth, percentage
2000	509,519.5	0.0
2001	517,676.1	1.6
2002	510,711.6	− 1.4
2003	512,055.0	0.3
2004	514,223.0	0.4
2005	517,893.7	0.7
2006	517,794.4	0.0
2007	526,608.6	1.7
2008	537,793.6	2.1
2009	532,968.4	− 0.9
2010	535,290.3	0.4
2011	550,602.1	2.9
2012	558,338.0	1.4
2013	568,931.5	1.9

IBISWorld Industry Report 44511, Supermarkets & Grocery Stores in US (2015)

customers should regularly shop at its stores. Among the alternatives, how much room was there for a high-priced health-food purveyor like Whole Foods?

Walmart's partnership with Wild Oats

Walmart's announcement that it would carry items from Wild Oats was an important step in the evolution of the organic food usually associated with Whole Foods from the fringe to a $35 billion a year industry.[11] A dozen years earlier, organic food sales were just $8 billion, but by 2014, nearly 80 percent of US families reported that they purchased organic foods some of the time. Growing sales were associated with the desire by people to have healthier life styles.

With a public increasingly suspicious of the foods it ate, a USDA organic label made a difference. Introduced in 1990 after the passage of the Organic Foods Production Act, the label did not mean the foods consisted of fresh vegetables or whole grains. Nor did the label guarantee that organic foods were healthier than non-organic fare. It just pledged that the foods did not contain artificial or sewage-based fertilizers, pesticides, GM organisms, and most hormones and antibiotics. Nonetheless, this pledge provided consumers with confidence that they knew what they were getting when they shopped organic.

Believing that it could appeal to customers outside its blue-collar core, Walmart first entered the organic market in 2006. Hoping it could lure consumers who were willing to spend more on food than its typical penurious shopper, it stocked more than 1,600 organic items on its shelves by 2014. A leading seller of organic milk, it sold its own organic fresh produce under the Marketside label.

In 2014, Walmart partnered with Wild Oats to sell packaged organic foods. A major category within organic foods was packaged goods. In the United States sales doubled from $5.77 billion a decade earlier to $12 billion in 2013, while the overall sale of packaged foods rose just 25 percent in the same time period.[12] The press release accompanying the partnership between Walmart and Wild Oats read:

Originally introduced in 1987, Wild Oats will re-launch at Walmart starting this month with a new, more affordable price point on quality products covering a broad variety of categories – from salsa and pasta sauce to quinoa and chicken broth. Customers will save 25 percent or more when comparing Wild Oats to national brand organic products.[13]

Wild Oats Marketplace Organic products included everything from canned vegetables to spices such as paprika, curry powder, and ground cinnamon. Walmart priced these products at a level equivalent to national non-organic brands, with its own Great Value private-label line, which was not organic, still holding the lowest price position.

Some commentators saw in Walmart's move the potential to reduce the gap between the ability of rich and poor people to enjoy healthy foods. The oft-made critique was that the poor had to shop based on price and convenience and the only options they had were bad quality, unhealthy fare. Walmart's strategy could open up better eating habits for society's less fortunate. While the need to do the right thing for society undoubtedly was important to Walmart, its main motivation was to increase traffic and interest in its stores, which had been dropping, as indicated by nearly regular quarterly declines in same-store sales. Walmart also had to keep up with its major rival, Target, which also had launched an organic and natural product line, called Simply Balanced. Target had 120 natural and organic products, highlighting 17 celebrated brands that were found exclusively at the company's stores for a period of six months or more. Troubled by a security breach and poorly executed move into Canada, Target, like Walmart, was looking for ways to grow. In 2013 natural and organic foods were a bright spot, with above-average growth in organics over the previous year of 15 percent.[14]

Walmart research found that 91 percent of Walmart's shoppers would consider purchasing affordable organic products, if the products were priced appropriately and came from a well-respected brand.[15] Wild Oats was a well-respected brand that offered a product that featured simple and real ingredients. It put together these ingredients in a ready-to-prepare skillet meal at just $1.50 for 5.8 ounces. With Wild Oats promising additional low-priced and organic items of this nature, the partnership between Wild Oats and Walmart could put a dent in the large price premiums Whole Foods charged for similar items.

Eliminating these price premiums was not going to be easy, however. Mainly concentrating on items such as tomato paste, chicken broth, and cinnamon applesauce, Walmart would be able to carry the Wild Oats label only in its pantry section. More than 90 percent of the products in this section would be organic, while the rest would adhere to Wild Oats' standards of natural ingredients and additives. Limiting the launch of organic packaged foods was necessary because Wild Oats had to make sure it had ample supplies of organic ingredients. Globally there was insufficient organic raw material and processing capacity. To ensure adequate supply Walmart would have to enter into long-term contracts with growers and processors, locking them in for a considerable period of time since demand would grow if Walmart kept its prices low. Because supply of organic ingredients was in doubt, Walmart restricted the launch of the Wild Oats brand to about half of its US stores.

Walmart's moves intensified competition among sellers to access the trustworthy organic suppliers. With less exclusive access to suppliers, shareholders already were concerned that Whole Foods might lose its strong position in organics. Besides Walmart, conventional supermarket giants like Kroger that sold organic products sought access to organic suppliers. Kroger had 170 items in its Naturally Preferred product line to stock. Sprouts Farmers Market, which had gained ground and was eroding Whole Foods' organic market share, also competed with Whole Foods for supplier access. In 2014, Whole Foods' comparable store sales growth was declining, while Sprouts' were growing.

Table 9.4 *Comparative prices*^{a} of organic food sold at Walmart and at other supermarkets

Product	Walmart prices, $	Local supermarket prices, $	Walmart's price advantage, percentage cheaper
Basil leaves	42.24	145.16	71
Cayenne pepper	17.19	57.49	70
Ground cinnamon	19.84	63.89	69
Black beans	0.94	2.79	66
Ketchup	1.19	3.42	65
Tomato sauce	0.94	2.69	65
Garlic powder	15.57	42.60	63
Oregano	63.36	169.28	63
Cinnamon applesauce cups	1.32	2.99	56
Creamy peanut butter	2.27	4.99	55
Marinara sauce	2.41	3.68	35
Tomato paste	1.55	2.13	27
Chicken broth	1.98	2.50	21
Extra-virgin olive oil	12.39	15.41	20
Kidney beans	0.94	1.02	8

^{a} All prices are per pound except for marinara sauce, chicken broth, and extra-virgin olive oil, which are per quart.
© 2014 by Consumers Union of U.S., Inc. Yonkers, NY 10703-1057, a nonprofit organization. Reprinted with permission for educational purposes only.
Taken from Consumer Reports, "Get lower-cost organic groceries with Walmart's Wild Oats Marketplace line," *Consumer Reports* (2014): www.consumerreports.org/cro/news/2014/04/get-lower-cost-organic-groceries-with-walmart-s-wild-oats-marketplace-line/index.htm

At the same time that it had become more difficult to access the supply base, Whole Foods was under pressure to lower its prices. *Consumer Reports* did a comparison of the prices on organic products sold in Walmart to organic products in other local supermarkets and found that Walmart's prices were substantially lower.[16] In two-thirds of the comparisons, the differential was greater than 50 percent (see Table 9.4).

Because Whole Foods had high margins, there might be room for it to lower its prices. Customers, however, did not shop at Whole Foods just because of the prices. They shopped there because they enjoyed the experience more than if they had to shop in a vast and shabby Walmart. Achieving lower prices might compromise the look and feel of Whole Foods' stores as it would mean less lighting and fewer elaborate displays. Because Whole Foods had so much overhead invested in its showy stores, it was not in a position where it could easily lower prices. Nor was the company as big as Walmart and therefore it was not in a positon to extract additional concessions from suppliers. Walmart or Kroger could sell organic foods as loss leaders to get consumers into their stores but Whole Foods could not do the same. If it regularly underpriced organics that might signify low quality.

Whole Foods retrofitted about 70 stores and opened about 30 new stores per year. Every time it retrofitted or opened a store, it tried to innovate in ways that made the shopping experience more sat- isfying. It could offer services such as home delivery and customer pickup in key markets, introduce an online subscription club, and ship major food categories to customers' homes, but would these services lead consumers to have a greater appreciation for the company? They had become standard at many chains and customers expected them. Did customers care enough about them to compensate for Whole Foods' large price differential? It was not at all clear what Whole Foods should do to stand out. Self-checkout counters were becoming increasingly popular. Should the company add Pay By Touch scan- ners, which made checkout payment even quicker and safer? Through the system, a customer could set up an e-wallet that contained the customer's bank account, reward card, and credit card information. Payment took place by simply scanning a fingerprint and keying in a password linked to account details. Consumers who bought just a few items might prefer the system because of its convenience but like other new technologies this one faced hurdles. Despite the hurdles, the sys- tem was likely to become standard practice among grocers, because it eliminated cashiers and lowered costs. Whole Foods' plan was to inau- gurate its first-ever national media campaign. The campaign would focus on its values and a new rating system for its products, but was this plan likely to bring the kind of avid customer loyalty the firm needed?

Industrial-scale distribution

For Walmart, with its massive scale, the question was whether the organic suppliers on which it had to depend could reliably deliver large

amounts of organic products cheaply. Subject to heavy industry lobbying, the US government, when it established guidelines for organic
food, allowed for a loophole. It left out the word "local" from the
formula that determined if a product was organic, an omission that
worked to Whole Foods' and Walmart's advantage since they could
line up supply agreements for large-scale shipments of organics at low
prices from distant places. Walmart's agreement with tomato farmers
was of this nature. The organic tomatoes found in Walmart stores did
not come not from local farmers. Walmart obtained guaranteed purchases at low costs from large bulk shippers and growers far from its
stores.

To keep organic prices low, Walmart had to assist in further stream-
lining the supply chain. Its mastery of supply-chain methods would
have to be applied to organic foods. As it accounted for a third of all
US grocery sales, it was well equipped to use its size to work with its
suppliers to lower prices. With economies of scale it could eliminate
extra channels that were common in the organic food market. Most
organic producers still relied on other companies' processing facilities,
which also handled conventional food, thus requiring that the processing facilities be shut down and cleaned out and incoming and outgoing
products segregated. Larger volumes, that would allow organic food
processors to run 100 percent organic all the time, could cut costs by
as much as 20 to 30 percent. Less expensive organic food would create
additional demand, which would allow for further price reductions
and more supply-chain efficiency.

This transformation would take time, however. The question was
whether further consolidating the still fragmented organic-food supply
chain under the aegis of Walmart's distribution system, and giving
manufacturers the chance to operate on a larger and more efficient
scale, really would work. Just getting the additional farmland certified
to create the crops to feed an expanded system would take years. It
was not at all clear if farmers who did not use synthetic pesticides and
industrial fertilizers could be as productive as farmers that did. Even if
the supply chain became more efficient would organic farmers be able
to compete with non-organic farmers at the scale Walmart needed?
The acreage of organic farmland in the United States able to supply
the demand for organic food had to grow.

In the meantime much of the organic food found in US stores
would come from abroad. To fill the gap it would be necessary to
rely on imports. Walmart had induced many of its suppliers, including

such well-known companies as Huffy, Levi Strauss, and Master Lock, to relocate factories and jobs abroad to lower costs. Would Walmart's involvement push organic suppliers similarly to relocate? Laws of disclosure on organic food imported into the United States were weak. Purveyors of this food were under no obligation to reveal from where the food came and under what conditions it was produced. Would this shift in the source of organic products undermine organic standards?

Even if Walmart's goal to produce organic food more cheaply than it had been produced in the past was achieved, critics would not be pleased. They did not want people to buy organics because they cost less but because of the underlying ethical values that organics represented. Walmart with its industrial-scale distribution system was likely to contradict these values. Walmart's critics maintained that in buying organic goods in such large quantities, Walmart was not supporting an ethic in which small local family farmers played a large role. By incentivizing large-scale production, Walmart undermined this ethic. Production on the scale Walmart needed would deplete soil health and lead farmers to abandon land when the soil did not yield ample harvests. To achieve low-cost organic, producers would adhere to minimum standards, if they adhered to them at all.[17] For Walmart the issues were from where would the organic products it wanted come, how they would be produced, and would Walmart be able to reveal the true story behind the product label.

Social responsibility

Walmart and Whole Foods had to compete on their vision of social responsibility as well as on the products and services they offered. With regard to this vision, Whole Foods was far ahead of Walmart, but what about with regard to execution? Was Walmart better able to execute its vision than Whole Foods?

Whole Foods' vision

Whole Foods' vison focused on its values. For instance, on its website, the firm declared:

Whole Foods Market's vision of a sustainable future means our children and grandchildren will be living in a world that values human creativity, diversity, and individual choice. Businesses will harness human and material resources without devaluing the integrity of the individual or the planet's ecosystems. Companies, governments, and institutions will be held accountable for their actions. People will better understand that all actions have repercussions... It will be a world... where people are encouraged to discover, nurture, and share their life's passions.

The company was aspiring to make its business matter to customers and society in more ways than the bottom line. Founder Mackey co-authored a book called *Conscious Capitalism* in which he proclaimed that he believed that economic freedom and entrepreneurship were the best ways to end poverty, increase prosperity, and evolve humanity upward.[18] Safer Way, the store out of which Whole Foods evolved, was supposed to offer shoppers an alternative to evil profit-seeking corporations.

However, Mackey admitted that his worldview shifted when he had to run a real business and discovered that while business and capitalism were not yet perfect they were fundamentally good and ethical. Mackey's philosophy was to do good and make money, and the more money he made he believed the more good he could do. If Whole Foods sold good products and treated its employees, shareholders, customers, and suppliers well, it would spread goodness simply by thriving.

As a mission-based sustainable firm, there was no inherent reason why it could not be ethically and socially responsible and profitable. Whole Foods' core values provided it with commitments to the fulfillment and equitable treatment of all of its stakeholders – customers, employees, investors, and suppliers. The company's obligations extended to the entire population, to the food system, and to the Earth.

A fan of Milton Friedman, Ronald Reagan, and Ayn Rand, Mackey also was a forthright libertarian and mainstream believer in free markets. Based on these beliefs he questioned Obama's health-care initiative in a *Wall Street Journal* opinion article, asserting that many health-care problems were self-inflicted and every person should be responsible for their own health. Overweight and obese Americans had made bad choices and society should not suffer on account of them.

Pushback quickly came from many of Whole Foods' customers and suppliers who saw the problems of overeating in much different terms, as societal as well as individual, and found Mackey's comments offensive. His *Wall Street Journal* article inspired a Boycott Whole Foods campaign on Facebook with more than 27,000 members. Could a company whose CEO espoused such beliefs be trusted?

Whole Foods set up its own Facebook group to support Mackey who defended himself by pointing out that just because he had made known his opposition to the Obama health-care initiative did not mean that he did not support a host of causes that directly appealed to his socially conscious customers. He was pro-choice, in favor of legalizing marijuana and gay marriages, protecting the environment, enforcing strict animal welfare protection laws, allowing for a safety net for the poor and disabled, and in favor of a drastically reduced defense budget and US military presence, but he opposed socialism because in his opinion it took away economic and civil liberties and increased global poverty.

Whole Foods won many awards for social responsibility.[19] They included the Natural Products Association's 2009 Socially Responsible Retailer Award for excellence in integrating social responsibility into multiple aspects of its business. The Ethisphere Institute in 2010 recognized the company for being one of the world's most ethical. In 2013 Whole Foods ranked 19th in *Fortune* magazine's list of most admired companies. The company had a policy of donating five percent of after-tax profits to charities. A number of foundations were the recipients of its generosity. The Whole Planet Foundation gave micro-credit to poor people in communities that supplied its stores. Whole Kids Foundation improved children's nutrition by means of grants to schools for salad bars. The Animal Compassion Foundation was dedicated to improving the quality of life for farm animals.

Though accused of selling overpriced luxuries for finicky eaters, Whole Foods tried to expand its value offerings and narrow the pricing gap between the food it sold and the food that conventional grocers sold. It tried to accelerate its growth by serving anyone that aspired to a healthy lifestyle. The company recognized that there was a limit to how much it could expand its business if it just served wealthier individuals. It engaged in an experiment in serving less advantaged people by setting up a store in Detroit, but was uncertain how much revenue it could expect to obtain in poor, inner-city neighborhoods.

Walmart's vision

The vision of Walmart's founder, Sam Walton, was a more modest one than that of John Mackey. His desire to change the world was to attend to the needs of underserved populations. Walmart's attempts to draw in the affluent with cheap chic design largely failed. Affluent customers tended to skim low-margin items off the top of its shelves and buy their big-ticket items elsewhere. Walmart's core customer was blue collar or lower middle class.

Like Whole Foods, the company had a very active foundation that donated more than $1 billion in cash and in-kind donations to positively impact local and global communities. It quickly came to the aid of disaster victims. It did more than its part to hire veterans, putting more than 100,000 of them at work in its stores. Nonetheless, the company regularly was attacked by activist groups that claim that its stores harmed local retail districts and independent retailers and grocers. Its big boxes produced traffic congestion and sprawl. It forced US firms to ship high-paying manufacturing jobs overseas. It engaged in corrupt practices to further its business interests in countries such as Mexico, where it resorted to bribes to secure construction permits, and India, where it engaged in illegal lobbying and foreign currency violations.

Two areas where the social responsibility undertakings of Whole Foods and Walmart could be further compared were labor relations and the environment and energy.

Whole Foods' labor relations

Whole Foods had been ranked many times as one of *Fortune's* 100 Best Companies to Work for in America. In 2007, it launched a Whole Trade Guarantee, a purchasing initiative emphasizing the ethics and social responsibility of its products imported from the developing world. The criteria included fair prices, environmentally sound practices, and better wages and labor conditions. One percent of proceeds from the Whole Trade certified products would go to the Whole Planet Foundation. In addition, Whole Foods introduced a Responsibly Grown rating system to assist customers in making well-informed buying choices with regard to worker welfare and other qualities that its flowers and produce had.

The average CEO of a large company in the United States earned over 330 times that of the average worker, but at Whole Foods, no one including the CEO was allowed to have a salary more than 19 times the average employee. However, the salary of top management was amply supplemented by bonuses and stock options that typically amounted to extra millions of dollars per year for most executives. Whole Foods' lowest earners averaged barely above minimum wage levels of $13.15 an hour, which led some to characterize its business model as being one of high prices and low wages.[20] Whole Foods did provide its employees with health-care and additional benefits, but the health insurance plan had high deductibles for general medical expenses and prescriptions. Only after an employee met the deductibles, did the insurance cover 80 percent of the medical costs and the prescriptions. Medications for mental illness were not covered. To compensate, employees did receive per year personal wellness expenditures depending on years of service.

Whole Foods' employees, whom it considered the soul of the company, had been organized into thousands of self-managed, interlocking teams.[21] Every person, from entry-level positions all the way up to management, was hired on a temporary basis for 30 to 90 days until team members voted them in as permanent employees. To achieve full-time status as a Whole Foods' employee, the candidate had to receive a two-thirds positive vote from team members. Team members helped decide what products to stock. They were encouraged to share their thoughts and give advice to management. Each team reported its sales, costs, and profits daily and these were publicly shared and compared with the results of other teams. Competition among teams was fierce because only the best performing teams had a share in company profits. Though subject to unrelenting financial pressure, the participative approach seemed to yield high morale.

Whole Foods steadfastly opposed unions.[22] Union organizers tried to move in on its stores in Berkeley in 1990 and in Austin in 1998 but were unsuccessful. The only store they successfully unionized was in Madison, Wisconsin and the company then dismissed the store manager. Labor activists in Wisconsin accused Whole Foods of union busting, but a 2004 ruling by the National Labor Relations Board (NLRB) upheld Whole Foods' actions. When truck drivers at the San Francisco-based distribution center voted to unionize in 2006, Whole Foods fired two of the drivers, altered its sick-leave policies, froze wage increases, refused to provide information to the union to negotiate a contract, and otherwise was found by NLRB investigators to have harassed and disciplined employees. The NLRB concluded that Whole Foods had engaged in retaliatory measures to discourage union activity. After an out-of-court settlement Whole Foods had to reinstate the employees and reverse its policies.

The United Farm Workers (UFW) criticized Whole Foods for its refusal to support a campaign by on behalf of strawberry field workers. The UFW in the late 1990s convinced several large supermarket chains to support improved wages and working conditions for the pickers. Whole Foods instead held a National 5% Day where five percent of that day's sales were donated to farmworkers' social services. When the UFW passed out literature at a store in Austin, the company called the police and had the people involved arrested. Embarrassed by the public outcry, Whole Foods promised to support a UFW grape boycott, but then broke the promise and passed out literature to customers blasting the farmworkers.

Mackey clarified his personal views about unions by commenting he was not opposed to labor unions that had served important historical purposes.[23] He agreed that employees should have the right to unionize, but they should not be coerced to join unions or pay union dues against their will. They also should have the legal right not to join unions.

In 2013, Whole Foods again ran afoul on labor issues. It suspended two workers in its Albuquerque store for speaking Spanish. It turned out that Whole Foods had a policy of speaking English only to customers and fellow workers, which was against the law.

Walmart's labor relations

Walmart's relationship to its workforce was complicated. The company had a very demanding culture in which its non-unionized employees, called associates, were expected to work very hard for low wages. However, because they were guaranteed some compensation in company stock, they could become very rich if the company's stock price went up substantially. Nonetheless, the company's reputation was low because of miserly hourly wages, fractious relationships with unions, and documented failures to extend to women the same pay and promotion opportunities as men.

The company did try to do more to help its part-time associates, for whom it did not provide health-care benefits, by helping them find full-time jobs and careers at Walmart. Walmart also launched a Women in Factories program, a five-year initiative to empower the more than 60,000 women that supplied products to Walmart and other retailers and worked in factories in India, Bangladesh, China, and Central America. The program trained women in communication, hygiene, reproductive health, and occupational health and safety.

Not much distinguished Walmart from Whole Foods in the companies' anti-union stances, however. Walmart regularly faced attacks from unions and lawsuits from angry, underpaid, overworked, and harassed workers.[24] In 2009 it paid $640 million to settle wage and hour class-action lawsuits. In 2010, it paid $86 million to settle this type of suit. Between 2005 and 2011, the settlements cost the company more than $1 billion. Temporary workers once again filed a lawsuit against the company in 2012 alleging that it forced them to work more hours than those for which they had been hired. Employees in California initiated a class-action suit in 2013 claiming that the company did not provide suitable seating for cashiers. Walmart regularly experienced the ill effects of these lawsuits, which diverted large sums of money in settlements.

On the other hand, Walmart helped to spawn the supplier auditing industry. After a scathing NBC Dateline report in 1992 uncovered child labor at a supplier in a Bangladesh that supplied Walmart, the company created a supplier code of conduct that outlawed child and prison labor among its suppliers. Other large companies joined, which created a market for auditors to inspect factories, scrutinize wage records, and interview workers about labor, health, and safety violations.

The effectiveness of the auditors, however, was repeatedly questioned. Walmart admitted that there were serious problems. Auditors could be bribed and many abetted the cheating of the factories they inspected by allowing the factories to outsource much of the work to other factories with mediocre or poor records. Officially, Walmart allowed factories to outsource more than half the work but they often outsourced much more to unregulated shadow factories. Auditing, in any case, was a cat-and-mouse game between suppliers and the auditors, with the suppliers often keeping two sets of books – the actual books and doctored-up versions.

Whole Foods, the environment, and energy

Whole Foods had much to its credit in the area of the environment and energy. It purchased renewable-energy credits from wind farms to offset 100 percent of the electricity used in its facilities in the United States and Canada, the largest wind-energy credit purchase by a company in these countries.[25] The acquisition of these credits made Whole Foods the only *Fortune* 500 firm to purchase enough credits to offset all the electricity it used. The company estimated that this initiative was equivalent to taking about 60,000 cars off the road or planting 90,000 acres of trees. In 2007, the US Environmental Protection Agency (EPA) applauded Whole Foods' actions for stimulating the development of renewable energy. In 2004, 2005, 2006, and 2008, the agency granted Whole Foods the status of Green Power Partner of the Year for its environmental contributions.

In 2013, the company started to build the first commercial-scale rooftop greenhouse in the United States above its Brooklyn store. In 2008, Whole Foods became the first US supermarket chain to commit to the complete elimination of disposable plastic grocery bags. Many Whole Foods' stores served as collection points for the recycling of plastic bags. Like other co-ops and health-food stores, it promoted the purchase of bulk food and other products in reusable packaging. To its customers it offered Better Bags made chiefly from recycled bottles. The company received the first Green Building award in Austin, Texas in 1998 for the expansion and renovation of its corporate headquarters. Because of the 42 percent waste reduction, the EPA profiled the building as a trend setter.

Yet unlike many other companies, Whole Foods had not issued an environmental report with concrete goals. Instead, in its report it had vague statements like respecting the environment and reducing waste whenever possible. As a result of the absence of goals, there were no benchmarks of how well the company had implemented its values. It did report carbon emissions to the Carbon Disclosure Project, but with a score of 61 it was not close to the leaders who scored above 95.[26] The words global warming and climate change were hardly found on its website and the company had no explicit climate change policy, which was not accidental given the public statements that Mackey made about the issue.[27] Mackey asserted that no scientific consensus existed regarding the causes of climate change and it would be a pity to allow hysteria about warming to result in higher taxes and increased regulation that in turn would lower standards of living. Historically, he maintained that prosperity correlated with warmer temperatures. Though he argued that global warming was perfectly natural, he claimed he was not a climate change sceptic.

Whole Foods also was criticized for the implied environmental messages in the signage in its stores.[28] Glossy pictures of local farmers standing near their crops in Whole Foods stores were meant to educate shoppers about the advantages of organics. However, small, family farmers who grew their products locally made up a very small percentage of what Whole Foods sold. A banner in its stores provided reasons to buy organic by explaining that local farms relied on natural fertilizers like manure and compost rather than chemical ones and thereby avoided energy waste in the production of the fertilizers. However, most of the organic food Whole Foods sold came from gigantic operations owned by big food conglomerates that were thousands of miles from its stores. This system was wasteful in its use of energy to transport these foods to the stores.

An area where Whole Foods stood out was in its activities on behalf of animal rights. For example, it educated customers about the killing of dolphins in the pursuit of tuna and it worked with canneries to buy from fisheries that used methods that did not result in dolphin deaths. The company belonged to the Marine Stewardship Council (MSC), a global non-profit organization that promoted sustainable fisheries. It began to sell MSC-certified seafood in 2000. In 2006 it chose to stop selling live lobsters and crabs, but in 2007 made an exception for a Portland, Maine supplier that met its standards.

Nonetheless, People for the Ethical Treatment of Animals (PETA) protested at Whole Foods' stores. They opposed the company's practice of purchasing duck liver from force-fed ducks the tip of whose bills were removed, and some people criticized Whole Foods for selling meat at all. In response, the company agreed to overhaul its procurement of meat. It no longer sold traditionally raised veal and worked with ranchers on behalf of more humane methods and educated customers about the cruelty of animal testing of body-care products.

In 2011, Whole Foods adopted a five-step animal welfare rating system promoted by the Global Animal Partnership. This system provided transparency about the conditions of farm animals used in the company's products. Independent, third-party observers audited and certified farms with regard to their animal welfare practices. According to the quality and compassion standards Whole Foods adopted, it did not allow the pulling of feathers from live ducks, bill trimming, bill heat treatment, toe punching, slitting the feet webs, and toe removal. It prohibited ducks from being treated with antibiotics or antimicrobials, cloned, genetically modified, or not allowed medical treatment. Whole Foods also created an Animal Compassion Foundation. In 2014 it started a pilot program to sell rabbit meat in some of its stores. Because rabbits were the third most common mammal pet in the United States the House Rabbit Society boycotted the firm. Protestors started a petition drive against the sale of rabbit meat and held national protests against the company's stores, despite the many policies for animal protection it had adopted.

Walmart, the environment, and energy

Unlike Whole Foods, Walmart had very quantifiable energy and environmental goals. The three goals were: (1) to be supplied 100 percent by renewable energy; (2) to sell products that sustained people and the environment; and (3) to create zero waste. The turning point in the company's environment and energy policies was in 2004 when the company again had been fined for environmental infractions. Then CEO, Lee Scott, was fed up with the firm's image as an environmental plunderer.[29] Scott was convinced that inefficiency and waste were ubiquitous and even in a company as efficient as Walmart they did damage to the environment and the company's bottom line. In 2005, Scott gave a Twenty-First Century Leadership address to all the company's stores and suppliers in which he affirmed the belief that being a good steward of the environment and an efficient and profitable business were one and the same. Without being sure how to achieve them, he set forth Walmart's three goals, which it continued to pursue. Walmart had its suppliers condense products such as laundry detergent into more easily packed and shipped containers. It retrofitted large trucks with small motors so that drivers did not run their engines to keep cool while they slept. It reduced the amount of cardboard and plastic the company used in packaging. It started to buy directly from farmers to ensure cheaper, fresher, and more reliable produce. The company's hope was that these actions would save money as well as protect the environment.

When Michael Duke succeeded Scott as CEO in 2009 he reaffirmed the goals Scott had set. The company aspired to rethink processes, use smarter packaging, recycle, and reduce plastic bag use so as to create zero waste. Its actions as the world's largest retailer had the potential to save customers money, help safeguard the world, and produce financial benefits for the company. On its website the company declared that sustainability was an essential part of its business responsibility and success. Walmart had many successes, including getting dairy farmers to use low-carbon cattle feed and methane digesters, and Hollywood studios to use slimmer DVD packaging. It increased its truck fleet's efficiency by 60 percent, eliminated hazardous materials in most of the electronics it sold, and reduced plastic bag use by more than 20 percent since 2007. Walmart completed the setting up of three solar power systems in Hawaii. It committed to eliminate 25 percent of solid waste from its US stores by 2008.

In 2011 Walmart reported that it had reduced its waste by 64 percent. It accelerated the widespread adoption of compact fluorescent light bulbs, an action that reduced carbon emissions and slowed the pace of global warming.[30] In 2012, it reported that it kept 80.9 percent of its waste from US landfills and achieved cost savings from recycling. It expected to eliminate all waste from US landfills by 2025. It reported that in China and Brazil, it diverted 52 percent of its operational waste from landfills. In 2011 the UK chain ASDA sent zero food waste to landfills. It revealed that it cut its plastic shopping bag waste by more than 35 percent from the 2007 baseline.

In the United States, Walmart was the second-largest onsite power generator and was the top corporate user of on-site solar power. More than 180 Walmart sponsored renewable-energy projects were in operation including Texan and Californian wind farms and Californian fuel-cell sites. In 2013, Walmart reported that its wind-energy projects, fuel-cell installations, and zero-waste programs had added $150 million to its bottom line.

Walmart's record, nonetheless, was not perfect. At its global stores and distribution centers Walmart met just half of its goal to reduce greenhouse gases by 20 percent by 2012. After US cap-and-trade legislation failed to pass and the Copenhagen climate talks fell into stalemate, the environmental organization Environmental Defense Fund (EDF) looked to Walmart and businesses like it to make progress. Though the company made strides on some of goals, its performance still left much to be desired.

In 2008, Walmart promised to boost energy efficiency by 20 percent per unit produced at 200 of its Chinese factories. In April 2011, it revealed that just 119 factories had met this goal.[31] EDF, which had been a partner in the effort, exited the program because of what it referred to as Walmart's lack of cooperation. At the end of the year the program came to a halt.

China was an especially difficult challenge. The company's total carbon footprint – from stores, distribution centers, offices, corporate jets, and without its suppliers – was already more than that of half the world's countries in 2010, according to data Walmart had given the Carbon Disclosure Project.[32] The company's more than 100,000 suppliers from Alabama to Uzbekistan deposited an untold number of additional greenhouse gases into the atmosphere. Some made products according to Walmart specifications. Others were brand-name producers who sold their own products to Walmart but both relied heavily on subcontractors, shadow factories that were largely out of anyone's control. These shadow factories produced some of most carbon-intense and climate-harming emissions. If all transport of goods and services among Walmart's suppliers also was counted it would be nearly impossible to estimate the company's total carbon footprint. In China alone, more than 30,000 factories manufactured for Walmart.

CEO Scott tried to move this group to become more conscious of its carbon footprint, but despite the participation of the EDF and other environmental organizations it was very hard to achieve real mastery over all this activity. In 2008, Scott met with the CEOs and managers of more than 1,000 suppliers at a Walmart Sustainability Summit and told them that he recognized the importance of low prices, but that customers cared more and more about the entire life cycle of a product – how it was made, sold, used, and recycled.[33] For this reason, all factories in the supply chain had to be responsible environmental stewards, cognizant of climate change, and preservers of energy. Scott insisted that meeting social and environmental standards was not optional and that he was not ready to tolerate companies that cheated on their labor, environmental, or any other practices. Walmart wanted to work with all the companies in its supply chain. If they did not meet their goals they had to have a plan to fix the problems, and if they did not improve after the inspection of outside auditors they would be cut off from making products for Walmart. If costs had to rise, then consumers would be willing to pay a small amount more.

China's government seemed to be supportive of Scott's initiative. Rather than unfettered development they too were moving in the direction of more environmentally responsible development. Their move in this direction came for obvious reasons – the growing alarm over illegal chemical substances in Chinese foods, the rampant air pollution, and threatened water supplies. Chinese consumers, when they could afford it, also were buying organically grown food because they believed it might be purer than conventional varieties. Walmart had been suspected for its involvement in the problems that China faced and the turn to sustainable solutions appeared to please China's leaders.

However, dealing with issues in China was far harder than Walmart anticipated. Though most environmentalists did not doubt the company's sincerity, the task of coordinating the behavior of so many suppliers and subcontractors simply was beyond the capability of a single company, even one as large as Walmart. Walmart made admirable though unexceptional progress on some of its goals, but with the global economic recession hurting the company and its many suppliers doing much more with less, to act without seriously hurting suppliers' profit margins became impossible. The momentum for making massive changes dissipated. Thankful for Walmart's assistance, suppliers remained uncertain if they could accomplish the company's goals. The investment to reduce energy and water use and reduce emissions was greater than they expected. They still were being pressured to lower prices by three to five percent per year. Operating on the thinnest of margins, Walmart's Chinese suppliers were unable to invest in green projects even when the pay-off seemed forthcoming.

At Walmart's 2008 sustainability conference in China, it promised to get Chinese suppliers on board for compliance with environmental and labor standards by 2009 or 2011 the latest, but in the company's 2011 Global Responsibility Report, it could report no substantive progress other than to admit that its compliance agreements with its suppliers were being strengthened. In many instances, Walmart lost patience and it stopped asking for reports on such critical aspects of its program as energy usage. Making the decision to reduce their energy use had proven to be too demanding for many of the suppliers. Should they really implement a solution that added a few cents to their products because it eliminated the use of unsafe chemicals, or should their focus be as it always had been on lowering costs? Despite all the encouragement Walmart provided it could not give them a straight answer to this question.

Walmart's accomplishments did not penetrate deeply into the supply chain. Where the company was most successful was in measuring its own energy use and the waste of its own stores, lowering them, and saving substantial amounts of money in improving the efficiency of its operations. Walmart made simple product changes such as taking the water out of a detergent product. It asked for employee initiatives and listened to employee recommendations, like turning off the lights in the Coca-Cola machines when they were not in use. From 2005 to 2011, the total square footage of its stores and facilities increased 40 percent and sales grew by 44 percent, but the company's greenhouse gas emissions increased by only 10 percent. This result came about because Walmart streamlined its operations. It innovated in the use of alternative energy in its stores and became a major user of green power but it could not induce its suppliers and their suppliers to make the same kind of decisions.

Walmart again turned its attention to its suppliers. It created greater employee awareness and started to put the life-cycle metrics in place that might help it in a second round of trying to make the supply chain more sustainable. It also launched a supplier sustainability index that asked suppliers specific questions about their operations that might result in significant changes in the 125,000 to 150,000 products that typical stores stocked.[34] Walmart intended to rank the suppliers, from best to worst, and share this information with its buyers who, in turn, would be compensated in part based on the sustainability performance of a category. The goals were to improve the environmental perfor- mance of its most popular products, further integrate sustainability by giving buyers responsibility, drive productivity in a way that would benefit customers, and increase trust in the company. Among the ques- tions it hoped its suppliers could answers were how could wheat be grown with less water and fertilizer? How could chemicals be removed from toys? How could mining to extract copper, gold, and silver for computers and jewelry be improved? How could the number of tele- visions sold that were Energy Star certified be increased? How much water could be cut in the production of a pair of polyester pants?

To make agriculture more sustainable, Walmart might ask suppliers probing questions about the grains they used. What percentage came from farmers that tracked fertilizer use and had goals to optimize fertilizer use? What percentage from farmers that monitored soil fertility and had goals to minimize degradation and erosion? What about the fuel and water use of the farmers? What were they doing to reduce it? Could the grapes in a bottle of wine come from a farm with a biodiversity management plan?

The origins of Walmart's new sustainability drive started in 2009 with the involvement of the Sustainability Consortium, a non-profit coalition at the University of Arkansas and Arizona State University that had been established to provide the technical foundation to support the effort.[35] A number of other retailers – Tesco, Kroger, Ahold, and Best Buy and consumer product companies such as Coca-Cola, Disney, Kellogg's, Mars agreed to participate. Walmart obtained pledges from eight of the world's biggest food companies to place up to eight million acres of farmland under sustainable agriculture programs, a move that could eliminate six million metric tons of greenhouse gas emissions according to Walmart's estimates. Working with the consortium, the company sent questions to suppliers in about 200 product categories. Each year it aimed to survey more of its suppliers with the ultimate goal of including about half the products Walmart sold in this system.

Walmart had learned from its mistakes. A prior survey of suppliers had been too long and burdensome and there was no follow-up like handing the results to buyers and having them use the results in purchasing. Walmart's intention was to grade each supplier against its peers with a score of one to a hundred. In a particular category the buyers would be able to compare companies. In cereals, for instance, they could compare Kellogg's, General Mills, Post, and Quaker. In soft drinks, they could compare Coca-Cola, Pepsi, and Dr. Pepper. Buyers could discuss performance with suppliers and encourage them to do better.

Buyers could not guarantee rewards for best companies or punishment of laggards. In the end, Walmart had to grant suppliers discretion to improve on their own. The company did not have the legal authority to compel them to make changes. It was not a government agency. By the end of 2017, the company promised to buy 70 percent of the goods it sold in US stores and US Sam's Clubs from suppliers who answered the Sustainability Index questions.

Walmart received positive media attention for this initiative but it had to prove that it was more reality than hype. Advocacy groups continued to doubt its sincerity. They did not let up the pressure they applied to the company. The Institute for Local Self-Reliance charged that Walmart's greenhouse gas emissions had continued to grow since 2005, while the percentage of power it drew from renewable sources lagged behind other major corporations.[36] Others asked no matter what Walmart's sustainability efforts entailed, just how sustainable was its business model. The company was under intense pressure to grow while decreasing its environmental impact. It hoped that, by 2020, it would not only flat-line its greenhouse gas emissions, but it would start to see a decline even as the number of its stores continued to grow.

Much to prove

In the realm of sustainability, Whole Foods and Walmart still had much to prove. To what extent were they on the right track? How could they make real and credible progress? How could they better align their sustainability goals with their business strategies? Who would stand out more in heroically changing the world: the mission-based Whole Foods or the mainstream Walmart?

Notes

1 J. Mackey and R. Sisodia, *Conscious Capitalism* (Boston, MA: Harvard Business School, 2013).
2 See CSRHUB: www.csrhub.com
3 *Ibid.*
4 B. Blatt, "Unacceptable Ingredients," *Slate* (2014): www.slate.com/articles/life/culturebox/2014/02/whole_foods_and_walmart_how_many_groceries_sold_at_walmart_would_be_banned.html
5 A. Antenucci, "Whole foods sued for understating amount of sugar in yogurt," *NY Post* (2014): http://nypost.com/2014/08/29/whole-foods-sued-for-understating-amount-of-sugar-in-yogurt
6 N. Paumgarten, "Food fighter: does Whole Foods know what's best for you?" *New Yorker* (2010): www.newyorker.com/magazine/2010/01/04/food-fighter
7 M. Dapen-Baron and C. Nordhielm, *Whole Foods Market: What Now?* (Ann Arbor, MI: Ross School of Business, 2010).

8 C. Marquis, M. Besharov, and B. Thomason, *Whole Foods: Balancing Social Mission and Growth* (Boston, MA: Harvard Business School, 2011).

9 John Mackey's Blog (2007): www.wholefoodsmarket.com/blog/john-mackeys-blog/whole-foods-market-wild-oats-and-federal-trade%C2%A0commission

10 See W. McKitterick, Supermarkets & Grocery Stores in the US. IBIS-World Industry Report 44511 (2014).

11 Walmart "Walmart and Wild Oats launch effort to drive down organic food prices," *Walmart News Archive* (2014): http://news.walmart.com/news-archive/2014/04/10/walmart-and-wild-oats-launch-effort-to-drive-down-organic-food-prices

12 Organic Trade Association, "American appetite for organic products breaks through $35 billion mark" (2014): www.organicnewsroom.com/2014/05/american_appetite_for_organic.html

13 Walmart "Walmart and Wild Oats launch effort to drive down organic food prices."

14 See US Department of Agriculture Economic Research Service, "Organic market overview" (2014): www.ers.usda.gov/topics/natural-resources-environment/organic-agriculture/organic-market-overview.aspx#.VEbaX_ldXTo

15 Walmart "Walmart and Wild Oats launch effort to drive down organic food prices."

16 See "Get lower-cost organic groceries with Walmart's Wild Oats Marketplace line," *Consumer Reports* (2014): www.consumerreports.org/cro/news/2014/04/get-lower-cost-organic-groceries-with-walmart-s-wild-oats-marketplace-line/index.htm

17 A. Gupta, "How Walmart threatens organic food," *In These Times* (2014): http://inthesetimes.com/article/16785/how_walmart_threatens_organic_food. In 2006, the public interest group Cornucopia caught Walmart putting organic signs in sections of its stores that had non-organic foods. For organic milk, it charged that Walmart relied on agribusinesses such as Horizon Milk and Aurora Dairy that typically confined 4,000 cows or more to pens in a single facility. The dairies responded that for the bulk milk purchases Walmart wanted it was impossible to provide the cows with pasture while milking them multiple times a day. In the complaint Cornucopia filed against Horizon's former parent company, Dean Foods, it accused the company of being in violation of organic standards, using conventionally raised cows, and violating laws about putting additives to its milk. The public interest group protested that these practices allowed Horizon and Aurora to undercut small organic dairies and drive them out of business.

18 Mackey and Sisodia, *Conscious Capitalism.*
19 See the Whole Foods website: www.wholefoodsmarket.com/mission-values
20 M. Bluejay, "Whole Foods Market: what's wrong with Whole Foods?" (2013): http://michaelbluejay.com/misc/wholefoods.html
21 Marquis, Besharov, and Thomason, *Whole Foods: Balancing Social Mission and Growth.*
22 See Bluejay, "Whole Foods Market."
23 R. Cummins and D. Murphy, "Exposed: how Whole Foods and the biggest organic foods distributor are screwing workers," *AlterNet* (2013): www.alternet.org/food/exposed-how-whole-foods-and-biggest-organic-foods-distributor-are-screwing-workers?paging=off&current_page=1#bookmark
24 S. Hochberg, "Conscious capitalism vs. unions? A look at Whole Foods," *onlabor* (2013): http://onlabor.org/2013/10/01/conscious-capitalism-vs-unions-a-look-at-whole-foods
25 P. Brady, "Energy credits fund new wind farm," The Official Whole Foods Markets blog (2009): www.wholefoodsmarket.com/blog/whole-story/energy-credits-fund-new-wind-farm
26 See Carbon Disclosure Project (2014): www.cdp.net/en-us/Pages/CDPAdvancedSearchResults.aspx?k=whole%20foods
27 C. Franzen, "Whole Foods CEO John Mackey: climate change 'not necessarily bad'," *TPM* (2013): http://talkingpointsmemo.com/livewire/whole-foods-ceo-john-mackey-climate-change-not-necessarily-bad
28 M. Pollan, "My letter to Whole Foods," *Michael Pollan* (2006): http://michaelpollan.com/articles-archive/my-letter-to-whole-foods
29 M. Gunther, "The green machine," *Fortune* (2006): http://archive.fortune.com/magazines/fortune/fortune_archive/2006/08/07/8382593/index.htm
30 Walmart, "Global responsibility report," (2014): http://corporate.walmart.com/global-responsibility/environment-sustainability/global-responsibility-report
31 A. Kroll, "Are Walmart's Chinese factories as bad as Apple's?" *Mother Jones* (2012): www.motherjones.com/environment/2012/03/walmart-china-sustainability-shadow-factories-greenwash
32 S. Mitchell, *Walmart's Assault on the Climate*, (Institute for Local Self-Reliance, 2013): www.ilsr.org/wp-content/uploads/2013/10/ILSR-_Report_WalmartClimateChange.pdf
33 A. Zimmerman and M. Fong, "Wal-Mart suppliers face energy, other mandates," *Wall Street Journal* (2008): http://online.wsj.com/articles/SB122463357082356711; A. Aston, "Wal-Mart: making its suppliers go green," *BloombergBusinessweek* (2009): www.businessweek.com/magazine/content/09_21/b4132044814736.htm

34 See Walmart website, "Sustainability index," (2014): http://corporate.walmart.com/global-responsibility/environment-sustainability/sustainability-index

35 See the Sustainability Consortium website (2014): www.sustainability consortium.org

36 Mitchell, *Walmart's Assault on the Climate.*

10 | *Sustainability's next frontier: DuPont and Monsanto*

What steps should DuPont and Monsanto next take in their sustainability journeys? Should DuPont, a more diversified company than Monsanto, focus more exclusively on food and agriculture? Should it become more like the mission-based Monsanto, whose focus was almost exclusively in these areas? Which products should DuPont and Monsanto make? Which markets should they serve?

No matter which products and markets they chose, they would have to defend themselves. What were the implications of DuPont's and Monsanto's product and market choices for society? To what extent would the next steps in their sustainable journeys affect their growth and profitability? To what extent should these companies dedicate themselves to playing a leading role in eliminating world hunger? DuPont and Monsanto had to decide what they should do next.

DuPont's and Monsanto's sustainability journeys

In its 2013 sustainability report, DuPont wrote that its journey had evolved from environmental compliance, to reducing its operational footprint, to market-driven efforts to produce sustainable solutions for the world.[1] It identified its future business opportunities in terms of sustainability goals: (i) harnessing renewable energy sources; (ii) protecting ecosystems; (iii) reducing fossil fuel dependence; and (iv) safeguarding the environment. These goals were meant to motivate the company's employees to exercise their technical prowess in researching and solving the problems of society.

DuPont's journey to these goals had been a long one. In the 1980s its core chemical businesses had been under great stress because of newly enforced Environmental Protection Agency (EPA) regulations; as much as 80 percent of its capital expenditures had been devoted to meeting these requirements. Edgar Woolard, the company's CEO from 1989 to

1995, paved the way for DuPont's movement toward sustainability.[2] An outspoken environmentalist, he rose through the ranks becoming DuPont's vice-president for environmental affairs before assuming the top leadership position. As CEO, Woolard expanded DuPont's environmental commitments. He presided over the early greening of the company's portfolio, its voluntary exit from chlorofluorocarbon (CFC) production, in light of the controversy over ozone depletion, and its introduction of the SUVA brand of refrigerants and coolants, which were less harmful to the environment. In the mid-1980s, the company created a profitable business selling substitutes for the CFC refrigerants that were depleting the Earth's protective ozone layer.[3]

DuPont next tackled climate change, voluntarily lowering its emissions in 1994 and choosing to cut them by 40 percent from 1990 levels by 2000.[4] After meeting this target, the company established the goal of a 65 percent reduction in greenhouse gas emissions by 2010. Rather than costing money, curbing greenhouse gas emissions had cut energy use and improved the firm's bottom line. Despite producing 30 percent more goods, DuPont used seven percent less energy than it had in 1990, saving more than $2 billion.

In 2005, DuPont topped a *Business Week* ranking of green firms. By 2007, it was a leader in shifting the climate debate from science to political action, lobbying heavily for a US carbon emissions cap that would not have been limited to utilities, the biggest emitters of greenhouse gases, but would have covered all sectors of the economy. The more industries under a cap, the more customers there would be for DuPont's goods and services for emission reduction.

Notwithstanding Congress's opposition to the cap, DuPont continued to launch new products that consumed fewer materials and produced less waste. These products were used in lightweight autos, solar and fuel cells, and wind turbines. The company replaced nylon in active wear fashion with the renewably sourced material Sorona®, the production of which consumed 30 percent less energy and reduced greenhouse gas emissions by 63 percent in comparison to similar amounts of nylon. The lightweight materials that it sold to automakers allowed them to design more fuel-efficient, low-emission, safe vehicles. The company estimated these products lowered vehicle weight by as much as ten percent and, at the same time, reduced greenhouse gas emissions and yielded six to eight percent better fuel economy.

DuPont also was a major supplier to the solar-power industry, having agreements with Suntech and Yingli to furnish them with photovoltaic materials and technologies, including the protective back sheet for solar modules that were made with DuPont Tedlar® polyvinyl fluoride (PVF) film (see Chapter 3). The company spent $295 million to expand its capacity to produce Tedlar® in order to meet the needs of this industry. Furthermore, DuPont had a cellulosic ethanol plant in Iowa, expected to be operational in 2014, which relied on biotechnology to convert non-food biomass into ethanol and lignin. It would offer a commercial-scale demonstration of the firm's integrated feedstock-to-fuel approach and produce 30 million gallons (c. 114 million L) of ethanol annually. The facility was the foundation for DuPont's biorefinery strategy, which was meant to capture value by licensing technology and selling enzymes and fermentation microbes.

Ending hunger

Ending hunger was another business opportunity tied to sustainability to which DuPont was committed. Its goal was to help make available enough healthy and nutritious food to feed the world's growing population. The company's commitment to this goal had been largely stimulated by a desire to catch up with Monsanto.

In a 1996 *Harvard Business Review* interview, Robert Shapiro, then Monsanto's CEO, articulated a vision of a world entering into a period of unprecedented discontinuity for which business had to plan with cold and rational logic.[5] Because of population growth the demand for food in the world was expected to increase by 40 percent by the year 2020.[6] By about 2050, the world's population would approach nine billion people. With that number of people on the Earth, there would be even more mouths to feed. Because about a quarter of the world's population lived in poverty and many of these people were malnourished, feeding them would be an immense challenge. The only feasible approach was to obtain additional productivity from each acre of soil harvested.

According to Shapiro, Monsanto's role was to spur this revolution by using biotechnology to create more valuable foods, without adding to the burden on the land and water and using excessive amounts of fertilizers, pesticides, or other chemicals. Intellectual capital in understanding genes would replace physical capital needed to grow crops. Genetic modification of seeds enabled human beings to increase soil yields with fewer physical inputs.

Shapiro set Monsanto on a course that transformed it into a biotechnology powerhouse. Farmers always had saved seeds of plants that lasted, looked better, tasted sweeter, and grew more vigorously.[7] If the cross-breeding of plants to create more robust hybrids was common, there was no reason not to believe that it made sense to accelerate this process by shooting snippets of DNA into plant walls with tungsten-coated gene guns.

Monsanto's spring 2014 Sustainability Progress Report announced the creation of a new crop research program that would focus on growing more food on less land in an environmentally friendly way.[8] The company would work with the National Corn Growers Association Soil Health Partnership to develop ways to improve soil health and water quality. Its goal was to reduce its own water usage 25 percent by 2020.

Monsanto, according to *Newsweek*'s 2014 green rankings of 500 companies, was in 68th place in the United States and 130th place globally. Nonetheless, the Internet was filled with sites like "Monsanto-Sucks" and references to "MonSatan."[9] The Union of Concerned Scientists was very critical of the company's GM seeds, claiming that they promoted pesticide resistance, spread gene contamination, increased herbicide use, expanded monoculture, and fell far short of feeding the world's hungry. Organizations such as Greenpeace urged Monsanto to give up on biotech and embrace organic farming.

DuPont's CEO in 1998, Chad Holliday, also announced that DuPont would cut back capital for its chemical businesses and make food biotechnology a centerpiece of the company.[10] DuPont used similar methods of creating seeds capable of delivering greater yields in stressed environments, and crop protection products that were better able to control insects and improve crop quality with less environmental damage. By 2014 its food businesses touched upon food cultures, probiotics, emulsifiers, and natural sweeteners. Brew makers optimized production with its enzyme LAMINEX® MaxFlow 4G. DuPont owned Solae, a company that made soy-based ingredients. The future growth of the company was tied to the integration of biology and agronomy with chemistry, materials science, and engineering.

Agricultural technology

Thus the demand for food played a prominent role in the sustainability journeys of both DuPont and Monsanto. Agricultural technology was the key.

In 1970, Norman Borlaug won the Nobel Prize for research in high-yield agriculture that allowed farmers to obtain more food from the same amount of land or less.[11] The green revolution he inaugurated increased crop yields throughout the world.[12] Educated at the University of Minnesota, he had been a DuPont employee from 1942 to 1944. Among his accomplishments were shuttle breeding, which sped immunity between strains of crops, and the perfection of dwarf spring wheat, stout short-stalked kernels that expended less energy in growing inedible sections and more in growing valuable grain. Largely because of his work, Pakistan became self-sufficient in food production in 1968 and India in 1974. India, indeed, became the world's second largest producer of wheat and rice. Pakistan went from 3.4 million tons wheat grown annually to 18 million and India from 11 million tons to 60 million. Dwarf rice yields in China were 1.6 tons per acre, close to the world's best yields of 2.0 tons per acre.

In 1950, the world required 1.7 billion acres to grow 692 million tons of grain to feed 2.2 billion people. In 1992, total acreage was virtually the same (1.73 billion acres) but the world was growing almost three times as much food (1.9 billion tons of grain) to feed twice the number of people (5.6 billion).[13] As global grain yields shot up from .45 tons per acre to 1.1 tons per acre, average daily per capita calorie intake grew from 2,063 calories to 2,495. Malnutrition, still a problem, was reduced, at the same time that obesity grew. The greater crop yields per acre also meant that there was less deforestation occurring in order to open up new land for farming.

Since the 1980s, however, crop yield growth has started to decline.[14] The world's population was increasing by 73 million persons per year. By the year 2020, it was projected that there would be 7.5 billion people living on the planet and that world demand for rice, wheat, and maize would grow by 40 percent. In some regions of the world, it was difficult for farmers to get access to the fertilizer and chemicals needed to grow crops. The high-yield crops, which Borlaug and his colleagues created, did not prosper without fertilizers and other chemicals. Water for irrigation also was becoming increasingly scarce, as the water table had been substantially depleted. Because of soil salinity and erosion and there has been loss of arable land since the late 1970s.

To improve yields it was thought that genetic engineering would be the solution. Scientists could use biotechnology to code plants against insects so that farmers would not have to spray toxic pesticides. They would be able to devise plants that could survive in salty soil or dry conditions. As well as making plants more pest resistant and more tolerant of adverse weather, it might be possible to pack more protein and minerals into foods people ate. The potential was to add input traits to crops that would make farmers more productive and to add output traits such as more nutrition and better taste.

Monsanto's move to biotechnology

In the late 1990s, Monsanto made the commitment to use biotechnology to bring GM foods to the market.[15] As a company, Monsanto was not new to controversy. Some of the products with which it had been associated over the years were saccharin, aspirin, fertilizers, carpets, PCBs, dioxin, and the defoliant Agent Orange. Under Richard Mahoney, Robert Shapiro's predecessor at Monsanto, it assembled a high-quality group of molecular biologists to explore biotechnology. It began to develop internal organizational capabilities to transplant DNA from organisms such as bacteria into plants that would be able to make the plants hardier, better tasting, higher yielding, and more resistant to pests and disease.

In the early 1990s Monsanto had a series of off-site meetings that brought together critical thinkers within the firm. This group had about 80 employees, who formulated a new approach for appraising the company's business opportunities. Eventually another 60 employees were involved. They organized themselves into seven sustainability teams, three concerned with enhancing agricultural productivity, three concerned with new product development, and one concerned with communicating the results of their decisions. The eco-efficiency team was devoted to measuring and optimizing raw material use. The full-cost accounting team's mission was taking into account the full environmental costs of a product during the product life cycle. The index team was committed to establishing metrics to balance other economic, social, and environmental factors. There also was a general new product development team devoted to meeting global water needs and, of especial importance given the decisions Monsanto made, a team dedicated to solving the problem of world hunger. Integrating the efforts of all these teams was the one that communicated the new vision of the company to employees and offered them the opportunity to play a role. Within the company, the movement that these employees began was contagious. The decision to make the move into biotechnology was a bottom–up effort.

Since 1953, when James Watson and Frances Crick discovered the structure of the DNA that carried the information cells needed to build proteins, scientists had generated detailed maps of the genes of hundreds of organisms and the data-analyzing capabilities to understand and use them. Genetic modification was a set of technologies that allowed human beings to alter the make up of living organisms including animals, plants, and bacteria. Scientists were able to cut bits of DNA from one cell and splice them into another to make GM products. When insulin started to be made this way in 1983, it became an accepted practice in medicine. Biotechnology, a more general term for this type of engineering, was using living organisms or their components to make products of any kind. The products made in this way, or in the pipeline to be made in this way, included vaccines, foods, food ingredients, feeds, fibers, and medicines.

Monsanto's CEO after Mahoney was Robert Shapiro. Shapiro catalyzed the effort to make the company a biotech powerhouse. To enhance the firm's capabilities in biotechnology, Monsanto spent $8 billion on a series of acquisitions, joint ventures, and partnerships. In 1996, it bought Calgene for $50 million dollars because the company had developed a gene for a slow-ripening tomato. In the same year, it bought DeKalb Genetics for $160 million, because of the corn seeds DeKalb was creating. In 1997, it bought Holden Foundation Seeds for $945 million for the company's seed marketing and sales capabilities. In 1998, it bought Cargill's international seed operations for $1.4 billion for this reason. These acquisitions gave Monsanto the ability to do research and development, to manufacture, and to market genetically enhanced seeds.

Monsanto therefore was the first on the market with these seeds and moved to the top spot among companies in agricultural biotechnology. In 1997, 14 of the 24 genetically engineered seeds US regulatory agencies had approved in the prior two years were from Monsanto and its partners. In addition, Monsanto formed a joint venture with

Cargill, called Renessen, for the purpose of creating and marketing new products using GM crops. This joint venture had a specific focus. For what market would the new crops be most suited? Not for direct human consumption, for that might raise anxiety among people, but for enhancing the quality of the corn, soybean, and canola that animals ate. A goal of the Cargill–Monsanto partnership was to increase the amino acid levels in animal feed and thereby diminish the need for additional enhancement.

Monsanto at the time was a conglomerate that had chemical, pharmaceutical, and food divisions as well as its biotechnology and crop protection division, but the agriculture division was growing the most rapidly. Its growth rate was three times the rest of the company and the margins on the seeds Monsanto introduced were very high in contrast to the commodity chemicals that Monsanto also sold. In 1997 therefore Monsanto decided to spin off the company's slower growing chemicals operation to shareholders as a separate concern. This new firm was called Solutia and had $3 billion in revenues. Monsanto used the proceeds from this divestiture to buy additional biotechnology companies, such as Ecogen, which had a large library of the bacterium *Bacillus thuringiensis* (Bt) genes; Synteri, which had access to gene expression analysis technology; Millenium Pharmaceuticals, which had developed genetic markers for corn and soybeans; and Mendel Biotechnology, which also had technical capabilities in agricultural genomics.

After the spin off, Monsanto had annual revenue of about $7 billion dollars and three remaining divisions. The first of them was agriculture. It sold the new GM seeds and the herbicide Roundup® and produced about half of the company's revenues. It had revenues of over $2 billion dollars in 1998 and provided about 40 percent of the company's total operating earnings. The second division was pharmaceuticals. It had the company's G. D. Searle subsidiary whose main product was Celebrex®, an arthritis drug. This division produced about a third of the company's revenues. The final division, food products, was dominated by artificial sweetener NutraSweet®. This division constituted about 20 percent of the company's revenues.

Roundup® was Monsanto's cash cow. Monsanto scientists had devised corn, soybean, and canola seeds that made crops that did not perish when exposed to Roundup® herbicide. Farmers did not have to plow to eliminate weeds left from the prior year's harvest before planting, thus ensuring that there would be less topsoil erosion. After the new plants sprouted, the farmers again could spray without having to worry about the herbicide killing their crops.

Monsanto modified its seeds with Bt. Naturally found in the earth, Bt made a poison that harmed the digestive tracts of various pests, but did not hurt other living things. Organic farmers had used it for decades. Rachel Carson, the environmentalist who created the modern environmental movement with her best selling book, *Silent Spring*, had been a proponent of its use. The problem was that when Bt was applied manually, it decomposed in sunlight and was washed away in rain. A far better idea was to insert Bt genes in a plant, thus protecting the Bt and making its use more effective.

Monsanto scientists also had made breakthroughs in cotton and potatoes. Bt cotton, which Monsanto scientists had bioengineered, repelled a destructive budworm that otherwise had to be destroyed by spraying. It eliminated the ten to twelve times each growing season that farmers had to spray cotton, reduced risk, and left no poisons in fragile ecosystems. The company's scientists bioengineered the NewLeaf® potato to protect it against a destructive beetle. It was capable of eliminating the manufacture and application of millions of tons of potent pesticides manufactured from oil-based raw materials. The pesticides typically were sprayed from the air with less than five percent actually coming into contact with target insects. The rest were toxic wastes that sat for long periods of time in an inert and hard to break down form in the soil.

From 1994 to 1997, Monsanto's stock nearly tripled in value. In a 1997 *Fortune* article, then CEO Shapiro declared that if Monsanto and other companies were able to bring environmentally better products that people wanted to the market faster and at lower costs, they would have tremendous marketplace success.[16] The future path on which Monsanto was headed was to create new food, drug, and combined food–drug (neutraceutical) products. One day, it might be possible to put a vaccine for hepatitis B and for diarrhea into the cells of a banana. The advantages in countries short on refrigerators, sterile needles, and hygiene, were immense. Another possibility was incorporating vitamin A into rice and thus reducing or eliminating the problem of millions of children worldwide, who lose their eyesight or die from infections caused by vitamin A deficiencies.

By the year 2000, biotechnology based crops were grown commercially or in field trials in over 40 countries on more than 100 million acres.[17] The countries at that time that grew 99 percent of the GM crops were the United States (68 percent), Argentina (23 percent), Canada (7 percent), and China (1 percent). The principal crops grown were herbicide- and insecticide-resistant soybeans, corn, cotton, and canola. Other crops that were grown commercially or being field tested were a sweet potato resistant to a virus that could decimate the African harvest, rice with increased iron and vitamins that could alleviate malnutrition in Asia, and a variety of plants that would be able to survive weather extremes.

On the horizon were bananas that produced human vaccines against infectious diseases such as hepatitis B; fish that developed more quickly; fruit and nut trees that matured earlier; and plants that yield feedstock for plastics. These GM crops offered the promise that they would be able to meet the twenty-first century's greatest food challenges, but like all new technologies, they posed various risks and generated controversy surrounding human and environmental safety, ethics, labeling, access, and intellectual property rights (see Table 10.1).

DuPont follows

DuPont was the world's largest chemical producer in 1997.[18] Its 1997 sales were $46.7 billion. It had profits of $2.4 billion and 98,000 employees. Its mission was to put science to work to solve problems in ways that made life better and safer. Founded in 1802, primarily as an explosives company, the company's focus had turned to chemicals, materials, and energy. Its products were in such areas as health care, apparel, safety and security, construction, electronics, and transportation.

DuPont prided itself in its ability to adapt and change and be an innovative company, and at the same time to remain committed to core values such as safety, health, and the environment. DuPont like Monsanto made herbicides, insecticides, and fungicides that farmers used to keep weeds, insects, and fungi at bay. Aware of the turnaround carried out by Shapiro, the company chose to move in the direction of biotech. The aim was to execute a complex corporate transformation, changing the 197-year-old company from a highly regarded, but at the time humdrum, chemical firm into a leading-edge bioengineering corporation.

For DuPont, this transition was a long one. In 1981, it acquired Conoco, the world's ninth largest petrochemical company. It bought

Table 10.1 *Benefits and controversies about genetically modified products*

Benefits	Controversies
Crops	**Ethics**
• Enhanced taste and quality	• Mixing of genes from species
• Reduced maturation time	to species
• Increased nutrients, yields, and stress	**Labeling**
tolerance	• Should it be mandatory?
• Greater resistance to disease, pests, and	**Access and intellectual property**
herbicides	• Conservation of soil, water,
• New products and growing	and energyNeed to protect
techniques	intellectual property rights of
Animal	developers while at same time
• Increased resistance, productivity,	providing access to farmers in
hardiness, and feed efficiency	developing countries who are
• Better yields of meat, eggs, and milk	most in need
• Improved animal health and diagnostic	
methods	
Environment	
• Reduced use of herbicides, insecticides,	
and fungicides	
• Conservation of soil, water, and energy	
Society	
• Increased food security for growing	
populations	
Saftey	
• Unintended transfer of genes through	
cross-pollination	

Adapted from A. Marcus, *Winning Moves, Cases in Strategic Management*

Conoco at the tail end of an oil shortage to secure a steady supply of raw materials. Then it sold Conoco, in the largest IPO for a US company at that time. In Conoco's place, it spent $7.7 billion to buy the remaining 80 percent that it did not yet own of Pioneer Hi-Bred, the biggest seed maker and marketer in the world. Pioneer was dominant in US corn seeds. This acquisition enabled Pioneer's research scientists to interact more freely with DuPont's on gene technology.

To capitalize on the synergies available in pharmaceuticals and biotech, DuPont also spent $2.8 billion to buy Merck's share of a joint pharmaceutical venture. As Monsanto at the time also had a pharmaceutical division, these acquisitions fortified DuPont in the ongoing competition it would have with Monsanto. DuPont's acquisitions opened up an array of possibilities. Coming out of scientific discoveries in the workings of the gene, there was the potential to create many new products. The company always had been at the forefront of technology. It had switched from making gunpowder to chemicals at the end of the nineteenth century and then had risen to prominence based on innovations from its labs such as nylon, Dacron®, Rayon®, Teflon®, Mylar®, and Lycra®. DuPont understood itself to be an R&D company, not a chemical company.

In the late 1980s, though, DuPont had fewer than 100 scientists engaged in biotech work at its central research department in Wilmington. The research was exploratory and coordination with crop protection was not taking place. One of the first moves DuPont made in the biotech area was to merge its biotech researchers with crop protection. The company obtained several patents and established research agreements with other firms and universities, and in 1992 marketed a herbicide resistant to tobacco seed sold by Northrup King. The crop protection market was attractive because of the patenting needed, the proprietary knowledge on which it was based, and the high margins achievable when a product was under patent. DuPont pursued the market, lured by the high potential margins and the research-intensive nature of the business.

In 1986 DuPont purchased Shell's chemical protection business. More than 60 percent of the crop protection market at that time consisted of herbicides, another 25 percent insecticides, about 10 percent fungicides, and the rest miscellaneous.[19] Because of patenting a company kept the position it acquired in a specific crop application for a long period. The research to achieve such a position was protracted and the risks great; however, no more than two percent of chemicals tested were effective. The EPA supervised testing for safety and efficacy and the process, an expensive one, could take more than five years to complete. After approval, a product's remaining patent life was about ten years.

By 1997, 30 percent of DuPont's 10,000 research scientists were engaged in work on crop protection and genetically modifying seeds.[20] The remaining 70 percent did work for which DuPont was more typically known: in polymers, electronics and imaging, and other areas.

At Pioneer's headquarters in Des Moines, scientists evaluated corn varieties that could improve yield and reduce disease. They tried to create chicken feed that made poultry taste better and reduced chicken manure's phosphorous smell.

Breakthroughs seldom took place as planned. DuPont tried to introduce more predictability in the process. It reviewed ongoing research projects to determine their commercial potential and when they might come to market. The company did an inventory in 1997 and determined that about 400 projects had the potential for commercial application. The projects were complicated and drew on a variety of disciplines. The company prioritized the 100 most likely to succeed for further development. It then chose the ten from among the 100 that had the most potential.

The company was working both on traits that would allow crops to withstand damage from pests as well as traits that would add to the products' taste, color, consistency, and nutritional content. The company examined nutraceuticals, potential health enhancers increasingly called functional foods, because signs of change already were in groceries – calcium-fortified orange juice, herbal tea with antioxidants, and eggs with fish-derived fatty acids to avert heart disease. The margins were high for functional foods and the market could explode. Tumor-stopping chemicals could be introduced into wheat, corn, or other grains. People would get cancer protection from the foods they ate. Research suggested that men with early prostate cancer might be able to slow the disease's progress by eating GM soy.

Soybean research also became an important DuPont priority. Soybeans were found in many foods including baked products, egg and meat alternatives, and animal feed. Next to corn, they were the most commonly grown US crop. DuPont scientists made a seed that produced soybeans with 80 percent oleic acid content as opposed to 24 percent previously. The oil was more stable, and cheaper to make. It was healthier and tasted better. It also added between $25 and $115 to a farmer's income for each acre grown.

At a Ralston Purina unit in St. Louis, Protein Technologies International (PTI), which DuPont acquired in 1997, DuPont continued its research on improving soybean's taste and its consistency. Protein Technologies International had cost DuPont $1.5 billion. Next to Pioneer Hi-Bred, it one was one of the largest acquisitions DuPont made in its transition from commodity chemicals to sustainable products.

A cyclical downturn in commodity chemicals combined with a decline in sales in Asia hurt the company's 1999 earnings and reinforced the sense of urgency that DuPont had to leave this area. Its entry into biotechnology was late compared to Monsanto and its approach different. Rather than selling off its mature businesses like nylon and polyester right away, as Monsanto did when it divested its commodity and specialty chemicals group, and becoming almost entirely dependent on agricultural technology, DuPont aimed to use the surplus cash from the mature businesses to fund biotech research.

Besides emphasizing such applications as agricultural, pharmaceuticals, food, and health, as Monsanto did, DuPont had hopes that biotech could replace polymer chemicals as a feedstock for its chemicals. For such DuPont staples as polyester, auto paints, films, resins, and industrial chemicals, the company could rely on GM crops. If successful, the company would be less reliant on non-renewable resources, whose prices fluctuated unpredictably, and more reliant on renewable resources that put less stress on the environment.

Obstacles to biotechnology's advances

By 2001, GM crops were in very wide use in the United States. More than 30,000 products from these crops were sold.[21] They included soy sauce, bread, pasta, ice cream, candy, meats, and corn flakes. Genetically modified seeds had been planted on 76 percent of cotton acres, 74 percent of soybean acres, and 27 percent of corn acres. Monsanto's GM corn was shown to increase yields by 13.5 bushels per acre on average. It also had lower levels of fungal toxins, a possible human carcinogen. Genetically modified papaya resisted the ring rot virus, which regularly devastated the Hawaiian crop.

Additional innovation, however, was not going to be easy because a number of serious issues emerged. One issue was that Monsanto charged more for the protection its seeds offered. The justification usually was economic. For example, even a slight corn borer infestation could reduce corn yield by a very large amount. Monsanto made farmers sign agreements that they would not resell seeds, keep them without planting, or set them aside from one harvest to the next. Most US farmers accepted these conditions. They were used to repurchasing seeds every year because even the non-GM seeds that they used lost their vitality if they came from last year's crop. However, farmers in developing countries counted on using last year's seeds for each new harvest. Thus using Monsanto's seeds in most foreign nations was not as easy as using these seeds in the United States.

In the United States there was some opposition as well. Farmers did not like the way Monsanto protected its intellectual property. Those that used Roundup® had to put up with unannounced audits to guarantee compliance with Monsanto's rules. If they were caught violating these rules, they could be fined as much as $10,000. In 2003, a Federal court in St. Louis awarded Monsanto $780,000 in a patent infringement suit against a farmer that had saved seeds for planting next year. Farmers, like the one charged in the Missouri court, who chose to defy Monsanto faced bankruptcy.

Environmentalist opposition

Another obstacle to the further diffusion of GM seeds was the opposition of environmentalists. The Union of Concerned Scientists (UCC) issued working papers against the technology. They raised the possibility that the pests frustrated by new plant strains eventually would adapt. Once they adapted, super pests would create a hazard that would be nearly impossible to control. The UCC papers raised the possibility that Roundup® ready seeds could mix with related weed species on a field's edge and that these weeds would be impossible to eradicate.

Monsanto maintained that there was a solution, its requirement that farmers create refuge areas – adjacent fields with non-GM seeds of the same crop. Pests and weeds that grew resistant would mate with those that were not resistant and the resulting offspring would not inherit resistance that was impossible to control. In 1997, when a Canadian farmer reported that Roundup® ready seeds had escaped and created a super weed conventional weed killers could not kill, Monsanto put the blame on the farmer who had neglected to establish the safe refuge area. In the developed world, the threat was not large since weeds similar to crops rarely were found next to most crops, but in the developing world crops often had close relatives growing nearby. These close relatives could morph into the super weeds that concerned scientists.

Environmentalists also publicized research by a Cornell University scientist in 1999 that showed that eggs of the monarch butterfly could perish if exposed to Bt-modified corn pollen. The pollen destroyed three-day-old monarch larvae 44 percent of the time in a laboratory study. Other scientists pointed out that a lab study did not reproduce conditions in the field. They again pointed to the refuge area that Monsanto required around the field as an antidote that restricted the Bt-modified corn to a small area.

When it came to human consumption, environmentalists insisted on a precautionary principle, so long as risk of any kind existed, the burden was on the introducer of a new product to demonstrate complete safety. They argued that GM seeds had been rushed to the market without adequate independent testing. The testing done was not able to pick up negative results in cases of small numbers. If the seeds affected less than one in a million persons they would not be noticed. Environmentalists claimed that the negative health effects were significantly felt by a small minority of hyperallergic persons. They also pointed to an incident in 1995 when Pioneer Hi-Bred had spliced together a Brazilian nut gene with soybeans to increase the level of the amino acids methionine and cysteine. The splicing together of the genes of these plants produced a more nutritious animal feed; however, humans allergic to Brazil nuts might die if they accidentally consumed a soybean or a soybean product with the spliced gene. After protests Pioneer HiBred took the seed off the market.

Another controversy ignited when Delta & Pine Land Company, the biggest US cottonseed producer in 1998, filed for a patent from the US Department of Agriculture for a set of molecular switches that could turn genes off and on. Among the genes that the switches could turn off and on were those for reproduction. The Canadian environmental organization Rural Advancement Foundation termed these switches "terminator" genes after the mechanical murderer that Arnold Schwarzenegger portrayed in movies. Monsanto, at the time, was in the midst of negotiations to acquire Delta & Pine. Using the terminator gene, Monsanto could protect its intellectual property without having to audit and inspect farmers. Environmentalists maintained that poor people in the developing world had to save seeds from one growing season to another.

Monsanto responded that the gene in question had uses other than turning on and off plant reproductive systems. Among the uses was that it solved the troublesome problem that GM seeds might cross-pollinate with related species. Once a plant lost its ability to reproduce, it could not transfer its genes to other plants. In addition, the switches were valuable because they could be used to turn on or off many other characteristics, such as the ability of a plant to fight drought, repel frost, be protected from the sun, or absorb the sun's rays. They were a step in the direction of designer seeds in which farmers would pay for the precise traits they wanted.

The pressure on Monsanto to withdraw its offer to buy Delta & Pine was intense. Gordon Conway, an agricultural ecologist, was the head of the Rockefeller Foundation at the time. His foundation had funded many projects to assist poor farmers in developing countries.[22] He was a public supporter of GM seeds, because they had the potential to lift these people out of poverty, but he urged Monsanto to give up on buying Delta & Pine. Monsanto was best served if it left this controversy behind it. In response to such advice, Monsanto, for the time being, gave up on its intention to acquire the company.

The European roadblock

In Europe, arguments about the importance of GM crops for feeding the world's poor had not made much of a dent. Many Europeans were fearful of new technology that tampered with the food supply, especially after such incidents as mad-cow disease and an attempted government cover-up of tainted chicken and eggs in Belgium. In developing countries almost 40 percent of the fruit and vegetables rotted in fields and never made it to the market. In developed countries refrigeration was common and inexpensive and good transport that got produce to the market on time was available. Putting restrictions on GM crops also allowed Europeans to protect domestic agriculture against US agribusiness. The European media tended to brand Monsanto as a global manipulator that created grotesque "frankenfoods."

The European Union (EU) recognized the consumer's right to information to make informed choices about GM ingredients and issued a directive that required labeling on all foods containing, consisting of, or derived from GM organisms in 1997. David Byrne, the Commissioner for Health and Consumer Protection for the EU, in a 2002 speech to the European Parliament recommended that Europe should require the mandatory labeling of food, food ingredients, and feed produced from a GM crop, even when the modified material was not directly detectable in the food, feed, or in the ingredient. The example he gave was table oil that came from maize, soybeans, or rapeseed. Though all modified material was removed in the refinement process, Byrne argued for labeling to inform consumers and to allow them to exercise choice.

The ruling that if any DNA or protein resulting from genetic modification was present, a product was subject to labeling requirement led to a virtual moratorium on the importation of products that contained genetically modified organisms into EU countries. The Swiss pharmaceutical company, Novartis, and the British pharmaceutical company, AstraZeneca, combined their agricultural divisions and created a third company called Syngenta, which they divested. Syngenta was solely devoted to biotechnology, seeds, and agricultural chemicals. It had no other revenue except the revenue it derived from these sources. Monsanto was soon to follow suit and become a pure bioengineering firm. To justify the decision that Novartis made to stop using GM soy and corn in its Gerber baby food, its CEO Daniel Vasella declared that his company was not a missionary. There was no use trying to sell products if customers did not think they were safe and good for them.

Other large European companies – Unilever, Nestlé, and Cadbury – announced they would no longer use GM products. UK food retailer Sainsbury removed these foods from its shelves. Food processors, distributors, and supermarkets in Europe had to provide signed affidavits showing that their products had not been contaminated. Deutsche Bank told its clients not to invest in companies that made products that were bioengineered. Domestic Chinese consumers began to show a preference for food that was not genetically modified. The country showed signs of shifting from wanting to be the developing world's leader in biotech to fearing that it would lose key export markets in Europe and the rest of the world if it pushed ahead too quickly.

Most US consumers did not have these concerns, but in 1999, the FDA held a series of open meetings based on surveys that showed that 70 percent of US public wanted labeling. The problem with labeling was how far it should go. In the United States products made from GM grains had an extensive reach. Corn- and soy-based products were ubiquitous. Worldwide opposition to GM crops, nonetheless, left a mark on the United States. United States' food manufacturers, such as

Heinz and Frito-Lay, asked suppliers for products that were non-GM. McDonald's purchased only non-GM potatoes but fried them in GM canola oil. ADM asked farmers to segregate modified crops and haul them to market in separate containers. Natural food companies such as Whole Foods announced that they would not sell GM products in the future (see Chapter 9).

Concerned that Europe might reject their agricultural exports, six African nations affected by drought refused US food aid in 2002 because the food had been genetically modified. The US government formally challenged EU policies in 2003, arguing that the EU's precautionary approach had gone too far. United States' Trade Representative Robert Zoellick maintained that the EU moratorium hindered US shipments to countries outside the EU even when they were in dire straits and desperately needed the food.

Patrick Moore, a co-founder of Greenpeace argued in his blog that the environmental movement's campaign against bioengineering exposed its "intellectual and moral bankruptcy."[23] Moore pointed to the EU's own research –eighty one scientific studies on GM organisms (GMOs) conducted by over four hundred research teams at a cost of 65 million dollars that showed no evidence of negative human health effects or environmental concerns. Moore characterized the campaign against GM foods as one of fear based on fantasy and a lack of respect for science and logic.

Monsanto's restructuring

At the height of the controversy, Monsanto's key product, Roundup, came off patent. Once off patent, its US market share –once above 80 percent –was about to fall and the company's revenues inevitably would shrink. As a result, from 1998–2000, Monsanto's stock lost half its value. The company therefore instigated talks with a number of other companies about a merger.[24] It came to an agreement with Pharmacia, which wanted the drug Celebrex. Pharmacia transferred the agricultural assets to a separate company called the new Monsanto which it divested. The new Monsanto, like Syngenta, had but one focus –biotech traits, seeds, and agricultural chemicals. Its sole mission was agricultural productivity.

In 2002, sixty one percent of Monsanto's earnings came from Roundup. The CEO of the new Monsanto, Hendrik Verfaille's maintained that it should end its dependence on the herbicide.[25] Less than thirty percent of its revenue should come from Roundup, twenty four percent should come from other agricultural productivity products, seventeen percent from seeds, and thirty percent from the genetic traits its scientists produced.

In response to the ongoing opposition to genetic engineering Verfaille tried to be more forthcoming and engaging. He admitted that the top managers at Monsanto never quite understood why the firm aroused such strong rejection. People feared frozen foods when they were first introduced and tried to ban them. Advances like antibiotics and vaccines were opposed because they entailed risk. Aspirin contributed to many diseases and even deaths yet it was universally accepted.

Verfaille argued that Monsanto was willing to listen, respect, and consider legitimate concerns. He maintained that the shift from traditional agricultural to biological approaches still was in its infancy. The first wave of GM products had been designed to improve farmer efficiency and productivity. The next wave of breakthroughs would be in applications that delivered more direct benefits to consumers. Monsanto for instance was developing a product that added omega-3 fatty acids to foods. As well as being able to enhance the protein, vitamin, or mineral quality of animal feeds, this product could help people fend off heart disease.

In response to Roundup's coming off patent, Monsanto lowered its costs and tried to create improved formulations. These moves were intended to repel aggressive Chinese manufacturers who had entered the market with generic products. Roundup® had two purposes. The first was to clean a field before planting, a low-tech use of the product, where cost was the key concern and generic brands competitive. The second was after crops started to grow; in this instance spraying without harm to the crops was difficult and required a very precise product formulation. For the initial use of Roundup, Monsanto developed a more concentrated version that allowed for extended spraying from a single tank that was cheaper to use. For the later use, it developed a new patentable formula and mixture that could continue to fetch a high price. Monsanto also started to license use of Roundup's primary ingredient, glyphosate, to other companies. Glyphosate allowed crops to withstand spraying by herbicides like Roundup. The companies licensing glyphosate included DuPont.

Monsanto also again tried to acquire Delta & Pine Land, but DuPont and Syngenta protested.[26] Delta & Pine Land had a fifty percent market share in cotton seeds in the United States and a 92 percent share in the Southern part of the country where most cotton was grown. The crop was the fifth largest grown in the United States. DuPont and Syngenta viewed Monsanto's attempted takeover of Delta & Pine as an attempt to reduce competition. Syngenta lobbied Congress to stop the deal. DuPont sued Monsanto.

Delta & Pine had just pulled back from its dependence on Monsanto genes. A month before Monsanto approached Delta & Pine, the company had reached agreements with DuPont's Pioneer Hi-Bred division to license DuPont's genes for weed killing immunity and Syngenta's genes for insect resistance. Before regulators allowed Monsanto to complete the acquisition, they made Monsanto agree to respect Delta's licenses to use the DuPont and Syngenta genes. They also made Monsanto divest its Stoneville cottonseed business which had a 12 percent share of the US market.

DuPont's renewed focus on biotech

During this period, DuPont's dilemma was whether to focus more exclusively on biotech or to continue to use its commodity chemical businesses as a cash cow to finance biotech. Would it be better for it to be a more mission based biotech firm like Monsanto and Syngenta? In 2003, DuPont agreed to sell its textiles unit to Koch Industries for $4.4 billion. The sale of the nylon, polyester, and Lycra fiber businesses came during a sharp decline in the US textile and apparel industries that came about because of foreign competition. It reduced DuPont's dependence on high-cost raw materials made from petroleum byproducts and signaled an intent to focus more on biotechnology. In 2002, the textiles unit had $6.3 billion in revenue and 18,000 worldwide employees. It was the source of about a quarter of DuPont's annual revenue, but it was the company's least profitable unit and had been subject to job cuts and plant closings. DuPont's CEO Holliday promised that the company would become more committed to crop protection and food.

DuPont became more focused on biotech, but remained more diversified than Monsanto or Syngenta (see Table 10.2). Unlike these companies, it had other business units with different goals. Besides

Table 10.2 *Major divisions of Monsanto, Syngenta, and DuPont, 2006*

Monsanto	Syngenta	DuPont
Seeds and Genomics	Crop Protection	Agriculture & Nutrition
Agricultural Productivity	Seeds	Coatings & Color Technologies (auto paint)
		Electronic & Communication Technologies (display & fluorocarbons)
		Performance Materials (polymers)
		Safety & Protection (consulting)

Derived from Company Annual Reports

Agriculture and Nutrition, it operated in these other segments: Coatings and Color Technologies; Electronic and Communication Technologies; Performance Materials; and Safety and Protection. Coatings and Color Technologies was a large global auto paint supplier. Electronic and Communication Technologies sold advanced display materials and products. It was the world's largest maker of both fluorochemicals (refrigerants, blowing agents, aerosols) and fluoropolymers (teflon resins and coatings). Performance Materials engineered polymers for auto, electrical, consumer, and industrial uses and sold packaging and polyester films. Safety and Protection did safety and other types of consulting as well as making safety products.

The Agriculture and Nutrition segment was dominated by Pioneer Hi-Bred, which constituted 46 percent of its sales. Pioneer Hi-Bred was the world's largest seed company and a major global supplier of crop protection chemicals. However, in 2006, the sales of DuPont's Agriculture and Nutrition Division were down by one percentage point and its profits were off 41 percent in comparison to the previous year. Pioneer Hi-Bred had lost ground in the US corn market. Monsanto had boosted its share of the US seed-corn market to 25 percent from around 10 percent in 2000, while Pioneer Hi-Bred's market share fell to about 31 percent from approximately 38 percent in 2000.

DuPont licensed and paid royalties to Monsanto for the herbicide tolerance trait glyphosate. The superiority of Monsanto's seeds was that they were triple-stacked to provide (i) nutrients, (ii) pesticide resistance, and (iii) herbicide resistance. Famers paid for the seeds by their traits. If DuPont did not license Monsanto technology it would not have a product as highly differentiated as Monsanto and it could not command a similar price. Monsanto's role in its partnerships with DuPont tended to be to provide development assistance and licensing in product commercialization, while DuPont's role tended to be to provide sales, marketing, and distribution assistance. Many similar cross-licensing arrangements existed in this industry. Monsanto, because of its firm hold on a strong portfolio of proprietary technology, was a dominant player in traits. Its partners included BASF, Bayer, Cargill, Merck, Novartis, Pharmacia, Pfizer, Solutia, and DuPont and Syngenta, while DuPont's partners included Bayer, Alcoa, BP, Dow, Lilly, Johnson & Johnson, Merck, Rohm and Haas, Monsanto, and Syngenta.

To better compete with Monsanto, DuPont cutback on its low-growth nutrition and crop protection operations and eliminated about 1,500 jobs. It invested $100 million of the savings in research and global marketing. It engaged in long term research that focused on such areas as drought tolerance, stalk rot resistance, and nitrogen use efficiency and invested in new sales managers, experienced seed company representatives, and promotional activity, committing heavily to Brazil which was the world's second largest soybean grower and the world's third largest corn grower. Unlike Monsanto, DuPont probed the biofuel space (see Chapter 1), working on a seed that was genetically engineered to yield more ethanol from corn in partnership with the Department of Energy. It worked with a company called Broin on methods to produce ethanol from parts of the corn other than the kernels and cob and had an alliance with BP to make a fuel called biobutanol that had higher energy content and could be used for air transport.

Alternatives to biotech

While in Europe GM foods were controversial, in the United States by 2006 89 percent of soybeans, 83 percent of cotton and 61 percent of corn were cultivated this way.[27] Corn's uses as animal feed, sweetener, and cereal continued to grow. By the end of 2006, corn prices were up by 55 percent, a price increase that had a ripple effect on the price of all grains including soybeans, oats, sorghum and barley. The alternative fuels industry in the United States also was booming – 106 ethanol plants were in operation in the United States and another 48 were under construction.[28] The ethanol industry consumed about a fifth of all corn harvested in the United States, an increase of more than 60 percent in two years.

The EU's 1998 moratorium on approving new types of GM crops for import ended in 2004 and the use of GM seeds in Europe also was growing.[29] By 2006, Spain had 148,200 acres of GM corn under cultivation, the largest amount grown in Europe. More French farmers planted GM seeds because it lowered their costs and increased pest protection; the pesticides savings could surpass $38 an acre. In 2006, French farmers grew 12,350 acres of GM corn, more than 10 times as much as they did the previous year, despite opposition from environmental activists and politicians. Other countries such as the Czech Republic, Portugal and Germany also increased their cultivation of GM crops. Total spending on GM seeds in the EU was 15 percent of the world's spending, but still the EU produced less than one percent of all GM crops.

Turbo charged selective breeding

To achieve sought after gains in agricultural productivity Monsanto and DuPont explored a number of alternatives to biotechnology.[30] Turbo charged selective breeding (TCSB) meant finding plants with desirable traits and mating them without gene splicing. Rather, rows of robotic devices examined slices of DNA from thousands of plants. Scientists examined the slices to find genetic differences that might explain why some plants were better than others at dealing with such conditions as cold weather, insect suppression, drought survival, or reproduction. With this knowledge, they created better plants by breeding and not genetic transfer.

This new method greatly reduced the time it took breeders to create marketable seeds. It was not necessary to wait until the plant matured. Companies relied on mathematic Ph.Ds to create predictive algorithms to project what would happen. The plant's traits were tested before planting in a field. The technology spread rapidly when instrument maker Applied Biosystems Group lowered scanning equipment costs. DuPont worked on stalk rot resisting corn, Syngenta on drought-resistant corn, and Monsanto developed soybean oil for fast-food restaurants that was not hydrogenated and did not create artery-clogging trans fats. Food companies like Heinz were interested in greater longevity and improved plant processing quality. ADM was interested in better pinto and lima bean varieties. Working with the Defense Department, which spent about $500 million a year on produce, companies tried to breed lettuce and tomatoes that stayed fresh longer. If the shelf life of lettuce and tomatoes could be doubled the Defense Department could save millions of dollars. Organic farmers used TCSB to investigate ways to prevent wheat fungi infestation. Monsanto relied on it to develop and market its new brands of fruits and vegetables such as the Melorange®, an extra-sweet cantaloupe; EverMild®, a less weepy onion; Frescada®, a lettuce sweeter and crunchier than romaine that stayed fresh like iceberg; BellaFina®, a small pepper in a single-serve sizes that reduced leftovers; and Beneforté®, a broccoli that had three times the antioxidant boosting compound.[31]

However, by 2013 the percentage of genetically modified US crops continued to rise. Pervasive suspicion about these crops had not deterred wide-scale diffusion. Ninety percent of the corn and cotton and 93 percent of the soybeans planted were genetically modified.[32] Corn, cotton, and soybeans were commodity crops with uses such as animal feed and ethanol. To the extent humans consumed them mainly it was as high fructose corn syrup (HFC), a sweetener in beverages and other products, or as a protein and stabilizer supplement. Public opposition had not entirely abated. Vermont passed a law that required labeling in 2014, while ballot initiatives that would have mandated labeling barely lost in California and the state of Washington.

Precision agriculture

Another alternative to increasing crop yields that did not rely on genetic modification was precision agriculture. With the analysis of large amounts of data transforming many fields from retail logistics to dating, agriculture was no exception. Monsanto applied these methods to farming. It was involved in improving farm productivity by providing farmers with such data. The unit of application for this type of agriculture was a square yard of soil, not the farm or field. With precise data at this level, yields could be improved in more environmentally sound and less energy-intensive ways. The amount of chemicals and fossil fuels used could be reduced.

Through the purchase of two companies, Precision Planting and the Climate Corporation, Monsanto began to offer software and hardware products that gathered and processed temperature, rain, soil, and pest data. The founders of the Climate Corporation (see Chapters 1 and 2) were Google engineers, David Friedberg and Siraj Khaliq. They created the software and brought together the climatological data. The Climate Corporation offered a new kind of crop insurance as well. It had no claims process but automatically compensated farmers if the company's models showed that the weather would hurt yields. For a fee per acre, the Climate Corporation offered farmers software that told them what, when, and how deep to plant, whether to irrigate, which fertilizer to apply, and where to reapply the fertilizer. The 40 to 50 factors that farmers who grew corn had to consider were amalgamated in a model designed to eliminate early mistakes that cascaded and affected later choices.

DuPont also entered this market in 2014 with services it called Encirca. It was its own suite of whole-farm decision aids to help improve the productivity and profitability of agricultural operations. DuPont's service could be delivered through local certified services agents who helped farmers improve yields by offering them advice to inform their crop planting decisions. As well as direct access to the DuPont experts, the service had mobile applications. DuPont's revenues, like Monsanto's, came from the different packages of services that farmers bought. A monthly subscription fee included market news and analysis including weather forecasts. The top of the line service was flexible, and tailored to a farmer's specific requests. According to DuPont, there was significant potential for these services to help improve productivity for North America corn and soybean growers and for the company to extend them globally to a range of different crops and markets.

Performance and choices

As of August 2014, DuPont had the best five-year stock market performance among the companies in this sector. It was the only one that did better than the S&P 500. The accounting results, however, tended to favor Monsanto (see Table 10.3). Its margins were superior

Table 10.3 *Agriculture chemical company financials compared, August 2014*

	DuPont	Monsanto	Syngenta
Market cap ($)	59.67 b	59.11 b	31.76 b
Employees	64,000	21,900	28,000
Quarterly revenue growth (%)	−0.02	0.00	0.01
Revenue ($)	35.49 b	15.43 b	14.81 b
Gross margin	0.37	0.54	0.45
Operating margin	0.12	0.26	0.15
Net income ($)	2.94 b	2.63 b	1.63 b

Compiled from publicly available quarterly report data of the companies
b = billions

Table 10.4 *Sustainability scores of major chemical companies, September 2014*

	Overall	Community	Employees	Environment	Governance
DuPont	62	54	66	64	62
Syngenta	61	53	69	60	60
Monsanto	50	38	61	51	51
All Chemical Companies	55	53	57	57	52
All Agricultural Companies	54	54	57	55	55
All company average	54	53	56	56	51
US company average	54	55	56	57	50

CSRHub: www.csrhub.com

to either DuPont or Syngenta. None of these companies saw much revenue growth in the second quarter of 2014. With regard to social performance DuPont also had the top overall rating and Monsanto the worst (see Table 10.4). The contest between DuPont and Monsanto presented many challenges to both companies and they had choices to make about what to do next.

DuPont's aims under Ellen Kullman

Since Ellen Kullman took over as CEO of DuPont in 2009, she stressed the need for constant reinvention.[33] She pushed the company to diversify into faster growing product areas such as high-tech seeds, photovoltaic cells, and Kevlar® body armor. DuPont, in Kullman's view, was a market-driven global science company. Its focus was to use science to improve the world. It had to match its research and development and capital expenditures against megatrends.

At 32 percent of the company's $36 billion total revenues in 2013, the agriculture segment constituted the major share of DuPont's 2013 sales. This segment was a leader in developing, producing, and marketing corn hybrid and soybean varieties with traits that allowed them to resist herbicides and pesticides. These seeds could be targeted toward biofuel production. DuPont's merger and acquisition activity was focused on expanding these businesses. It was collaborating with other companies on R&D in the development of such products as seeds with high oleic content, multiple levels of herbicide tolerance, and insect protection.

Yet DuPont was a more diversified firm than either Monsanto or Syngenta. Because it was diversified, its US revenue did not suffer much during the recession. While growth slowed in 2009 and 2010, the company quickly bounced back. From 2008 to 2013 DuPont's agriculture segment grew by an average of 12 percent per year, a growth rate higher than its competitors, but the company achieved substantial earnings increases and operating margin improvement across other segments as well including safety and protection, electronics and communications, nutrition and health, and industrial biosciences (see Table 10.5). The exception was performance chemicals. Because of the slow and uncertain demand for titanium dioxide, one of this segment's major products, DuPont chose to spin it off. The spin off freed up capital for other investments. DuPont was able to spend $7 billion to buy Danica, a Danish enzyme maker in 2011. It also invested in increasing the speed with which it introduced new materials used for solar cells, plastics, and industrial coatings.

In 2014, DuPont's agriculture earnings began to suffer because of lower corn-seed revenue as a result of harsh weather in the United States and less corn planting. Popular sentiment in the United States remained a challenge. Even though attempts to pass mandatory GMO labeling requirements mostly failed, the commitment of food sellers such as Whole Foods not to sell food grown with GM seeds (see Chapter 9) was an indicator that DuPont and other sellers of these seeds could lose market share to non-GMO technologies and methods. In North America and Europe there was increasing adoption of

Table 10.5 *DuPont's segments, products, markets, and sales, 2013*

Segment	Products	Markets	Percentage of 2013 sales
Agriculture	Pioneer, crop protection	Seeds, agricultural protection	32
Nutrition and health	Food ingredients	Nutritional products	10
Industrial biosciences	Industrial enzymes	Biobased materials	3
Electronics and communications	Photovotaics, advanced printing	Consumer electronics, displays	7
Performance chemicals	Titanium, chemicals, and fluoroproducts	Industrial, chemical, construction, transportation, plastics	19
Performance materials	Performance polymers, industrial polymers	Packaging, transportaion, electronics	18
Safety and protection	Protection technologies, buildings	Sustainability, industry, construction, military, transportation, consumer	11

Derived from 2013 Company Annual Report

integrated pest management strategies, organic farming, the development of biopesticides, and the more selective use of herbicides.

The costs of complying with environmental laws and regulations associated with crop protection were likely to go up. Some products might be banned or phased out by the EPA. Continued concerns about the impact of pesticides meant that Kullman was considering putting more emphasis on environmentally benign and low-risk products. Product advancement and innovation were needed in low-dose, better applied technologies that had less toxicity.

Given the problems that the agricultural business might face, Kullman was of the opinion that DuPont should look overseas for growth. International opportunities existed in developing nations as they adopted US habits for eating protein-rich meat. Demand for meat increased the demand for grains with GM seeds. Companies such as

DuPont that specialized in these crops could take advantage of this opportunity. They also could take advantage of the opportunity from the mounting global demand for fuel in addition to food.

The DuPont–Monsanto partnership

DuPont and Monsanto had regularly sued each other for anti-trust violations and patent infringement. Monsanto accused DuPont of violating the licensing agreement for the use of glyphosate, and after a billion dollar jury verdict against DuPont, the two companies agreed to drop claims against each other and forge a partnership. The DuPont–Monsanto agreement was a multi-year, royalty-sharing license that allowed DuPont to gain access to Monsanto's next-generation technologies. DuPont could use Monsanto's Genuity soybean brand that dealt with herbicide-resistant weeds spreading across the US and Canada starting in 2014.[34] In exchange for this right DuPont had to make four annual fixed royalty payments to Monsanto, totaling $802 million, from 2014 to 2017. Beginning in 2018 it would pay royalties on a per-unit basis.

The agreement broadened DuPont's soybean line-up and gave it increased flexibility to develop its genetic and trait combinations on its own. Monsanto, in return, gained access to DuPont's marketing capabilities, which were greater than Monsanto's in soybeans. The partnership was based on recognition of mutual strengths, DuPont also obtained Monsanto's assistance in maintaining regulatory approvals for technologies coming off patent that were already incorporated into DuPont corn and soybean varieties, while DuPont granted Monsanto licenses to some of its disease-resistance technology and patents.

Monsanto's ongoing reputational problems

Monsanto was devoted solely to its agricultural businesses. Under the DeKalb, Asgrow, and Seminis brands, it produced conventional and GM seeds and supplied biotech traits for plant protection from insects and herbicides. Its biggest markets were in corn and cotton. Yield data for its soybean seeds were positive, with the soybean seeds having many advantages. Monsanto sold these products directly to farmers and licensed them to third parties. Its biotech traits enabled crops to defend themselves against a variety of parasites and pests.

The company, however, faced ongoing public opposition due to suspected adverse effects on human and animal health, other plants, and the environment. A 2013 Harris Poll measuring the reputation quotient of major companies had Monsanto in 49th place out of 60 companies.[35] Farmers complained that Monsanto engaged in strong-arm tactics to protect its intellectual property. In annual marches in cities worldwide, protestors blasted the company for fighting efforts to mandate labeling. They charged Monsanto with polluting organic crops with GM pollen. They complained that it sued organic farmers for intellectual property theft and that it relied on the terminator gene to make crops sterile. Dressed as bees, protestors blamed the company for the alarming death rate of this insect that was so critical to the success of so many US crops. Among protestors, the company's name was shorthand for villainy.

Nonetheless, eminent scientists from many prestigious organizations had found no compelling evidence that the GM foods were not safe to eat. Organizations that came to this conclusion included the National Academy of Sciences, the American Medical Association, the World Health Organization, Britain's Royal Society, the European Commission, and the American Association for the Advancement of Science.

David Friedberg, the chief executive of the Climate Corporation became a public defender of the company.[36] He touted his own long-standing environmental credentials and denounced critics who charged him with treason:

I am not the kind of person that would take easily to partnering with a company that 'poisons the world's food system,' lays waste to the land, puts farmers out of business, or creates a monoculture that threatens the global food supply ... Humans have genetically engineered seeds for 11,000 years, primarily through seed breeding, where we "got rid of" the traits we didn't want and introduced the traits we did. Modern advancements in science have allowed for those genetic advances to be much more organized and specific, rather than haphazard, over time. The notion of introducing specific genes into specific places to create a protein that did not evolve through a natural process has been a breakthrough – one that is hard to understand and comprehend, but powerful in its implications. ... I think Monsanto has created amazing and safe technology.

Robert Fraley, Monsanto's chief technology officer, stated that though Monsanto opposed mandatory labeling because it would create unnecessary costs and confusion, the company was supportive of voluntary labeling. He challenged critics to find better ways to increase crop yields to meet the world's growing demand for food.

Demand for genetically modified seeds and next steps

Demand for GM seeds spiked in the middle years of the first decade of the twenty first century when US legislators passed the Energy Policy Act 2005, which mandated increasing levels of biofuel in gasoline. The Energy Independence and Security Act 2007 supported growth in domestic biofuel production. However, demand for agricultural products, especially corn and cotton, went down during the recession. Corn prices in the United States in 2013 were weak at about three dollars a bushel after they had reached a high of more than six dollars a bushel in 2011. Corn generated more than a third of Monsanto's revenue and a significant portion of its profits. Though Monsanto had not lost market share to DuPont, Syngenta, or other competitors, in the face of declining corn sales, it had been unable to raise prices.

Soybeans fetched over ten dollars a bushel in the United States. The high prices provided producers with an incentive to grow more soybeans and less corn. In 2013 the number of acres of corn that farmers planted declined by 3.8 percent compared to the previous year, while the number of acres of soybeans they planted went up by 8.3 percent.[37] Monsanto's concern was that farmers would continue to switch from corn to soybeans where its products were not as competitive. Another issue was that in the United States, where Monsanto did the bulk of its business, certified organic acreage had grown by an average annual rate of 12.5 percent from 2003 to 2013.[38] Demand for organic foods limited Monsanto's capacity to increase its US sales. Monsanto therefore looked to strengthen its position in soybeans in Brazil, Argentina, and other South American nations. It launched a new soybean seed called Intacta that could be used with Roundup® and established a partnership with DuPont to sell seeds in these countries

After years of focusing on genetically engineered crops, Monsanto had other options. More of its annual research budget was assigned to traditional plant breeding. The company researched the targeted use of bacteria, fungi, and other living organisms to protect and nourish seeds using technologies borrowed from organic agriculture. Genetic engineering was expensive and time consuming, so the firm relied on it less and employed TCSB methods more. Monsanto's vegetable division Seminis had greater than $800 million in sales in 2013.[39] It introduced many new brands of fruits and vegetables such as Performance Series Broccoli in 2012 that had a shape different than conventional broccoli and permitted cheaper and faster mechanical harvesting. The vegetable market in which Seminis competed might have the potential for very fast growth. Climate Solutions also was exceeding Monsanto's expectations and had the potential to become a billion dollar or more a year business.

The question Monsanto therefore faced was how committed it should continue to be to GM seeds and crop protection. Climate change still could make it very difficult to feed the world and GM seeds still could make a difference.[40] Blight-resistant potatoes were an example. Without a genetic defense against this disease, 15 percent or more of the world's potato harvest would be destroyed. Blight and other plant diseases, such as stem rust, a fungal disease of wheat, had spread through Africa and the Arabian Peninsula. They threatened growing regions in Asia. Bananas died because of wilt disease. Climate change could make these problems worse, bringing high temperatures and wetter conditions that spread infestations, and drought. Genetic engineering had the potential to create seeds that could withstand such risks. An expanding global population still was in need of new food sources.

What approach should companies like Monsanto and DuPont take to tackle these problems? To what extent should they push forward with GM crops to help solve them or retreat because the set of opportunities they had were better elsewhere?

Notes

1 See DuPont, "Science meets sustainability," (2013): www.dupont.com/content/dam/assets/corporate-functions/our-approach/sustainability/documents/2013DuPont%20Sustainability%20Report_web.pdf

2 A. Marcus, *Winning Moves: Cases in Strategic Management* (Lombard, IL: Marsh Publications, 2009): pp. 139–71.

3 See the DuPont website: www.dupont.com and the Monsanto website: www.monsanto.com/pages/default.aspx

4 A. Aston, B. Helm, M. Arndt, A. Barrett, and J. Carey, "The race against climate change," *Business Week* (2005): www.businessweek.com/stories/2005-12-11/the-race-against-climate-change

5 R. Shapiro, "Growth through global sustainability," *Harvard Business Review*, (1997): http://hbr.org/1997/01/growth-through-global-sustainability-an-interview-with-monsantos-ceo-robert-b-shapiro/ar/1; also see J. West, *E.I. du Pont de Nemours and Company (A) and (B)*, (Boston, MA: Harvard Business School, 1999); E. Simanis, *The Monsanto Company: Quest for Sustainability* (Washington, DC: World Resources Institute, 2001); R. Goldberg, *Monsanto: Leadership in a New Environment* (Boston, MA: Harvard Business School, 2003); M. Watkins, *Robert Shapiro and Monsanto* (Boston, MA: Harvard Business School, 2003).

6 R. Shapiro, "Growth through global sustainability."

7 J. Graves, "Designer genes go for your plate," *Fortune* (1995): http://archive.fortune.com/magazines/fortune/fortune_archive/1995/07/10/204241/index.htm; D. Stipp, "Engineering the future of food," *Fortune* (1998): http://archive.fortune.com/magazines/fortune/fortune_archive/1998/09/28/248704/index.htm; F. Reinhardt, *Agricultural Biotechnology and its Regulation* (Boston, MA: Harvard Business School, 2001).

8 *Monsanto's Spring Sustainability Progress Report* (2014): https://s3.amazonaws.com/SustainabilityCSR/CSR_PROGRESSREPORT_FINAL.pdf

9 N. Schwartz, "Monsantophobia," *Fortune* (1999): http://archive.fortune.com/magazines/fortune/fortune_archive/1999/03/29/257380/index.htm

10 A. Barrett, "At Dupont, time to both sow and reap," *Business Week* (1997): www.businessweek.com/stories/1997–09–28/at-dupont-time-to-both-sow-and-reap; A. Taylor III, "Why DuPont is trading oil for corn," Fortune (1999): http://archive.fortune.com/magazines/fortune/fortune_archive/1999/04/26/258748/index.htm; West, *E.I. du Pont de Nemours and Company (A) and (B)*.

11 G. Easterbrook, "Forgotten benefactor of humanity," *The Atlantic* (1997): www.theatlantic.com/magazine/archive/1997/01/forgotten-benefactor-of-humanity/306101

12 *Ibid.*

13 *Ibid.*

14 M. Specter, "The pharmageddon riddle," *New Yorker* (2000): www.newyorker.com/magazine/2000/04/10/the-pharmageddon-riddle

15 Simanis, *The Monsanto Company: Quest for Sustainability*; Goldberg, *Monsanto: Leadership in a New Environment*; Watkins, *Robert Shapiro and Monsanto*.

16 L. Grant and A. Moore, "Monsanto's bet: there's gold in going green," *Fortune* (1997): http://archive.fortune.com/magazines/fortune/fortune_archive/1997/04/14/224981/index.htm

17 Marcus, *Winning Moves: Cases in Strategic Management.*
18 see West, *E.I. du Pont de Nemours and Company (A) and (B).*
19 *Ibid.*
20 *Ibid.*
21 Marcus, *Winning Moves: Cases in Strategic Management.*
22 G. Conway, "The voice of reason in the global food fight," *Fortune*, (2000): http://archive.fortune.com/magazines/fortune/fortune_archive/2000/02/21/273846/index.htm
23 See P. Moore, "Confessions of a Greenpeace dropout," *MercatorNet* (2011): www.mercatornet.com/articles/view/confessions_of_a_greenpeace_dropout
24 D. Stipp, "Is Monsanto's biotech worth less than a hill of beans?" *Fortune* (2000): http://archive.fortune.com/magazines/fortune/fortune_archive/2000/02/21/273844/index.htm
25 *Ibid.*
26 S. Kilman, "Foes of Monsanto deal dig in: unusual backlash germinates within crop-biotech industry to proposed Delta & Pine union," *Wall Street Journal.* (2006): http://online.wsj.com/articles/SB116579960468646062
27 Marcus, *Winning Moves: Cases in Strategic Management.*
28 S. Kilman, "Corn is booming as ethanol heats up: crops fetch new highs, ranchers, food makers fret; silver lining for taxpayers?" *Wall Street Journal* (2006): http://online.wsj.com/news/articles/SB116260858542413472?mod=hpp_us_pageone&mg=reno64-wsj
29 J. Miller, "Stalk-raving mad: French Farmers, activists battle over rise in genetically altered corn," *Wall Street Journal* (2006): http://online.wsj.com/articles/SB116061998330490157
30 S. Kilman, "New leaf: seed firms bolster crops using traits of distant relatives; gene maps permit breeding better varieties quickly without a 'GMO' stigma; mathematicians in the field," *Wall Street Journal* (2006): http://online.wsj.com/articles/SB116226333799308526
31 D. Bennet, "Inside Monsanto, America's third-most-hated company," *Bloomberg Businessweek* (2014): www.businessweek.com/articles/2014-07-03/gmo-factory-monsantos-high-tech-plans-to-feed-the-world
32 M. Kelly, "Top 7 genetically modified crops," *Huffington Post* (2012): www.huffingtonpost.com/margie-kelly/genetically-modified-food_b_2039455.html
33 R. Kikland, "Leading in the 21st century: an interview with Ellen Kullman," *McKinsey & Company* (2012): www.mckinsey.com/insights/leading_in_the_21st_century/an_interview_with_ellen_kullman
34 C. Gilliam, "Monsanto, DuPont strike $1.75 billion licensing deal, end lawsuits," *Reuters* (2013): www.reuters.com/article/2013/03/26/us-monsanto-dupont-gmo-idUSBRE92P0IK20130326

35 See "The Harris Poll Reputation Quotient®" (2013): www.http://harrisinteractive.com/vault/2013%20RQ%20Summary%20Report%20FINAL.pdf

36 M. Specter, "Why the Climate Corporation sold itself to Monsanto." *The New Yorker*, (2013): www.newyorker.com/tech/elements/why-the-climate-corporation-sold-itself-to-monsanto

37 See AG WEB: www.agweb.com/crops

38 United States Department of Agriculture Economic Research Service, "Organic production," www.ers.usda.gov/data-products/adoption-of-genetically-engineered-crops-in-the-us.aspx#.VEgzH_ldXTo

39 See Monsanto website: www.monsanto.com/products/pages/seminis.aspx

40 D. Rodman, "Why we will need genetically modified foods," *Technology Review* (2013): www.technologyreview.com/featuredstory/522596/why-we-will-need-genetically-modified-foods

Concluding observations: the journey continues

That a high percentage of the sustainable innovations discussed in this book have not yet borne fruit or even failed should not be a deterrent to sustainability innovators. Clearly, the need for this type of innovation remains compelling.[1] Over seven billion people inhabit the planet and by the year 2050, this number is likely to grow to more than nine billion before world population plateaus and falls off.

This fantastic flourishing of the human species puts an extreme strain on nature to adequately and equitably provide for the amenities humans need. Technologically, humans are very sophisticated, which may permit the expansion of the carrying capacity of the Earth, but people also are divided into belligerent groups that make it hard for governments to take the collective action needed to sensibly address common problems. These problems are dire and involve not only protecting nature but a full array of additional issues often discussed under the rubric of sustainable development, such as fuel and food.

The premise of this book has been to examine the oft-made arguments that contributing to the solution of these problems provides business organizations with a way not only to help society but to profit. The journey to sustainability is an evolutionary process with some firms surviving and others failing. An imperfect fitness screening process, affected by political and institutional biases, sorts out the winners and losers. All of the organizations involved in sustainable innovation are subject to risk and uncertainty. They suffer because of imperfect selection.

All of the organizations involved in sustainable innovation in this book placed bets on the future survival of their organizations and of the planet. There was no guarantee that the investments that they made would succeed either financially or in providing the needed global benefits. Their experience, in fact, was not unusual in that all strategic decision making – whether related to pricing, product features, acquisitions and divestitures, globalization, or technology and business model transformation – involves risky decision making in environments of uncertainty.[2]

Though popular business writing and the media tend to focus on the few truly outstanding cases of exceptional success like Apple, the bulk of the carefully done statistical studies in the empirical literature suggest that the strategic choices business organizations make fail more often than they succeed.[3] For example, almost every careful study done of mergers and acquisitions shows that the failure rate is very high, yet that has not stopped organizations from engaging in more and more mergers and acquisitions in wave after wave of this activity.

Risky decision making carried out in an evolutionary setting of imperfect selection means that not every choice that organizations make work out perfectly. Yet the willingness to make such choices despite the obvious risks is critical not only for the continued profitability and viability of particular organizations but for society at large. The most important point that this book makes is that the journey to sustainability has not been an easy one; nonetheless it is an important one that is still ongoing and will continue to necessitate that business organizations make risky choices in an uncertain environment.

This book has invited its readers to participate in thinking through the decisions that must be made as this journey proceeds from the perspective of the business leaders and the employees of other organizations, especially those in government policy making positions and non-profit advocacy groups, who must make these decisions. The vital takeaway of the book is the open-ended character of this decision-making process. Decision makers have many choices they can make about financing sustainable innovations, developing business models, coping with shifts in external conditions, seeking sustainable customers, and competing with other firms that may be more or less focused on a sustainable mission than themselves.

The purpose of this book has been to invite readers into the actual day-to-day mind set of those responsible for making these decisions. The movement toward a more sustainable society is still at a relatively early stage. The likelihood that it ever will be achieved in its entirety is low. Pushback is inevitable, yet decisions still must be made if the attempt to achieve greater sustainability is to make progress and continue to move forward.

This book introduces a new realism into the study and practice of sustainable business management. It takes us from the win–win hype and does not just portray innovation successes but depicts the risky character of innovation decision making. Moral obligations to society on the part of businesses must be combined with the recognition that these obligations are in no way privileged.

In fact, it is not just markets that thwart their realizations. Government policies and social pressures also play a role. Their role should be apparent to the readers of this book. Cases involving solar and wind power show the power of government to create and destroy markets. Cases involving sustainable food show the power of social pressures to encourage and erect barriers.

The difficult battle for the implementation of sustainable innovation is an uphill struggle that depends on the degree to which tough-minded people can by the force of their will, their shrewdness, and some luck demonstrate that in some instances, certainly not all, moral obligations do indeed yield financial benefit. This demonstration requires the application of business acumen and skills that in no instance are perfect. If the selection process were entirely rational, this outcome might be different.

No matter how worthwhile sustainable innovation is from a planetary perspective, there will be a hard-boiled sorting out of the fallible ideas that entrepreneurs and innovators are trying to commercialize. Only some of these ideas will survive the process. Even mature ideas that have achieved some success will encounter ongoing difficulties. The journey toward sustainability is by no means inevitable. To the extent that sustainable innovations are introduced it is in uneven patterns. No teleology is at work, no ultimate triumph of what some are firmly convinced are the best solutions.

Promising developments

Sustainable innovation then is clearly not simple. It is among the most challenging quests that the world faces. The big financial pay-off that some of the organizations in this book were seeking has yet to happen, but it is not outside the realm of possibility that it still could take place. In the midst of so many stories of failed expectations, the most promising development this book chronicled might be the rise of the Tesla.

The rise of this company has the potential to revolutionize not only personal transportation and the auto industry, but also for its battery technology to be used to revolutionize the electric power industry. The battery technology on which Tesla is working can reduce dependence on fossil fuels from unstable and dangerous regions of the globe. It also may be able to lower greenhouse gas emissions and lessen climate change damage.

Early investors in Tesla, including its founder Elon Musk, already have reaped substantial economic rewards. Nonetheless, the story of Tesla is not over. Many pitfalls still lie ahead for the company and its financial backers. The future is nothing but uncertain and contingencies could arise that could rapidly erase any business advantages Tesla so far has built. Like the other companies in this book it has to prepare for managing these uncertainties. Its ability to get through market uncertainties and its own internal challenges largely will determine how successful it ultimately will be and the extent to which its contribution to society grows or diminishes.

Another development of great promise chronicled in this book has been the expanding frontiers of food technology. Conventional breeding, bioengineering, precision agriculture, and organic farming all are likely to play an essential role in feeding people. The increased agricultural productivity these technologies yield can bring about progress in dealing with hunger, the most critical problem that humanity always has confronted.

Firms such as DuPont and Monsanto are well positioned to profit from these changes in technology regardless of the choices they make. These companies already have built strong business models in the areas of agricultural productivity that have rewarded shareholders, perhaps not at the level of Tesla, but at a strong level nonetheless. If the past is any guide to the future, advances in this domain will not be linear in nature because of market and technological barriers, and economic and social considerations. As societies balance the risks and rewards of the application of different technologies, there will be serious issues and setbacks.

Even if food becomes more ample, its distribution will remain an issue. Who will get the bulk of this food, the malnourished in the world or the overnourished? Though world hunger is the more pressing issue, the problems of overeating and obesity also have been intractable. Controversy does not abate over the extent to which healthy eating is a matter of personal accountability or societal and food-industry responsibility.

With the definition of healthy eating still evolving, whether the food industry can profitably transition to a different model is still a question. The future economic viability of the companies in this industry will depend on how well they address the issue. They cannot sustain their revenue growth if they just stick to business as usual.

Consensus capitalism implies that all firms face the dual burden of remaining economically viable and socially responsible. Every business organization is caught in this web. Many of the business organizations discussed in this book have seriously addressed fuel and food issues, but their journeys along this path are far from over. The evolutionary path that they have undertaken is a hard one. Some comments about the stages in this journeys are an apt way to conclude the book.

Financing

With respect to financing startup sustainable enterprises, a distinction must be drawn between private venture capital funding of less advanced but more risky technologies, and corporate venture capital funding of more advanced but presumably less risky technologies. By and large, the range of investments that Khosla Ventures and KPCB made were very wide and covered a host of promising technologies, very few of which actually made much headway – mainly because the time span of private venture capital is typically limited to no more than ten years.

Worth recapitulating are avenues that Khosla Ventures and KPCB explored. Khosla Ventures specialized much more than KPCB in funding biofuel ventures. Its investments spanned the gamut of biofuel possibilities from using woodchips as a fuel stock (Kior) to municipal waste (Coskata) to sugar (ETH Bioenergy) to novel approaches to degrading the feedstock (Aemetics) and making useable products from it (Geva). To the extent that KPCB invested in biofuels it often was with Khosla Ventures and its investments were of a more conventional nature. The two VC firms partnered in corn ethanol (Altra Biofuels) and design microbe (Amyris) investments.

With respect to energy efficiency, KPCB's investments – inspired by a vision of greater coordination of the electric power production and distribution system that would lead to greater efficiency – were more extensive than Khosla Ventures'. They included dynamic glass (View), networked thermostats (Nest), social comparison feedback (Opower), electric power control software and products (Silver Spring Networks and Echelon), facility energy management (OSIsoft), stacked fuel cells (Bloom), and AC/DC power converters (Transphorm). Khosla Ventures invested in LED lighting (Soraa) and the two companies partnered in investing in more efficient integrated circuit manufacturing (eAsic).

With respect to solar, KPCB's investment also were more extensive than Khosla Ventures. They included multifunction thin-film cells (Amonix), a sputtering process to make thin-film cells (MiaSolé) and a flexible thick-film cell that did not have to be supported by a frame (Solexel). Together KPCB and Khosla Ventures invested in solar-thermal Fresnel reflectors (Areva). Khosla Ventures also invested in multifunction thin-film cells (Stion).

The investments of these VCs covered promising paths that solar power could take, but none really took off because of inroads into the market by inexpensive Chinese solar panels. The Chinese manufacturers effectively exploited existing technology, while VCs such as KPCB and Khosla Ventures explored for more advanced approaches. When startups that KPCB, Khosla Ventures, and other VCs funded faltered, the Chinese companies often acquired the startups and the technologies that the VCs had supported.

Similar to solar power, KPCB's transportation and battery investments were more extensive than Khosla Ventures. KPCB invested in a firm (Next Autoworks) that relied on the internal combustion engine (ICE) to try to create a more ecofriendly vehicle, a plug-in hybrid company (Fisker), and an electric bus and charging station firm (Proterra). It also invested in the successful energy storage company Aquion that relied on sodium-ion technology and the zinc-fluoride battery company Primus Power Flow. Its investments covered a broad spectrum of the promising paths open in transportation and battery technologies.

Khosla Ventures' investments were more limited. It invested in an opposed piston opposed cylinder firm (Ecomotors) and solid state lithium-ion rechargeable battery firm (Sakti3). As was the case with solar power, Chinese firms often purchased companies and technologies that US VCs had backed but that failed to take off.

The wind and agriculture investments KPCB made also were more extensive than those of Khosla Ventures. KPCB invested in a NASA-inspired covered wind turbine startup (Ogin), a natural and organic fungicides and pesticides company (Jiangxi Tianren), a firm that sold organic food in China (Tony's Farm), and a firm that created high-yielding seeds (Kaiima). Khosla Ventures invested in a two-bladed wind turbine startup (Nordic Windpower) and a company that focused on biobased egg replacements (Hampton Creek Foods). Together the two companies backed the data-driven agricultural productivity and insurance firm the Climate Corporation that was acquired by Monsanto for $1.1 billion.

The differences in the two VCs' investment styles were that one firm was more focused (Khosla Ventures) and one was more diversified (KPCB). One might argue that one firm was more conservative (Khosla Ventures) and one was more adventuresome (KPCB). Within the biofuels realm in which Khosla Ventures specialized, it did back a variety of different methods and systems. Clearly, a way to mitigate risk is to spread investments around and experiment. If the future is inherently unknown, then intelligent diversification is a good strategy, but whether this way of mitigating risk worked for either Khosla Ventures or KPBC is worth debating. With hindsight it is easy to criticize choices they made, in particular Khosla Venture's decision to focus on biofuels.

The evolutionary stage toward which private equity and corporate venture capital contributed was variation. They tried many technologies and business models but few succeeded.

The investments of the corporate venture capital firms Intel Capital and Google Ventures tended to be more late stage than those of Khosla Ventures and KPCB. Success therefore should have been more likely. They were driven by business goals the parent companies Intel and Google had, and by these companies' environmental commitments, as much as by a desire for a purely financial return.

SpectraWatt was an internal spin off of Intel's New Business Initiative Group. It was supposed to take advantage of Intel's competence in manufacturing in order to make solar cell manufacturing more efficient. Solecture, another solar company Intel Capital backed, evolved into a firm that was trying to sell thin-film solar cells for building integration and not utility-scale projects because for utility-scale projects Solecture's panels were not cost effective. Nexant, still another company Intel Capital supported, was an energy management software provider and consultant. The company Icontrol that Intel Capital supported had a personalized digital home platform for energy management, security, and healthcare. None of Intel Capital's investments were blazing successes. SpectraWatt and Solecture went bankrupt. Nexant and Icontrol faced intense competition.

Google Ventures, as a relative newcomer to venture capital investment, prided itself in being more analytical and data driven than other venture capitalists. Unlike Intel Capital it was more willing to acquire startups such as Nest, which it backed. It financed solar-thermal firm eSolar that mass produced advanced heliostats and the software that ran these heliostats. It backed geothermal company AltaRock that had capabilities for enhanced geothermal recovery that would allow geothermal to be applied more broadly than to sites particularly well suited to this technology.

However, Google Ventures also backed away from funding startups with unproven technology, which it referred to as science experiments. It avoided investments where the risk was very high and returns low, and invested heavily in wind- and solar-power projects where the risks were lower and likely returns higher because the project sponsors had long-term power purchase agreements from utilities. These investments were more lucrative than investing in young startups with immature technologies. In this way Google Ventures hedged its bets.

Nonetheless, the companies with which it partnered in these projects were not run of the mill. They provided Google with access to business partners and technologies it otherwise might not have been able to access. It invested in the solar projects of Recurrent Energy, which was owned by Japanese electronics company Sharp. It invested in the solar projects of SolarReserve, which had unique technology for molten-salt solar storage that had been developed by United Technology and the US federal government.

Google Ventures also made a big commitment to the ridesharing service Uber. Like its acquisition of Nest, this commitment had many purposes. Nest opened up another way other than the Internet to gather information about individual behavior. The commitment to Uber was not only for its current ridesharing services but for the future promise that its software could play an increasingly important role in coordinating a more autonomous transportation system made up of driverless cars.

Khosla Ventures, KPCB, Intel Capital, and Google Ventures did important work in exploring for promising technologies and testing new ideas, even if most of their investments did not lead to a successful commercial application. When the investments were made a good case could have been made that they were likely to pay off. Who could have predicted that the US Congress would not pass climate-change legislation, that Chinese companies would rush into global solar and wind markets and there would be trade wars, that fracking would bring such a cornucopia of energy resources to the United States, that the European economy would not fully recover from its economic malaise, and that its backing for renewables would falter?

These outside events often were matched by disappointments mostly technological in nature in which products, processes, and broader systems at the stage of scale-up to a commercial stage simply did not work as expected. A future analysis of which played a bigger role – the external events or the internal disappointments – would be worth pursuing.

The selection landscape ruled out most of the investments that VCs made. Does this reveal problems in VCs decision making or in the selection environment? To what extent were there inherent flaws in the companies and technologies that the VCs backed, and to what extent were they overwhelmed by external events over which no one had real control?

Business models

Sustainable ventures were subject to a strict selection environment in which enterprises that survived variation tried different business models in an effort to succeed. The business models differed on a number of dimensions: how companies were financed, the technologies on which they relied, the scope of their goals and how attainable these goals were, and the aggressiveness with which they pursued their objectives

First Solar and Suntech, for instance, relied on different business models to advance their solar power businesses and, to a point, these different models both were commercially successful. With regard to First Solar the first factor to keep in mind was that it had solid and dependable financial backing from the Walton family. The family was patient about nurturing the company through the ups and downs of a turbulent environment where technological issues, government subsidies, and trade policies played a role.

The company's choice of specializing in thin-film solar technologies also was a factor. It protected First Solar from the erratic movement of silicon prices. However, this choice might be a liability in the long run as the industry standard has moved toward thick-film silicon cells. First Solar was an early thin-film adopter. The technology was entrenched in the company and it might be hard for it to switch.

Suntech had the backing of the Chinese city of Wuxi. Its business model was based on the idea of an initial heavy infusion of capital in order to rapidly scale up the production of thick-film silicon panels to meet the demands of the highly subsidized European market. In going in this direction Suntech at first succeeded beyond anyone's expectations, making its founder very rich.

However, Suntech seriously overextended itself and became involved in shady business deals. Along with the trade tariffs imposed on it by the US government and other countries, these practices led to its bankruptcy. Rescued by the city government of Wuxi, because of the employment it provided, it still had the capacity to be a major industry player.

The different business models used by First Solar and Suntech represented different US and Chinese approaches to innovation. The US model is to be a first mover, obtain patient capital, and over time develop a following for a particular technology. The Chinese model allows firms to be very aggressive and opportunistic second movers that can quickly enter markets and disrupt them by massively introducing technology no matter what its technological readiness. Quickly manufacturing at scale, like Suntech did, has its costs as well its benefits. The costs were fierce price competition and premature market saturation.

Different business models have resulted in Tesla's success so far and Better Place's bankruptcy. The most obvious lesson is the importance of having concrete and staged business goals. Tesla's model was to build a sports car, use that money to build an affordable car, and use that money to build an even more affordable car. It executed on the first stage of the model at a high level. Confidence was built and funding extended.

Better Place's business model of separating the car from battery ownership may have been more brilliant and creative than Tesla's business model. However, after raising so much venture capital money, Better Place could not demonstrate concrete success in applying this model. Granted it did not have the right partner in providing an auto that would allow its business model to work. Renault did not give it a flashy vehicle with a battery that had sufficient range. In this way, Better Place was at an extreme disadvantage in comparison to Tesla.

Moreover, Better Place did not obtain sufficient assistance from the Israeli government, unlike Tesla, which received a half billion dollar loan from the US government. However, Better Place also got lost by trying to initiate multiple projects in many different countries before successfully completing any of them. Its visionary and charismatic founder Shai Agassi simply was not a very good manager.

The lesson that can be learned from this comparison is to keep the business model relatively simple, get the pieces in place for executing it, adjust it repeatedly, be opportunistic to developments that take place along the way, and regularly create confidence-building wins that can be carried on to the next stage. The Tesla model was ambitious from the start but the ambition was well executed. Tesla was able to expand what it was trying to do as each confidence-building goal it set for itself was achieved. Whether it ultimately will succeed is yet to be seen.

The macroenvironment and industry context

The macroenvironment and industry context also have important implications for sustainable business innovation. These play critical roles in the selection stage of the innovation journey.

The bets major auto companies such as Toyota and GM made on sustainable transportation options such as hybrids and plug-in hybrids were conditioned on certain assumptions about future fossil fuel availability. These assumptions were that petroleum would become scarcer in the world, prices would rise, and drivers would seek alternatives to the ICE. These assumptions may yet become true, but as of 2014 a glut in hydrocarbons suddenly overtook the world and put a damper on alternative transportation plans.

The lesson of this comparison is that companies must carefully manage these perturbations in the macroenvironment and industry context. They alter perceptions of the risks of making investments in alternatives to the ICE. To succeed, companies must hedge their bets and plan for different scenarios, some of which will mean that oil prices remain relatively stable and inexpensive and some of which signify volatility and rising prices.

Even if abundant, if hydrocarbons cause extreme damage to the Earth's climate the pressures to reduce their use will go up. This damage cannot be subtle and indirect, however, as the forces of denial are strong and stand in the way of a global response. Aware of what might take place, the auto companies must consider alternative futures and have vehicles that do not rely only on the ICE in their portfolios.

The macroenvironment and industry conditions also played a role in the Vestas–GE comparison. The wind turbine industry in which Vestas and GE participated very rapidly became mature. Some sustainable innovations like wind mature relatively quickly, while others like solar germinate slowly, but when they do take off as the First Solar–Suntech comparison attests, their take off can be very rapid.

Vestas and GE were early movers in the wind industry. By the year 2014, they confronted a viable substitute in natural gas that was not intermittent and whose price was declining. They faced a changing set of demanding global customers that shifted from nation to nation depending on the provision and elimination of government subsidies. They had to be close to markets but moving their facilities from one geographical region to another one was anything but easy. In many markets, new low-cost Chinese entrants operated at a scale that enabled them to underprice Vestas and GE. Moreover, Vestas and GE had to deal with a shortage of productive on-shore wind sites, skilled workers, and critical materials such as steel at sufficiently low prices.

These factors reduced Vestas' and GE's room for maneuver. These companies were squeezed into a corner where they had to make fundamental choices. These choices were manifold – about product quality and cost, where in the value chain to compete, and most critically whether to participate at all in an industry that had so many unattractive features.

Exiting the industry was not really an option for the undiversified Vestas. The diversified GE, on the other hand, had many ways to make money in the energy sector. As well as exiting the wind industry entirely, it could limit its participation in wind. With a market on the verge of contracting and so much competition, consolidation seemed inevitable. What decision would Vestas and GE make if this consolidation continued to gain momentum?

Finding customers

Sustainable innovation only can take place if there are sufficient customers. Finding a sufficient number of customers is essential for the retention of sustainable innovation. This kind of innovation must move from a narrow niche category and became more mainstream.

To become more mainstream, companies that offer sustainable products have to have a broad customer base, but does this broad customer base really exist?

Since the late 1960s, General Mills and Kellogg's had been vigorously attacked for loading up their ready-to-eat cereals with sugar and relentlessly advertising these cereals to impressionable young children. Both companies had depended upon the sugar-laden cereals for a high percentage of their revenue and profits.

To admit that there was a problem with the consumption of the cereals might push parents from buying them and serving them to their children. Yet, for whatever reason – and it might just be changing eating habits, less time, and the desire for more convenience – the amount of ready-to-eat cereal that people consumed was going down. For General Mills and Kellogg's to move into a market space occupied by healthier alternatives might mean to admit its critics were right.

Finding a market space in which to move that had the same strong broad appeal as ready-to-eat cereals was not going to be easy. Innovating in this space might not be what either General Mills or Kellogg's were capable of accomplishing. It might not be a strong fit with their acquired capabilities.

The firms could claim that they were only giving consumers what they wanted. They did not have to eat indulgent treats in excess. They could eat the healthier foods that General Mills and Kellogg's also sold. These companies could maintain they were not responsible for the obesity epidemic, it was due to their customers' gluttonous desires. But with watchdog groups carefully weighing their prioritization of healthy and less healthy alternatives and regularly publicizing the results on the Internet, any room for maneuver for General Mills and Kellogg's was limited.

For these companies the uncertainties lay in both finding the healthier alternatives – what should they sell now that people were less likely to eat cereal for breakfast – and fully committing to them as opposed to the other foods they sold. Since they often were sued for misleading advertising, they had to be very careful about how they promoted new products. Under the watchful eye of consumer groups whatever claims they made had to be accurate.

The Pepsi and Coca-Cola challenge was very similar to that of General Mills and Kellogg's. Retention of sustainable innovation means that firms must find sufficient customers to move this type of innovation from the margins and to the mainstream. Because of health concerns, people were abandoning these companies' mainstay sugary soft drinks in developed country markets. Could they revive these brands or were they better off trying to sell different types of beverages in other parts of the world?

Pepsi and Coca-Cola already had made inroads into global markets for tea, sports and energy drinks, bottled water, and juices, but their dominance in these drinks was nowhere close to their dominance in the carbonated soft drink (CSD) market. In the market for non-CSD beverages they faced strong global competitors such as Danone and Nestlé and many vital local brands that were propped up for national reasons or because of ethnic pride and religious resentment.

Pepsi had snacks upon which to fall back, but snacks also did not meet with acceptable health criteria. Coca-Cola had nothing but beverages to sell. It dominated over Pepsi in nearly every country in the world in almost every beverage category, but on which beverage categories did it make the most sense for it to concentrate in the future? Did it make sense for Pepsi and Coca-Cola to try to expand the market for sugar-based soft drinks in developing countries, while at the same time the market for these drinks was contracting in developed nations?

Both companies declared that they were committed to sustainability. They both carried out sustainable projects globally in the areas of water and climate change. Yet neither company could lift their current sales substantially by only selling healthier beverages and snacks. To grow their businesses, they resorted to buying back their bottlers. Coca-Cola also acquired or partnered with rising industry stars such as Monster, but whether these moves were the right ones for either of the companies or for society was still uncertain.

Competition between mission and non-mission based businesses

Retention of sustainable innovation often ends in a competition between mission and non-mission based companies. Whole Foods was the quintessential mission-based firm, dedicated to uplifting a person's values and way of life and not just meeting a person's everyday need for nourishment. Its grandiose mission should have set it far apart from the plebian Walmart, but nothing of the sort took place.

Both companies felt similar pressures. For Whole Foods they meant lowering its prices and reducing margins so it could compete on a more even playing field with Walmart; and for Walmart they meant raising the quality of the food it sold so that it could compete on a more even playing field with Whole Foods. This convergence signified a shift toward consensus capitalism in which all companies march in step to the dual demands of the market and social responsibility.

The tough anti-union policies of the two companies were similar; yet both companies tried to provide their employees with a voice and sense of ownership so that they would be dedicated and work hard at achieving corporate goals. Whole Foods took many important actions with regard to energy use, packaging, recycling, and animal rights, but with regard to its greenhouse gas emissions its founder John Mackey denied the seriousness of the problem and the company lacked concrete goals. Walmart, on the other hand, had very concrete goals, that two of its CEOs reaffirmed. No matter how intense its effort to achieve these goals, however, it still was far from accomplishing them.

A major difficulty was Walmart's size. To put goods on its shelves required an international supply chain of immense proportions consisting of subcontractors, subcontractors of the subcontractors, subcontractors of the suncontractors' subcontractors, and so on. What took place in this supply chain simply was too hard for a buyer of even Walmart's immense girth to control.

Both Whole Foods and Walmart had the capability to bring sustainability more into the mainstream. It also was in their interest to do so, but the task was so large and the business constraints so great that it was easy for them to lose their way.

DuPont never really set out to be a mission-based business and never completely became one. Monsanto's movement in this direction, on the other hand, was more deliberate. It made the conscious choice under CEO Robert Shapiro that it no longer was going to be a commodity-based chemical company but rather was going to become a high-tech bioengineering firm whose mission was to feed the world.

Monsanto carried out a series of mergers and acquisitions and was involved in a major divestiture that resulted in it being solely dedicated to agricultural productivity. DuPont leaned toward this focus but always had a broader agenda. It more slowly divested its slow-growing chemical businesses and more gradually acquired bioengineering capabilities.

In lean years this diversification served DuPont very well, but technically it never completely caught up with Monsanto, which had been the first large company to move to biotech. Though in the marketing of seeds DuPont dominated over Monsanto, in some areas it still had to partner with its rival to obtain key genetic material.

However, because of Monsanto's focus, it bore the brunt of protestors' criticism, while DuPont largely escaped this criticism. DuPont's main goals as a scientific and technical company were reset to be more mission-like in nature, again illustrating the power of convergence and of consensus capitalism to move sustainable innovation to the frontier of the conventional. DuPont, once the world's largest chemical company, now had an explicit mission that involved it in feeding the world's hungry and in nearly every aspect of renewable energy.

The next frontier

The next frontier in the sustainable journey of these companies and others covered in the book is yet to be determined, and will depend on the ensuing choices they make to meet the twin goals of social responsibility and business growth. These choices are both risky for the planet and for the organizations involved. Not all the choices these organizations will make will be good ones. No matter what they do they will not escape public criticism. The selection process is far from over. If the past is a guide to the future the route to continued sustainable innovation will be a rough one, but one that is well worth taking.

Notes

1 A. Marcus, and A. Fremeth, "Green management matters regardless," *Academy of Management Perspectives* (2009): http://scholar.google.com/scholar?hl=en&q=alfred+marcus+and+adam+fremeth&btnG=&as_sdt=1%2C24&as_sdtp=

2 *Ibid.*

3 *Ibid.*

Index

Figures and tables are shown in **bold** typeface.

60 Minutes (television show), 21–22

A Calorie Counter (website), 217
A123 Systems (battery company), 38, 117, 163
ABB Ltd. (technology company), 29
Abe, Shinzo, 168
Abound Solar, 73
Academy of Nutrition and Dietetics Foundation, 215
Accel Partners (venture capital), 22
Acer Inc., 58
advertising controversy, 218–23
Advertising Standards Authority (ASA), 219
Aemetis (biofuel company), 42
Aerodyn Energiesysteme, 187
After Greenwashing (book), 1
Agassi, Shai, 110, 124–35, 342
agricultural technology. *See* food biotechnology
agriculture. *See also* food biotechnology
    and Monsanto, 298–99
    and Walmart, 290
    CVC investment in, **55**
    healthy food investment, 203–23
    precision, 320–21
    TCSB, 319–20
    venture capital investors, 45–47
Ahearn, Mike, 90
Ahold (retailer), 291
Aikosolar, **74**
Airbnb, 80
Aje Group (carbonated soft drinks company), 243–45, **245**
Alcoa, 318

Alexander, Lex, 268
Alfalfa's Market, 268
AlgaeCake Technologies (biofuel company), 44
Alpha Beta (food store), 269
Alstrom (manufacturing company), 193, 196
AltaRock Energy (geothermal), 68, 70–71, 339
Alternative Energy Systems Consulting (AESC), Inc., 38, 117
AltraBiofuels, 41
Amatil (Australian bottler), 253
Amazon, 15, 262
Amdocs (billing company), 129, 133
American Association for the Advancement of Science, 326
American Electric Power, 181
American Energy Alliance, 178
American Heart Association, 205, 212, 226–27
American Medical Association, 326
American Recovery and Reinvestment Act, 178
Amonix (solar power company), 22, 32–33
Amyris (biofuel company), 42
Animal Compassion Foundation, 286
animal rights, 285–86
Apple Inc., 58, 79, 333
Applied Biosystems Group, 319
AQT Solar, **74**
Aquion Energy, 38
Archer Daniels Midland (ADM) (food company), 320
Areva (solar company), 31
Argonne National Labs, 38

ARM (microprocessor company), 58
Ascent Solar, **74**
Asia Silicon, 97
AstraZeneca (pharmaceutical
    company), 313
AT&T, 30
Atlantic Wind Connection, 65
Attune Foods, 209
Australia
    electric vehicles in, 131, 133, 140
    solar energy, 99
    wind energy, 179
Avancis (solar company), **74**

bacterium *bacillus thurungiensus* (BT),
    303, 304, 311
Ballard Fuels (fuel cell company), 128
Bank of America, 30
Barrett, Craig, 57
BASF, 318
batteries
    cost of, 137–39
    GM electric vehicle, 113
    hybrid vehicles, 35, 37–40, 158–61,
        168
    swapping stations, 125, 130,
        135–36, 139
    Tesla, 110–13, **111**, 116–18, 135–36
Bayer (pharmaceutical company), 318
Bechtolsheim, Andy, 16
Belkin (consumer electronics
    company), 61
Best Buy (retailer), 61, 291
Better Place (electric automobile
    company)
    battery technology, 117
    business model evolution, 5, 110,
        111, 124–35, 341
    financing, 115
Beyond Meat (plant protein company),
    23
biofuels
    assessing venture capital investments
        in, **24**
    CVC investment in, **55**
    demand for, 327
    Dupont and, 318
    venture capital investors, 40–44,
        336
biomass energy cost, 175

Bloom Energy (energy efficiency
    company), 29–30
Bloomberg, Michael, 226
Bluebonnet Natural Foods Grocery,
    267
BMW (automobile company), 128,
    140
Borlaug, Norman, 300
bottled water consumption, 232–34,
    233
Bowen, F., 1
Branson, Richard, 80
Braskem (oil company), 42
Bread & Circus (food store), 267
Bread of Life (food store), 267
British Petroleum (BP), 43, 318
Bronfman, Edgar Sr., 126
Buffet, Warren, 181
buildings (energy efficiency of), 26–31,
    251
Burkle, Ron, 269
buses (electric), 37
Bush, George W., 19, 268
business model evolution
    and social responsibility, 259
    Better Place, 111, 124–35
    Coca-Cola company, 226–55
    DuPont, 322–25
    First Solar, 89–95, **94**
    Google Ventures, 59
    Intel, 56–59
    mission based, 263–75
    Pepsi, 226–55
    stages, 4–8, 338
    Suntech, 95–99
    sustainable ventures, 340–45
    Tesla (electric automobile company),
        110–42
    venture capital investors, 336–40
Business Week (magazine), 297
Butamax (biofuel company), 43
Byrne, David, 312

cadmium, 100
cadmium telluride (CdTe), 99–101
Calgene (biotechnology company),
    302
California Public Employees
    Retirement System (CALPERS),
    14, 17, 249

California State Teacher's Retirement System, 17
Cambridge Associates (investment company), 20, 25
Canada
 oil reserves in, 151, **151**
 tea market, **230**
Canadian Solar, 67, 95
capacitors, 39
CapGemini (French IT consulting), 61
Carbon Disclosure Project, 251, 284, 288
Carbon War Room, 125
carbonated soft drinks
 Coca-Cola domination in, 234–36, **236**
 global competition, 242–47, **244**, **245**, **247**
 in Muslim countries, 245–47, **247**
 markets for, 226–27, 229, 344–45
Cargill (biotechnology company), 302, 318
Carson, Rachel, 304
Cascadian Farm, 203
Center for Science in the Public Interest (CSPI), 226, 241
Centre for Science & Environment (India), 242–43
Champions for Healthy Kids grants, 215
Charles River Ventures, 23
Chesapeake Energy, 197
Chevron, 34
China
 agriculture technology in, 46–47, 313
 and Walmart, 288–90
 approach to innovation, 341
 bottled water consumption, **233**
 clean energy investment, 21
 clean transportation investment, 114, 139–40
 future energy demand, 150
 hybrid vehicles, 157, 166
 juice consumption, **235**
 solar energy investment in, 19, 33–34, 66, 72, 78, 95–99, 337
 solar trade wars, 87–89, **88**, 102–06

 tea market, **230**
 wind energy, 179, 181–83, **182**, 184, **185**, 185–87
China Development Bank (CDB), 97, 104
Chobani (food company), 220
Cialdini, Robert, 28
Cilion (biofuel company), 42
Cisco Systems, 51
Citrix Systems, 15
Clarksville Natural Grocery, 266
clean energy
 and trade wars, 105
 CVC investment in, 52–56, **55**, **56**, 71–81
 private venture capital investment, 24, 15–47, 48
 public policy on, 19–20, 103
clean transportation
 CVC investment in, **55**, 80–81
 electric cars, 110–42
 fuel-cell vehicles, 166–69
 hybrid vehicles, 155–66
 macroenvironment assumptions, 342–43
 private venture capital investors, 35–37
Cleantech Group, 68, 82
climate change
 and clean transportation public policy, 114, 148–50
 Coca-Cola and Pepsi, 250–52
 DuPont, 297
 Monsanto, 328
 Walmart, 287
 Whole Foods, 284–85
Climate Corporation (agriculture company), 45–46, 52, 321, 326–27, 338
Climate Savers Computing Initiative, 63
coal. *See* fossil fuels
Coalition for Affordable Solar Energy (CASE), 107
Coalition for American Solar Manufacturing (CASM), 106–07
Coca-Cola company
 and carbonated soft drinks market, 344–45
 and Walmart, 291

business model evolution, 226–55
clean energy investments, 30, 43
Cohen, Dan, 133–34
Comcast Cable, 76–77
Compaq (computer company), 15, 115, 141
Compass Technology Partners (venture capital), 114–15
competition
  between mission and non-mission based companies, 345–47
  between Whole Foods employees, 281
  carbonated soft drinks, 242–47
  food retailer, 259–63, 264
  solar energy, 88, 87–89
computer technology
  and Intel, 56–59
  venture capital success in, 15
Conoco (petrochemical company), 305
conscious capitalism. *See* consensus capitalism
Conscious Capitalism (book), 278
consensus capitalism, 259, 336, 346
Consumer Reports (magazine), 120, 266, 274
Convey Computer, 60
Conway, Gordon, 312
Cook, Libby, 268
copper indium gallium selenide (CIGS), 32–35, 71–76, **74**
Core Power (food company), 228
Coriolis Wind (power company), 45
Corning, 26
Corporate Social Responsibility ranking (CSR), 250
corporate venture capital (CVC). *See also* private venture capital investors, Intel Capital, Google Ventures
  costs to companies, 54–58
  principles of, 51–54
  uncertainty in clean energy investment success, 336–40
Coskata (biofuel company), 41
Costco, 261, 270
costs
  clean energy implementation, 19

genetically modified (GM) foods, 309–10
hybrid vehicles, 156
levelized energy, 174–77
  of CVCs to companies, 54–56
  of solar in China, 99
  organic foods, **274**
  solar power, 71–76, 87
  Tesla battery, 110–12, **111**, 137–39
  wind energy, 189–92
Coulomb Technologies (charging system company), 129
CPower (energy efficiency company), 60
Crick, Frances, 302
CSRHub (assessment group), 264
CVC. *See* corporate venture capital
Cypress Semiconductors, 15

Daimler, 120, 122, 128, 137
Danica (Danish biotech company), 323
Danish Oil & Natural Gas (DONG Energy), 130
Danone (food company), 234, **245**, 345
De Gucht, Karel, 105
DeKalb Genetics (biotechnology company), 302
Dell (computers), 58, 141
Delta & Pine Company (food), 311–12, 316
Denmark (electric vehicles in), 127, 129–31
Deutsche Bank, 313
Diageo (food company), 207
Disney Corporation, 291
diversification. *See also* innovation
  General Electric (GE), **174**
  Kleiner Perkins Caufield & Byers (KPCB), 338
  Monsanto, 316–18, 346–47
  solar energy, 93
Doerr, John, 22–23
dominance (business), 4–8, 54–55, 234–36, **236**
Dominick's (food store), 269
DotOrg (Google non-profit), 61–62
Dow, **74**, 318
Dow Jones Sustainability Index, 252

Draper Fisher Jurvetson, 16, 115
Duke, Michael, 287
DuPont
  and Monsanto, 316, 325
  and TCSB, 319
  diversification, 316–18, 346–47
  example of retention stage, 5
  financials, 321
  food biotechnology, 299, 305–09
  precision agriculture, 321
  promising future of, 335
  sustainability, 296–98
dynamic random access memory
  (DRAM), 57

early-stage startups
  Google Ventures, 68–71
  Intel Capital, 66–68
eAsic (transistor efficiency company),
  31
Eberhard, Martin, 115
Echelon Corporation (smart-grid
  company). *See* Spring Networks
Ecogen (biotechnology company), 303
EcoMotors, 36
economic performance. *See* financials
Edison, Thomas, 171
EI Solutions (solar energy), 65, 96
electric vehicles
  background of, 112–14
  hybrid, 155–66
  technology, 134–35
Electronic Arts, 15
Elektromotive (charging system
  company), 129
Enercom (wind power company), 194
Enerdel (battery company), 38
energy efficiency investment
  CVC, 55
  Intel Capital, 68
  venture capital investors, 24, 31, 38,
  336
  Walmart, 290
Energy Independence and Security Act
  (2007), 327
Energy Policy Act (2005), 327
Energy Solutions, 97
energy storage
  CVC investment in, 55
  venture capital investors, 37–40

Enertech Capital, 16
enhanced geothermal systems (EGS),
  70–71
Enron Corporation, 91, 171
environmental commitment
  Coca-Cola and Pepsi, 247–52
  food companies, 207
  Google Ventures, 61–66
  Intel Capital, 59–61
  Monsanto, 310–12
  Walmart, 286–92
  Whole Foods, 284–86
Environmental Defense Fund, 288
Environmental Protection Agency,
  175, 284, 296. *See also* public
  policy
Envision (Chinese wind power), 186
Ericsson (telecom company), 58
eSolar, 68–70, 339
Esty, D., 2
ETH Bioenergy (biofuel company), 42
ethanol. *See* biofuels
Ethisphere Institute, 279
Europe
  and genetically modified (GM) crops,
  312–14
  carbonated soft drinks in, **236**
  clean transportation investment, 114,
  140–41
  hybrid vehicles, 157, 164
  public environmental policy, 128
  solar energy in, 33, 90, 95
  tariff on China solar, 105–06
  wind energy, 179, 182, 192, 194
European Commission, 326

Facebook (internet social network), 22,
  64
Fadell, Tony, 23
Fairfield Semiconductor Company, 15
FedEx (shipping company), 30
Financial Recovery Act, 103
financials
  agriculture chemical companies, 321
  automaker, 123
  Coca-Cola and Pepsi, 252–55
  Monsanto, 314–16
  ready-made cereal, 205–07
  wind energy, 194–95
financing. *See also* funds

clean transportation, 115, 124–26
First Solar, 89–90, **94**
startups, 336–40
Suntech, **94**, 94–95
Tesla, 138
First Solar
and trade wars, 87–89, **88**
business model evolution, 89–95, **94**,
340
competition, 78, 95
efficiency of, 34
financials, **94**
selection onset stage, 5
technology, 73–74, 99–102
Fisker (electric automobile company),
22, 36–37, 122
Fisker, Henrik, 36–37
fitness landscape, 4, 5
Flodesign Wind Turbine. *See* Ogin
Florida Power & Light, 28
Food and Drug Administration (FDA),
219, 221, 231, 313
food biotechnology. *See also*
genetically modified (GM) foods,
agriculture
DuPont, 299, 305–09
Monsanto, 301–05
obstacles to, 309–19
promising future of, 335
TCSB, 319–20
Forbes (journal), 21, 23, 56, 95
Ford Motor Company, 156, 159, 160,
161, 165
Forsythe, Tom, 213
Fortune (magazine), 279, 280, 284,
304
fossil fuels
and clean energy, 13, 147–48,
154–55
and climate change, 148–50
demand and supply of, 150–53, **151**,
342
dependence on foreign, 114
levelized energy costs, 175
subsidies, 177
Fox, Vicente, 244
Fraley, Robert, 326
Freeman, Sullivan & Company (FSC),
68
Fresh Fields Markets, 267

Friedberg, David, 46, 326
Friedman, Milton, 278
Frontline (TV show), 212
fuel cell
and batteries, 139
investment in, 197–98
vehicles, 166–69
Walmart, 287
funds. *See also* financing
clean transportation, 114–16, 120
pension, 17
venture capital in clean energy, 14,
52–56
wind energy, 172–74, **174**
Fuze (food company), 228

gallium arsenide (GaAs), 102
gallium nitride (GaN), 30
Gamesa (wind energy company), 194
Gates, Bill, 39
Gateway Computer, 141
Gatorade (food company), 227–28,
231
Gemini Solar, 97
General Electric (GE)
energy investment options, 195–98
wind energy, 171–74, **174**, 182,
189–93, 343
General Electric Ventures, 26, 69, 76
General Mills
advertising controversy, 218–23
cereal nutrition, 211–12, 216–18,
344
economic performance, 205–07
example of retention onset stage, 5
healthy food investment, 203,
212–15, 291
sales, 209–11
snack foods, 236
General Mills Foundation, 214–15
General Motors (GM)
clean technology investment, 61,
147–48
electric vehicle, 113–14, 128
fuel-cell technology, 139, 166–67
hybrid vehicles, 5, 34, 156, 159, 160,
162–66, **165**
macroenvironment assumptions,
342
General Motors Ventures, 38

genetically modified (GM) foods. *See
   also* food biotechnology
   alternatives to, 319–21
   and Monsanto, 301–09
   costs, 309–10
   demand for, 327–28
   environmentalist opposition, 310–12
   global usage of, 318–19
   in Europe, 312–14
geothermal power, 70–71, 175, 176
Gevo (biofuel company), 43
Ghosn, Carlos, 119, 126, 127
Gilliland, Mike, 268
Gilster-Mary Lee (food company), 209
Glaceau (food company), 228
Global Animal Partnership, 285
global dimensions
   genetically modified (GM) foods,
      318–19
   nutrition, **204**, 204–05
   of sustainable choices, 4
   wind energy, 181–87, **182**, **185**
Global Food Safety Initiative (GFSI),
   265
Global Greenhouse Gas Register, 251
Global Solar Energy, **74**
Global Star Fund (GSF), 97
Global Water Challenge, 249
glyphosate, 315, 325
Goldwind (Chinese wind power),
   185–86, 193
Gooch, Sandy, 268
Google Green campaign, 62
Google Ventures. *See also* startups,
   corporate venture capital
   and Bloom Energy, 30
   and Nest, 23, 26
   business model evolution, 59
   CVC investments, 30, 36, 45, 52, 55,
      56, 54–58, 338–40
   early-stage startups, 68–71
   environmental commitment, 61–66
   late-stage investing, 77–81
   variation stage, 5
Granoff, Michael, 125
Graphene Energy, 39
Great Atlantic & Pacific Tea Company
   (A&P), 270
green buildings, 251
green gold, 2

Green Mountain (food company), 254
Green Mountain Coffee (food
   company), 228
greenhouse gases. *See* climate change
Greenpeace (environmental group), 62,
   63, 66, 299, 314
Grid Net (smart grid company), 60
Gross, Bill, 70
Grove, Andy, 57
guaranteed purchasing agreement
   (PPA), 181
Guodian United Power (Chinese wind
   power), 186

Hallo (transportation sharing
   company), 80
Hampton Creek Foods, 46
Hanergy (solar power company), 34,
   74, **74**
Hansen Juices. *See* Monster
Hansen, Peder, 171
Hanwha (solar energy company), 78
Harbin Electric Machinery (Chinese
   wind company), 183
Hareon (solar company), 95
Harnett, Tony, 268
Harper's Magazine, 62
Harvard Business Review (journal),
   20, 298
Healthy Weight Commitment
   Foundation (HWCF), 214–15
Hearthside Food Solutions, 209
Heinz, 320
HelioVolt, **74**
Henry's Marketplace, 268
Hewlett Packard, 15, 58, 67, 124
Hidden Villa Ranch (food distributor),
   269
high fructose corn syrup (HFC),
   263–66, 320
Hitachi, 38, 117
Holden Foundation Seeds
   (biotechnology company), 302
Holliday, Chad, 299, 316
Honda
   fuel-cell vehicles, 166–67
   hybrid vehicles, 158–61
Honest Tea (food company), 228
Honeywell, 29
Horowitz, Andrew, 80

HSBC (bank), 131
Hughes, James, 91
hybrid vehicles. *See also* internal
    combustion engine (ICE)
    market for, 155–66
    selection stage, 5
    venture capital investors, 35–37
hydropower energy costs, 175
Hyundai (car company), 159, 160,
    161, 161

Iberdrola (wind energy), 181
IBM (computer company), 30, 67, 141
Icontrol (energy efficiency company),
    60, 76–77, 338
IdeaLab (business incubator), 70
Immelt, Jeff, 171
imports (organic food), 275–77
income. *See* financials
independent power producers (IPPs),
    181
India
    carbonated soft drinks in, 242–43,
        244
    electric vehicles in, 140
    solar energy, 92, 93, 99
    solar trade wars, 89
    water issues in, 253
    wind energy, 184, 187
*Influence: The Psychology of
    Persuasion* (book), 28
initial public offering (IPO)
    and venture capital, 14, 47–48, **48**
    clean energy numbers of, **56**
    Tesla, 122
Innocent (food company), 228
innovation. *See also* sustainability,
    diversification
    battery technology, 116–18, 137–39
    Chinese approach to, 341
    electric vehicle, 141–42
    fuel cell, 167–68
    hybrid vehicles, 155–56
    petroleum exploration, 152
    solar energy technology, 99–102
    uncertainty in, 1–8
    wind energy, 193, 196
Institute for Local Self-Reliance, 292
Intel Capital. *See also* startups,
    corporate venture capital

business strategy history, *56–59*
CVC investments, 30, 34, 45, 55, **56**,
    54–56, 141, 338–40
early-stage startups, 66–68
environmental commitment, 59–61
late-stage investing, 71–77
variation stage, 5
internal combustion engine (ICE),
    35–36, 113–14, 116–18, 139,
    342–43. *See also* hybrid vehicles
International Energy Agency (IEA),
    182
International Organization for
    Standardization (ISO), 128
Internet
    bubble burst, 16
    dominating CVC investing, 54–55
Intuit, 15
Isdell, E. Neville, 247
Israel, 126, 129–31, 342
Israel Cleantech Ventures, 126
Israel Corporation, 125, 133
Izze (food company), 228

JA (solar company), 95
Japan
    and solar energy investment, 78–79
    electric vehicles in, 131, 140
    export market for Chinese solar, 98
    solar energy in, 89–90
    tea market, **230**
    wind energy, 179
Jiangxi Tianren Ecological Industrial
    (Chinese agriculture company),
    46
Jinko (solar company), 95
Johnson & Johnson, 318
Johnson Controls, 29, 117
Joy, Bill, 16
JP Morgan Partners, 115
juice market, **235**
Juniper Networks, 15

Kaiima (agriculture company), 47
Kashi, 203, 219–20
Kauffman Foundation, 20
Kellogg, John Harvey, 211
Kellogg's
    advertising controversy, 218–23
    and Bloom Energy, 30

Kellogg's (*cont.*)
  cereal nutrition, 211–12, 216–18, 344
  changes to fight obesity, 214–15
  economic performance, 205–11
  example of retention onset stage, 5
  healthy food investment, 203
  snack foods, 236
  sustainability, 291
Kent, Muhtair, 252, 253
Kholsa, Vinod, 16
Khosla Ventures. *See also* startups, corporate venture capital
  agriculture, 45–47
  and biofuels, 40–44
  and clean energy, 20–22, 31–35, 44–45, 47–48, **48**
  assessing venture capital investments in, 23–25, **24**
  clean transportation, 35–36
  energy efficiency investment, 31, 38
  energy storage, 37–40
  example of variation stage, 5
  founders of, 16
  investors in, 14
  private venture capital investors, 336–37
Kior (biofuel company), 40–41
KKR (investment firm), 78
Kleiner Perkins Caufield & Byers (KPCB). *See also* startups, corporate venture capital
  agriculture, 45–47
  and biofuels, 43–44
  and solar power, 31–35
  assessing venture capital investments in, 23–25, **24**
  criticism of clean energy investment, 22–23
  energy efficiency investment, 31, 38, 76
  energy investment future, 47–48, **48**
  energy storage, 37–40
  founders of, 15
  transportation, 35–37
  variation stage, 5
  venture capital funds, 14
  venture capital investors, 336–37
  wind energy, 44–45
Kleiner, Eugene, 15

Koch Industries, 316
Kola Real (carbonated soft drinks company), 243–45
KPCB. *See* Kleiner Perkins Caufield & Byers
Kravis, Henry, 78
Kroger (food retailer), 261, 273, 291
Kullman, Ellen, 322–25
Kyocera, 90
Kyoto treaty, 149–50

labeling
  genetically modified (GM) foods, 313
  Monsanto and, 326
labor relations
  Walmart, 282–83
  Whole Foods, 280–82
Land O'Lake, 43
late-stage investing
  Google Ventures, 77–81
  Intel Capital, 71–77
Latin America
  food industry, 210–11
  solar energy, 92, 99
  wind energy, 179, 182
Lauckner, Jon, 162
Lazard Asset Management, 131
LDK (solar company), 95
Leadership in Energy and Environmental Design (LEED), 251
Leonard Green & Partners (private equity firm), 270
levelized energy costs, 174–77
LG Chemical (Korean car parts company), 38, 117, 163
light emitting diode (LED), 25, 77, 337
Lilly, 318
lithium-ion batteries, 38, 116–17, 141, 161, 168
Luberski (food distributor), 269
Lucent Technologies, 58
Lufthansa (airline), 43
Lutz, Robert, 162
Lyft (transportation sharing company), 80
Lynch, Michael, 56

Mackey, John, 259, 266, 268–70, 278–79, 282, 284–85, 346

Magenn Power (wind power
  company), 45
Mahoney, Richard, 301
Makani Power (wind energy), 64
malnutrition, **204**, 204–05, 240
Malt-O-Meal (food company), 209
Maniv Energy Capital, 125
Manz, **74**
Marine Stewardship Council, 285
market
  carbonated soft drinks, 226–27
  electric vehicles, 119, 139–41
  sports drinks, 231–32
  tea, **230**
  wind energy, 179–83
marketing. *See* sales, advertising
  controversy
Mars (food company), 291
Mascoma (biofuel company), 22, 43
Mathlouti, Tawfiq, 246
Mayer, Jean, 212
McNealy, Scott, 16
Mecca Cola (soft drinks company),
  246
Mendel Biotechnology, 303
Mercedes-Benz, 140
Merchant of Vino (food store), 267
Merck Pharmaceutals, 306, 318
Merrill Lynch, 30
Metropolitan Life (insurance
  company), 78
Mexico
  carbonated soft drinks, 243–45, **245**
  juice consumption, **235**
MiaSolé (solar company), 34, 74, **74**,
  99
microprocessors. *See* computer
  technology
Microsoft Corporation, 51, 141
MidAmerican Energy (wind energy),
  65, 181, 194
Mill Valley (food store), 267, 268
Millenium Pharmaceuticals, 303
Mingyang Wind Power (Chinese), 186,
  187
MinuteMaid (food company), 228
mission-based business model, 263–66
Mississippi Development Authority, 33
Mitsubishi Industries, 193
MMA Renewable Ventures, 96

mobile device technology, 58–59
Monsanto
  and Climate Corporation, 45–46
  and TCSB, 320
  diversification, 316, 318, 346–47
  ending hunger committment, 298–99
  environmentalist opposition, 310–12
  example of retention stage, 5
  financials, 321
  food biotechnology, 301–05, 313
  genetically modified (GM) foods,
    309–10, 327–28
  partnering with DuPont, 325
  precision agriculture, 320–21
  reputation, 312, 325–27
  restructuring of, 314–16
Monster (food company), 254–55, 345
Moore, Gordon, 57–58
Moore, Patrick, 314
Morgan Stanley (financial planning),
  126, 131
Moss, Michael, 212–14
Motorola, 58, 59
Mrs. Gooch's Natural Foods Markets,
  268
Musea Ventures, 126
Musk, Elon, 93, 110, 114–16, 119
Muslim countries
  carbonated soft drinks, 245–47, **247**
  oil production in, 150–53, **151**
Muslim Up (soft drinks company), 254

Naked Juice (food company), 228
Nanosolar (solar company), **74**, 99
Narain, Sunita, 242
Nation Highway Traffic Safety
  Administration (NHTSA), 164
National Academy of Sciences, 326
National Labor Relations Board, 281
natural gas
  levelized energy costs, 174–77, 343
  technology in, 197
Nature Conservancy, 249
Nature's Heartland (food store), 267
Nature's Northwest (food store), 268
Navetas (energy efficiency company),
  61
NEC (technology company), 117
Nest (energy efficiency company), 23,
  26, 51, 52, 77, 339

Nestlé
  bottled water, 234
  carbonated soft drinks, **247**, 345
  economic performance, 205–06
  tea, 228
Netscape (web portal), 15
New York Times (newspaper), 63
Newsweek (magazine), 299
Nexant (energy efficiency company),
    68, 338
Next Autoworks, 36, 52
NextEra Energy (wind energy), 181
NGEN Partners, 16
Nokia, 58
Nooyi, Indra, 237–40, 243, 252–53
Nordic Windpower, 44
Norway, 121–22
Novartis (pharmaceutical company),
    313, 318
Noyce, Robert, 57–58
Nth Power, 16
NUMMI (car manufacturing plant),
    120
nutrition. *See also* organic foods
  and obesity, **204**, 204–05
  and snack food consumption, 237
  cereal, 211–18
  Pepsi investment in, 237–40
NuvoSun (solar company), **74**

Oak Street Market, 267
Obama, Barack, 19, 107, 278
Obama, Michelle, 226
obesity
  and exercise, 240
  and nutrition, **204**, 204–05
  and sugar intake, 212
  food companies changes to fight,
    214–15
  from carbonated soft drinks, 226–27
  tea for, 230
Odak, Perry, 268
Odebrecht Agroindustrial (Brazilian
    conglomerate), 42
Odersun (solar company), **74**
Odwalla (food company), 228
Ofer, Idan, 125, 132
Ogin (wind energy company), 44–45
Ogiso, Satoshi, 167
oil. *See* fossil fuels

Olmert, Ehud, 125
Opower (energy software company),
    23, 28
OptiSolar, 91
organic foods. *See also* nutrition
  Walmart, 271–77, **274**
  Whole Foods, 271–75
Organic Foods Protection Act, 271
Organization for Economic
    Cooperation and Development
    (OECD), 150
Organization of Petroleum Exporting
    Countries (OPEC), 150–53, **151**
OSoft Electric, 29
Otellini, Paul, 58

Pacific Gas and Electric Company, 28,
    181
Panasonic, 38, 116–18, 120, 138, 163
Parle Bisleri (Indian water company),
    244
Partnership for a New Generation of
    Vehicles (PNGV), 156
Pathmark (food store), 270
PayPal, 114, 115
Peltz, Nelson, 236
Pentadyne Power, 40
People for the Ethical Treatment of
    Animals (PETA), 285
Pepsi, 206, 226–55, 291, 344–45
Peres, Shimon, 125, 126
performance. *See* financials
Perkins, Thomas, 15
Pfizer (pharmaceutical company), 318
Pharmacia (drug company), 314, 318
photovoltaics (PVs), 31, 34, 68–69,
    77–79, 93, 96, 99, 298
Pickens, T. Boone, 36
Pillsbury, 207
Pioneer Hi-Bred (seed company),
    305–08, 311, 316, 317
Planar Energy Devices, 40
Post, 209, 211–12, 217, 291
PowerLight, 96
PowerMap (energy efficiency
    company), 61
Powerthru (energy storage company),
    40
Powervation (energy efficiency
    company), 60

precision agriculture, 320–21
Precision Planting (biotech company),
    321
Premier Nutrition, 209
PrimeStar, 73
Primus Power Flow, 38
private venture capital investors. *See
    also* corporate venture capital
    and clean energy, 52–56
    and global economy transformation,
    15
    and late-stage investing, 50–51
    and startups, 13–15
    in clean energy, 15–48
    in clean energy startups, 23–25, **24**
    uncertainty in clean energy
        investment success, 14–15,
        336–40
Procedia Food Science (journal), 216
Proctor and Gamble, 207
protein, 221–23
Protein Technologies International
    (biotechnology company), 308
Proterra (electric bus company), 37
public policy. *See also* Environmental
    Protection Agency
    and battery vehicles, 36, 163,
    165
    and building efficiency, 26–27
    and clean energy, 50–51
    and climate change, 148–50
    and electric vehicles, 112–14
    and solar power, 90–91, 96
    Chinese solar, 98
    European, 128
    oil subsidies, 177–78
    on carbonated soft drinks, 226
    sustainability, 4
    wind energy, 179, 185–86, 191
    WTO, 104
Public Utility Regulatory Policies Act
    (PURPA), 178
Putin, Vladimir, 152

Q-Cells (solar energy company), 17

Ralphs Grocery, 269
Rand, Ayn, 278
Range Fuels (biofuel), 41
Reagan, Ronald, 278

Recurrent Energy (solar power),
    77–79, 339
Reinemund, Steven, 238
Reliance Group (Indian company), 187
Renault (car company), 127
Renessen (biotechnology company),
    303
renewable energy certificates (RECs),
    251, 284
renewable portfolio standards (RPS),
    179
renewable power
    investment return on, 20
    Walmart, 287
    Whole Foods, 284
retention stage, 5
Reuters (news service), 22
REVA (electric car company), 129
risk. *See* uncertainty
Robb, Walter, 268
Roberts, George, 78
Rockefeller Foundation, 312
Rocketdyne (engine company). *See*
    United Technologies Corporation
Rockport Capital Partners, 16
Rogers Cable, 77
Rohm and Haas (chemical company),
    318
Royal Society, 326
Russian oil production, 151, **151**

Safer Way (food store), 266, 278
Saft (battery company), 38, 117
Sainsbury (food retailer), 313
Sakti3 (battery company), 38
sales
    Better Place, 127, 130, 135
    bottled water, 232–34, **233**
    carbonated soft drinks, 228, 229
    food retailers, 261
    General Mills, 209–11
    hybrid vehicles, **165**
    juice, **235**
    Kellogg's, 209–11
    retail food industry, **271**
    snack food, 236–37, **237**, **238**
    tea, 230, **230**, 230–31
    Tesla, 118–24, **122**, 136–37, 139–40
    wind power, **172**
Salt, Sugar, and Fat (book), 212–14

Salzman, Alan, 132
Samsung, 58, 138
Sandia National Laboratories, 31
Sanger, Stephen, 213–14
SAP (software company), 124, 125
SBAE Industries (biofuel company), 44
Scheuten Solar (solar company), 74
Schneider (electric), 29
Scott, Lee, 286, 288
Secret Tesla Motors Master Plan
  (blog), 110
Securing America's Future Energy
  (advocacy group), 125
selection onset stage
  and macroenvironment, 342–43
  business model evolution, 5
selection stage, 5
semiconductor energy efficiency, 31,
  32
Shanghai Electric (Chinese wind
  power), 193
Shapiro, Robert, 298–99, 302, 305,
  346
Sharp Corporation, 72, 78–79, 90,
  339
Siemens, 29, 39, 193, 194
Silent Spring (book), 304
silicon
  and solar power, 32, 34, 67, 90
  compared to thin-film technology,
    71–76, 93, 99–102, 340–41
  supply, 95–96, 97
Silver Spring Networks. *See* Spring
  Networks
Sinovel (Chinese wind power), 186,
  193
SJF Ventures, 16
SK Energy, 38
SK Innovation, **74**
Skiles, Mark, 266
Skytron Energy (solar company), 93
Smitty's (food store), 269
snack food consumption, 236–37, **237**,
  238
SoBe (food company), 228
social media investing, 22
social responsibility. *See* sustainability
Sodastream (soft drinks company), 253
sodium
  and snack food consumption, 237

in batteries, 38–39
software (investing in), 54–55
Solar City, 93
solar energy. *See also* wind energy
  CVC investment in, 55, 77–81
  DuPont, 298
  Google Ventures, 68–70
  hybrid vehicles, 155–66
  levelized energy costs, 175
  thermal, 31, 66, 68–70, 79, 175
  venture capital investment, **24**,
    31–35, 337
  Walmart, 287
  world competition in, 85–89, **88**
Solar Energy Industries Association
  (SEIA), 107
solar-thermal (ST) power, 31, 66,
  68–70, 79, 175
Solarion (solar company), **74**
SolarReserve (solar company), 79–80,
  339
SolarWorld (German solar company),
  87, 104, 106
Solecture (solar company), 71–76, **74**,
  338
Solexel (solar power company), 34
Solibro (solar company), 74, **74**
Solutia (biotechnology company), 303,
  318
Solyndra (solar company), 19, 21, 32,
  74, **74**, 99
Sony, 61
Soraa (energy efficiency company), 25
Soros, George, 30
South Africa
  and solar power, 79–80
  electric vehicles in, 140
  nutrition, 205
  solar energy, 99
South America. *See* Latin America
Southern California Edison, 181
SpaceX (space travel company), 115
Spark Capital, 23
SpectraWatt (solar energy company),
  66–67, 338
sports drinks market, 231–32
Spring Networks (smart-grid
  company), 22, 29
Sprouts Farmers Market (food
  company), 260, 261, 273

stages
  corporate investment in, 50
  evolution model of business
    innovation, 4–8
startups. *See also* Kleiner Perkins
    Caufield & Byers, Khosla
    Ventures, Intel Capital, Google
    Ventures
  evolution stages of, 5
  sustainability, 336–40
  venture capital investors, 50–51,
    66–81
Stion (solar power company), 33
Straubel, J. B., 117
subsidies (energy), 177–78, 191
sugar
  and carbonated soft drinks, 226–27
  and obesity, 212, 219
  in cereals, 214–18
  in ready-made cereals, 211–12
Sulfurcell. *See* Solecture
Sun Microsystems, 16
Sungen (solar company), 72
SunPower (solar energy company), 17,
    78, 95
Suntech
  and DuPont, 298
  and trade wars, 87–89, **88**, 106
  business model evolution, 95–99,
    340–41
  financing, 17, **94**, 94–95
  selection onset stage, 5
  solar supplier, 79
  technology, 99–102
supply chain
  Walmart, 289–92
  wind energy, 187–93
sustainability. *See also* innovation
  and carbonated soft drinks
    companies, 226–55
  business evolution stages, 4–8, 259
  business models, 340–45
  clean energy, 13–48
  DuPont, 296–98
  food retailers, 264
  major chemical companies, 321
  path to, 1–8, 332–34, 336–40
  Walmart, 280
  Whole Foods, 277–79
Sustainability Consortium, 291

Suzlon (Indian wind energy), 187
swapping stations (battery), 135–36
Symantec, 15
Syngenta (biotechnology company),
    313, 316, 318, 319, 321
Synteri (biotechnology company), 303

Taiwan, 88
Tandem Technologies, 15
Tantie, Tulsi, 187
Target, 261, 262, 265, 272–73
Tauber, Gayle, 219
Tauber, Philip, 219
TCSB. *See* turbo charged selective
    breeding
tea sales, 229, **230**, 230–31
technology. *See* innovation
Tendril (energy efficiency company),
    76
Tennessee Consolidated Retirement
    System, 14
Tesco (retailer), 291
Tesla (electric automobile company)
  and Fisker, 36
  business model evolution, 110–42,
    341–42
  collaboration with Toyota, 168
  promising future of, 334
  selection onset stage, 5
Tesla, Nicola, 114
Tetrick, Josh, 46
TFG Radiant, **74**
thin-film cells
  and solar power, 32–35, 67, 95
  business model evolution, 71–76, **74**,
    93, 340
  technology of, 99–101
Think (electric automobile company),
    122
Think Global (electric car company),
    129
Thornley, Evan, 133
Three Capers Community Market, 268
Tianwei (solar company), 95
Time Magazine, 63
Time Warner Cable, 76–77
Tony's Farm (Chinese agriculture
    company), 46
TopTier (web portal company), 124
Total (gasoline company), 43

Toyota
  and Tesla, 120, 140
  environmental commitment, 147–48
  example of selection stage, 5
  fuel-cell vehicles, 138–39, 167–69
  hybrid vehicles, 156–61, **161**, **165**
  macroenvironment assumptions, 342
TPI (wind energy supplier), 192
trade wars (solar), 87–89, **88**, 102–06
Transform (semiconductor efficiency
  company), 31, 32
Transforming Global Transportation
  (white paper), 124
transportation
  CVC investment in, 55, 80–81
  electric cars, 110–42
  hybrid vehicles, 155–66
  macroenvironment assumptions,
  342–43
  venture capital investors, 35–37
Trina (solar company), 72, 95, 106
Tropicana (food company), 228
True North (venture capital), 90
TSMC (Taiwanese semiconductor
  company), 33
turbo charged selective breeding
  (TCSB), 319–20, 328
Turner (solar company), 91
Twitter (social networking site), 23

Uber (transportation sharing
  company), 80–81, 339
Ulukaya, Hamdi, 220
uncertainty
  in clean energy venture capital
  investment success, 14–15, 56
  in solar energy investment, 20
  in sustainability future, 1–8, 332–34
  of fossil fuel supply, 154–55
Unicorn Village (food store), 267
Unilever, 228, 313
Union of Concerned Scientists, 299,
  310
unions
  and Walmart, 282–83
  and Whole Foods, 281–82
United Farm Workers (union), 282
United States
  bottled water consumption, **233**
  wind energy, 179–81

United States Department of
  Agriculture, 216, 265, 311
United States Department of
  Commerce (DOC), 104, 106–07
United States Department of Energy
  (DOE), 120, 122, 153, 175, 193,
  196
United States Federal Trade
  Commission (FTC), 269
United States Food and Drug
  Administration (FDA), 265
United States Green Building Council,
  251
United States Insurance Institute for
  Highway Safety, 157
United States National Highway
  Traffic Safety Administration
  (NHTSA), 157
United States Securities and Exchange
  Commission (SEC), 250, 268
United Technologies Corporation
  (UTC), 79
US Renewables Group, 79

Valero Corporation, 43
values. *See* mission-based business
  model
VantagePoint Capital Partners, 115,
  126, 131, 132
variation stage, 5
venture capital investors
  corporate, 51–58, 336–40
  private, **24**, 13–48, 336–40
Verfaille, Hendrik, 314
Vestas Wind Systems, 171–74, **174**,
  178, 189–93, **194–95**, 343
View (energy efficiency company), 25
Vogel, D., 2

W. K. Kellogg Foundation, 214–15
Wall Street Journal (newspaper), 95,
  278
Walmart
  and Wild Oats, 271–75, **274**
  as mission-based business, 263–66,
  346
  being inexpensive, 270
  competition, 259–63, 264
  environmental commitment, 286–92
  food, 209–10

in Mexico, 244
labor relations, 282–83
organic food imports, 275–77
retention stage, 5
sustainability, 280
Walton family, 94
Walton, John, 88, 90, 91
Walton, Sam, 280
Wang Yuan, 186
Wanxiang Group (Chinese company),
    37
water
  bottled, **233**, 232–34
  environmental stewardship, 247–50
  in India, 242–43, 253
Watson, James, 302
Weihl, Bill, 63–64
Welch, Jack, 171
Weller, Craig, 266
Wellspring Grocery, 267
Whirlpool, 61
Whole Foods
  and Wild Oats, 268–71
  as mission-based business, 263–66,
    346
  competition, 259–63, 264
  environmental commitment, 284–86,
    323
  expansion of, **271**, 266–71
  labor relations, 280–82
  retention stage, 5
  sustainability, 277–79
Whole Planet Foundation, 279, 280
Whole Trade Guarantee (initiative),
    280
Wild Oats (food company), 260,
    268–74
Wilson, Andrew, 66–67
wind energy. *See also* solar energy
  business model evolution, 2009, **172**,
    174, 171–74
  competition in, 183–94
  CVC investment in, **55**
  global markets, 179–83
  Google investment in, 64
  jobs, 189
  levelized energy costs, 175

macroenvironment assumptions, 343
offshore, 192–93
private venture capital investors,
    44–45, 337
subsidies, 177
Walmart investment in, 287
Whole Foods investment in, 284
WindAid (wind power company), 45
wins
  for Whole Foods and suppliers, 263
  in sustainability, 1
Winston, A., 2
Wolfensohn, James, 126
Woolard, Edgar, 296
World Business Council for
    Sustainable Development, 251
World Economic Forum, 251
World Health Organization, 326
World Resources Institute, 251
World Trade Organization (WTO),
    104
WTO. *See* World Trade Organization
Wuerth Solar, **74**

X.com (financial services email
    company), 115
Xcel Energy (wind energy), 181
XEMC (Chinese wind power), 186
XFINITY Home, 76
Xtreme Energetics (solar company), 67

Yale Rudd Center for Food Policy and
    Obesity, 215–16
Yingli (solar company), 35, 72, 79, 95,
    298
Yoki Alimentos (Brazilian food
    company), 211
Yucaipa (private equity firm), 269

Zam Zam (soft drink company), 246,
    247
Zarur, Andrey, 124, 126, 132
Zhengrong Shi, 88, 89, 95
Zico (food company), 228
Zip2 (software company), 115
Zoellick, Robert, 314
Zoltek (wind energy supplier), 192

Printed in the United States
by Baker & Taylor Publisher Services